DELIVERING MOTHERHOOD

DELIVERING MOTHERHOOD

Maternal Ideologies and Practices in the 19th and 20th Centuries

Edited by KATHERINE ARNUP, ANDRÉE LÉVESQUE AND RUTH ROACH PIERSON

with the assistance of Margaret Brennan

ROUTLEDGE
London and New York

First published 1990
by Routledge
11 New Fetter Lane, London EC4P 4EE

Simultaneously published in the USA and Canada
by Routledge
a division of Routledge, Chapman and Hall, Inc.
29 West 35th Street, New York, NY 10001

Printed and bound in Great Britain by
Biddles Ltd, Guildford and King's Lynn

British Library Cataloguing in Publication Data

Delivering motherhood: maternal ideologies and
    practices in the 19th and 20th centuries.
    1. Canada. Motherhood. Social aspects history
    I. Arnup, Katherine, 1949–   II. Lévesque, Andrée,
    1939–   III. Pierson, Ruth Roach, 1938–   IIII.
    Brennan, Margaret
    306.8'743'0971

Library of Congress Cataloging-in-Publication Data

Delivering motherhood.
    Includes bibliographies and index.
    1. Motherhood – Canada – History. 2. Human reproduction
    – Social aspects – Canada. 3. Childbirth – Canada –
    History. 4. Birth control – Canada – History. I. Arnup,
    Katherine, 1949–   . II. Lévesque, Andrée.
    III. Pierson, Ruth Roach, 1938–   . [DNLM: 1. Abortion
    – history – Canada. 2. Family Planning – history –
    Canada. 3. Midwifery – history – Canada. 4. Mothers –
    history – Canada. 5. Obstetrics – history – Canada.
    WQ 11 DC2 D3]
    HQ759.D43   1989   306.874'3   89-10297

ISBN 0-415-02018-2

Any royalties generated by the

sale of this book will be contributed to

Jessie's Centre for Teenagers

CONTENTS

NOTES ON CONTRIBUTORS

Rona Achilles completed her doctoral work at the Ontario Institute for Studies in Education in Toronto, Canada. Her doctoral thesis is a study of participants in donor insemination programmes. She is currently a free lance researcher in Toronto.

Florence Kellner Andrews is Associate Professor of Sociology and Anthropology at Carleton University. Her present major research projects are a study of the La Leche League and an analysis of data on alcohol consumption in Canada.

Katherine Arnup is completing her doctoral dissertation in the Department of History and Philosophy at the Ontario Institute for Studies in Education. The title of her thesis is "Education for Motherhood: Women and the Family in 20th Century English Canada." She teaches Canadian history on a part-time basis at Trent University.

Cecilia Benoit is an Assistant Professor in Sociology at the Memorial University of Newfoundland. She completed B.Ed., B.A. and M.A. (Sociology) at Memorial University and a Ph.D. in Sociology at the University of Toronto. Her research interests are in the sociology of occupations and organizations, and she has conducted extensive interviewing with midwives. Among her publications is "Uneasy Partners: Midwives and Their Clients" *The Canadian Journal of Sociology* 12, 3 (1987). Her current research concerns a sociological understanding of clients of midwives.

C. Lesley Biggs currently teaches in the Department of Sociology at the University of Saskatchewan. She is receiving her Ph.D. from the Department of Behavioural Science at the University of Toronto and her dissertation is on the professionalization of chiropractic in Ontario. Her teaching and research activities focus on the sociology of health and health care in Canada.

Dianne Dodd is a Ph.D. candidate at Carleton University studying Canadian women's history. She has published several articles on the Canadian birth control movement of the 1930s in *L'histoire sociale/Social History* and *Ontario History*. She is currently working on a study of domestic electrical technology in Ontario and its impact on women in the 1920s and 1930s.

Deborah Gorham is Associate Professor of History at Carleton University in Ottawa and author of *The Victorian Girl and the Feminine Ideal* (London: Croom Helm; Bloomington: University Press, 1982). Her present major research project is a study of the English feminist writer Vera Brittain.

Andrée Lévesque is an historian teaching at McGill University in Montréal. She is the author of *Virage à gauche interdit: Les communistes, les socialistes et leurs ennemis au Québec, 1929-1939* (Montréal: Boréal Express, 1984), as well as of numerous articles on the history of women in Québec and in New Zealand. She is currently researching the discourse on women, particularly deviant women, in Québec in the interwar period.

Jane Lewis is a lecturer in the Department of Social Science and Administration at the London School of Economics. She is the author of many articles, edited collections and books on women's history, including *The Politics of Motherhood: Child and Maternal Welfare in England, 1900-1939* (London: Croom Helm; Montreal: McGill-Queen's University Press, 1980), *Women in England 1870-1950: Sexual Divisions and Social Change* (Sussex: Wheatsheaf Books; Bloomington: Indiana University Press, 1984), and (ed.) *Labour of Love: Women's Experience of Home and Family 1850-1940* (Oxford: Basil Blackwell, 1986).

Angus McLaren teaches history at the University of Victoria and is the author of numerous articles and several books dealing with attitudes towards fertility control.

Arlene Tigar McLaren teaches sociology at Simon Fraser University and has written several articles and books including (with Angus McLaren) *The Bedroom and the State: The Changing Practices and Politics of Contraception and Abortion in Canada, 1880-1980* (Toronto: McClelland and Stewart, 1986).

Kathryn McPherson has an M.A. from Dalhousie University in Halifax, Nova Scotia, and is currently a doctoral student in history at Simon Fraser University in British Columbia, working on Canadian nursing in the 1920s and 1930s.

Jo Oppenheimer completed her Ph.D. in the Department of History and Philosophy at the Ontario Institute for Studies in Education. She is now at York University at the Centre for the Study of Computers in Education, researching the writing process and the computer. She continues to pursue her main interests, qualitative research and the holistic/spiritual perspective of education, and is actively involved in the alternative school movement.

Ruth Roach Pierson teaches women's history and feminist studies at the Ontario Institute for Studies in Education. She is the author of *"They're Still Women After All": The Second World War and Canadian Womanhood* (Toronto: McClelland and Stewart, 1986) and editor of *Women and Peace: Theoretical, Historical and Practical Perspectives* (London: Croom Helm, 1987).

Sherene Razack wrote her master's thesis in the History Department of the University of Ottawa on the education of Quebec girls for marriage and motherhood. She is currently at the Ontario Institute for Studies in Education, working on a doctoral thesis on Canadian feminist activities of the 1970s and 80s.

Veronica Strong-Boag teaches history and Women's Studies at Simon Fraser University in British Columbia. Her recent publications include *Rethinking Canada: The Promise of Women's History* (Toronto: Copp Clark Pitman, 1986), edited with Anita Clair Fellman, and *The New Day Recalled: Lives of Girls and Women in English Canada, 1919-1939* (Toronto: Copp Clark Pitman, 1988).

INTRODUCTION

Ruth Roach Pierson,
Andrée Lévesque and Katherine Arnup

In the course of the nineteenth and twentieth centuries motherhood in Canada, as elsewhere in the western world, became contested terrain. Male medical practitioners vied with midwives and midwives with nurses,[1] while reform-minded middle-class women joined with eugenically-minded state officials in efforts to control the quantity and quality of the population. As reproduction gained in importance as a political as well as a religious issue, motherhood moved to the centre of debate over public health and welfare policies and formed the cornerstone of both feminist and anti-feminist ideologies. At the same time the discourse on motherhood, in its manifold dimensions, became increasingly elaborate. From the limitation of fertility, whether termed 'voluntary motherhood' or birth control, through the differentiation of ante-natal, peri-natal, and post-natal stages of childbirth, to the lengthening years of child rearing, motherhood could no longer be understood, if it ever had been, as a single phenomenon. Although theirs have been the bodies and work processes struggled over, the mothers themselves have often been relegated to the sidelines, particularly if further distanced by class, race or ethnicity from the ruling strata of society. The papers collected together in this volume capture chapters in the history of this complex development where control over the different stages of reproduction, from conception to delivery to childcare, has shifted from the central figure of the mother to experts and professionals.

In her opening review of the recent historical literature on motherhood, Jane Lewis puts turn-of-the-century maternal ideologies and practices in the context of the scientific discourses being articulated at the time. Neither the doctors' beliefs and practices nor the women's responses, she argues, can be understood without reference to an orthodoxy of sex differences[2] under formulation by the emerging disciplines of sociology and sexology. The early twentieth-century Swedish maternalist and pacifist Ellen Key, the subject of Ruth Roach Pierson's chapter, serves as an example of a writer whose ideas on women's sexuality and reproductive role owed much to the theories of social Darwinism, eugenics, and sex reform circulating as the common intellectual currency of her day. Throughout those theories runs an undercurrent of tension between faith in the progress of cultural evolution and commitment to the necessity for sex role differentiation.

As Lewis suggests, the triumph of male-dominated

gynaecology and obstetrics over female-dominated midwifery has been interpreted by historians as a major step in women's loss of control over the reproductive process. C. Lesley Biggs' chapter traces the negative impact on midwives in Ontario of the development of a science and a profession of medicine from which women were excluded. In a parallel chapter, covering approximately the same period, Hélène Laforce sketches the process whereby midwives in Québec were eliminated from their traditional role in childbirth as doctors extended their hegemony over both medical practice and medical knowledge. Both authors show how successful doctors were in influencing the state to enact legislation confirming their dominance over delivery and post-natal care. According to Laforce and Biggs, the doctors achieved this success, however, not without opposition in the form of a sustained debate over midwifery. In the end, only in outlying regions where doctors feared to tread were midwives considered to be an acceptable medical alternative. As Cecilia Benoit notes, outport Newfoundland remained a region where midwives continued to exert influence and control long after they had been driven out of most of Canada.

Women's displacement from authority over childbirth has come to be subsumed under the term 'medicalization',[3] a many-faceted process for which the disappearance of midwives paved the way. A logical next step was hospitalization. Those who advocated moving the site of delivery from home to hospital promised a safer environment for mother and child and hence a reduction in both maternal and infant mortality.

The death rate for new born babies in Canada was alarmingly high throughout the nineteenth into the twentieth century. In 1882 the newly formed Ontario Board of Health could regard as a major achievement of the past one hundred years the reduction of infant mortality "from 75 per cent of all births to a little over 25 per cent."[4] Over-crowded cities, without proper sanitation, sewage disposal systems, or clean water supplies, were particularly lethal environments, serving as breeding grounds for epidemics of smallpox, typhoid, diphtheria, influenza and other communicable diseases. In turn-of-the-century Montreal, considered to be the most dangerous city in the Western world, one in three babies died before reaching the age of one;[5] and in 1909, in the city of Toronto, one hundred and eighty out of every thousand newborns never lived to see their first birthday.[6] While residents of slums, often lacking proper nutrition as well as adequate housing, might have been the hardest hit, epidemics knew no class. Middle-class mothers, like Adelaide Hoodless, who lost their children to preventable disease, spearheaded campaigns for state regulation of the purity of water, milk and other foods, and for the provision of domestic science instruction to mothers-to-be.[7] In response to a widespread social reform movement pressuring government to take measures to reduce infant mortality and improve public health, provincial boards of health grew into full-fledged departments or ministries that in turn spawned specialized divisions of child welfare.

"Toronto Milk Campaign," T. Eaton Company (1921).

Source: Ontario Archives, RG 10, 30-A-2 (1.8.3)

Domestic Science Class, Y.W.C.A. Montreal, 16 February 1938, photograph by Conrad Poirier.

Source: Archives Nationales du Québec, Centre Régional de Montréal, 06-M, P48/8/22750.

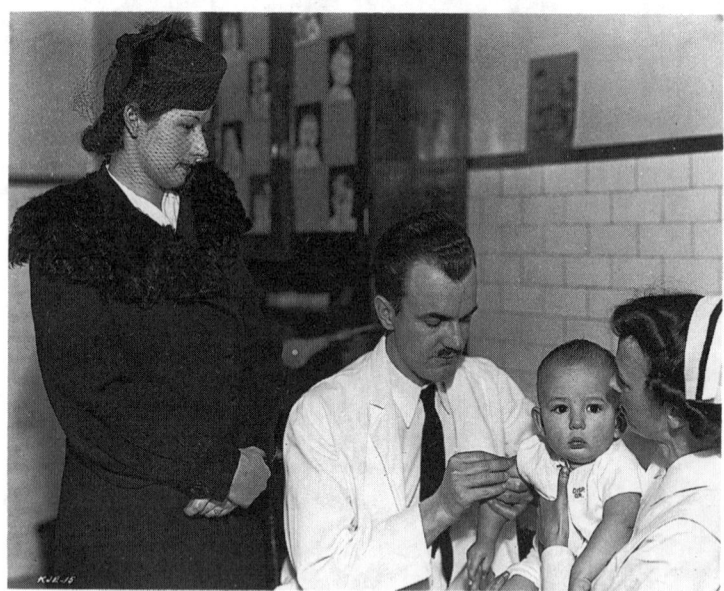

"Vaccination of unidentified baby," Ottawa, Ontario, December 1939, photograph by Eugene Michael Finn, Canadian Government Motion Picture Bureau (National Film Board of Canada), for possible use in *The Canadian Mother and Child*.

Source: National Archives of Canada, PA-163917

The devastating impact of the Great War and its aftermath compounded concerns about the health and size of Canada's population.   During the First World War, Canada sustained 230,000 casualties, of which over 60,000 were fatal, out of a total population of only about eight million.[8] The Spanish influenza epidemic of 1918/1919 struck a further blow, as an estimated 50,000 Canadians died from the disease brought to Canada by the returning troops.[9] Largely in response to these two population disasters, the Federal Department of Health was established in 1919 and its Division of Child Welfare in 1920. With doctors in positions of leadership over staffs of public health nurses and in possession of the germ theory and the means to inoculate with vaccines against a number of infectious diseases, the public health movement made great strides. As a result not of hospitalization per se but rather of improvements in sanitation, pre-natal care, pasteurization of milk, refrigeration, and the medical scientific discovery of immunization, the infant death rate declined from 102 per thousand live births in 1922 to 75 per thousand in 1932.[10] Nor, before the Second World War, did the hospitalization of childbirth do much to improve expectant mothers' chances for survival. As Veronica Strong-Boag and Katherine McPherson point out in their study of the institutionalization of parturient women in British Columbia in the 1920s and 30s, "relatively high levels of hospitalization appear to have preceded any substantial reduction in maternal mortality." Similarly Jo Oppenheimer's study of the shift of birth location from home to hospital in Ontario by 1938 has discovered little positive correlation between safer deliveries and hospitalization. What does correlate positively, according to Strong-Boag and McPherson, is the drive of a male-dominated medical profession for control of the field of childbirth. In the opinion of Dr. Hector Sanche of the *Hôpital de la Miséricorde* of Montreal in 1939, "delivery, during which the patients' submission must be total, is much better controlled in the hospital."[11] Increased control translated into increased obstetrical intervention.

Only with the introduction of sulfonamide drugs in the late 1930s did Canada begin to see a significant decline in maternal mortality.[12] Meanwhile, locating women's confinement within hospitals catered to the convenience of the usually male medical practitioner. As decision making passed into the hands of professionals, the scope of women's freedom of choice contracted. Race and poverty, McPherson and Strong-Boag indicate, further limited choice. Many factors influenced expectant mothers to acquiesce in hospitalization: fear of dying in childbirth, the authority of science claimed by the doctors, and their disparagement of alternative methods.

The first lying-in hospitals, we learn from Oppenheimer, were for indigent women pregnant out of wedlock. The need for such 'charitable' institutions has persisted and will persist so long as society inflicts poverty and shame on the unwed mother. From documentary and statistical records, Andrée Lévesque has carefully reconstructed the treatment meted out to the unfortunate women who were admitted during the Depression to the refuge in Montreal run by the Soeurs de Miséricorde. Shrouded in anonymity to protect their future reputation and subjected to a punitive regime of atonement for sin, these mothers not infrequently accepted the death of their babies as a 'blessing'. These women suffered a loss of control over their reproductive lives second only to dying from a botched abortion.

Deaths due to abortion, Angus McLaren and Arlene Tigar McLaren tell us in Chapter Seven, contributed significantly to keeping the maternal mortality rates high in British Columbia from the 1920s to the 1950s. That so many women were compelled to resort to illegal, back-street abortionists or equally dangerous home remedies, the McLarens conclude, attests to the lack or inadequacy of other available means of fertility control. That so many women in the past died while seeking to abort, the McLarens further conclude, speaks eloquently to the need for safe, legal abortions.

As this books goes to press, abortion has again moved to the centre of the political stage in Canada. On Thursday, January 28, 1988, the Supreme Court of Canada ruled five to two that the federal abortion law is unconstitutional, i.e., in violation of the Charter of Rights and Freedoms. Section 7 of the Charter guarantees the "life, liberty and security of the person." Section 251 of the Criminal Code of Canada made all abortions illegal except those performed in "accredited or approved" hospitals after a duly constituted "therapeutic abortion committee" had decided in the case of an individual pregnant woman that "the continuation of the pregnancy would or would be likely to endanger her life or health." According to Chief Justice Brian Dickson and Mr. Justice Antonio Lamer, "Forcing a woman, by threat of criminal sanction, to carry a fetus to term unless she meets certain criteria unrelated to her own priorities and aspirations, is a profound interference with a woman's body and thus an infringement of security of the person." Madam Justice Bertha Wilson argued that Section 251 also violated a woman's liberty in the sense of freedom of decision. At the same time these members of the majority decision clearly signaled their opinion that a reasonable limit on the rights of women might be in order in the late stages of pregnancy in the interests of protecting the foetus. Thus the ground on which the question of abortion has been debated in Canada is shifting from concern with women's rights to concern with foetal protection.[13]

The ability to exercise control over if and when to bear children, and how many, has been, of course, fundamental to women's control not only of motherhood but also of self-identity and destiny. From 1892 until 1969, the advertisement, sale and/or distribution of information about, or devices for, preventing pregnancy were outlawed under provisions of the Criminal Code of Canada.[14] Racist and classist eugenic concerns, mixed with patriarchal resistance to women's self-determination, fueled the opposition of Canada's leaders to contraception. The cry from nationalist clerics and politicians in Quebec was for a *revanche des berceaux* to maintain French Canada's position against the high tide of Anglo-Saxon immigration.[15] Meanwhile Anglo-Saxon Canada was gripped by the fear of 'race suicide'.[16] Since the late nineteenth century, as urbanization progressed and children passed from being assets in rural society to liabilities in industrialized cities, the birth rate has declined among Anglo-Saxons resident in towns, despite the illegality of contraceptive technology. Judged against the higher fertility of first-generation immigrants of non-British and particularly peasant origins, Anglo-Saxon women of the 'better classes' were chastised for shirking their reproductive duty.

The Great Depression brought a measure of respectability to the Canadian birth control movement, Dianne Dodd informs us in her chapter on the Hamilton, Ontario, clinic of the 1930s. Some representatives of the business interests of Protestant Canada adopted a eugenicist and neo-Malthusian perspective on contraception. Widely regarded today as the 'father of birth control' in Canada, Kitchener industrialist A. R. Kaufman, for example, found the solution to poverty and unemployment, and hence the safeguard against social revolution, to lie in the dissemination of simple contraceptive information and materials to the poor. Dodd contrasts this population control approach with the more woman-centred motives of the middle-class women active in the Birth Control Society of Hamilton.

Developments in pre-natal care of pregnant women derived from concern with infant mortality, and it was only after infant mortality rates had declined significantly that attention turned to maternal mortality. Similarly, the state's twentieth-century programme to educate mothers took its cue from interest in infant survival and child welfare, as Katherine Arnup explains in her examination of such government advice literature between the wars. Indeed, seeking to reduce infant mortality by educating mothers rather than attacking the poverty and malnutrition suffered by many of those who lost their infants to disease, was in some degree tantamount to blaming the victim.[17]

For all the Victorian era's talk of 'the maternal instinct', the nineteenth century firmly established the belief in women's need to be educated for motherhood. In the evolving ideology of motherhood, the rearing of babies and children was held to be the 'natural' task of mothers in the home at the same time as they were regarded as requiring training to carry out this assignment. The proliferating literature on child care contributed to the developing 'professionalization' or 'vocationalization' of motherhood during the nineteenth and twentieth centuries.[18] The work of mothering intensified as legislation restricting child labour and enforcing compulsory schooling prolonged the period of children's dependence and mothers were expected to devote increasing amounts of time to child rearing.[19] In the early Victorian period, child care literature tended to be religious in origin and to deal principally in advice to middle-class mothers about the moral and spiritual welfare of their children.[20] With industrial capitalism's growing need for a healthy work force, and, as Arnup notes, the military's alarm at the poor health of recruits during the Boer War and World War I, maternal advice literature shifted its focus to working-class mothers and the physical well being of the child. As responsible child rearing became the national duty of the "modern mother," the state instructed her to ignore the advice of female friends and relatives and heed instead the precepts of medical and psychological experts on how to mother 'scientifically'.

Sherene Razack's chapter on the *instituts familiaux* in rural Québec in the forties and fifties analyzes an institution that took education for motherhood to the level of personality training. True to the traditions of clerical and conservative Québec nationalism, the schools called on women as mothers to preserve the culture and numerical strength of French Canada. Beyond their uniquely Québec constitution, however, the *instituts familiaux* were also, Razack argues, expressions of more widespread post-war anti-feminism and concurrent psychological theories positing fulfillment in the roles of wife and mother as women's only path to happiness.

Within the context of that ideology, a woman can experience infertility as a denial of her very womanhood. Cashing in on the woman = mother equation are promoters of new reproductive technologies that can, Rona Achilles warns us in "Desperately Seeking Babies," raise hopes to dangerous heights with their promise of the capacity to overcome "those (once) seemingly immutable processes of conception and gestation." The unregulated development and marketing of these technologies by physicians on a free enterprise basis also threaten to increase the medicalization of motherhood to an unprecedented degree. To their long-held powers over life and death, some doctors are now adding the power of "choosing the reproductive partner" and of deciding whom to admit to fertility: those with the ability to pay over those without and the heterosexual married pair over the lesbian couple or the single woman.

The history of motherhood in the last two centuries, however, has not been simply a tale of women's loss of control. As Adrienne Rich set forth in her now classic study *Of Woman Born*, it is necessary to distinguish between the "institution" of motherhood and the "experience" of mothers.[21] This distinction parallels those drawn between discourse and practice or between prescription and behaviour. Most problematic to the historian, as Arnup points out, is what occurs at the point of intersection between prescriptor and prescriptee. The majority of the chapters in this volume concentrate more on the institutional and discursive organization of motherhood than on the experience of individual mothers. Nonetheless, it is necessary to remember that, as Lewis observes and as many of the following chapters give evidence, neither medicalization nor other prescriptions of the state-supported medical establishment were "simply imposed upon women"; they were rather "negotiated." Women have been the recipients of prescriptions to reproduce exclusively within marriage, not to abort nor to practise any form of artificial birth control, to give birth in a certain way in a certain setting, to rear children according to the dictates of the experts, to educate themselves specifically for motherhood, to breastfeed or to bottle feed, and, most recently, to overcome infertility and conceive against all odds. Whether because poverty made compliance impossible or class privilege bred a sense of entitlement, women did not always fall neatly into step with the scientifically prescribed and state-enforced norms. Instead women attempted to prevent conception, resisted the elimination of midwives, engaged in pre-marital sexual intercourse, and either resorted to abortion or gave birth out of wedlock. Even women as alienated from their own reproductive labours as the inmates of the Montreal l'Hôpital de la Miséricorde in the 1930s were capable of acts of passive resistance and insubordination, according to the findings of Lévesque.

But a mere listing of resistances gives an oversimplified picture of the nature of the interaction between the prescribers and the women/mothers who were/are the objects of prescription. As Deborah Gorham and Florence Kellner Andrews' study of the La Leche League from a feminist perspective clearly illustrates, women themselves can be divided against one another when the resistance to prescription on the part of one group is perceived as a new form of prescription calling forth resistance by another. On the one hand, in its valorization of breastfeeding and "home-centred values," the La Leche League represents a reaction to medicalized, modern motherhood. On the other hand, in its opposition to mothers of young children working outside the home, the League flies in the face both of existing economic realities and of feminism's critique of the patriarchal family.

In the media-saturated consumer society of the 1980s, it is difficult to conceive of a residuum of experience untouched by popular or professional discourse. Cecilia Benoit's investigation of mothering in a Newfoundland community at the beginning of this century, however, has uncovered evidence of women who, within their religiously prescribed and economically assigned roles of "'procreators' and 'homemakers'," were able to create a sub-culture of maternal agency. Given voice through the oral interviews Benoit has conducted, these pre-modern Newfoundland mothers recall sharing the "genuine joys" as well as sorrows of maternity.

The recent history of women and mothering can be charted as a seesaw of gains and losses. Women of the post-war baby boom have benefitted from an age of relatively 'safe', albeit medicalized, motherhood. The decriminalization of birth control and the invention of the 'pill' has brought liberation for many from unwanted pregnancies, but at the cost, for some, of new health hazards. Nor are the positive advances of medical science distributed evenly throughout Canadian society. While for most Canadians the infant and maternal mortality rates have been reduced to negligible levels, they remain unconscionably high for the poor and the native women of Canada.[22] And even as we write, motherhood is undergoing profound changes in the very means and relations of reproduction. "'The revolution in reproduction can be compared only to the splitting of the atom,' says Margrit Eichler," organizer of the Canadian Coalition for a Royal Commission on New Reproductive Technologies.[23] It is entirely possible that within this century a baby may be conceived and developed entirely outside of a woman's body. What this would mean for women--as mothers and as citizens--we can only speculate. We do believe that, in the face of these changes, an understanding of the historical conditions of and ideas about motherhood becomes vitally important.

Notes

[1]Suzann Buckley, "Ladies or Midwives? Efforts to Reduce Infant and Maternal Mortality," in Linda Kealey, ed., *A Not Unreasonable Claim: Women and Reform in Canada, 1880s-1920s* (Toronto: Women's Press, 1979), pp. 131-49.

[2]Rosalind Rosenberg, *Beyond Separate Spheres: Intellectual Roots of Modern Feminism* (New Haven and London: Yale University Press, 1982), pp. 1-12, 40-3, 68-72.

[3]For an excellent general discussion of 'medicalization', see Wendy Mitchinson, "The Medical Treatment of Women in Canada: An Historical Overview," in Sandra Burt, Lorraine Code, and Lindsay Dorney, eds., *Changing Patterns: Women in Canada* (Toronto: McClelland and Stewart, 1988).

[4]Ontario, Board of Health, *Annual Report 1882* (Toronto, 1883), xi.

[5]Victoria Dickenson, co-ordinator, "Mother and Child: History of Mothering from 1600 to the Present," exhibit at the Ontario Science Centre, 11 December 1986 to 30 April 1987. See also Terry Copp, *The Anatomy of Poverty* (Toronto: McClelland and Stewart Ltd., 1974), p. 93.

[6]Michael J. Piva, *The Condition of the Working Class in Toronto--1900-1921* (Ottawa: University of Ottawa Press, 1979), table 29, p. 114.

[7]Terry Crowley, "Madonnas before Magdalenes: Adelaide Hoodless and the Making of the Canadian Gibson Girl," *Canadian Historical Review* 67, 4 (December 1986), 520-47; Patricia Saidak, "The Home

Economics Movement in Canada," unpublished M.A. thesis, Carleton University, 1987; and Robert M. Stamp, "Teaching Girls Their 'God Given Place in Life'," *Atlantis* 2, 2 (Spring 1977-Part I), 18-34.

[8]Desmond Morton, *Canada and War: A Military and Political History* (Toronto: Butterworths, 1981), pp. 81-2. Canada's population in 1918 was 8,148,000. F. H. Leacy, ed., *Historical Statistics of Canada*, 2nd ed. (Ottawa: Statistics Canada, 1983), Series A1.

[9]One sixth of the entire Canadian population contracted influenza during the years 1918-19. See Janice P. Dicken McGinnis, "The Impact of Epidemic Influenza: Canada, 1918-19," in S. E. D. Shortt, ed., *Medicine in Canadian Society: Historical Perspectives* (Montreal: McGill-Queen's University Press, 1981), pp. 447-77.

[10]Leacy, ed., *Historical Statistics of Canada*, 2nd ed., Series B51-58.

[11]Andrée Lévesque, "Méres ou malades: les Québécoises de l'entre-deux-guerres vues par les médecins," *Revue d'histoire de l'Amérique française* 38, 1 (été 1984), 29.

[12]C. Lesley Biggs, "The Response to Maternal Mortality in Ontario, 1920-1940," unpublished M.Sc. thesis, University of Toronto, 1983.

[13]"Upsetting a law of the land," *Globe and Mail*, 29 January 1988, A7. Meanwhile, deploring the Supreme Court ruling as legalizing "abortion on demand," the Social Credit Premier of British Columbia, "a fervent Roman Catholic and anti-abortionist," has announced that the government of his province will not extend health insurance coverage to abortions. John Cruickshank, "B. C. won't pay abortion costs, Premier pledges," *Globe and Mail*, 8 February 1988, A1-2.

[14]Angus McLaren and Arlene Tigar McLaren, *The Bedroom and the State: The Changing Practices and Politics of Contraception and Abortion in Canada, 1880-1980* (Toronto: McClelland and Stewart, 1986), p. 9.

[15]Marie Lavigne, "Réflexions féministes autour de la fertilité des Québécoises," in Nadia Fahmy Eid and Micheline Dumont, eds., *Maîtresses de maison, maitresses d'Ecole* (Montréal: Boréal Express, 1983), pp. 319-38.

[16]For the response of Canada's most vocal suffragist to anti-suffrage manipulation of this fear, see Nellie McClung, *In Times Like These*, with an Introduction by Veronica Strong-Boag (Toronto: University of Toronto Press, 1972; reprint of 1915 original edition), p. 87.

[17]Jane Lewis, "'The Ignorance and Fecklessness of Mothers'" and "Educating the Mothers," Chapters 2 and 3 of *The Politics of Motherhood: Child and Maternal Welfare in England, 1900-1939* (London: Croom Helm; Montreal: McGill-Queen's University Press, 1980), pp. 61-113.

[18]See, inter alia, Julie A. Mattaei, "The Development of the Homemaking Profession, and of Women as Homemakers," Chapter 8 of *An Economic History of Women in America: Women's Work, the Sexual Division of Labor, and the Development of Capitalism* (New York: Schocken Books; Brighton: Harvester Press, 1982), pp. 157-86.

[19]Anna Davin, "Working or Helping: Children's Economic Contribution in the Late Nineteenth Century," paper delivered at the Ontario Institute for Studies in Education, November 20, 1987.

[20]Deborah Gorham, *The Victorian Girl and the Feminine Ideal* (London: Croom Helm; Bloomington: Indiana University Press, 1982), pp. 65-6.

[21]Adrienne Rich, *Of Woman Born: Motherhood as Experience and Institution* (New York: W. W. Norton and Company Inc., 1976). According to Hester Eisenstein, Rich's theoretical position involves a tripartite distinction between and among the "institution" of motherhood under patriarchy, the day-to-day "experiences" of mothers under patriarchy, and the potential "experience of women in motherhood when it could be detached from, and freed of, the bondage imposed by male domination." Hester Eisenstein, "The Cultural Meaning of Mothering: I. As Experience and Institution," Chapter 7 of *Contemporary Feminist Thought* (Boston: G. K. Hall & Co., 1983), pp. 69-78.

[22]"Compared with the national average, the infant mortality rate is twice as high, deaths from infectious diseases are 2.5 times more common and accidental deaths are twice as common among children of low-income families." Chandrakant P. Shah, Meldon Kahan, and John Krauser, "The health of children of low-income families," *Canadian Medical Association Journal* 137 (September 15, 1987), 485. On the basis of an investigation of infant mortality on Indian reserves in five Canadian provinces for the period 1976-1983, it was found that "Indian reserve neonatal mortality was over one third higher than that experienced by the comparable non-reserve population, while postneonatal mortality was almost four times higher." H. I. Morrison, R. M. Semeciw, Y. Mao, and D. T. Wigle, "Infant Mortality on Canadian Indian Reserves 1976-1983," *Canadian Journal of Public Health* 77 (July/August 1986), 269.

[23]Ann Pappert, "*In vitro*, in trouble, critics warn," *Globe and Mail*, 6 February 1988, A2.

"Group of baby dolls," Child Welfare Council of Canada, Ottawa, Ontario, July 1929, photograph by Eugene Michael Finn, C.G.M.P.B. (NFB).

Source: National Archives of Canada, PA-163916

Chapter One

'MOTHERHOOD ISSUES' IN THE LATE NINETEENTH
AND TWENTIETH CENTURIES

Jane Lewis

Very broadly, two major approaches may be discerned in the
historical work of the last decade and a half treating women's
experience of and ideas about motherhood. The first has focussed
on an explanation of women's behaviour in the family in an effort to
reconstruct the fabric of women's lives and to explain the nature of
the balance they achieved between work outside the home on the
one hand, and childbearing, child rearing and household tasks on
the other. The second has tended to concentrate on the view from
above, exploring the legal, professional and bureaucratic structures
acting upon women and using prescriptive literatures to explore the
ideology of motherhood.

The women's history published in the early and mid-1970s
concentrated particularly on the way in which women were denied
access to birth control information and on the 'heroic' gynaecology
and obstetrics of the late nineteenth century, which succeeded in
turning the "uterus into a toybox."[1] Women were portrayed above
all as victims at the hands of male physicians and policymakers.
The doubtful quality and unpleasant nature of some (it is difficult
to say how much) late Victorian medical practice towards women
patients is not at issue, nor is the fact that doctors have
increasingly dominated crucial life events, such as childbirth. More
recent work, however, has raised the important question of what we
mean by the oft-used term 'medicalization' and whether it is correct
to see control emanating solely from doctors.[2] At the least, the
process of medicalization must be carefully differentiated. It
comprises advances in technology which become the province of
professionals; intra-professional issues of the status according to,
say, doctors over midwives; the nature of the patient/doctor
relationship and the greater authority exerted by the doctor: and
the place of treatment, which has increasingly become the hospital
rather than the clinic or the home. It is a mistake to see women as
passive recipients or victims of these changes. Recent work shows
that early twentieth-century women fought hard for particular

measures of medical intervention, such as anaesthesia, which some women now deplore, and resisted others in ways that may not be immediately obvious.[3] For example, Ann Oakley has suggested that women's non-attendance at ante-natal clinics today should be understood as a form of resistance to the organization and content of ante-natal care.[4]

In respect to fertility control, it would seem that the strictures of physicians against contraception were systematically ignored by large numbers of the population, for the birth rate began to decline steadily during the late nineteenth century. Indeed, some historians have argued strongly that the falling birth rate signals the degree to which women were asserting control over their lives.[5] But the issue of 'control' is as fraught with difficulty as 'medicalization'. The contraceptive methods used in the late nineteenth and early twentieth centuries--mainly withdrawal and the sheath--did not require medical direction, thus the question becomes more one of whether women were able to exercise decision-making power within the family. Only with the contraceptive pill and legal safe abortion were women provided with sure methods of controlling their fertility. It has been the medical profession, however, who have dictated the terms of their use.

This introductory essay looks at the position of late nineteenth and early twentieth-century women and suggests that it is necessary to understand the context both for doctors' beliefs and practices and for women's responses and concerns in order first, to interpret them correctly, and second, to assess how and why the nature of the debate has changed. The empirical material used is English, but I attempt to interpret it in the light of similar, primarily North American, work. The first section demonstrates the extent to which medical prescription was determined by contemporary ideas about sexual difference and the proper position of women, as well as by the state of medical technology and expertise. The second section shows that medical prescriptions were not simply imposed upon women, but rather were negotiated. The issue of birth control reveals the complexity of the factors that must be considered in understanding the decision to use contraception, while developments in the management of childbirth demonstrate women's support for some aspects of medicalization and resistance to others. Their behaviour can only be understood in relation to their material conditions.

The final part of the chapter begins to explore how 'motherhood issues' in the late twentieth century stand in relation to earlier developments. Today, the authority of the medical profession has increased and the medical technology is more sophisticated. The material circumstances of women have also changed: pregnancies are fewer, household labour is less heavy and paid work more common. Issues of medicalization and control are still paramount, although their content has changed over time, and the way in which they are now being negotiated is very different.

I. Late Nineteenth and Early Twentieth-Century Medical Beliefs and Practices in Context

For the main part, doctors during this period did not choose to make contraceptive information available to those women who were in a position to seek and pay for medical advice, notwithstanding the fact that physicians were members of an occupational group recording a low fertility rate. At the same time, doctors preached motherhood as women's highest calling and most important duty, and in their professional practice engaged in a lengthy battle with midwives for dominion over childbirth.

Doctors' attitudes on reproductive issues were part and parcel of a larger set of beliefs about the relationship between women's physiology and natural abilities which were linked in turn to developments in biological and anthropological research. Darwinistic Victorian science conflated sex and gender differences and derived psychological and cultural difference between men and women (such as women's observed greater tenderness, generosity, and intuition) from male and female biology. Such a belief system tended to elevate women's capacity for reproduction into a moral and social duty. Obviously women succeeded in neglecting that duty insofar as the birth rate declined, although the Women's Co-operative Guild's collection of letters from its members about their maternity experience testified to the suffering of women denied all access to information about contraception.[6] Nevertheless, in large part it was doctors who mediated the new scientific doctrines on sex differences and sex roles and who succeeded in becoming the new moral arbiters.[7] Not only did the medical profession deny women control of their own sexuality, but in promoting motherhood as women's natural task, they both reinforced assumptions regarding sexual divisions and asserted their fitness to 'manage' pregnancy, childbirth and childbearing.

Much of the recent work on Victorian and Edwardian science has shown how an emotional commitment to women's place in the home underpinned research into sex differences. Victorian scientists undertook a "massive exercise in circular reasoning."[8] Having stopped women acquiring certain capacities, science provided the justification for refusing rights on the grounds that those same capacities were 'naturally' absent. Havelock Ellis, himself by no means unconvinced that sex differences were biologically based, observed the way in which preconceived ideas led scientists to distort or ignore evidence. For example, the frontal region of the brain was held to be the seat of the intellectual processes but until the idea was discredited by the discovery that the ape exceeded man in this respect, it was impossible to acknowledge the fact that the frontal regions of women's brains also exceeded those of men.[9] Perhaps the most influential work on sex differences on both sides of the Atlantic during the late nineteenth century was that of Herbert Spencer, whose analysis neatly justified the position of the middle-class Victorian woman as he found it.[10] He argued that sex roles were a product of mankind's successful adaptation to social survival. Thus the sexual division of labour was a hallmark of social progress and a reflection of organic law. He also held that women's arrested individual development enabled them to conserve their energies for the development of their reproductive systems. The more highly developed the society the more differentiated would be the sex roles and the more able women would be to produce better offspring. Spencer thus condemned any attempt to change women's position in society, just as he opposed any state intervention to safeguard the position of the poor and the weak.[11] This would be to interfere in the natural process of evolution and natural selection which ensured social progress.

Towards the turn of the century, scientific (and political) thought turned away from the brutal competition implicit in Spencerian Darwinism and began to stress the possibilities of harmonious co-operation. In regard to sex difference, two biologists, Patrick Geddes and J. Arthur Thomson, derived a theory which preserved the immutability of separate spheres but stressed the complementarity of sex roles and co-operation between men and women. The emphasis was no longer placed on male domination, but rather on women's 'equal but different' attributes. Psychological and cultural difference was still grounded in biology, indeed Geddes and Thomson believed sex difference to be psychological, which held out even less possibility for change than did Spencer's explanation based on evolution. The womanly qualities of nurturance and domesticity, however, were now considered of vital importance, not just within the confines of the home, but to society as a whole.[12] Geddes and Thomson wrote enthusiastically of the possibility of women extending their motherly role to the wider society as charity organizers and carers of the sick.[13] In some measure, this shift in attitude reflected the fact that women had already moved into new occupations such as teaching, nursing and social work; Karl Pearson, Galton Professor of Eugenics (defined as the science of better breeding) at University College, London, admitted that he found women very useful as research assistants. Jill Conway and Flavia Alaya have pointed out how eagerly women active in philanthropy adopted this view of women's role.[14] The strong scientific justification that was given to sexual divisions was both influential and long lived; Geddes and Thomson's ideas were still in circulation when de Beauvoir criticised them in *The Second Sex*.[15] Moreover, there are obvious links between Spencer's theory of sex roles as a product of evolution and Parsonian functionalism, which argues that male and female roles have become increasingly differentiated and that this sexual division of labour has best served human development, particularly in terms of socializing children.[16]

Against this background, it is not surprising that more attention was paid to encouraging and controlling motherhood, rather than giving women the power to control their own sexuality. Many physicians believed that birth control would impair women's capacity to reproduce. Geddes and Thomson, writing in 1889, thought that artificial contraception would open the floodgates to sexuality. Like Spencer, they believed that progress in culture took place at the expense of sensual gratification. Victorians were in fact profoundly ambivalent about female sexuality. Women were either Madonnas or Magdalens, and remained madonnas only by virtue of the purity that attached to total ignorance,[17] thus middle-class women were denied knowledge about their bodies.[18] But artificial contraception was not just morally dangerous, it also posed a racial threat. It represented an interference in the evolutionary process, all the more deplorable since the 'wrong' people were limiting their families. The only late nineteenth and early twentieth century rationale for birth control was provided by the neo-malthusians who wished to rectify the balance by promoting contraception among the poor. Social Darwinists, particularly strict hereditarian eugenicists, nevertheless remained suspicious of birth control, regarding it as an essentially dysgenic mechanism.[19]

The prescriptive literature of the period was therefore chiefly devoted first, to the best way of achieving the healthy development of women's reproductive systems and second, to the management of pregnancy, childbirth and infant care. By the 1870s, the medical treatment of women reflected belief in the centrality of their role in biological reproduction. Building on Spencer's ideas, doctors wrote of the importance of adolescent girls conserving their limited energies in order to ensure the development of their reproductive organs.[20] Women's duty to the race meant that other activities, particularly in respect to education, had to be sacrificed. "The gigantic power and influence of the ovaries over the whole animal economy of women"[21] meant that women's constitutions were believed to be inherently unstable throughout the life cycle. The dangers of adolescence gave way to the possibilities of puerperal insanity following childbirth, and the "climacteric paroxysms" of menopause.[22] With menstruation and pregnancy regarded as "the borderline of pathology,"[23] medical treatment focussed on women's reproductive system and many historians have described the 'heroic' measures of leeching, ovariotomy and clitorectomy that were practised during the nineteenth century.[24] Too often explanations for such practices have been reduced to the simple hostility of male doctors towards their female patients, when the state of medical knowledge and the capacity of doctors to cure, together with their marginal social status also require consideration.[25] Angus McLaren has pointed out that doctors had professional reasons for withholding birth control information, the provision of condoms having been long associated with quacks.[26] Nevertheless, the evidence would not seem to support the totally 'revisionist' thesis of Jacques Donzelot, that doctors and mothers formed an alliance during the period.[27] To be sure, the framework of Darwinistic science and particularly eugenics, offered women a positive role as mothers. During the early twentieth century, as anxieties regarding the decreasing birth rate of middle-class Anglo-Saxons and the poor physical condition of babies born to working-class mothers increased, doctors in private practice and medical officers of health employed by local government addressed more attention to the management of childbirth and child-rearing practices. But the result was arguably not so much an alliance between doctors and mothers as an increasing domination by the medical profession.

Many leading physicians were environmental eugenicists, who, while believing in the importance of a science of better breeding, felt that social reform had as important a role to play as inheritance. These male doctors turned their attention to the quality of motherhood and the problem of infant mortality. All women were encouraged to breastfeed, but particular attention was paid to the working-class mother who was condemned for her fecklessness and carelessness, and in whose education was thought to lie the solution to the infant mortality problem.[28] Educating mothers in infant care was a cheap solution, but amounted to little more than an exercise in blaming the victim (also a feature of the early ante-natal care provided between the wars).[29] The fault lay not in offering mothers information on child rearing, which they welcomed,[30] but in subordinating the material conditions of their lives--the poverty and insanitary living conditions--which were also at the root of the problem and which the early twentieth-century medical reports adequately diagnosed, to an individualist solution.[31] Carol Dyhouse has neatly pointed out the paradox of the medical profession's position, whereby middle-class girls and women were to be protected and encouraged not to take their health into their own hands, but working-class women were to be encouraged to take on the guardianship of the health of the whole family.[32] The consistent strand was the denial of autonomy, something that also permeated the movement of childbirth from home to hospital, the curtailment of female midwifery and the prohibition of female lay attendants.[33]

By the inter-war years, the infant mortality rate was showing a steady decline and it was the persistence of a high and, in Scotland, increasing maternal mortality rate that made motherhood a social problem. As with infant mortality, the preferred remedies were clinical, but in the case of maternal mortality this was at least a more appropriate response. Recent careful research[34] has confirmed earlier suggestions[35] that the key to problem-free childbirth lay in a high standard of clinical practice. It remains an issue for debate as to whether this was achieved more frequently by doctors than by midwives, or in hospitals rather than homes. As Nancy Schrom Dye has remarked of the early twentieth-century United States, obstetrical instruction was scarcely uniform.[36] Certainly doctors were slow to adopt strict aseptic and antiseptic procedures in childbirth cases, while some bodies of midwives, for example the Queen Victoria Jubilee Institute, showed an impeccable record of safe deliveries. Furthermore, Neal Devitt's study of twentieth-century hospital births in the USA suggests that hospitalization did not significantly lower either maternal or infant mortality.[37]

Thus while late nineteenth and early twentieth-century medical and social science put an ever increasing emphasis on the importance of women's reproductive role and doctors sought both to encourage motherhood and to play a more dominant part in supervising pregnancy and childbirth, medical intervention was not spectacularly successful. Motherhood had become a social problem but the physician's approach to that problem was both narrowly clinical and, in regard to maternal mortality, often misguided. During the course of the twentieth century, however, the medical profession has succeeded in consolidating its authority by more sophisticated clinical expertise, culminating in techniques such as ultrasound.

The pro-natalism of the first half of the twentieth century insisted on the importance of motherhood, but based assessment of women's needs as mothers on a functional definition of motherhood. The behaviour of the medical profession in this regard should be seen alongside that of government who directed policies towards improving the welfare of mothers and children more out of regard for the 'national health' than out of regard for the welfare of individual mothers.[38] Thus in the case of British national health insurance, introduced in 1911, coverage was extended to workers in insurable trades, but not to housewives and mothers and not to children. The assumption that husbands would support their families through the family wage system (including payment of medical expenses for wives and children) and that married women would and should devote themselves to full-time wifehood and motherhood underpinned a wide range of social security and employment as well as health policies throughout the twentieth century.[39] The next section takes up the question of women's material reality and the ways in which they negotiated their position, while the final section returns to the issue of conceptualizing women's real needs.

II. Birth Control and Childbirth Negotiated

The average working-class mother of the 1890s, married in her teens or early twenties, had ten pregnancies and spent fifteen years in a state of pregnancy and nursing, compared to the four years so spent after the Second World War.[40] The letters collected by the Women's Co-operative Guild on the maternity experiences of their 52,000-strong membership--for the most part respectable married working-class women--allow us to penetrate behind these bare bone statistics to women's social reality. One woman who spent almost exactly fifteen years either pregnant or nursing wrote:

I had been married eighteen months when I had my first baby, when I had a trying time, being only an eight-months baby. My water broke five weeks before, and caused what the doctor calls "dry labour." He only lived twelve hours. The second came three years and nine months afterwards. I had a straight labour, but I flooded afterwards, and if the doctor had not been there I should have lost my life; it caused me three months' doctoring afterwards. The third one, which came two years and one month after, I had a fairly good labour. Over this one my sufferings were mostly before it came. I had varicose veins in the right leg right away. . . and the irritation was most distressing; I used to walk the bedroom most nights during the last month. The fourth came two years and three months after the third, and the doctor put me an elastic band on my leg, and of course I did not suffer so much over that one. . . .

Between the fourth and fifth I was four years and eleven months, and then the sixth I went five years and eleven months, and was forty-two when I had him. Of course, I think I am suffering now for some of it, as I have always had to do my own work up to the last. . .I must say that I have had a good husband to help me through. . .I don't think my husband's wages averaged no more than 28s a week.[41]

This woman also had a miscarriage, which again meant calling in a doctor, something she could ill afford.

Having babies in itself is not necessarily detrimental to health, but in the conditions of the early twentieth century, when housework was very much hard labour and money was short, there is no doubt but that frequent pregnancy taxed women's health severely. The members of the Women's Co-operative Guild, who would have done quite a bit better than the very poor, expected to have what they called 'womb problems' after childbirth, most had varicose veins and swollen ankles and very few had a complete set of teeth. None of these were likely to cause premature death. But taken together, they added up to a serious amount of ill-health among working-class women during the early part of this century.

Working women's experience of wifehood and motherhood was dominated by their responsibility for managing the family economy and solving the food/rent equation, which they often did only by going short of food themselves. One investigation of family budgets in Lambeth just before the First World War showed many wives making do with what they called 'kettle bender'--a piece of dry bread soaked in hot water--while husbands, who had to be kept fit enough for hard manual labour, sat down to a small meat ration and children to a meal that was neither as poor as that of their mother's or as good as that of their father's.[42] Another inquiry into the conditions of families in Middlesborough reported that girls began to ail as soon as they began to menstruate.[43] In view of the fact that we now know that healthy childbirth depends in large part on a woman's diet throughout her life, it is perhaps not so surprising that twentieth-century women experienced difficulty with their pregnancies. The threat posed by frequent pregnancies to women's health and the financial stress imposed by each new arrival were considerable. The latter point is captured in an interview conducted by Elizabeth Roberts, where a working-class mother referred to the visits to the pawnshop that were occasioned whenever she 'fell' for another baby.[44]

Compared with today, very few married women were employed full time. This was hardly surprising in view of the toll taken by pregnancy and childbirth and the nature of housework in this period. Water often had to be drawn from a communal tap and then heated in a copper. Clothes had to be pounded by hand in the 'dolly tub'. There were no modern scouring agents or soap powders; furthermore, soap itself was relatively expensive. Soda was considerably cheaper, if less effective, and was sometimes even used to wash the children's hair.[45] Very few working-class houses had indoor lavatories before World War I. A government return of 1914 showed that as many as 54 per cent of households in Hull and 15 per cent in Liverpool were still making do with privies of one kind or another.[46] Alice Foley, growing up in Bolton at the turn of the century, remembered the plague of houseflies emanating from the privies in summer.[47] Flies were a major source of the diarrhoeal disease, which also helped to keep the infant death rate high during the first decade of the century.

As well as taking responsibility for hard household labour, women would also go out charring for a few hours, or take in mangling in order to earn a few shillings to supplement the family budget. Kathleen Woodward remembered her mother's bitter complaints about washing: "Wash, wash, wash; it's like washing your guts away. Stand, stand, stand. I want six pairs of feet and then I'd have to stand on my head to give them a rest."[48] Other women took in homework--covering tennis balls, machining shirts or making match boxes. This was laborious and ill-paid work, but, women could combine it with looking after a household, indeed children could make a contribution to many tasks.[49] Several of the women writing in reply to the Women's Co-operative Guild's request for information about their maternity experiences said that they continued to take in work right up to the point of childbirth. Some of the most famous accounts of working-class life during the early part of the century made a point of commenting on the wife's apparent lack of leisure.[50] Generally, women had much less opportunity than men for either reading or exercise. Indeed, many women had no shoes suitable for walking beyond the local shops-- boots were an expensive item and once again it was usually the women who went without. This, then, is the context within which working-class women got pregnant and had their children. Most knew little or nothing about methods of birth control or even about their own physiology.

The material position of middle-class women was, of course, very different. Expected to be 'angels of the home', they could count on domestic service and certainly the attendance of a physician in childbirth. The nineteenth-century novel is nevertheless replete with the image of the ailing woman on the sofa and the female hysteric. Carroll Smith-Rosenberg has suggested that hysteria represented an escape from the hopeless task of reconciling frequent and painful childbirth and the difficult job of supervising a household with the image of the angel in the home.[51] If this is correct, then middle-class women's greater access to medical care was unlikely, given the medical beliefs and practice described above, to provide any relief.

Something that all social classes of women shared in the late nineteenth century was frequent pregnancy and again doctors were unlikely to tell their middle-class female patients how to avoid it, although they may have divulged more information to husbands. In the case of working-class women lack of privacy and lack of indoor sanitation made it very difficult for them to use female methods of birth control and for many, fear of another pregnancy made sexual pleasure impossible. A significant percentage of women resorted to abortion, often by taking one of the potions advertised in newspapers of the day, for example:

"Ladies only. The Lady Montrose miraculous Female Tabules. Are positively unequalled for all FEMALE AILMENTS. The most obstinate obstructions, irregularities, etc. of the female system are removed in a few doses."[52]

How many women attempted to abort or how effective these kinds of pills were is impossible to know with any certainty.[53]

It is clear that late nineteenth-century and early twentieth-century women of all social classes desired smaller families. Such sentiments are recognizable in the famous statement of Queen Victoria that she would prefer not to be the "maman d'une nombreuse famille"; in the case made by Dora Russell on behalf of working-class women to male socialist leaders that, irrespective of the better living standards that might be expected under socialism, women would not want a baby every year;[54] and in the recipe for home-made pessary of cocoa butter, boric acid and tannic acid found in the papers of the Canadian feminist Violet McNaughton.[55] What is not clear is whether the main strand of historical argument to the effect that men rather than women took the lead in decision making about family size is correct. J. A. Banks has argued that it was the burden of child rearing, not childbearing, that worried the middle-class male and that his economic concerns were a vastly more important factor than his wife's preoccupations regarding the pain and safety of childbirth.[56] Others, however, have stressed the strong desire of women for 'voluntary motherhood'.[57] The voluntary motherhood hypothesis stops short at establishing the precise dynamics of fertility decision making and, in particular, the extent to which the decrease in fertility was achieved with or without the co-operation of men. For example, female textile workers were among the first occupational groups to limit their families, probably by a mixture of contraception and abortion. Whether this behaviour was the result of a desire to work in order to contribute to the family economy and was supported by husbands, or whether, in line with Edward Shorter's arguments,[58] work before marriage had emancipated the female operative, who then wished to continue work after marriage for reasons of personal autonomy, is unclear.

What has become apparent from recent work is that while economic conditions and societal norms regarding family size--reflected, for example, in government housing policies, the tax system and the like--influence fertility decisions, they do not necessarily determine them. At the individual level the meaning attached to family becomes all important and meanings may change over time or be negotiated. It is also clear that couples may not share meanings. Diana Gittins' research on the fall in working-class fertility in the inter-war years showed that couples with joint role relationships were more likely to achieve their ideal family size, that is, smaller families tended to result when husband and wife negotiated the issue of birth control.[59] But many women remained trapped by ignorance or their husbands' opposition, in a cycle of frequent pregnancies.[60] However, even if it is unlikely that women exercised full decision-making power regarding the use of contraception during this period, it is equally unlikely that they remained the passive pawns of their husbands. It was not until the 1960s that women got ready access to birth control information through family planning clinics, but increasingly the use of contraception had to be negotiated not only with partners, but with doctors.[61]

When it came to childbirth itself, most working-class women relied on a midwife for attendance, the cost being about half an unskilled labourer's wage; a doctor would cost more still. At the beginning of the century there was no pain relief available to poor women delivering, as most did, at home. The usual practice was to knot a towel round the bed rail and to pull on it when the pains came. Motherhood was undoubtedly a dangerous business; as late as the 1930s mothers ran a greater risk of mortality than did coalminers. As Judith Walzer Leavitt has pointed out, to talk of women having more 'control' over childbirth in such circumstances is difficult.[62] A North American pioneer woman might have delivered herself and survived, but she remained at the mercy of her body. Women feared the pain of childbirth and they feared death. From the perspective of women facing frequent pregnancy and

11

childbirth in homes that were often far from ideal, it made sense to campaign for more medical assistance, especially to ease the pain of childbirth, and even for hospital births. Women's groups, including the Women's Co-operative Guild, campaigned particularly strongly for anaesthesia, although the pre-First World War records of a London lying-in hospital reveal that some working women themselves remained suspicious of pain relief in childbirth as being in some way 'unnatural'.[63]

The Women's Co-operative Guild's collection of letters about maternity was itself part of the Guild's campaign to make motherhood safer. The Guild campaigned for every woman to be attended by a fully qualified midwife and doctor and for more hospital beds for maternity cases. Part of their support for hospital births was determined by their desire to see childbearing women get proper rest away from their families. They therefore also asked that every woman entering hospital should be supplied with a home help to ensure that she was freed from anxiety about the welfare of her husband and other children. The women who campaign for home births today do so on the basis of very different material conditions, but just as the medical profession has failed to respond to their current concerns, so in the early twentieth century there was little attempt to meet women's demands. The move to hospital births was dictated more by professional developments and the changing status of obstetrics as a specialty than by women's campaigns, although the latter were invoked to legitimize the change.[64]

The hospitalization of childbirth was undoubtedly a particularly crucial element in the medicalization of childbirth. For while births took place at home, women could exercise considerable control over the conditions under which they gave birth. Leavitt has documented the way in which women sought the support of other women during childbirth, regardless of whether a doctor was present, and from the records of the New York Medical Dispensary, Schrom Dye has found evidence of women calling midwives as well as doctors and not always submitting to the authority of the doctor.[65] In hospital, medical authority became absolute and the paturient woman was isolated from friends and relatives. Again, the idea of women as passive victims is far from the truth. Edward Shorter portrays women waiting patiently for a safe and painless childbirth delivered by a medical profession growing in skill and competence.[66] The reality is much more complicated. The competence of doctors was by no means uniform and their ability to meet women's needs limited by their narrowly clinical vision (home helps for women giving birth in hospital were never part of the obstetrician's agenda), while women's negotiation of the issue was both active and meaningful in terms of their material conditions. Women undoubtedly participated in 'medicalizing' childbirth, but, as Leavitt has commented, this becomes understandable when account is taken of the degree of suffering in their lives.[67] Today, the question has become how women's authority may be strengthened and yet the benefits of many of the new medical techniques retained.

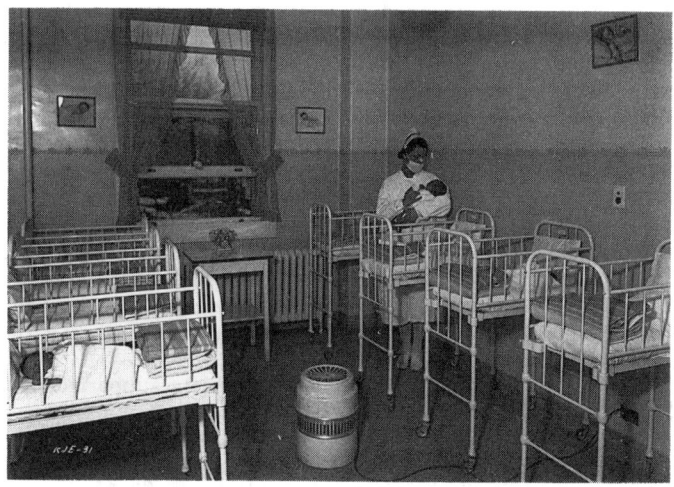

"Nursery, Ottawa General Hospital," Ottawa, Ontario, 18 December 1939, photograph by Eugene Michael Finn, for possible use in *Canadian Mother and Child*.

Source: National Archives of Canada, PA-163912

III. Feminism and Motherhood

It is therefore possible to see how women's responses to issues of contraception and childbirth were not simply dictated by men. Documenting women's suffering in childbirth, early twentieth-century women's groups campaigned for women to receive the best quality care available, which meant medical attention that was beyond the reach of most working-class women. In part these demands must have been provider-led. The Women's Co-operative Guild began its maternity campaign before World War I with a demand for qualified midwives. By 1917, it was asking for doctors and hospital beds. To some extent, women inevitably demanded what they were told was best by medical experts. But what is more striking is the way that women's groups, unlike the medical profession, addressed the broad fabric of women's needs as mothers. In pre-World War I England, the Women's Co-operative Guild and Fabian Women's Group supported the idea of family allowances in order to provide women with a measure of economic independence and so to improve the material welfare of women and children. Issues of diet, housing conditions, and household help for women during this period of childbirth were all part of women's campaign for better motherhood and arose directly out of the circumstances of the lives of the majority.

Today, women's material conditions have changed. The labour participation rates of married women have risen at least five-fold in most western countries, while the number of years spent in childbearing have declined dramatically and the conditions of domestic labour have improved. In these circumstances, it is not surprising that many women are demanding the right to give birth at home. But the medical domination of all aspects of reproduction has increased. Amniocentesis and ultrasound are symptomatic of the high-technology birthing that has become the norm. Rates of inductions have more than trebled since the 1960s. Female methods of birth control, especially the pill and access to abortion, are controlled by doctors. Jean Aiken Swann has shown how doctors use social criteria, such as evidence of a steady boyfriend, in assessing whether a woman 'deserves' an abortion.[68] And most recently medical science has extended its dominion in the field of artificial reproduction, which depends on some of the most sophisticated medical technology.[69]

Medical prescription is no longer explicitly supported by the kind of ideas about sexual difference that were current in the late nineteenth century, but as the criteria for access to abortion show, Ann Oakley is probably correct when she argues that the wombs of women are containers to be captured by ideologies.[70] In face of the consolidation of medical authority over reproduction, feminists have, in the main, resorted first to arguing for the individual rights of women to control over sexuality and in particular for the right to choose to have an abortion; and second, to demanding alternative forms of therapies, including natural childbirth, which are often organized on a self-help basis. Most recently women have found themselves squeezed in the battle between the mechanistic scientific advance of the medical profession and its determination to push back the frontiers of reproductive engineering, and the moralistic opposition of the New Right, whose support for foetal rights would put limits on the development of in vitro fertilization techniques and at the same time pose new threats to women's access to abortion.[71]

The late twentieth-century medicalization of reproduction is formidable in terms both of its technological sophistication and authority. While the life chances and opportunities of women are greater than early in the century, the issue of autonomy and control remains vexed. Early twentieth-century feminists fought in large part for greater access to medical expertise. Late twentieth-century feminists have sought to negotiate a way out, either at the level of the individual patient/doctor relationship (as in the case of abortion), or by rejecting medical technology altogether, as in the case of the home-birth movement. It is not clear that either represents an adequate response. Access to abortion needs to be argued on social rather than on individual grounds. Making abortion 'a matter for a woman and her doctor' will not in and of itself secure a safe abortion. It may be that the doctor's right to decide is upheld at the expense of that of the woman. It is therefore important to conceptualize abortion as a social right, not as a necessary evil, but as a positive necessity for women's health and welfare, arising from particular social economic conditions.[72] Rejection of medical technology in childbirth runs the risk of denying women the relief of pain and the increased safety in childbirth that was so hard won. Women need greater control over the way in which medical technology is used, but this too can only be argued for in the context of a more holistic approach to the needs of mothers.

Feminist economists have perceived that focussing on the issue of how to care for and support children leads to an entirely different set of policy responses from the more traditional labour market approaches. The social need of women to be able to choose when and if to have a child, to claim social support in the form of maternity pay and day care, and to combine paid and unpaid work, require a fundamental restructuring of women's position in society and revaluing of reproductive work. When medical attention is offered to mothers in a society in which access to resources is profoundly gendered, women's needs as mothers are defined in terms of a functional definition of motherhood rather than on the basis of women's real circumstances. As long as this is so then wombs will indeed be containers to be captured by the ideologies and practices of others.

Notes

[1]For example, G. J. Barker-Benfield, *The Horrors of the Half-Known Life: Male Attitudes Toward Women and Sexuality in Nineteenth-Century America* (New York: Harper and Row, 1976).

[2]J. Walzer Leavitt and Whitney Walton, "'Down to Death's Door': Women's Perceptions of Childbirth in America," in J. Walzer Leavitt, ed., *Women and Health in America* (Madison: University of Wisconsin Press, 1984), pp. 155-65.

[3]J. Walzer Leavitt, "Birth and Anaesthesia: The Debate over Twilight Sleep," *Signs* 6, 1 (Autumn 1980), 147-64.

[4]Ann Oakley, *The Captured Womb* (Oxford: Blackwell, 1984).

[5]Patricia Branca, *Silent Sisterhood* (London: Croom Helm, 1975).

[6]Margaret Llewellyn Davies, *Maternity: Letters from Working Women* (London: Virago, 1978, 1st ed. 1915). See also the letters written to the birth control pioneer, Marie Stopes: Ruth Hall, *Dear Dr. Stopes* (London: Deutsch, 1978).

[7]Jacques Donzelot, *The Policing of Families* (London: Hutchinson, 1977) stresses the way in which many of the priest's functions were taken over by the doctor. Wendy Mitchinson, "Historical Attitudes towards Women and Childbirth," *Atlantis* 4, 2 (Spring 1979), 13-34, has observed how doctors spoke on matters of 'social' as well as 'medical' health.

[8]Elizabeth Fee, "The Sexual Politics of Victorian Anthropology," in Mary S. Hartman and Lois Banner, eds., *Clio's Consciousness Raised* (New York: Harper and Row, 1974), pp. 86-102.

[9]Susan Sleeth Mosedale, "Science Corrupted: Victorian Biologists Consider the Woman Question," *Journal of the History of Biology* 11 (Spring 1978), 1-55.

[10]On Spencer see, Jill Conway, "Stereotypes of Femininity in a Theory of Sexual Evolution," in Martha Vicinus, ed., *Suffer and Be Still* (Bloomington: University of Indiana Press, 1973), pp. 140-54; and Janet Sayers, *Biological Politics* (London: Tavistock, 1981).

[11]Herbert Spencer, *Man Versus the State* (London: Williams and Norgate, 1884).

[12]Patrick Geddes and J. Arthur Thomson, *The Evolution of Sex* (London: Walter Scott, 1901, 1st ed. 1889), and *Sex* (London: Williams and Norgate, 1914).

[13]For a discussion of the work of Ellen Key, maternalist social reformer and wholesale subscriber to these ideas, see Ruth Roach Pierson, "Ellen Key: Maternalism and Pacifism," in this volume, pp. 270-83.

[14]Flavia Alaya, "Victorian Science and the Genius of Women," *Journal of the History of Ideas* 38 (April-June 1977), 261-80; and Conway, "Stereotypes of Femininity."

[15]Simone de Beauvoir, *Le deuxième sexe* (Paris: Gallimard, 1949); *The Second Sex*, trans. and ed. by H. M. Parshley (New York: Alfred A. Knopf, 1953).

[16]Talcott Parsons and Robert F. Bales, *Family, Socialisation and Interaction Process* (London: Routledge and Kegan Paul, 1956).

[17]See Eric Trudgill, *Madonnas and Magdalens: The Origin and Development of Victorian Sexual Attitudes* (London: Heinemann, 1976); and Peter Cominos, "Innocent Femina Sensualis in Unconscious Conflict," in Vicinus, ed., *Suffer and Be Still*, pp. 155-72.

[18]Jean L'Esperance, "Doctors and Women in Nineteenth-Century Society: Sexuality and Role," in J. Woodward and D. Richards, eds., *Health Care and Popular Medicine in Nineteenth-Century England* (London: Croom Helm, 1977), pp. 105-27.

[19]On eugenics, neo-malthusianism and birth control, see Linda Gordon, *Woman's Body, Woman's Right* (Harmondsworth: Penguin, 1977), and Angus McLaren, *Birth Control in Nineteenth-Century England* (London: Croom Helm, 1978). It is important to distinguish among the many different types of eugenicists; see Charles Webster, ed., *Biology and Medicine, 1840-1940* (Oxford: Oxford University Press, 1981).

[20]Particularly influential were E. H. Clarke, *Sex in Education, or A Fair Chance for Girls* (Boston: J. R. Osgood, 1873); and H. Maudsley, "Sex in Mind and in Education," *Fortnightly Review* 15 (1874), 466-83.

[21]Dr. Bliss (1870), quoted in Sara Delamont and Lorna Duffin, eds., *The Nineteenth-Century Woman: Her Cultural and Physical World* (London: Croom Helm, 1978), p. 35.

[22]Elaine Showalter, "Victorian Women and Insanity," *Victorian Studies* 23 (Winter 1980), 157-82.

[23]Jeffrey Weeks, *Sex, Politics and Society: The Regulation of Sexuality since 1800* (London: Longmans, 1981), p. 43.

[24]Barker-Benfield, *Horrors of the Half-Known Life*; and Ann Douglas Wood, "'The Fashionable Diseases': Women's Complaints and Their Treatment in Nineteenth-Century America," in Hartman and Banner, eds., *Clio's Consciousness Raised*, pp. 1-22.

[25]Regina Morantz, "The Lady and the Physician," in Hartman and Banner, eds., *Clio's Consciousness Raised*, pp. 38-53; and Martha Verbrugge, "Women and Medicine in Nineteenth Century America," *Signs* 1, 4 (Summer 1976), 957-72.

[26]McLaren, *Birth Control*.

[27]Donzelot, *Policing of Families*.

[28]See especially Anna Davin, "Imperialism and Motherhood," *History Workshop Journal* 5 (1978), 9-65; Carol Dyhouse, "Social Darwinistic Ideas and the Development of Women's Education in England, 1880-1920," *History of Education* 5 (1976), 41-50; and Jane Lewis, *The Politics of Motherhood* (London: Croom Helm, 1980).

[29]Lewis, *Politics of Motherhood*; and Oakley, *The Captured Womb*. Katherine Arnup comes to a similar conclusion, based on Canadian evidence, in "Educating Mothers: Government Advice for Women in the Inter-War Years," in this volume, pp. 190-210.

[30]See, for example, the moving autobiography of Hannah Mitchell, *The Hard Way Up*, ed. by Geoffrey Mitchell (London: Virago, 1977, 1st ed. 1968).

[31]Deborah Dwork, *War is Good for Mothers and Young Children* (London: Tavistock, 1987) has offered a spirited defence of doctors' behaviour in regard to infant mortality, but notwithstanding the bacteriological advances made, this basic point remains.

[32]Carol Dyhouse, *Girls Growing Up In Late Victorian and Edwardian England* (London: Routledge and Kegan Paul, 1981), p. 138.

[33]See especially Jean Donnison, *Midwives and Medical Men* (London: Heinemann, 1977); Lewis, *Politics of Motherhood*; Richard W. Wertz and Dorothy C. Wertz, *Lying-In* (New York: Free Press, 1977).

[34]Irvine Loudon, "Deaths in Childbed from the Late Eighteenth Century to 1935," *Medical History* 30 (January 1986).

[35]Lewis, *Politics of Motherhood*.

[36]Nancy Schrom Dye, "History of Childbirth in America," 6, 1 *Signs* (Autumn 1980), 97-108.

[37]Neal Devitt, "The Transition from Home to Hospital Birth in the United States, 1930-1960," *Birth and the Family Journal* 4

17

(Summer 1977), 47-58. For a discussion of the Canadian experience, see Jo Oppenheimer, "Childbirth in Ontario: The Transition from Home to Hospital in the Early Twentieth Century," in this volume, pp. 51-74.

[38]This point is made by John MacNicol, *The Movement for Family Allowances* (London: Heinemann, 1981) and is elaborated into a theory of welfare by Robert Pinker, *The Idea of Welfare* (London: Heinemann, 1979).

[39]Jane Lewis, "Dealing with Dependency: State Practice and Social Realities, 1870-1945," in J. Lewis, ed., *Women's Welfare/Women's Rights* (London: Croom Helm, 1983).

[40]Richard Titmuss, *Essays on the Welfare State* (London: Allen and Unwin, 1958), pp. 88-103.

[41]Llewellyn Davies, *Maternity: Letters from Working Women*, pp. 54-5.

[42]Magdalen Stuart Pember Reeves, *Round about a Pound a Week* (London: Bell, 1913).

[43]Lady F. Bell, *At the Works* (London: Thomas Nelson, 1911).

[44]E. A. Roberts, "The Working Class Family in Barrow and Lancaster, 1890-1930," unpublished Ph.D. thesis, University of Lancaster, 1978.

[45]Elizabeth Roberts, *A Woman's Place: An Oral History of Working-Class Women 1890-1940* (Oxford: Blackwell, 1984).

[46]Local Government Boards, *Returns as to Scavenging in Urban Districts* (London: HMSO, 1914).

[47]Alice Foley, *A Bolton Childhood* (Manchester: Manchester University Extramural Department, 1973).

[48]Kathleen Woodward, *Jipping St.* (London: Longmans, 1928), p. 12.

[49]Jenny Morris, *Women Workers and the Sweated Trades* (London: Gower, 1986).

[50]B. S. Rowntree, *Poverty: A Study of Town Life* (London: Longmans, 1922, 1st ed. 1901), p. 108.

[51]Carroll Smith-Rosenberg, "The Hysterical Woman: Sex Roles and Conflict in Nineteenth-Century America," *Social Research* 39 (1972), 652-78.

[52]McLaren, *Birth Control*, p. 323.

[53]For a discussion of abortion deaths in Canada, see Angus McLaren and Arlene Tigar McLaren, "Discoveries and Dissimulations: The Impact of Abortion Deaths on Maternal Mortality in British Columbia," in this volume, pp. 126-49.

[54]Dora Russell, *The Tamarisk Tree* (London: Virago, 1977).

[55]Linda Rasmussen, et al., *A Harvest Yet to Reap: A History of Prairie Women.* (Toronto: The Women's Press, 1976).

[56]J. A. Banks, *Victorian Values* (London: Routledge & Kegan Paul, 1981).

[57]Gordon, *Woman's Body, Woman's Right*; McLaren, *Birth Control*; and Branca, *Silent Sisterhood*.

[58]Edward Shorter, *The Making of the Modern Family* (New York: Basic Books, 1975).

[59]Diana Gittins, *Fair Sex: Family Size and Structure 1900-1939* (London: Hutchinson, 1982).

[60]For example, N. Dennis, I. Henriques and C. Slaughter, *Coal is Our Life: An Analysis of a Yorkshire Mining Community* (London: Tavistock, 1956).

[61]For a discussion of the birth control movement in Canada in the 1930s, see Dianne Dodd, "Women's Involvement in the Canadian Birth Control Movement of the 1930s: The Hamilton Birth Control Clinic," in this volume, pp. 150-72.

[62]Leavitt and Walton, "'Down to Death's Door'."

[63]Lewis, *Politics of Motherhood*, p. 130.

[64]*Ibid.*, Chaps. 4 and 5. See also Oppenheimer, "Childbirth in Ontario" and Veronica Strong-Boag and Kathryn McPherson, "The Confinement of Women: Childbirth and Hospitalization in Vancouver, 1919-1939," in this volume, pp. 51-74 and pp. 75-107.

[65]Nancy Schrom Dye, "Modern Obstetrics and Working Class Women: The New York Midwifery Dispensary, 1890-1900," *Journal of Social History* 20 (Spring 1987), 549-64.

[66]Edward Shorter, *A History of Women's Bodies* (New York: Basic, 1982).

[67]Leavitt and Walton, "'Down to Death's Door'."

[68]Jean Aitken Swann, *Fertility Control and the Medical Profession* (London: Croom Helm, 1977).

[69]For a discussion of recent developments in reproductive technology, see Rona Achilles, "Desperately Seeking Babies: New Technologies of Hope and Despair," in this volume, pp. 284-312.

[70]Oakley, *The Captured Womb*.

[71]Jane Lewis with Fenella Cannell, "The Politics of Motherhood in the 1980s: Warnock, Gillick and the Feminists," *Journal of Law and Society* 13, 3 (Autumn 1986), 321-42.

[72]Rosalind Pollack Petchesky, *Abortion and Women's Choice* (London: Verso, 1986, 1st ed. 1985).

Chapter Two

'THE CASE OF THE MISSING MIDWIVES': A HISTORY
OF MIDWIFERY IN ONTARIO FROM 1795-1900[*]

C. Lesley Biggs

While pregnancy and childbirth have been the traditional domain of
female midwives in many parts of the world,[1] Canada has the
dubious honour of being one of nine countries (out of a total of 210
recently surveyed) to have no legislation regarding midwifery.[2] In
fact, midwifery has been illegal in most provinces of Canada since
the end of the nineteenth century. Attempts were made to
introduce a system of midwifery in the early decades of the
twentieth century by the National Council of Women to meet the
urgent needs of women in sparsely settled areas.[3] Their efforts,
however, were hampered by their own class and professional
interests as well as "the complex professional rivalries played out in
a male-dominated world."[4]

In recent years several histories of midwifery have been
written.[5] While they vary both in time and place, each study
reveals that the decline or elimination of the midwife can be
attributed to the emergence of a male-dominated medical profession.
Equally important, these studies demonstrate the role of patriarchal
ideology that fostered male control over a uniquely female
experience.[6]

This paper will analyze the relationship between the
monopolization of medicine and the decline of female midwifery in
Ontario. In order to do this, it will examine the major pieces of
legislation governing medical practice from 1795 to 1900. Changes
in the legislation reveal the medical profession's attempts to
regulate its members, control education and eradicate unwanted
competition. In addition, because the issue of who should practise
midwifery (i.e., female midwives or male physicians) became a
heated one, an opportunity arises to examine the attitudes of both

[*]Reprinted by permission of the Ontario Historical Society from *Ontario History*
75, 1 (March 1983), 21-35. The author wishes to thank Ruth Pierson, Wendy
Mitchinson and David Coburn for their comments and criticisms.

the medical profession and certain segments of the laity toward midwives. Finally, although the medical profession was successful in making midwifery illegal (except by a qualified practitioner), it does not automatically follow that attitudes would change. The last section of the paper examines the 'meddlesome midwifery' debate which reveals that physicians were able to dominate childbirth by redefining it.

The Impact of the Institutionalization of Medicine upon Midwifery

The first act to regulate the practice of physic and surgery in Upper Canada was passed on 6 July 1795.[7] This act made it illegal to practise medicine without a licence; only those who had university degrees or who were surgeons in the navy were exempt from licensing. But, the act was found irrelevant to the conditions of the times. The absence of any record of an Examining Board being convened would seem to indicate that the act was not enforced.[8] Robert Gourlay stated that there were few men who were eligible to take the examination, and even those who held a university degree would not practise medicine since it was not profitable.[9] Furthermore, Gourlay found the act particularly unfair to women since it prevented female midwives from practising:

> How absurd, how cruel, how meddling that a poor woman in labour could not have assistance from a handy, sagacious neighbour without this neighbour being liable to be informed upon and fined.[10]

Despite its unfairness, however, the act was not repealed until 1806. The next act was similar to the statute of 1795 but it also provided:

> that nothing in this Act contained shall extend or be construed to extend to prevent any female from practising midwifery in any part of the Province, or to require such female to take out such licence as aforesaid.[11]

This was the first piece of legislation to recognize female midwives as "legitimate healers."[12] It can be argued that by virtue of their femaleness (i.e., as both participants and observers in childbirth), female midwives' experience constituted acceptable and valuable knowledge in the eyes of the community. Hence, female midwives were exempt from licensing but male midwives were not. Even if this were not true, it was practical to exempt female midwives since there were approximately forty qualified medical practitioners to serve the needs of all of the Province in 1815.[13] Despite the importance of female midwives, there was some opposition to the practice of female midwifery as this anonymous letter from "W" to the *Kingston Gazette* (1815) illustrates:

21

An unfortunate female accoucheur, from ignorance or trepidation, separated the funis [umbilical cord] from the placenta, leaving the latter within the patient causing her death . . . . The vigilance of the magistrates, the contempt of the public, the scorn of all good men must root out these pretenders and make them feel if they cannot see.[14]

This letter prompted a number of responses opposing "W's" position. One subscriber said that without female accoucheurs "those who live in the back settlements . . . would be in a very distressing situation since the closest medical man was thirty or forty miles away."[15] Another letter from a "female accoucheur" expressed alarm that this critic "would shake the Province from one end to the other" and suggested that if it were not for midwives the writer might not have even been born.[16]

Female midwives continued to be exempt from licensing until 1865 when the provision in favour of midwives was dropped. This does not mean, however, that their work had gone unnoticed by the medical profession. Several attempts, albeit unsuccessful ones, were made to regulate the practice of midwifery. In 1845 a bill was introduced which required that, after one year from the passage of the act, every female candidate was "to be examined as to her qualification and ability to act as such Midwife."[17] In 1846 another bill was introduced requiring a similar measure, but it went into effect two years after the passing of the act.[18] Finally, in 1851, a bill was introduced to the legislature which excluded the licensing of midwives altogether; however, an amendment was later made to include such a provision.[19] All of these clauses were contained within acts which were aimed at creating a new College of Physicians and Surgeons and all were defeated.

An open letter to Dr. John Rolph (who founded the first medical school in Upper Canada in 1824 and later another in 1843) from the editors of the *Upper Canada Journal of Medical, Surgical and Physical Science,* "recommending that midwives should be obliged to gain a certain amount of practical and theoretical knowledge,"[20] and an editorial appearing in the *British American Journal of Medical and Physical Science* further indicate that the medical profession was concerned about this issue.[21] More importantly, the editorial illustrates the attitudes of the medical profession towards midwives and also how the licensing issue could have been used to eliminate female midwives from practice.

Taking a line of attack against midwives common to the emerging male medical profession, the editorial charged that female midwives were "very illiterate," thus confusing illiteracy with stupidity. It also invalidated experience as a legitimate source of knowledge. Consequently, if a midwife lost a life, her stupidity and ignorance were to be blamed; but if a medical man made a mistake, he was able to provide a "learned" explanation. Equally important, midwives were characterized as dangerous, as this statement from *The British American Journal* strongly suggests:

And when we consider the enormous errors which they [midwives] are continually perpetuating and the valuable lives which are frequently sacrificed to their ignorance, the more speedily some legislative interference is taken with respect to them, the better for the community at large.[22]

But despite these criticisms, the medical profession was very much aware of the effects of suddenly depriving women resident in "large tracts of country, scarcely or rarely visited by medical men," of the services of female midwives while they received formalized training. Therefore, the male doctors opted for "a more gradual manner," which entailed no specific course of study but required the women to submit to an examination (in this case, one year after the passing of the act). If we accept the medical profession's premise that midwives were illiterate, then this system of examination provided a politically expedient method of eliminating midwives. If it were a written examination, then they did not possess the skills to express themselves; if it were an oral examination, then they would probably lack the appropriate medical vocabulary. Furthermore, it would be difficult for midwives to submit to an examination since they were located in rural areas and the Board of Examiners tended to be located in major urban centres.

A brief review of the changes in the legislation between 1818 and 1865 reveals that the medical profession had made significant strides towards achieving dominance.[23] By 1865 the medical profession had established a system of licensing and registration, and medical education had gradually evolved from the old apprenticeship system to academic study in universities.

By 1869 the orthodox, eclectics and homeopaths had unified under one medical act. Prior to this time the eclectics and homeopaths represented distinct schools of thought with their own medical acts, licensing boards ,and schools. The amalgamation of these schools represented steps towards a convergence of medical theory and practice. In addition, the Act of 1869 provided for the establishment of a provincial College of Physicians and Surgeons which was empowered to administer licensing examinations, set entrance standards, and prescribe curriculum.

While it is quite clear that the medical profession had by no means consolidated its position of dominance, it is evident that it was rapidly moving towards self-regulated autonomy. At this point, the profession had some control over its members, and over the content of their work. Moreover, it appears that its status had considerably improved. Elizabeth MacNab, in her study of the legal history of the health professions in Ontario, states that, because the number of practitioners available had increased and the quality of services had improved, the passage of the Medical Act of 1869 became more acceptable and easier to enforce.[24] Finally, it is evident that each of the three divisions of medicine had been reasonably successful in obtaining the patronage of the social and political elite since all three groups had managed to get their own medical acts. After they amalgamated, this would prove even less difficult since they were no longer competing with one another.

Between 1869 and 1874, relations among the homeopaths, eclectics and orthodox practitioners proved to be quite contentious and a fierce debate developed around issues of examination, requirements for homeopaths and eclectics, and representation on the General Council (the governing body of the College). But by 1874, these internal difficulties would be resolved with the passage of yet another act.[25]

The Debate Over Midwifery

After 1874, the College was able to turn its attention to the prosecution of unlicensed practitioners (frequently referred to as "quacks" and "irregulars"). From the minutes of the annual meeting in 1874, MacNab reports that the Council had decided to appoint a prosecutor for each county. This proved to be too impractical, however, and, in the following year, it was agreed to appoint a public prosecutor for the province of Ontario.[26]

The actions of the Council did not go unnoticed. In fact, there seems to have been considerable opposition prompted by the prosecution of three individuals. An editorial in *The Globe*, entitled *"Medicus* on the War Path,"* reveals the vehemence of the debate:

> The Medical Council has flung away the scabbard, it has opened the campaign against unlicensed knowledge; blood has been drawn; for the moment monopoly has triumphed; one fallen trespasser has bitten the dust . . .[27]

The debate turned on the medical monopoly of knowledge. The opponents of the "regular" practitioners argued that there should be no compulsory curriculum and advocated "unrestricted" or "free trade" in the practice of medicine.[28] Some portion focussed directly on midwifery. An editorial appearing in *The Globe* stated:

> In no way does the restriction imposed by the medical act operate more harshly and unreasonably than in imposing the terms of the law between women and the assistance they are accustomed to rely upon from members of their own sex . . .[29]

Of major concern was the matter of "female delicacy." One writer regarded male practitioners attending women as the "quintessence of imposition" and that many women "shrink with horror from the interference of men at such times."[30] It was argued that, because women did not protest the presence of male practitioners, they approved of them, but *The Globe* made the point

that "it was easy to mistake quiet endurance for indifference!"[31]
The newspaper also pointed out that women were less likely to
confide in men and, therefore, more harm would result from the
suppression of certain facts (due to modesty or fear for their
reputation).

In the opposing camp, a country practitioner "sneered" at the
concept of female delicacy. He asked:

> Are the women of Canada more refined in their feelings or
> more sensitive in their address than the Queen or the
> Princess of Wales and other ladies of the Royal family?
> They could have had the services of thoroughly
> experienced midwives . . . yet they were all attended by
> professional men . . .[32]

This statement is revealing because it suggests that one way male
practitioners were able to gain control of midwifery was to align
themselves with and serve the interests of the upper classes. When
it became acceptable and even fashionable among 'genteel' women to
have male practitioners attend them during childbirth, these
attitudes would eventually filter down and be accepted by the 'lower'
classes.

Furthermore, with regards to female delicacy, the country
practitioner stated that "[he had] heard more vulgarity spiced with
a considerable amount of obscenity in some lying-in chambers than
[he had] heard in many a long day."[33] This last statement has, of
course, little to do with modesty as a way of justifying the
male practitioner's presence and, as *The Globe* most aptly pointed
out, showed that the Medical Act did not "punish obscenity."[34]

Not surprisingly, a significant proportion of the debate
centred on who should practise midwifery--female midwives or
medical men. In a curious confession, a "Country Practitioner"
suggested that the medical profession was not "enamoured with the
midwifery branch of their business, as a rule, they cordially detest
it." Yet in the next section of his letter, he berated midwives,
calling them "Goody Two-Shoes" and suggesting that their only
motives for participating in childbirth were "curiosity and the
chance of a night's gossip." Furthermore, he undermined the value
of their experience by citing their lack of knowledge in anatomy and,
lastly, he strongly suggested that midwives were dangerous because
of the "irremediable injury caused by their clumsiness."[35]

In support of midwives, *The Globe* observed that the medical
profession was not indifferent to the practice of midwifery since the
legislation distinctly identified midwifery as a branch of medicine
which could only be practised by a "qualified practitioner." Then,
The Globe suggested that, although mistakes might have been made
by midwives, it could also call to mind cases in which the "qualified
practitioner [had] grossly blundered."[36] The paper added:

> The qualified practitioner can generally cover up his
> mistakes with some learned explanation and has no one to
> expose his error. But the uneducated woman who loses a
> patient has all the doctors at once to publish her
> misfortune.[37]

Lastly, while *The Globe* acknowledged that midwives were
"extremely ignorant," they also recognized that this was easily
remediable through education.[38] The paper conceded, however, that
the only alternative under the present act was to attend university
and become a regular practitioner. In order to do this a woman
would have to "endure the almost insupportable ordeal, opposition
and persecution!" Therefore, they recommended circumvention of
the law. If a midwife were hired as a nurse and gave her assistance
when a crisis arose, she could not be prosecuted for *practising*
medicine.[39]
    The debate over midwifery was not only carried out in
newspapers but also in the medical journals. An editorial in the
Canada Lancet indicated that the medical profession followed the
debate in *The Globe* and was aware of the paper's position:

> Much surprise and regret have been expressed by many
> intelligent people, both medical and lay, in this city and
> throughout Ontario, at the singular course of *The Globe*
> newspaper, in its support and advocacy of quacks and
> quackery in the medical profession.[40]

It is clear from the editorial that the medical profession was
particularly concerned about female midwives and, in fact, appeared
quite incensed at *The Globe's* suggestion that only female midwives
should practice midwifery:

> We would like to know very much where *The Globe* gets its
> information regarding the desire of women to be attended
> by midwives . . . . The daily experience of medical men,
> however, is that women don't want midwives about them,
> as a rule they have no confidence in them.[41]

    Lastly, a letter to the editor of the *Canada Lancet* written "on
request of a number of physicians in the neighbourhood" reveals
that regular doctors feared the economic competition of midwives.
The reason given by the doctor, however, for the "dispensing of
midwives" was that doctors were more competent and that
midwives had "caused the death of many a woman."[42] Most of the
letter, however, was devoted to lamenting the loss of income to
midwives. The letter stated that the licensing of midwives was
"totally uncalled for in a country which is flooded with doctors" and
later the writer observed: "I do not know that I should object so
much to the passage of the clause alluded to if doctors were as
scarce and as difficult to obtain as they were years ago."[43]

These statements reinforce the view that doctors were tolerant of female midwives only while it was practical to be so. But by 1873 (when the above letter was written), the medical profession was growing rapidly and was well on its way to entrenching its monopoly. Clearly, the writer *believed* that there were enough doctors available to meet the needs of the community. Therefore, doctors were no longer dependent upon female midwives to provide these services. To the regular practitioners, then, female midwives represented a source of unwanted competition.

The writer felt that since doctors invested "the most valuable years of their lives as well as considerable money" in their education, then doctors should be "protected most stringently against the meddlesome interference on the part of old women."[44] In other words, one of the rewards of becoming a licensed practitioner was the right to maintain a monopoly over health care. Furthermore, the doctor writes that midwifery "is to many of us country doctors a very remunerative part of our business" and he expressed considerable irritation at the loss of income resulting from competition by midwives. According to the writer the amount of money lost to these "old bodies and a quack" would be a "decent living for [his] small family."[45] Female midwives were able to undercut the doctor's income because they charged two dollars for each case while the doctor charged five dollars.

Almost twenty years later, in 1895, the issue of medical monopoly was raised by the Patrons of Industry, an opposition party in the Ontario Legislature. According to Elizabeth MacNab, the Patrons, who tentatively drew their support from the working class, were opposed to business and the professions because they exploited the working class. In particular, they were opposed to the professional colleges because the colleges "prevented poor men's sons from joining their ranks. The Patrons advocated the abolition of these colleges and the 'free trade' in professional practice."[46] Having gained a presence in the legislature, the Patrons' first target was the medical profession. On 27 March 1895, the Patrons introduced what became known as the Haycock Bill, named after their leader.

One feature of the bill was to abolish the medical court and another was to license midwives. Midwives who attended ten cases of confinement would be eligible to practise midwifery upon paying a fee of one dollar for a licence. The reaction of the medical profession to the bill, in general, and to the clause regarding midwives in particular, was, as can be expected, overwhelmingly negative. An editorial appearing in the *Ontario Medical Journal* reflected this sentiment:

> The gist of the bill was ridiculous in the extreme, both from the standpoint of benefit to the profession and benefit to the general public. All the good clauses in the Act were to be repealed, and many others, almost

iniquitous ones, to be added, giving scope to any kind of quacks, fakirs and midwives.[47]

The fact that the bill was soundly defeated (71 to 15) indicates that the medical profession had strong support in the legislature. Furthermore, *The Globe*, which had been against the medical profession in 1875, had now reversed its position as the editorial below reveals:

> The Legislature did not go far wrong when considering Mr. Haycock's amendments to the Ontario Medical Act in making the public interest the final standard by which the proposed changes are to be judged. The Medical Act was passed for the protection of the public not for the purpose as some people suppose of creating medical practitioners of Ontario a closed corporation.[48]

So how successful was the medical profession in eliminating female midwives? We know from the Ontario *Sessional Papers* of 1899 that it was, in fact, making considerable headway against female midwives, although it had not yet eradicated the movement entirely.[49] Overall, 3 per cent of all births in Ontario were attended by midwives. Caution should be exercised in interpreting this figure, however, since, under the threat of prosecution, female midwives were not likely to report their presence. This figure, therefore, is probably an underestimate. Figures were given for the total number of births unattended by physicians in 1899 and this was 16 per cent of all births. It seems unlikely that all of these women had their babies without any assistance. Thus, we can infer that some of these births were attended by midwives but, as suggested, this was not reported.

These statistics, however, also reveal a rural-urban dichotomy in the delivery of health care. For example, in the counties of Algoma and Renfrew, it was reported that midwives attended 10 per cent and 12 per cent of the births (respectively) while approximately 50 per cent of the births in these counties were listed as unattended by physicians. Yet, in York, only 1 per cent of the deliveries were attended by midwives and 3 per cent were unattended by physicians. Thus, in the areas that were well established (such as York) and were densely populated, almost all of the births were attended by physicians and very few by midwives. We can conclude that the medical profession was most successful in eradicating the female midwife in the urban areas. In the newer, developing counties, however, there were few physicians available and, therefore, many births went unattended by physicians. It is difficult to imagine that 50 per cent of the women had no assistance in their deliveries; it is more likely that female midwives assisted with these births and did not report it. Thus, one can assume that midwives continued to practise in areas that were *unprofitable* for the medical practitioners.

The debate over midwifery as it was waged in the pages of *The Globe* and the medical journals reveals that in mid-nineteenth-century Ontario, it was a contentious issue. Medical practitioners' objections to female midwifery can be attributed in part to a desire to protect their own pecuniary interests. This is not surprising since, in the mid-nineteenth century, physicians were barely able to eke out a decent living. It seems clear that a major tactic of the profession was to undermine the credibility of the midwives by characterizing them as dirty, ignorant and dangerous. On the other hand, those who supported midwives seem to have done so for two reasons. First, they wished to protect female modesty, thereby reflecting the prudish Victorian values dominant at that time--values that the medical profession conveniently ignored when it came to the issue of midwives, yet indignantly espoused when the issue of female physicians came to the fore. Second, they did not seem to be convinced that medical monopoly of knowledge was beneficial to the community and therefore advocated free trade.

The opposition to medical monopoly tends to reinforce the view put forth earlier that, while the profession was moving towards a position of dominance, it had by no means achieved it. However, the changes in the position of *The Globe* on medical monopoly and the sound defeat of the Haycock Bill strongly suggest that by the early 1900s the medical profession's monopoly was largely complete.

One reason for these changes in attitudes may have been that there had been improvements in medicine which convinced people of the medical profession's superior role in health care. Equally important, however, may have been medicine's claims to being scientific in a period when the western world was enamoured with the rationality of science. It will become apparent that both of these developments would seem to have applied to changes in the "management of childbirth."

The "Meddlesome Midwifery" Debate

As discussed in the previous section, one method of changing attitudes was to undermine the credibility of midwives. A second, more subtle, method by which the medical profession came to dominate childbirth was by redefining it. The "meddlesome midwifery" debate is a reflection of this process.[50] The debate focussed on whether childbirth practitioners should take a 'laissez-faire' approach to labour and delivery and let nature take its course, or whether they should take an aggressive, interventionist role in assisting labour and delivery (i.e., "meddlesome").

The change in nomenclature from midwifery to obstetrics reflects the success of the interventionist approach. As one practitioner phrased it:

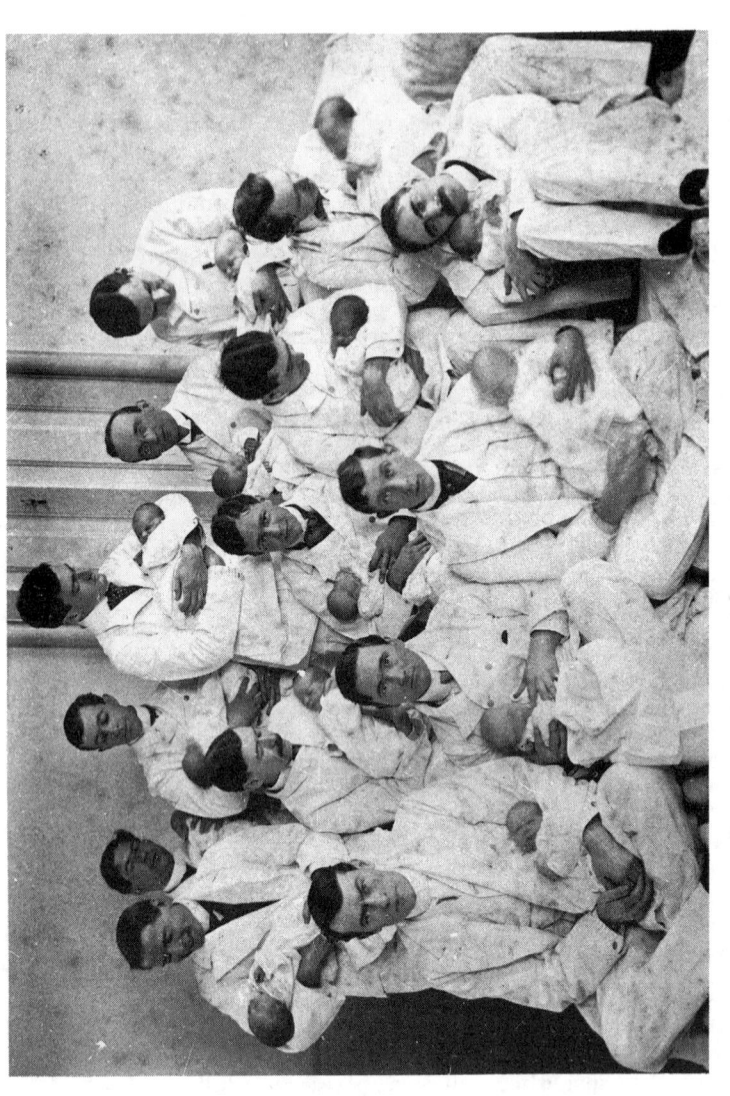

Medical interns holding infants, Toronto General Hospital, turn of the century, photograph the property of Lilian E. Lawrence, nurse-in-training at T.G.H.

Source: Ontario Archives, ACC 2444 S5695

The art of midwifery belongs to prehistoric times; the science of obstetrics is the latest recognition of all ancient sciences. No branch of medicine demands more skill, presence of mind or justifiable daring than midwifery.[51]

Thus, attendance at childbirth became 'scientific'! Barbara Ehrenreich and Deirdre English argue in *For Her Own Good: 150 Years of the Experts' Advice to Women* that, since in the late nineteenth century "science was well on its way to becoming a sacred national value, any group which hoped to establish itself as 'experts' in a certain area would have to prove that they were rigorously scientific."[52] Furthermore, the authors suggest that "making something scientific became synonymous with reform."[53] The development of various procedures, techniques and instruments (i.e., anaesthesia, antiseptics, forceps and Caesarean section) strengthened doctors' claims that childbirth was becoming 'scientific'. These new techniques were thought to be beneficial since they alleviated pain and lengthy labours. Moreover, only the experts were able to administer them. By taking an active role in the "management" of labour, the prestige of the doctor was further enhanced by his "justifiable daring."

The use of forceps provides a good example of the "meddlesome midwifery" debate. Forceps were first discovered by the Chamberlen family in England in the seventeenth century. Ann Oakley suggests that the mystique generated around the Chamberlens' use of the forceps "probably did a great deal to elevate the status of the male midwife."[54] In England by the 1720s, male midwifery became more fashionable among the upper classes, and male midwives began to compete with female midwives for normal cases of labour. (Prior to this male midwives only attended complicated cases of labour.) Since female midwives were prohibited from using forceps, "the use of surgical techniques even for normal labour was a means whereby male midwives were able to assert their superiority over the female practitioner."[55]

It is clear that, even in the mid-nineteenth century, forceps were infrequently used. "The rule which guided obstetric teachers was that meddlesome midwifery was bad," and the use of forceps was considered to be a "dangerous operation;" therefore, they were to be used only as a last resort.[56] Physicians were not encouraged to take their forceps with them because:

The impatience of the patient, the anxiety of the friends, and the doctor's wish to show that he was really doing something, would induce him to use the forceps before he ought . . .[57]

But, by the late nineteenth century, this maxim was being questioned. Many doctors claimed that this rule was "accountable for a great deal of suffering and a great many deaths."[58] One physician wrote that this convention was "to be utterly repudiated when applied to the skillful efforts of the educated accoucheur." He argued that once a doctor was satisfied that "Nature, unaided is unable to effect delivery within a safe period," then the forceps should be used. Furthermore, he denounced some of the guidelines taught in the 1850s (when he was in training) as no longer valid forty years later at the end of the nineteenth century.[59] As a result of this switch in attitude, there was a great change in the frequency of the use of forceps. Around 1855, one practitioner reported that over a three-year period, there were eighteen forceps cases for 6,634 deliveries (1/360).[60] By 1868-1874, however, there were 639 forceps cases for 7,027 deliveries (1/11).

At the same time, however, other doctors objected to the interventionist approach. As one wryly observed in *Canada Lancet* in 1885, "It is felt that at the present rate of advance we shall soon overtake Nature and relegate her to a back place."[61] These doctors suggested that forceps were often used too frequently and when they were uncalled for. Furthermore, one practitioner claimed that: "The forceps are sometimes used to save time, sometimes to gain a little notoriety, sometimes for a double fee, and sometimes from ignorance."[62] This particular doctor claimed that he had used forceps only a dozen times in twenty-five years of practice.[63]

The non-interventionists, however, did not win the day. The success of the interventionist approach is perhaps best reflected in the statistics of modern day obstetrical practice. In 1982-83, low forceps delivery (both with and without an episiotomy) was occurring in 18.9 per cent of all births in Ontario, and Caesarean section, in 18.6 per cent.[64]

The aim of this paper has been to examine the relationship between the institutionalization and monopolization of medicine by male doctors, and the demise of the female midwife. Male physicians' desire to eradicate the female midwife stemmed, in part, from the belief that female midwives were dangerous; and, in part, from the desire to eliminate economic competition. Male doctors were able to gain control of childbirth by operating on a number of different levels. First, the doctors were able legally to prohibit female midwives from practising. Second, male doctors were able to undermine the credibility of midwives by characterizing them as dirty, ignorant and dangerous. Finally, by claiming that childbirth was 'scientific' and by using technology, the male doctors were able to "assert their superiority" over female midwives and, in doing so, redefined childbirth.

Notes

[1]See Doris Haire, "The Cultural Warping of Childbirth," *Environmental Child Health* 27 (1973), 179-91; Margaret Mead and Niles Newton, "Cultural Patterning of Perinatal Behaviour," in S. A. Richardson and A. F. Guttmacher, eds., *Childbearing: Its*

Social and Psychological Aspects (Baltimore: Williams and Wilkins, 1967).

[2]Cited in *Midwifery Is a Labour of Love*, compiled by the Interdisciplinary Midwifery Task Force Association and the B. C. Association of Midwives (Vancouver, B. C.: Maternal Health Society, 1981), p. 83.

[3]Suzann Buckley, "Ladies or Midwives? Efforts to Reduce Infant and Maternal Mortality," in Linda Kealey, ed., *A Not Unreasonable Claim: Women and Reform in Canada 1880s-1920s* (Toronto: Women's Press, 1979), pp. 131-49.

[4]*Ibid.*, p. 149.

[5]*Ibid.*, pp. 131-49; Jean Donnison, *Midwives and Medical Men: A History of Inter-professional Rivalries and Women's Rights* (London: Heinemann, 1977); Barbara Ehrenreich and Deirdre English, *Witches, Midwives and Nurses: A History of Women Healers* (Old Westbury, N. Y.: The Feminist Press, 1973); Ann Oakley, "Wisewoman and Medicine Man: Changes in the Management of Childbirth," in Juliet Mitchell and Ann Oakley, eds., *The Rights and Wrongs of Women* (Harmondsworth, Middlesex: Penguin, 1976).

[6]Nancy Schrom Dye, "History of Childbirth in America," *Signs* 6, 1 (Autumn 1980), 98.

[7]William Canniff, *History of the Medical Profession in Upper Canada, 1783-1850* (Toronto: W. Briggs, 1894), pp. 19-21.

[8]*Ibid.*, p. 22.

[9]Cited by Canniff, p. 22.

[10]*Ibid.*

[11]Canniff, pp. 30-2.

[12]Elizabeth MacNab, *A Legal History of Health Professions in Ontario* (Toronto: Queen's Printer, 1979). MacNab cites the Act of 1795 as the first act to exempt midwives. The source of my information is Canniff, who cites the entire Act of 1795 which makes no mention of female midwives being exempted.

[13]Canniff, p. 31.

[14]Letter by "W" to the *Kingston Gazette*, 18 November 1815.

[15]Letter by "a subscriber" to the *Kingston Gazette*, 2 December 1815.

[16]Letter by "a female accoucheur" to the *Kingston Gazette*, 2 December 1815.

[17]The proposed bill was cited in an editorial *The British American Journal of Medical and Physical Science* 1 (1845), 57.

[18]The proposed bill was cited in an editorial in *ibid.* 2 (1846), 27.

[19]The proposed bill was cited in an editorial in the *Upper Canada Journal of Medical, Surgical and Physical Science* 1 (1851), 71-115.

[20]Letter appearing in *ibid.* 3 (1853-4), 271.

[21]An editorial appearing in *The British American Journal of Medical and Physical Science* 1 (1845), 195.

[22]Ibid.

[23]See MacNab, pp. 4-19 for further details. Also see Charles M. Godfrey, *Medicine in Ontario* (Belleville, Ontario: Mika Publishing Company, 1979) for a detailed description of the changes in medicine and particularly in medical education.

[24]MacNab, p. 10.

[25]Ibid., pp. 16-19.

[26]Ibid., p. 19.

[27]Editorial, *The Globe*, 24 August 1875.

[28]Ibid.

[29]Editorial, *The Globe*, 11 September 1875.

[30]Letter by "an observer" to *The Globe*, 6 September 1875.

[31]Editorial, *The Globe*, 11 September, 1875.

[32]Letter by "a country practitioner," *The Globe*, 11 September 1875.

[33]Ibid.

[34]Editorial, *The Globe*, 11 September 1875.

[35]Letter by "a country practitioner," *The Globe*, 11 September 1875.

[36]Editorial, *The Globe*, 11 September 1885.

[37]Ibid. See, for example, J. M. Penwarden, "Barbarous Treatment by a Midwife," *Canada Lancet* 4 (1872), 273-4.

[38]Ibid.

[39]Editorial, *The Globe*, 13 September 1875.

[40]Editorial, *Canada Lancet* 8 (1875), 58.

[41]Ibid., 60.

[42]Letter to the *Canada Lancet* 4 (1873), 150.

[43]Ibid.

[44]Ibid.

[45]Ibid.

[46]MacNab, p. 29.

[47]*Ontario Medical Journal* 3 (1893), 251-2.

[48]*The Globe*, 1 April 1895.

[49]Statistics are from Ontario, Report of the Registrar-General, *Sessional Papers* (1899), no. 32.

[50]See Wendy Mitchinson, "Historical Attitudes Toward Women and Childbirth," *Atlantis* 4, 2, pt. 2 (Spring 1979), 13-34.

[51]W. Symington, "Forty Years' Experience in Midwifery," *Canada Lancet* 17 (1885), 262.

[52]B. Ehrenreich and D. English, *For Her Own Good: 150 Years of the Experts' Advice to Women* (New York: Anchor Press, 1979).

[53]Ibid.

[54]Oakley, p. 36.

[55]Ibid.

[56]L. Athill, "Changes in Midwifery Practice and in the Treatment of Uterine Diseases During the Last Twenty Years," *Canada Lancet* 8 (1876), 171.

[57]Dr. Harrison, "Operative Midwifery as It was Taught to Me and as I Practise It," *Ontario Medical Journal* 1 (1892), 154.

[58]Athill, p. 171.

[59]*Ibid.*

[60]*Ibid.*

[61]"Meddlesome Midwifery," *Canada Lancet* 17 (1885), 25.

[62]Dr. Clark, letter the Editor, "The Use of Forceps," *Canada Lancet* 18 (1885), 73.

[63]*Ibid.*

[64]Percentages have been calculated from Statistics Canada, *Hospital Annual Statistics 1982-1983*, Catalogue No. 83-232 (Ottawa: Ministry of Supply and Services, 1983) and Statistics Canada, *Surgical Procedures and Treatments 1982-1983*, Catalogue No. 82-208 (Ottawa: Ministry of Supply and Services, 1983).

Chapter Three

THE DIFFERENT STAGES OF THE ELIMINATION OF MIDWIVES IN QUEBEC

Hélène Laforce

To establish that a profession has been eliminated, one must first ascertain that the profession did indeed exist. The profession also has to have been sufficiently well established and structured to withstand the normal interplay of supply and demand without being doomed to disappearance. The first part of this chapter contains a brief presentation of the practice of midwives in Québec up until their actual elimination. In the second part, we will study the various mechanisms of elimination and the slow conquest of obstetrics by the medical profession. In the third part we will examine the doctors' motives for proceeding with the elimination of midwives.

I. The Midwife in New France: 1650-1760

It is interesting to note that the country that colonized Québec in the seventeenth century was the most advanced in the field of obstetrics. French obstetrics had already gained international renown in the two previous centuries because of its unique maternity schools and the discoveries of its doctors and midwives.

The theorizations of these early French researchers were the first steps in the infant science of obstetrics. They proved to be fundamental to the understanding of the physical phenomena associated with childbirth and later to new teaching methods in the art of obstetrics. An example of this is that, by comparing the functioning of the uterus to a machine in the shape of a pump,[1] the French scientists were better able to prevent possible complications by using manual procedures. The purpose of the techniques developed during this period was to preserve the normal process of childbirth, while minimizing risks, rather than to intervene with instruments. The ideology that supported the superiority of instrumental intervention over all other techniques was therefore not the fruit of French thinking, even though it was easily adopted by the French.

Obstetrics was not the only field in which the French were pioneers. They were also the first to produce innovative medical treatises in which the art of medicine was divided into three distinctive branches: the domain of the doctors, that of the surgeons, and that of the midwives. Within this tripartite division, doctors occupied a position of importance and controlled the generation of medical knowledge and the arts of diagnosis, and treatment. The domain of surgeons was more technical: they were called upon each time an incision or a dressing was needed. The matrons or midwives were called upon whenever, for the sake of modesty, their eyes and their hands were needed to carry out examination of intimate parts.[2] This division of tasks was clear and precise. Each group was governed by rights and obligations and structured according to a strict hierarchy. Within the hierarchical structure of midwifery the *maîtres* and *maîtresses* were responsible for quality control; the *entretenus* and *entretenues* were paid by the King; the *ordinaires* and the *jurés* alone were allowed to give expert opinions in court and the *approuvés* enjoyed local privileges.

This professional infrastructure, with all its complexity, was transplanted to New France with the creation of French colonies in North America. By 1740, a network of midwives served the French colonists from Louisiana to Isle Royale (Nova Scotia). Each city (Québec, Montréal, Louisbourg, Nouvelle-Orléans) had its own *entretenue* midwife and its *matrones, maîtresses-sages-femmes* or *jurés*, each with a well-defined territory. Each village was proud to have an *approuvée* midwife around whom gravitated assistant-midwives and *accoucheuses* representing the new generation of obstetrical practitioners. The hierarchy was strict and well observed.

The profession of midwifery assembled under a single name a heterogenous group of practitioners with very different economic and cultural backgrounds. The higher up the practitioners were in the hierarchy, the richer and more cultured they were. The *entretenues* midwives were trained at the *Hôtel-Dieu de Paris* which was, at the time, the best maternity school in Europe, and their salaries were almost the same as that given the King's surgeon.[3] Country midwives inherited their knowledge from their mothers, aunts or grandmothers according to family tradition. Apprenticeship was practised everywhere and the records often contain the mention of an assistant-midwife. In the villages, midwifery was part of a self-help system, even though in the cities it was becoming a habit to pay for the service.

Despite their diversity, the midwives knew each other and worked together within charity organizations such as confraternities or poor relief bureaus. Though corporative groups were forbidden in the colony, the midwives succeeded in establishing a network of practitioners who placed abandoned children and put city children out to nurse in the country. Midwives seemed to have played as much of a social role as a medical one. In the villages, they were recognized as moral and public advisers. In the cities, the midwife who was paid by the King had to be available at all times, and even free of charge, to meet the needs of the poor.[4] This was a kind of pregnancy insurance in keeping with the social welfare policies of enlightened monarchies.

All things being equal, the small French colony overseas seems to have been better provided with midwives than the mother country which suffered a midwife shortage in the seventeenth and eighteenth centuries. The luxury of established civil servants, a very costly system overall, was characteristic of an absolutist regime that wanted every French subject, wherever he/she might be, to enjoy the same privileges. This beneficent attitude on the part of the mother country toward the colony was far from completely disinterested. Since Colbert's introduction of childbearing subsidies in the 1660s, it had been realized that the best way to populate a colony, without draining France, was to endow the colony with a good obstetrical system. The gamble seems to have paid off. The newborn and maternal mortality rates for this period prove that not only did women in New France bear more children, they also lost fewer babies than their counterparts in France.[5]

Adapting French customs to a new geographical and social environment created a unique situation. During the century of colonization, women of New France gained rights that were almost unknown to their European counterparts since it was no longer magistrates, lords or parish priests but women themselves who elected their midwives.[6] This was a privilege that gave women of New France real decision-making power in the field of childbirth.

Around 1720 a merciless war between surgeons and midwives began in France that was to last to 1760. In the small colonies of New France, meanwhile, both professions continued to practise without any conflict and with mutual respect. Far from denigrating midwives, surgeons and doctors on the contrary supported them, lodging a request with the authorities to send more. In practice, the midwives' territory seemed to be well respected. In 1730, a surgeon even refused to give a medical opinion in the area of childbirth because "that comes under the services of the midwives." It was not unusual for midwives to deliver the wives of surgeons. This cohesion was further reinforced in their private lives, especially if both surgeons and midwives belonged to the same socio-economic class. Working side by side, surgeons and midwives intermarried and their children married each other. The families of midwives and surgeons called on one another to share in godparenting, thereby strengthening the ties linking these two professional groups.[7]

Structured and organized into a hierarchy, well established in their community, efficient and highly skilled, midwives, unsurprisingly, were the ones to demand of the Minister of Colonies the creation of a school of midwifery in 1755.[8] This was an ambitious project that would have placed them in the forefront of the Canadian system, ready to be part of the quasi-technological change in European obstetrical knowledge during the eighteenth century. How then can one explain the ensuing disappearance of the profession? Could it have been one of the effects of the Conquest?

II. Midwives during the Conquest of Lower Canada (1760-1840): A Well-Adapted Profession

With the arrival of a new master, the context for the development of the system of obstetrics in the colony began to change. A detailed analysis, however, reveals that the old customs survived. These customs, nevertheless, had to conform to the new rules of the game introduced by the English conqueror.

England at the end of the eighteenth century brought more than new administration to the colony. England also brought a new way of looking at political and economic realities as influenced by developing liberalism, industrialization and the parliamentary system. English puritanism also introduced another way of viewing morality, the role of women in society and even science. The impact of protestantism, which favoured man's intervention in nature, had a significant effect on medicine and obstetrics.

In the England of the early eighteenth century, deliveries were performed within a kind of unregulated free market in which doctors and surgeons battled fiercely. Deliveries were still the midwives' domain but the introduction of forceps, invented by the barber-surgeon Chamberlen,[9] raised the stakes in the obstetrical field.

In 1760, at a time when the English were settling in Canada, the first debate over interventionism had just ended in Great Britain. For a few decades, in the maternity schools of London, Glasgow and Edinburgh, doctors and midwives pondered an important problem. What kind of knowledge was necessary to intervene in the normal process of childbirth? How and when should forceps be used? Since the use of forceps seemed to present real danger, even more so because the surgeons who used them tended to abuse them, the doctors of university faculties in agreement with an elite group of midwives concluded that the course of nature was usually adequate and that any intervention was liable to endanger women.[10]

It is on the basis of this consensus that doctors organized, at the end of the eighteenth century, a new legal framework for their system of obstetrics. The art of delivering babies became, to the detriment of surgeons, an enterprise shared by doctors, that is, learned men not much inclined to use their hands, and certified midwives.

This favourable prejudice towards midwives was no doubt the reason why the surgeons Blake and Fisher, who were consulted during the drafting of the first Act governing the practice of medicine in 1788, were in favour of the survival of midwives in the colony. Reflecting the values of their time, Blake and Fisher simply were giving, as were their colleagues in New England, the English doctors' point of view. Furthermore, would it not have seemed unfair to British midwives not to enjoy in an English colony the same privileges they had just acquired in their homeland? There are, however, other possible explanations, especially in Québec, for them to have been favourably considered, an important one being the verdict of incompetency rendered on Canadian practitioners by English surgeons as soon as they arrived on Canadian soil.[11] This judgement, even though confirmed by the surveys of 1819 and the controversial Durham Report of 1839, must be viewed with caution because of the generally disdainful attitude of the British towards the colonials.

The assessment of incompetency likely underlay the investigator-surgeons' recommendation in 1775 and in 1776 that city midwives be certified by the same authority that certified and granted legal recognition to doctors. They also proposed the creation of a school for midwives.[12] The school was never established but the profession of midwife was legalized by the Medical Act of 1788. Midwives were thus recognized as public officers by the Lieutenant-Governor and entered in the official gazette. They also had a specific place, in the official directory, in the medical practitioners' section. In the villages, midwives continued to be approved and controlled by the Church as well as recommended by doctors.

As far as the acquisition of knowledge is concerned, in the cities, midwives could enroll in courses given by obstetricians or continue their apprenticeship, as doctors did, with a doctor or a midwife. One can suppose that the knowledge of midwives who graduated from the new British schools surpassed that of Québec doctors who did not have access to specialized places of learning. This supposition is confirmed by the rather summary papers that Québec doctors presented from 1820 to 1822 at lectures of the Québec Medical Society.[13]

As far as efficiency and patient satisfaction are concerned the historical records offer, in fact, the best verdict one can find: that given by the patients themselves. Around 1820, two private institutions were founded in Quebec City in order to help and assist poor women during childbirth. They are the *Dispensaire de Québec*, created in 1818 by doctors with a clinical approach, and the *Société compatissante de Québec* (Female Compassionate Society of Québec), headed, as early as 1819, by women who paid for the services rendered by midwives. These two organizations operated according to the same model. The practitioners made house calls and offered their services free of charge, as long as the women were recommended by the sponsors of the organization. When the *Dispensaire* closed its doors a year later in 1819, its founder remarked that it was a pity that not a single pregnant woman had called on them for help. The *Société compatissante*, on the other hand, was swamped with requests from the first year of operation. In 1862, forty-two years after its inauguration, it still employed four midwives. The facts speak for themselves![14]

The profession of midwife, which was legalized, structured and competent, was therefore well established when the Corporation of Physicians was created in 1847. At this point, nothing seemed to forecast the subsequent disappearance of midwifery. Yet, the mechanisms that were to lead to its elimination were already in place.

III. The Disappearance of Midwives in Quebec

It seems as though the various interventions of doctors with regard to midwives were influenced by two major factors: periodic surpluses of doctors and the influence of the various types of international medicine. The interaction of these factors can be applied to Québec during two major phases. From 1760 to 1870, doctors attempted to share the field of obstetrics with midwives whose training they controlled as was the case in Europe. Then, from 1870 on, a new trend appeared which aimed at removing them completely from this field.

Firstly, a group of doctors, under the leadership of the doctor and Member of Parliament Pierre de Sales Laterrière, tried to establish a system to control midwives which would ensure their survival yet keep them under the supervision of doctors. This group of doctors tabled from 1790 to 1840 three bills that proposed the certification of country midwives by doctors who would see to their training, and the publication of handbooks aimed at their education. In 1818, the group attempted to organize courses for midwives at the *Dispensaire de Québec*.[15]

Although a textbook for country midwives was published and midwives were legally required to obtain certification from a doctor after 1800, these measures had little practical effect. After 1820, a new group of young doctors became increasingly influential and demanded more restrictive measures toward midwives. This development did not, however, prevent F.X. Trudel at the Ste-Pélagie (Montréal) Maternity Hospital and Dr. Trestler at the McGill Maternity Hospital from training many midwives. It was nevertheless a bad omen for the future of this female profession.[16]

It is difficult to imagine what would have become of midwives if the group of doctors that supported them (the traditionalists) had

41

won the struggle with their opponents (the radical doctors). Could midwives, put under the supervision of the traditionalists, have gained their independence as did dentists in 1870, veterinarians in 1905, homeopathic doctors in 1865 and pharmacists in 1870? No one knows for sure. We can nevertheless suppose that such supervision would have enabled these women to get together, organize and thus offer a legal alternative to the growing influence of medical knowledge in obstetrics.

Why, then, was not an association of midwives created in the middle of the nineteenth century? Two major reasons may explain this. Firstly, the socio-economic conditions of women deteriorated in the middle of the nineteenth century, causing women to be excluded from institutions of higher learning. They, therefore, did not have any way of grouping together to create a common front and defend their rights. Secondly, and without doubt most importantly, the surplus of doctors took on alarming proportions just when their field of practice was being eroded by the emergence of other healing professions. For example, doctors who had obtained a monopoly on the sale of drugs in 1863, lost it two years later with the legalization of the Association of Pharmacists. Consequently, they could not afford to let the obstetrical field elude them, for it had become more and more vital to their profession. This would have indeed happened if midwifery had become a profession.

If, from 1847 to 1870, doctors seemed tolerant, occupied as they were with firmly establishing their teaching institutions and forming a united profession, in 1870 they were solidly established and ready for action. From this moment on, practitioners were everywhere and at all levels making sure they were gaining ground. This included the surveillance and harassment of country midwives (1890-1980) as well as the control of midwives holding a diploma, be they midwives (1870-1920), midwife-nurses (1920-1980) or immigrant midwives (1920-1986). The doctors' control was the most tenacious and vigorous with respect to midwives holding a diploma, who were surely the most threatening.

Firstly, the Corporation of Doctors let self-educated midwives continue practising in the country, hoping that this group would disappear on its own with the coming of 'progress' and 'civilization'-- progress meaning doctors and civilization meaning hospitals. In fact, in the beginning, the Corporation attempted to have these women fined but was forced to show tolerance when the population came to the midwives' defence. In 1919, this is what happened in the village of Sacré-Coeur in the Saguenay region. The Corporation settled out of court so as not to establish any precedent.[17]

Secondly, a decision favourable to midwives in a trial, which took place in 1879, spurred the doctors into taking action to limit the field of practice of midwives holding a diploma. The trial came at time when doctors were so preoccupied with the surplus of doctors in cities that a midwife was able to achieve, through the courts, a significant gain for her profession. Basing his verdict on the deposition of Dr. Hingston, then president of the Corporation, the judge ruled:

> that the plaintiff has the right to give the care she has given, that the word "midwife" must be taken in its general sense, that midwives can practise during and before pregnancy and therefore they can see to it that a woman's organs are in a state conducive to conception and a normal pregnancy.[18]

Since this decision was an important one, "for it established a precedent that tended to broaden the privileges and rights of midwives,"[19] the Corporation acted swiftly. In an article published in 1880, Dr. Hingston declared that he had had no choice in his testimony since "the Bureau of Medicine had just given a definition of the term 'midwife' during its last meeting in May 1879"[20] which he had felt he could not deviate from in court. To counteract the 1879 court decision, the Bureau simply called another meeting in April of 1880 and amended the regulations to read as follows: "the midwife licence shall only give her the right to deliver babies and not to practise medicine even in cases resulting from childbirth."[21]

Thus restricted, the expansion of the profession proved to be impossible. The massive arrival of foreign midwives, better informed and better organized, could have brought new leadership to the profession. But here, too, the Corporation was vigilant.

To illustrate the power gained by doctors over immigrant midwives, we will use a fairly contemporary example, that of Anna Farina Colantini, an Italian midwife.[22] In 1961, this graduate of one of the best maternity hospitals in Italy, after having been assured by the Canadian Embassy in Rome that she would be able to practise the profession she had been practising for over fifteen years, was refused a certificate on the pretext that she had not completed six months of courses in a Canadian university as was required by Section 33 of the Medical Act. Sponsored by a doctor friend who came to her defence and hired a lawyer for her, this woman finally agreed to take the courses, but the courses in question were only given at the *Hôpital St-Sacrement de Québec* and reserved exclusively for missionary nuns. The case of immigrant midwives is a good example of the way doctors determined the fate of midwives in general.

The fact that such cases tended to be settled out of court gives us indirect insight into the nature of the process. In a letter to the registrar of the Corporation in 1963, Dr. Augustin Roy summarized the attitude of the Corporation:

> It seems as though the present policy of the College is not to give licences to midwives. In this case, I wonder if it would not be wise to eliminate the controversial Section 33 from our regulations. This section is time-worn and

goes against present-day customs. I think that such an action would spare the College future problems.[23]

Is it not significant that the Corporation never felt compelled to ask, at least not officially, to have Section 33 of the Medical Act repealed? While the law continued to recognize the midwives' right to practise, insurmountable obstacles were systematically placed in their way. This process could never have become a reality without its institutional counterpart: the control of teaching institutions by doctors.

From 1840 to 1870 is the crucial period during which doctors asserted control over medical knowledge. It is a time when university faculties of medicine were created. Rejecting the U.S. model of competing private schools which were riddled with conflicts and often not very viable because more concerned with making money than offering serious courses, the Québec legislators chose centralization. All schools of medicine had to be affiliated with a university which awarded the diplomas. Since there were few universities there were few faculties of medicine. In 1829, the Montreal Lying-In Hospital joined with the McGill Faculty of Medicine. L'Ecole de chirurgie et de médecine de Montréal united in 1845 with what was later to become the Université de Montréal. The Ecole de Québec opened its own Faculty of Medicine at Laval University in 1848. Bishops University did the same in 1871. Still today, there are only four faculties of medicine in Québec, at the Université de Montréal, McGill University, Université Laval and the Université de Sherbrooke.

This concentration is very important for it allowed for better control by the government as well as by the Corporation of these institutions and of their curricula. Although midwives still retained their place within this infrastructure--it was still a mistress midwife who taught the interns at the McGill Maternity Hospital until 1880 and interns could take courses at Ste-Pélagie up until 1920--they, nevertheless, slowly lost the administrative and official control of these same institutions.[24] If women in general, midwives and nuns in particular, had not been ousted from the real centres of decision making, the story that follows would no doubt have been a different one.

The influence of university faculties made itself felt as soon as these institutions got a foothold within maternity hostels headed by nuns, where, since 1840, unwed mothers had found refuge to give birth. First introduced as volunteers, French-speaking doctors gradually imposed their directives and their way of thinking through contracts they negotiated with the religious congregations. The nuns did not have much choice in the matter since they needed university funding. As for the doctors, they needed to make use of these maternity hospitals in order to provide teaching opportunities, as improvement in practical teaching became more and more important and the number of medical students grew.[25]

In the English-speaking community, the process was simpler. The doctors simply took over the Board of Directors of the McGill Maternity Hospital and caused the teaching midwife to resign in 1880. In the French-speaking community, the gradual gaining of control by doctors proved just as efficient. This resulted, after 1920, in the abolition of courses in midwifery and their replacement by courses in nursing.[26] In fact, one cannot really use the term 'abolition'. The process was more subtle. In 1913 and then again in 1915, the mother superior of Ste-Pélagie asked the Corporation's permission to extend the training courses for midwives so that they would be in conformity with the legal requirements. "This [was] in order to train more competent midwives who could administer quality care and neither put public safety nor the school's reputation in danger."[27] In an important brief, a group of nuns proposed the creation of an independent midwifery course that could serve as a retraining course for nurses. Since doctors were also asking for more hours of practical training in this same period, the Corporation never complied with the nuns' request. There was only room for one category of practitioner in obstetrics and it was decided that it would be that of the doctors.

The creation of university faculties had another less perceptible impact on the evolution of obstetrical knowledge. By gaining the right to control the admission of medical students, the doctors excluded women from francophone faculties of medicine until 1920. Women, therefore, had no say in these institutions of higher learning where gynaecology became firmly rooted after 1930. As in faculties of medicine, courses in midwifery were replaced by those in gynaecology.[28] It was under the influence of gynaecology that the modern concept of "female nature" was shaped, that childbirth was defined as a pathological and dangerous event and that the interventionist approach--anaesthesia, forceps, Caesarean section, pubiotomy and so on--was favoured and became the basis for the dehumanization of care.

Gaining wide circulation in the 1920s was the belief of Dr. DeLee, one of the renowned gynaecologists of the time, "That modern women were the nervous inefficient product of modern civilization."[29] According to that gynaecologist, the twentieth century, with its environment and education, had increased women's hypersensitivity--especially upper-middle-class women who were the target clientele of doctors of the time--causing the atrophy of their physical and emotional capacity. Women's worsened condition justified the growth of the specialization of gynaecology and, in the name of protection, the increasing intervention by doctors into childbirth.

This thesis, disputed in Europe by midwives who managed to retain a more normal approach to pregnancy by limiting the intervention of gynaecologists to high risk cases, was also debated in Québec by the traditionalists in the profession. The triumph of the radicals had great repercussions for women. Coincident with the rise of gynaecology occurred a widespread publicity campaign aimed at attracting women to hospitals thought to be safer than home delivery. Gynaecology's increasing ascendancy furthered the hospitalization of birthing women which, after 1960, became the norm. At the same time, the modern concept of female nature kept women doctors away from the practice of obstetrics. Their "physical weakness" and "tender hearts" would not allow them to face a sight so difficult for their sensitivity to endure. It is this same view of "female nature" that would be used as an argument to limit the field of practice of nurses specializing in obstetrics.

Nurses too became concerned with the field of practice of midwifery. The possibility of specialized training in obstetrics, which was offered to them sporadically from 1940 to 1972, and of a specialization in midwifery from 1962 to 1972 at the Hôpital St-Sacrement in Québec City, made them available if ever the profession of midwife regained legitimacy. What was the nurses' position in this debate?

From 1897 to 1920, the superintendent of the Victorian Order of Nurses, Charlotte Hanington, tried to convince nurses to become midwives. The Nurses Association of Canada refused to get involved because the housework included among the midwives' tasks, as outlined by Hanington, seemed irreconcilable with the Florence Nightingale mystique. Fearing competition to their own profession, nurses opposed the importation of British midwives, as proposed by Hanington in 1917.[30] The midwife was a potential competitor to the nursing profession still not well established, judging from the reaction of a group of nurses from Québec that requested the abolition of midwifery courses given by the Institut technique de Québec in 1930.[31]

On the whole, it is mostly because the nurses generally endorsed the idea that the doctor is best suited to intervene in obstetrical cases that they refused to back a profession that might have insured them a path to new independence. The debate is still alive today between the Victorian Order of Nurses and the different nurses' unions.

IV. The Reasons and Purpose of the Intervention of Doctors in Obstetrics

The elimination of the profession of midwife by doctors thus took place from 1840 to 1960. The reasons and mechanisms involved have been studied by researchers worldwide. Many historians, American, Australian and Canadian, have observed the same basic scenario in their own countries, and have all come to similar conclusions.[32]

Doctors ousted midwives from obstetrics because this field of practice became, as the surplus of doctors increased competition, the basis for establishing a clientele. This elimination did not depend on the superior efficiency of obstetrical practice compared to midwifery even though the criterion of efficiency was used after the fact to justify the process. On the contrary, rigorous studies have shown that the massive intrusion of doctors in obstetrics between 1900 and 1930, the period of the elimination of midwives, did not decrease the peri-natal mortality rate.[33] It seems, in fact, as though the mortality rate increased because of the type of intervention often practised by doctors. According to a 1983 American report, from 1915 to 1929 a 40 to 50 per cent increase in the number of infants who died because of injuries sustained in delivery and half the maternal deaths of women in childbirth were attributable to incompetent interventions.[34]

Furthermore, it would be incorrect to assume that the elimination of midwives was based on the unanimous agreement of practitioners of the healing arts. The positions of health practitioners with respect to midwives during the past hundred years have been very diverse and contradictory. Québec historians Jean-Marie Fecteau and Jacques Bernier and the American historian Howard S. Berliner have shown that one particular group of doctors, the *réguliers*, gained ascendancy within the field of medicine.[35] As seen above, these 'regulars' were dominated by the radical faction, as opposed to the traditionalist, within the Corporation of Doctors. The members of this particular group, by gaining influence within the legislature and other powerful social/political institutions,[36] succeeded in securing for the Corporation the power of regulation it enjoys today.

Notes

[1]This mechanistic model could have proved to be wrong. It happened to be right. Richard W. Wertz and Dorothy C. Wertz, *Lying-In: A History of Childbirth in America* (New York: Schocken, 1979), pp. 32-33.

[2]Claude De Ferrière, *Dictionnaire de la pratique de la médecine en France*, t. II (Paris: Delegrange, 1773), p. 222.

[3]600 French pounds for the highest ranking surgeon in the colony; 400 French pounds for the *entretenue* midwife. At a time when a practitioner's expert opinion in court was paid according to the person's quality, a surgeon received 20 *sols* and a 'midwife 15 *sols*. Hélène Laforce, *Histoire de la sage-femme dans la région de Québec* (Québec: Institut québécois de recherche sur la culture, 1985), pp. 195-6.

[4]See Hubert Charbonneau, *Vie et mort de nos ancêtres* (Montréal: Boréal Express, 1973), p. 210.

[5]Archives Nationales du Québec à Québec, Archives des colonies, série B, 25 janvier 1721, "Conditions de la dame Dorille, maîtresse sage-femme pour passer à la Louisiane," folio 403, p. 2.

[6]The parish priest called a meeting of women for the purpose of electing midwives. This election took place according to the *Quebec Ritual* in effect from 1713 until, in some places like Rimouski, 1930.

[7]Archives Nationales du Québec, Archives judiciaires, Inventaire d'une collection, 12 avril 1730. There was a case of a surgeon from Chateau Richer and his wife, the midwife of the area, who married their daughter, who was also a midwife, to a physician from Champlain and that couple in turn arranged a marriage of their daughter to another physician from Champlain.

[8]Archives des colonies, serie B, 2 mars 1755.

[9]*Le Petit Robert 2*, 1981 edition, has no entry under Chamberlen and that is unfortunate. If the forceps used at this time were an instrument that both saved and took lives, it remains certain that they were useful in difficult cases when used correctly. It is the way forceps were used more than the instrument itself that was deplorable. The premature use of forceps could cause damage, infection and hemorrhaging and very often crushed the infant's head. It does not seem that the use of forceps by midwives was illegal during this period as was the case in France, for we know that several famous midwives used them in Britain. The reluctance demonstrated by the majority of midwives towards this instrument can no doubt be explained by: (1) the cost and the physical strength needed to use the original instruments, (2) the real dangers involved and the anxiety suffered by women giving birth who had been warned against the destructive use of the instrument; (3) the fact that surgeons refused to sell forceps to midwives and that the midwifery tradition knew other methods anyway.

[10]This does not stop the surgeons from using forceps as often as possible, whether the delivery was a normal one or not. This practice reduced the length of labour and gave them a clear advantage over midwives. The instrument made the reputation of the obstetrician and in France surgeons were encouraged to display it. Jacques Gélis, "Sages-femmes et accoucheuses. L'obstétrique populaire aux XVIIe et XVIIIe siècles," *Annales ESC* 32, 15 (septembre-octobre 1977), 929-52.

[11]Surveys found in "Rapport du Comité concernant la population, l'agriculture et la colonisation, part no. 18." Archives publiques du Canada, *Documents constitutionnels 1759-1791*, p. 918.

[12]Archives publiques du Canada, Documents constitutionnels 1759-1791, "Rapport du Comité concernant la population, l'agriculture et la colonisation," Rapport Fisher 1775, pp. 918, 919.

[13]Laforce, p. 94.

[14]Archives de la paroisse de Notre-Dame-de-Quebec, *42e procès-verbal de la Société compatissante de Québec*, 1862.

[15]Archives publiques du Canada, Legislative Council Papers, 22 mars 1791, folio 483, p. 2. Archives de la Bibliothèque municipale de Montréal (Salle Gagnon), *Rapport du Comité spécial*

*formé pour amender la loi relative a la pratique et de l'art obstétrique
dans le Bas-Canada*, Québec, Assemblée législative (25 octobre
1852), 20. Von Iffland, *La Gazettte de Québec* (5 novembre 1819), 15.
[16]Archives des Soeurs de la Miséricorde de Montréal,
Chroniques des Soeurs de la Miséricorde, papiers privés, 68. Dr.
Trestler, "University Lying-in Hospital," *Montreal Medical Gazette* 1
(1844), 223.

[17]Montréal, Archives de la Corporation des Médecins, dossier
sage-femme (privé), Procès des Dames du Sacré-Coeur,
correspondance, 1920.

[18]"Des sages-femmes," *L'Union médicale du Canada* 9 (1880),
275.

[19]*Ibid.*, p. 277.

[20]"Des sages-femmes," *L'abeille médicale* 2 (1880), 255.

[21]"Des sages-femmes," *L'Union médicale du Canada* 9 (1880),
277.

[22]Archives de la Corporation des médecins, Correspondance,
"Dossier sages-femmes," cas de Anna Farina Colanti, 1961.

[23]*Ibid.*, letter written by Augustin Roy to J.-B. Jobin, April
1963.

[24]Archives of the Bibliothèque municipale de Montréal (Salle
Gagnon), fonds de l'Ecole de chirurgie et de médecine de Montréal,
Soeur Marie Saint-Hilaire to Mgr. Georges Gauthier, Vice-Rector,
Université Laval (October 1917).

[25]*Ibid.*, Dr. René de Cotret to Mgr. Georges Gauthier, 5
October 1917, 1-4.

[26]This question is dealt with in Rhona Kenneally, "The
Montreal Maternity, 1849-1926; Evolution of a Hospital,"
unpublished M.A. thesis, McGill University, 1983.

[27]Archives de la Miséricorde, letter written by the mother
superior to the secretary of the Corporation of doctors, May 8, 1915.

[28]Judith Walzer Leavitt, "Science Enters the Birthing Room:
Obstetrics in America since the Eighteenth Century," *Journal of
American History* 70 (September 1970), 281-304. According to
Summey and Hurst: "The first period, from 1920-1944, marks the
formal alliance of obstetrics and gynaecology in the United States
and the formation of its ideology." Pamela S. Summey and Marsha
Hurst, "Ob/gyn. on the Rise: the evolution of professional ideology
in the twentieth century," Part One, *Women & Health* 2, 1 (Spring
1986): 133.

[29]Summey and Hurst, 140.

[30]Suzann Buckley, "Ladies or Midwives? Efforts to Reduce
Infant and Maternal Mortality," in Linda Kealey, ed., *A Not
Unreasonable Claim: Women and Reform in Canada, 1880s-1920s*
(Toronto: The Women's Press, 1979), pp. 144-7.

[31]Archives de l'Université Laval, lettre de Mgr. Camille Roy à
M. Jean Bruchési, Université 500 no 153, 10 février, 1938. "Je
viens de recevoir une délégation de l'Association des gardes ou
infirmières diplômées de l'Université Laval. Les gardes me prient

d'intervenir auprès de l'honorable Secrétaire de la Province au sujet des cours de sage-femme et de garde-malades qui se donnent à l'Ecole technique de Québec aux jeunes chômeuses en vertu du plan Rogers-Bilodeau, ce, afin de les faire cesser, car ils font une concurrence déloyale aux infirmières."

[32]For Australia, see Evan Willis, *Medical Dominance: The Division of Labour in Australian Health Care* (George Allen & Unwin Australia Pty. Ltd., 1983). In the United States the bibliography on midwives contains numerous titles. We particularly recommend the excellent synthesis by Richard W. Wertz and Dorothy C. Wertz, *Lying-In: A History of Childbirth in America* (New York: Schocken, 1979) as well as that by Judith Walzer Leavitt, *Brought to Bed: Child-Bearing in America, 1750-1950* (New York and Oxford: Oxford University Press, 1986). Two classic articles in the field are Judith Walzer Leavitt, "Science Enters the Birthing Room: Obstetrics in America since the Eighteenth Century," *Journal of American History* 70 (September 1970), 281-304, and Frances Kobrin, "The American Midwife Controversy," *Bulletin of the History of Medicine* 40 (July-August 1966), 350-63. For Great Britain see Jean Donnison, *Midwives and Medical Men: A History of Inter-Professional Rivalries and Women's Rights* (London: Heinemann, 1977), and Jean Towler and Joan Bramall, *Midwives in History and Society* (London: Croom Helm, 1986). See also in this volume, Jane Lewis, Lesley Biggs and Jo Oppenheimer.

[33]Jo Oppenheimer, "Childbirth in Ontario: The Transition from Home to Hospital in the Early Twentieth Century," in this volume, pp. 51-74. Wertz and Wertz, p. 260.

[34]*Foetal, Newborn and Maternal Morality and Morbidity* cited in Wertz and Wertz, p. 161.

[35]Jean-Marie Fecteau, "Pauvres, indigents et assistés au Québec: modes successifs d'insertion de l'Etat dans le processus de réduction des discordances sociales," unpublished M.A. thesis, Université Laval, 1976; Jacques Bernier, "Les praticiens de la santé au Québec, 1871-1921, quelques données statistiques," *Recherches sociographiques* 20, 1 (janvier-avril), 41-58; Howard S. Berliner, "La consolidation du pouvoir médical au début du siècle: une nouvelle interprétation du rapport Flexnor," in *Médecine et société. Les anneés 80* (Montréal: Les Editions Saint-Martin, 4e édition, 1985).

[36]For the influence of the College of Physicians on the Quebec Legislature and on the Legislative Council, see Hélène Laforce, p. 110.

Chapter Four

CHILDBIRTH IN ONTARIO: THE TRANSITION FROM HOME TO HOSPITAL IN THE EARLY TWENTIETH CENTURY[*]

Jo Oppenheimer

Childbirth has always been a precarious experience. The apprehension that women have felt has been well justified when one considers that, similar to the statistics elsewhere, the maternal mortality rate in Ontario did not drop below one death per 1000 live births until 1950,[1] and that even today, more than one per cent of children in the province die before they reach their first birthday (1,795 children under one year old, including stillborns, died in 1986).[2] These figures do not begin to reflect the numbers of women who are permanently injured during childbirth or the numbers of children who survive in spite of birth defects and birth injuries. As dismal as these statistics seem, however, the nineteenth-century picture was far more sombre.[3] The first three decades of the twentieth century were as tragic in terms of maternal deaths as the late nineteenth century: there was a record high of 489 or 6.75 deaths per 1000 live births in 1920. Infant mortality rates were not significantly reduced until the 1920s.

For society in Ontario, and for most of North America, the most noticeable change in birthing custom from mid-nineteenth century to mid-twentieth century was the location of parturition; until 1938 most births in Ontario took place at home and after that date most births took place in hospital.[4] Although the number of maternal deaths declined at about the same time the shift took place in birthing location, analysis of other factors suggests that location was only coincidental and that the initial reduction of maternal and infant deaths was related to the generic well-being of the individual and the community through a better understanding of 'health' and by the practice of healthful living. The shift to hospital births appears to have been related to the convenience of

[*]Reprinted by permission of the Ontario Historical Society from *Ontario History* 75, 1 (March 1983), 36-60.

the obstetrician and his 'patient', and to the attempts of medical
men to quell the rising tide of public dissatisfaction over the
continuing high maternal and infant mortality rates.

Hospital care before the 1880s was quite primitive by today's
standards. The York Hospital, the first real hospital in Ontario and
the precursor of the Toronto General Hospital, was opened to the
public in 1829, primarily to treat the veterans of the War of 1812
and destitute immigrants. The buildings used before 1875 were
often overcrowded and ventilation and heating were constant
problems. It was commonly reported that the limited supply of
bedding was filthy and in a poor state of repair. Some members of
the staff, it was noted, evidently took full advantage of the patients'
brandy and whisky allowance and it was also noted that the women
who acted as nurses were "too often crude and uneducated."[5]
Although medical treatment of diseases varied from doctor to doctor,
bloodletting or leeching and poulticing were common prescriptions
for most ailments. Add to this the fact that during the periodic
epidemics many patients died in hospital, it is not difficult to
understand why people feared going to hospital. In the York
Hospital and Dispensary Report to the Legislature of 1832 it was
stated:

> It is worthy of remark that most of the lower orders have
> such an aversion to an hospital, that they will not submit
> to be removed until they are conveyed hither [sic] in a
> state of insensibility.[6]

Another commonly held fear that the medical men had difficulty
dispelling was that the doctors and medical students would use the
patients or their bodies for dissections and experimentation.[7] The
fact that the public mistrusted teaching hospitals was still a topic
for discussion in the early twentieth century.

If hospitals were only for the diseased and wounded and, more
specifically, only for those who could not afford to receive medical
care at home, how, one might ask, did birthing become a hospital
procedure? It happened as a result of several developments: first,
lying-in hospitals and homes for unwed mothers were established;
second, after non-medical midwifery was made illegal, women began
having doctors attend their births; and finally, the public, as their
awareness of health developed, demanded that the maternal and
infant mortality rates be lowered.

The first institution in Ontario for women needing care
during childbirth was established in 1820. The Society for the
Relief of Women during their Confinement[8] was organized as a
charity under the patronage of Lady Maitland (the wife of the
Lieutenant-Governor, Sir Peregrine Maitland). It provided clothing
for mother and child, a midwife-nurse, a physician if required, and
food for destitute women. The Society's report of 1825 notes that in
its first four years fifty women had greatly benefitted from the
services of the organization.

FIGURE I

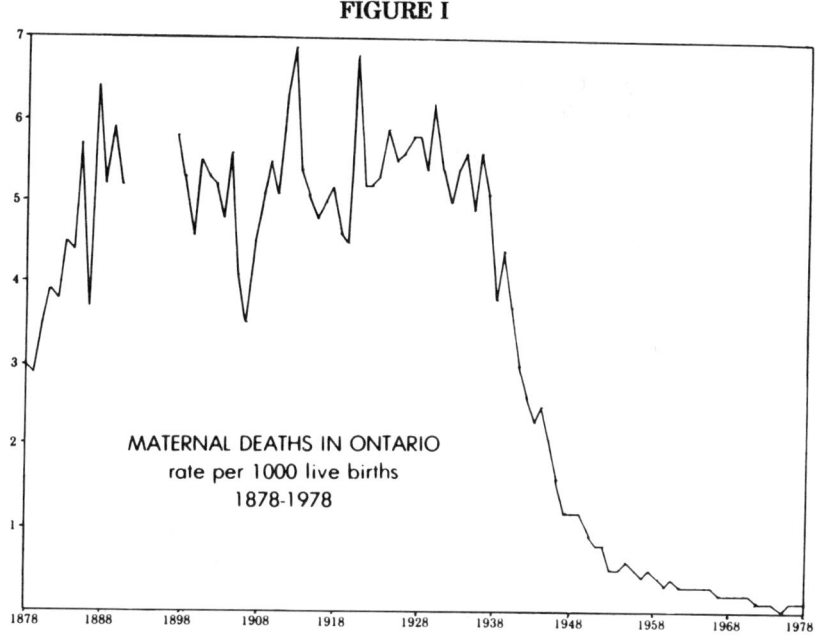

MATERNAL DEATHS IN ONTARIO
rate per 1000 live births
1878-1978

Source: Ontario Registrar-General, *Report Relating to the
Registration of Births, Marriages and Deaths, 1880-1892,
1897-1979.*

Since the society did not, however, provide shelter, except in
the case of a few orphans, those poor women who lacked housing
were forced to go to the General Hospital for their confinements.
The increase in the number of poor immigrants and the outbreak of
cholera in 1832 brought to the attention of the medical board of the
hospital the need for a more suitable institution to benefit destitute
strangers. It was also emphasized at that time that such an
institution was needed to train students and midwives.[9] By the
1840s the programme of medical studies offered at both the Rolph
School (later to become the Toronto School of Medicine) and the
King's College (later University of Toronto) Faculty of Medicine
included lectures on the principles and practice of obstetrics and the
M.B. (Bachelor of Medicine) degree required an apprenticeship of
six months' attendance at a lying-in hospital.
        It was not, however, until June, 1848, that the Toronto
General Dispensary and Lying-in Hospital was established for the
dual purpose of providing care for destitute women and an arena for
the preparation of medical midwives. *The Globe* announced the
opening of the new charity institution, making known to the public
that there were five beds prepared to receive patients and that

FIGURE II

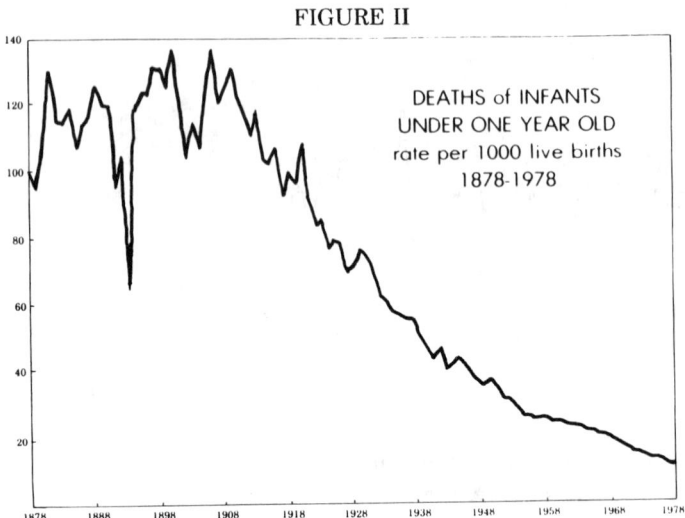

Source: Ontario Registrar-General, *Report Relating to the Registration of Births, Marriages and Deaths*, 1880-1979.

FIGURE III

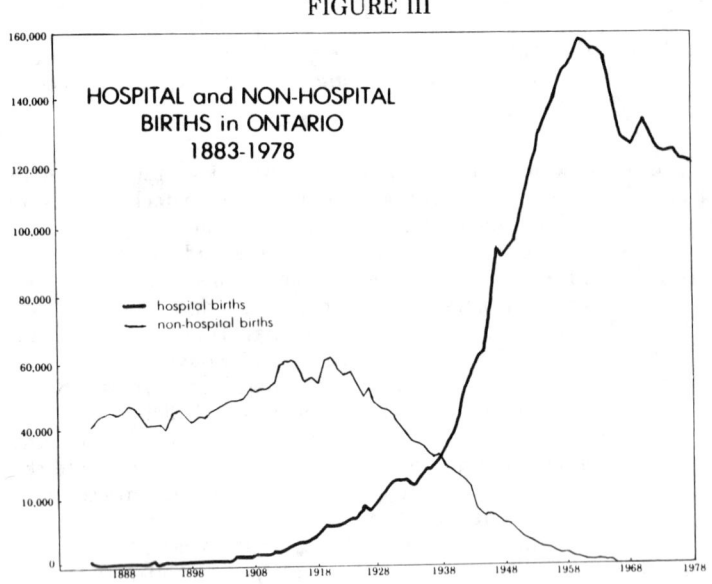

Source: Ontario Registrar-General, *Report Relating to the Registration of Births, Marriages and Deaths*, 1885-1979; Ontario, *Report of the Inspector of Hospitals and Refuges*, 1884-1926.

funds were urgently needed.[10]   The Trinity College Medical Faculty[11] circular of 1853, with reference to the Toronto General Dispensary and Lying-in Hospital, advertises that:

> The Lying-in Hospital in Richmond Street, with its abundant sources of information for sufficiently advanced pupils, that is to say, for those who have already attended one course of lectures on the subject, cannot be surpassed in Canada. The pupils have the advantage of reference to the Professor of Midwifery in all cases of difficulty, and he will from time to time give practical or clinical lectures on the cases of interest in the house.[12]

It seems that by 1856 the Toronto General Dispensary and Lying-in Hospital had become affiliated with Trinity College since the medical officers of the hospital were Trinity instructors. The Toronto Directory of 1856 lists two other institutions, the Maternity Lying-in Hospital and the General Dispensary and Vaccine Institution, stating that they provided similar services in association with the Toronto School of Medicine and Toronto University, respectively.[13]   By 1869 the three lying-in hospitals amalgamated and became known as the Burnside Lying-in Hospital. In 1877 the Burnside united with the Toronto General Hospital and in 1878 moved to new quarters beside the General on Gerrard Street between Sumach and Pine Streets.

The Burnside, true to the initial *raison d'être*, remained a training hospital for medical students, continued to serve charity patients, and acted as a treatment centre for diseases of women.[14] Until 1890, it was the only institution in Toronto where students could gain clinical obstetrical experience and where women could have their babies in hospital. The vast majority of women still had their babies at home with the help of doctors or, in some cases, midwives. Since hospital births were associated with high rates of puerperal fever and with charity, and an overall fear of hospitals still existed, most homes offered a preferable environment even when a doctor anticipated a difficult birth. Nevertheless, the way was set to train doctors in midwifery at lying-in hospitals.

A further development that led to the use of hospitals for birthing was the outcome of the Provincial Board of Health's recommendation in 1882 that female lock-hospitals (prisons with hospital facilities) be established to check prostitution.[15]   This suggestion does not appear to have been followed precisely. In 1885 the Board altered its recommendation slightly, this time suggesting that infant homes and well-equipped lying-in hospitals be established to reduce the very high incidence of death among foundlings and to prevent infanticide.[16] This recommendation was followed by legislation in 1887--the Act for the Protection of Infant Children--which required the registration in every local municipality of houses for the reception of infants.[17] In addition, the Salvation Army opened its first Rescue Home in Toronto on April 26, 1888. The original intent of the "rescue" was to provide a home and training for young women who had become prostitutes or who had been induced to live with men because they had no other means of support, and eventually to find more appropriate employment for them.[18] Similar homes were subsequently opened in Windsor, Hamilton, and Ottawa. Their function soon after their opening became that of small maternity hospitals and homes for unwed mothers.[19]

In 1897 the provincial legislation was revised to include the registration and inspection of maternity boarding houses and the requirement that "every birth which shall take place in such a house or hospital shall be attended by a legally qualified medical practitioner. . ."[20] The Medical Health Officer for Toronto, Dr. Charles Sheard, in 1899 acknowledged that permits had been issued for "seven Maternity Boarding Houses within the City. . ."[21]

Although these maternity hospitals were being established and were coming under the control of government and its agencies, they were strictly for "unfortunate women." While the number of hospitals in general had increased by the end of the nineteenth century, the number of babies born in hospitals had not increased substantially. There were 501 babies born in Ontario hospitals during 1883 and only 789 in 1899. Even when Women's College Hospital first opened, it was only a dispensary. It did not become fully a hospital until 1910, and it was not until 1911 that the first baby was born there. While the hospital was dedicated to the care of women by women, only 1,030 babies were born at the hospital in the ensuing ten years.[22]

What had changed during the latter part of the nineteenth century was that, since professional midwifery had been made illegal,[23] most births took place with the attendance of a physician. This was a very important second step in the final transition from home to hospital births. Out of 47,323 births in Ontario in 1897, only 7,794 were reported as having had no physician and 1,388 of these, mostly in remote districts, were attended by midwives.[24]

The third and final step in the transition to hospital births happened gradually over a fifty-year period. It was the result of increasing awareness of issues related to health and the demands by the public for better medical services. This process began in the 1880s with the re-establishment of the Provincial Board of Health in 1882 when it was noted that an enormous proportion of deaths in the province were "due to preventable causes."[25] In the light of that awareness, the Board, with extremely limited funds and manpower, set upon the colossal job of cleaning the cities, purifying water supplies, building sewage systems, inspecting food and buildings and educating the people "in the nature of the physical laws which govern their own bodies, as regards air, food, exercise, dress and the numerous other details which belong to the everyday life of the individual."[26]

In 1876, Louis Pasteur demonstrated the germ theory to be
true. This gave rise to the attempt to isolate the causes of the
zymotic, or infectious, diseases. In 1882 the cause of tuberculosis
was suspected and by 1887 the causes of diphtheria and typhoid
were both suspected. Since it was proven that the diseases that
were responsible for large numbers of deaths were contagious,
people with such a disease were either put into an isolation hospital
or quarantined at home. As a result, 19,617 patients were treated
in 47 hospitals in 1897 in contrast with only 4,372 patients
receiving treatment in ten Ontario hospitals nineteen years earlier
in 1878.[27]

The mortality rates associated with some contagious diseases
fell dramatically, with the introduction of new medical treatments,
as the following table illustrates:

TABLE I

Deaths Attributed to Contagious Diseases in Ontario

	Smallpox	Scarlatina	Diphtheria	Typhoid
1882-86	128	1929	5028	3027
1887-91	16	650	4774	3060
1892-96	7	993	4774	1642

Source· Ontario, Board of Health, *Annual Report, 1897,* 9.

It was soon discovered, however, that hospitalization was not
the only source of relief. Diphtheria and typhoid, it was found, were
spread through the use of contaminated water and milk. The
subsequent action of the Board of Health was to ensure that water
and milk (and other food products) were free from contamination.
While province-wide inspections of water, milk, and food were being
initiated, along with the passage of legislation regarding these
items, examination of all school children, especially absentees, was
begun.

With the decrease in deaths attributed to contagious diseases,
the principal cause of death changed, as shown in Table 2 below.

Note that pre-natal deaths increased and moved into first
place by 1896. Since at that time the connection between pre-natal
care and foetal development had not been made, the following
statement, without prescription, was the resulting official medical
reaction to these statistics:

. . .pre-natal stands first, and includes all stillbirths, all deaths returned as heart failure under one year, and those dying within two or three months of birth without any definitely assigned cause. This classification must be considered very unsatisfactory, but inasmuch as children delicate at birth continue throughout their brief life in a lingering death, and frequently are but casually seen by physicians, it is probably as fair to ascribe the cause of death to immature development as to anything else.[28]

TABLE II

Principal Causes of Death in Ontario, 1893-1896

1893 cause/no. of deaths		1894 cause/no. of deaths		1895 cause/no. of deaths		1896 cause/no. of deaths	
phthisis*	2552	phthisis	2379	phthisis	2474	pre-natal	2772
old age	2306	old age	2008	pre-natal	2266	phthisis	2752
pre-natal	1840	pre-natal	1839	old age	2053	old age	2543
pneumonia	1595	pneumonia	1487	pneumonia	1551	pneumonia	1638
diphtheria	942	diphtheria	1075	diphtheria	942	diphtheria	980

*TB

Source: Ontario Registrar-General, *Report Relating to the Registration of Births, Marriages and Deaths, 1895-1898.*

In 1906 the Registrar-General's Report introduced a new table, one which included the deaths of children in age groups under five years, given by individual disease. This table brought to the attention of physicians, public health workers, and others responsible for the welfare of children the seriousness of the problem as well as its specific causes. Figure IV illustrates the patterns of the four greatest causes of infant mortality according to these reports. Except for epidemics of communicable diseases (mainly whooping cough and influenza), infants died from pneumonia and bronchitis, diarrhoea and enteritis, and by far the greatest number as a result of malformations, congenital weakness and stillbirths.

Although pre-natal problems accounted for the greatest number of deaths, immediate attention was focused on child care and only later was pre-natal care introduced in the public health programme. Dr. Charles Hodgetts, the Deputy Registrar-General and Chief Health Officer set the direction for the early twentieth-century child care programme when he wrote in 1904:

Too often is it found that the life of the first-born is sacrificed during the early months of its life by reason of the lack of knowledge on the part of the parents in the care necessary in the feeding of this valuable portion of

FIGURE IV

Some Causes of Infant Mortality in Ontario 1899-1949
Rate Per 1000 Live Births

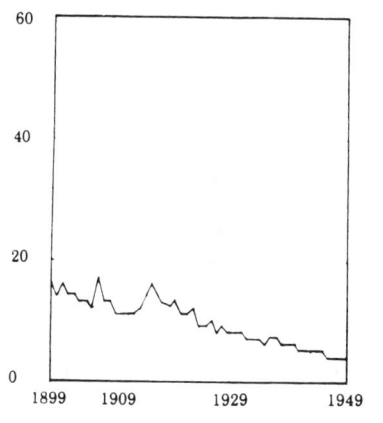

Diseases of the Respiratory System

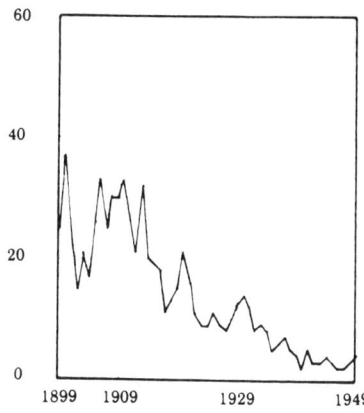

Diseases of the Digestive System

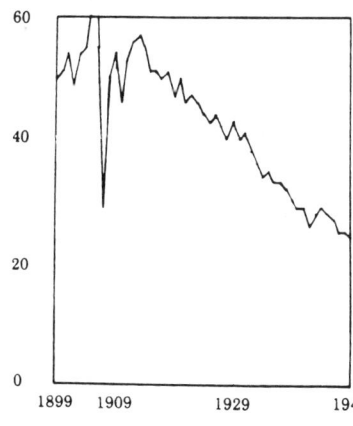

Malformations and Congenital Weakness

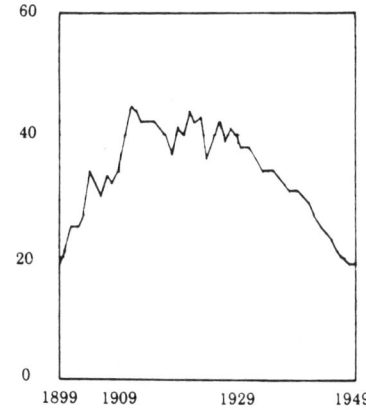

Still Births

Source: Ontario Registrar-General, *Report Relating to the Registration of Births, Marriages and Deaths*, 1900-1950.

our population, and a lack of knowledge as to the care in
the toilet and personal hygiene of these dear little
infants. . .
This Board of Health should impress upon the
Legislature, upon the educationists, upon the clergy . . .
even upon the medical profession, the growing need of this
neglected . . . subject being taken up and given a more
prominent place in our nation's life.[29]

It was not until 1910 that the first child care programmes
were started in an attempt to bring to a halt the 'slaughter of the
innocents'. Since it had been noted that infant deaths caused by
gastro-intestinal diseases nearly always occurred in bottle-fed
infants, an intensive movement to provide pure milk was begun. In
Ottawa four Infant Milk Stations were opened where milk was given
free to those who could not afford it (mothers were encouraged to
nurse their babies and drink the milk themselves) and where
doctors held a clinic once a week to give free care to infants.
Another part of the programme was the distribution of literature to
families through medical officers and teachers. The first annual
public health exhibit (which included a moving picture show) was
displayed at the Canadian National Exhibition in 1910. A number
of organizations were formed, for example, the Baby's Welfare
League, Little Mother's League, and the Baby's Milk Dispensary
Guild, to spread the word to mothers and to train young girls, the
future mothers, in infant care. Public health nurses had been hired
in a few cities and began inspecting the sanitation of homes where
newborns were reported and checking the feeding of infants.

By 1911 the Ontario Legislature passed an act requiring that
those selling milk in the province be licensed and their equipment
be inspected.[30] This was followed in 1912 by a new Public Health
Act which gave more power to medical health officers in terms of
ability to enforce legislation. The structure of the department was
also changed: seven districts headed by full-time, paid officers were
created. In 1914 the Division of Child Hygiene was added. This
division was responsible for the creation of "Mothercraft" classes
which were offered through the public health nurses.

A drop in the infant mortality rate from 129.7 per 1000 live
births in 1909 to 107.3 in 1916 was attributed to this first phase in
the child care movement. A second phase, a more effective
campaign against child deaths, began in 1917 when the Bureau of
Child Welfare advised the public that "this loss of life is a matter of
national importance in view of the large number of casualties in the
Canadian Expeditionary Force. . ."[31]

The Ontario Board of Health took up the challenge to reduce
child mortality further and in 1917 published *The Baby*, a pamphlet
on infant and child care. *The Baby* included not only instructions
on feeding, nursing and bathing the baby, but also introduced, for
the first time, care for the mother-to-be. Pre-natal care was still

part of a programme to reduce infant mortality. It had not yet become an issue associated with maternal mortality. *The Baby* recommended that:

As soon as you know a baby is coming place yourself under the care of your physician, and follow his advice. If you cannot afford a doctor, apply to a hospital or dispensary where experienced doctors and nurses will advise and care for you.

The care which every mother should insist upon receiving during this period should include all of the following:

1. Monthly examination of urine from the fifth to the ninth month.
2. Supervision of a private physician with monthly visits at least from 5th to 9th month.
3. Measurement of the pelvis in the first pregnancy.
4. General physical examination, including blood pressure, examination of the abdomen and heart and lungs.[32]

Child welfare work continued in the cities of Toronto, Hamilton, Ottawa, and Fort William. The travelling exhibits conducted by the public health nurses were expanded in terms of both the places visited and the information distributed. The Bureau recommended that children's wards be added to existing hospitals. And the topic of "infant mortality" was discussed in a number of conventions held in Canada and the United States.

In 1918 Ontario introduced the *Regulations for the Control of Babies' Sore Eyes* (the requirement for the insertion of silver nitrate into newborns' eyes to prevent blindness as a result of gonorrhoea), and distributed 25,000 copies of *The Baby*. The Chief Officer of Health, John W. S. McCullough, wrote,

In the absence of any Federal public health organization or the immediate prospect of such being inaugurated, it is imperative that Ontario should not only continue the efforts already made in the line of Child Welfare but that these efforts should be very materially increased.

To this end, he recommended the adoption of a motherhood plan similar to that of New Zealand, where women were invited as guests to hospital for a week or so where they could be given instruction in the care of the baby and of themselves. He also recommended the use of a system in which country nurses would organize local committees, aid in medical inspection of schools, give demonstrations of baby care to school girls and their mothers, assist in pre-natal care of mothers, and hold baby clinics and exhibitions.[33] The latter part of the plan was adopted; ten centres were organized to run clinics and co-ordinate child welfare work. Exhibits and special clinics were held at 24 sites and "Baby Week" lectures were given in conjunction with exhibitions. In 1919 the exhibits were brought to 13 centres and free physical examinations were given to babies and older children.

Within the Board of Health the Division of Public Health Education was established in September, 1920. This addition greatly aided in the distribution of health literature. Weekly articles were written and published in local newspapers (220 weeklies carried health articles in 1922) and Women's Institutes were employed to host demonstrations. The "Child Welfare Special," a truck designed to carry the exhibits, was purchased and used to tour the province. The Child Welfare Division of the Board was expanded and renamed the Division of Maternal and Child Hygiene, reflecting the recognition that child health depended on maternal health. The expansion included the hiring of eight public health nurses, one for each provincial health district. The Red Cross supplied eight additional nurses to be paired in each district. A full-time pediatrician was appointed, and sixteen other nurses entered training in public health work.

By 1921 the child and maternal hygiene programme was fully underway. Nineteen local public health nurses were hired and during the year made 767 pre-natal visits, 430 post-natal visits, and checked 6,004 children at 390 pre-school clinics.[34] Except for the influenza and whooping cough epidemics in 1920, the child mortality rate decreased noticeably after 1918.[35] The Board of Health reports constantly repeated, district by district, that the lower infant mortality rates were due to the work of the district nurses and increased attendance at the baby clinics. Again and again the reports stated that it was the job of the public health nurse to provide education and pre-natal care.

With a certain amount of assurance that child care was being brought under control, attention was finally turned to maternal mortality. In 1921 Dr. W. J. Bell, the pediatrician for the Board of Health presented a paper entitled "Maternal Mortality" at the Annual Meeting of the American Child Hygiene Association. In his report he stated that while the statistics showed an increase in maternal mortality, they actually under-represented the true number "owing to the fact that some physicians prefer to report death as due to almost any other cause rather than puerperal sepsis or one of the other causes of maternal mortality."[36] Along with declaring that the problem was far more serious than previously reported, Dr. Bell announced that "the Deputy Registrar-General is preparing a questionnaire for physicians, dealing with the death of every female between the ages of 16 and 49, to obtain information as to whether pregnancy or parturition was the direct or contributory cause of the woman's death."[37]

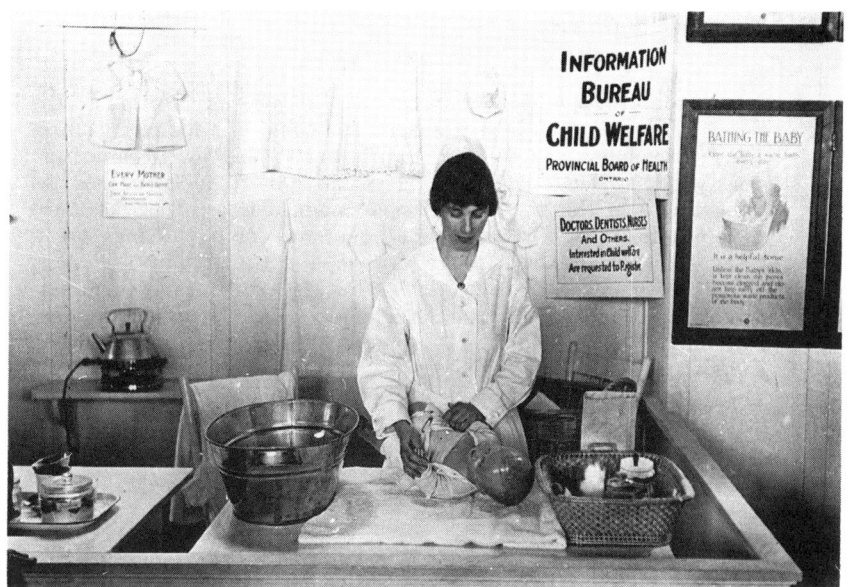

Public Health Nurse demonstrating "Bathing the Baby," at the Canadian National Exhibition Baby Clinic, September 6, 1918.

Source: Ontario Archives, RG 10, 30-A-2 (2.2.3A)

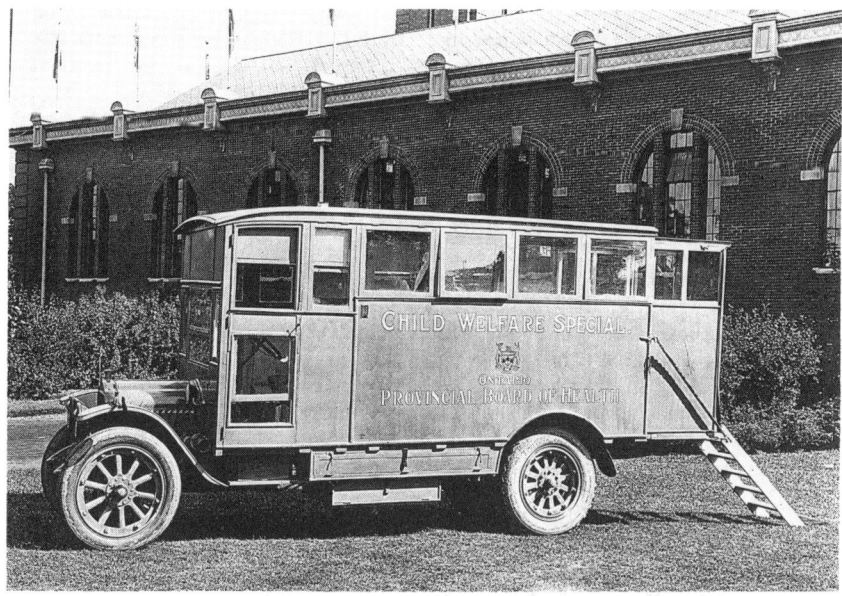

A sign attached to this converted truck, on exhibit at the 1918 Canadian National Exhibition, read: "This is a Child Welfare Clinic on Wheels. It is to visit the Cities, Towns & Villages of Ontario. A Doctor and Nurse in Charge. Ask for it if you would like it to call at your Town."

Source: Ontario Archives, RG 10, 30-A-2 (2.3.9)

From 1922 until 1924, the work and the orientation of the Board of Health remained primarily the same as they had been in the previous few years. In 1925, however, the health education work of the Department of Education was transferred to the Department of Health.[38] The Department of Health now assumed the responsibility for child, adult, occupational disease, chest, orthopedic, eye, dental, and ear, nose, and throat clinics. Along with these increased responsibilities, the Department also turned its attention to the sparsely populated regions. At the 1926 Canadian National Exhibition, the Department of Health exhibition emphasized industrial hygiene, vital statistics, and tuberculosis. The baby show, which had been so popular since its introduction in 1910, was not even included.

Although the Department's emphasis had changed, its policy with regard to birthing had not. The 1926 issue of the Department's *Health Almanac* stated:

> Child-bearing. . .demands adequate medical and nursing attention. All those in any way concerned must realize that practically all of the factors responsible for this loss of maternal life can be done away with by reasonable pre-natal care.[39]

The Division of Maternal and Child Hygiene's 1927 report reflected, however, a change in emphasis away from the nurses and foreshadowed the action which would be taken in the future for child and maternal care, namely to rely on doctors for medical supervision, both obstetrical and pre-natal.[40]

The concern over the high mortality rates continued to gain momentum. In 1927 Women's Institutes made the question of maternal mortality an important part of their programme plans for the following year.[41] The Federal Department of Health completed a special inquiry into the question of maternal mortality and concluded that Canada's rank as second highest among the reporting nations was not "an enviable one."[42] J. J. Fraser, the district Public Health Officer for Guelph, stated emphatically that "we know the causes of maternal mortality, and we know that at least 50 per cent of these deaths are preventable. That should be something to start from."[43] Pressure to do more to lessen mortality rates was coming from several directions.

The Division of Maternal and Child Hygiene's 1929 report spelled out the controversy that had begun to rage over the central issue of lowering maternal mortality rates. The report stated that sides were taken by "the proponents of pre-natal care," "those who stress the value of more extensive hospitalization," others calling for "better obstetrical training" and "some who insist that the more widespread extension of public health nursing throughout the province generally, is essential to the success of any measures established for the lessening of the maternal death rate."[44] The

Department's position was made clear: it openly supported doctors over the nurses and left the final details to the leaders in the obstetrical field. The previous emphasis on a strong programme of instruction in pre-natal care gave way to one on increased obstetrical care; the shift in emphasis was made by the "leaders in the obstetrical field." The Department's position was that it would try to bring about a "fully enlightened womanhood;" however, it would also await "with hope the early development of physicians skilled and painstaking."[45]

The 1930 Division's report more assuredly demonstrated that the Department of Health had chosen sides against the nurses and at the same time had chosen to place the responsibility for lowering the mortality rates on the doctors. The report stated:

> The whole question of lessening maternal deaths is one of adequate medical supervision during the pre-natal period, and the maximum of obstetrical service during labour. No health department can do any more than urge that the two parties concerned, namely, the expectant mother and the attending physician, should establish a professional contact at the earliest possible moment, and maintain such contact until well on in the post-natal period . . .[46]

The work of the Department then turned to the necessity of persuading the medical profession and the public that the problem was that of the doctors. In 1931 the Division declared:

> It is the hope of the Division that, following the evident interest on the part of the leaders in the field of obstetrics in the subject of maternal deaths, that a better conception of the relative importance of the various factors which contribute toward this higher-than-should-be death rate, will result.[47]

This was followed in 1932 by the assertion that:

> the lessening of the morbidity and mortality associated with maternity is primarily a task for the medical profession. No other agency can, willingly or otherwise, assume this responsibility. The interested woman can, however, materially lighten the load of the physician by consulting him at the earliest possible moment and by following his advice literally.[48]

The *Health Almanac* in its 1932 edition refers to the mother-to-be as a "patient," although much of the entry on birth still includes information for home confinements.[49] Instructions for home confinements (four pages listing equipment and its preparation) continued to appear in *The Baby* until at least 1948, but after 1940 it was stated that "it is becoming more common for women to have their confinement take place in hospital. It has many advantages, everything necessary in the way of equipment being at hand if any emergency should arise . . ."[50]

In 1933 a major study was conducted to investigate maternal mortality in the province. Following is a list of some of the findings of that study:

- There has been no significant reduction in mortality from puerperal causes during the last twenty-five years.
- Mortality due to pregnancy and childbirth is second only to tuberculosis in women of childbearing age.
- The estimated specific puerperal mortality among "urban" women was 5.7 per 1000 live births and 4.7 among women in rural areas. Practically all the difference was found in excess in mortality from puerperal sepsis and abortion in the urban group.
- By type of delivery, the estimated specific mortality was 8.2 per 1000 births in the "operative" group and 2.3 in the "spontaneous" group.
- The specific puerperal mortality rates for hospital (only those delivered in hospital and dying there) and domiciliary cases were 5.3 and 2.3 per 1000 births respectively. On the same basis, the death rates from puerperal sepsis were 1.7 and 0.7 per 1000 births respectively.
- In 18 per cent of delivered cases a Caesarean Section was performed. The incidence of Caesarean Sections among fatal delivered cases was found to be more than twice as high among urban than among rural mothers.[51]

The results of this survey are extremely important. They point out that while maternal mortality had not been reduced significantly in 25 years, it was also true that maternal deaths had increased in hospital deliveries. There were 5.3 maternal deaths per 1000 births in hospital as opposed to 2.3 maternal deaths per 1000 births in home births. It was found that deaths associated with sepsis and abortion had risen in the urban population, and that both were connected with hospitalization. There were 8.2 maternal deaths per 1000 births in women whose babies were delivered, that is doctor-controlled, as compared with 2.3 per 1000 births in women whose babies were born 'naturally'--without medical interference. It was further reported that 18 per cent of the births that were 'delivered' births were done by Caesarean Section and that these were twice as high among urban mothers who died than among rural mothers who died.

Hospitalization of childbirth continued to be advised, however, and the results of the survey were used to pressure hospitals to provide better services and doctors to improve obstetrical techniques. The fall in maternal mortality rates in the late 1930s thus was the result of changes made in birthing techniques, not location. This argument is further substantiated by looking at the causes of maternal mortality, illustrated by the graphs in Figure V. These graphs indicate that there was no significant reduction in any one area that could be associated with hospitalization. The drop in septicaemia, which accounted for the largest proportion of the decrease in deaths, was not due to hospitalization. In fact, sepsis was noted to have been substantially higher among women whose babies were born in hospital. Until World War II, maternal deaths were consistently lower among rural mothers who tended not to go into hospital. Widespread post-war employment of chemotherapy, particularly sulfa drugs and antibiotics, was used to treat infection, and for the first time deaths among urban mothers dropped below those in rural districts.[52]

The substantial decrease in maternal deaths after 1946 can, in part, be attributed to the fact that on 1 October 1946 legislation went into effect making available one complete medical examination during the period of pregnancy for any expectant mother resident in the province. The legislation reflected the rising awareness among doctors of the importance of pre-natal care. Remember, however, that the involvement of doctors with pre-natal care had been growing since 1927. The following table indicates the increase in the percentage of women who took advantage of the pre-natal care service.

TABLE III

Percentage of Women Receiving Pre-Natal Examinations, 1947-1953

1947	1948	1949	1950	1951	1952	1953
39.4%	49.4%	54.0%	60.0%	62.0%	64.7%	66.5%

Source: Ontario, Department of Health, *Annual Reports, 1949-1954.*

Since World War II the number of maternal deaths and especially peri-natal deaths has increasingly been a matter of concern. Throughout the period investigation of maternal deaths in childbirth has continued and changes have been made in hospital technique and medical intervention. The growing concern with maternal mortality resulted from the awareness that the well-being of the expectant mother is crucial not only to her own life but also

FIGURE V

**Principal Causes of Puerperal Deaths in Ontario 1910-1945
Rate per 1000 Live Births**

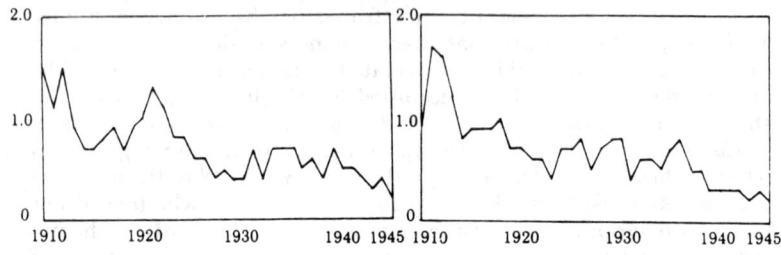

Accidents of Pregnancy   Accidents of Childbirth

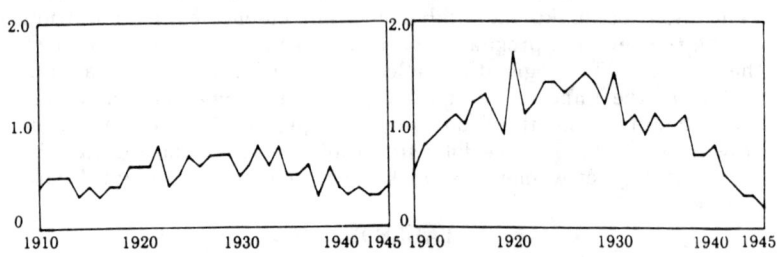

Haemorrhage   Albumineria

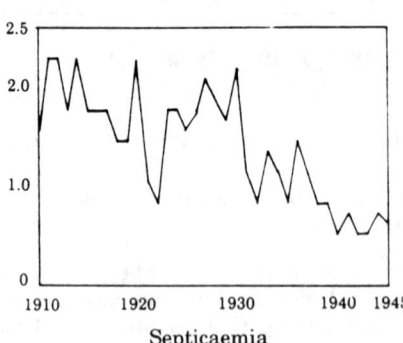

Septicaemia

Source: Ontario Registrar-General, *Report Relating to the Registration of
Births, Marriages and Deaths, 1911-1946.*

FIGURE VI

Maternal Mortality by Location 1931-1950
Rates per 1000 Live Births

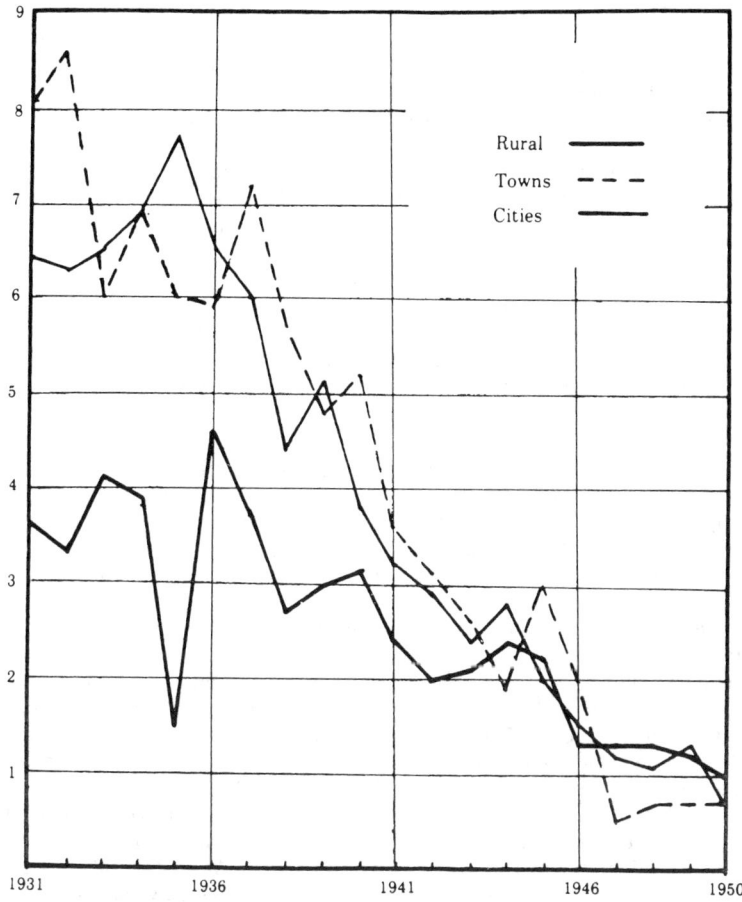

Source: Ontario, Registrar-General, *Report Relating to the Registration of Births, Marriages and Deaths, 1932-1951.*

to that of the child. Under the impact of the second wave of feminism in addition to the spiritual and 'back-to-the-earth' movements, the women's health movement has reasserted women's right to have control over pre-natal care and the conditions and location of childbirth. Nonetheless, the issue of pre-natal care has not yet been made a priority by the medical establishment. Virtually all pre-natal classes in the province are attended on a voluntary basis and have been taught solely by nurses, midwives and lay teachers. In 1979, a report recommending a pre-natal care education programme was actually rejected by the Medical Officer of Health in Toronto in favour of a computer-based programme to detect and monitor high-risk pregnancies.[53] And in response to the renewed interest in home births and the re-emergence of non-medical midwifery,[54] the College of Physicians and Surgeons of Ontario issued in January 1982 the following statement:

> Some physicians have been urged by their patients to attend them at home when they go into labour. The College would discourage this practice because it does not consider home births to be safe or in the patient's best interest.

This notice further stated that "it is professional misconduct for a member to permit, counsel or assist any person not licensed as a physician [e.g., a nurse, midwife or homebirth attendant] to engage in the practice of medicine [i.e., attend a homebirth]."[55]

Evidence mounted through the 1980s that homebirths, in carefully screened low-risk deliveries, are associated with low neo-natal mortality and result in significantly lower incidence of morbidity (such as, infection, respiratory distress, maternal hemorrhage) and of obstetrical interventions (such as, episiotomies and use of forceps).[56] Even in the face of this evidence, in March 1983 and again in May 1987, the College reiterated its belief that "out-of-hospital births should be discouraged because of potential additional risks to the mother and to the baby."[57]

Due to the increase in alternative health services, many of which were not included under the Health Disciplines Act, the Ontario Ministry of Health finally admitted by August 1983 that its legislation governing health professions was "patchwork" and "in need of amendment" and accordingly appointed the Ontario Health Disciplines Act Review Board. Significant to the review were questions surrounding midwifery. The Task Force on the Implementation of Midwifery in Ontario was subsequently organized with a mandate to address such issues as the education and qualifications of midwives, scope, standards and locations of practice, and patient access. The Task Force's submissions to the Review Board have brought to light many issues related to childbirth. Legislation stemming from the Review Board's report (due late 1987) is likely to broaden the range of options in pre-natal care, childbirth and post-natal care. Although the possibility of resolution appears to be better now than ever before, the childbirth problem is still with us.

Notes

[1]See Figure I.

[2]Ontario, Registrar-General, Statistics Department. See Figure II for earlier statistics.

[3]". . . within a hundred years infant mortality has been reduced . . . from 75 per cent of all births to a little over 25 per cent . . ." Ontario, Board of Health, *Annual Report 1882* (Toronto, 1883), p. xi.

[4]See Figure III.

[5]C. K. Clarke, *A History of the Toronto General Hospital* (Toronto: W. Briggs, 1913); W. G. Cosbie, *The Toronto General Hospital 1819-1965* (Toronto: Macmillan of Canada, 1975), pp. 1-61, 70-5.

[6]Cited in Ontario, Board of Health, *Annual Report 1891* (Toronto, 1892), p. 4.

[7]Clarke, p. 49.

[8]*Report of the Female Society for the relief of poor women in childbirth* (York: Printed by J. Carey, 1825), copy in the library of Marion V. Royce, Toronto.

[9]Cosbie, pp. 95-6.

[10]"Toronto Lying-in Charity," *The Globe*, 20 May 1848.

[11]The Medical Faculty of Trinity College was renamed and reorganized several times during the nineteenth century. It was the University of Trinity College Medical Department from 1872 to 1876; Trinity Medical School from 1877 to 1888; and Trinity Medical College after 1888.

[12]University of Toronto Archives, Trinity College, *Faculty of Medicine Circular* (Toronto, 1853).

[13]*Toronto City Directory* (Toronto, 1856), p. xxxix.

[14]Cosbie, pp. 94-100.

[15]Ontario, Board of Health, *Annual Report 1882* (Toronto, 1883).

[16]Although there was only one reported infanticide in 1882, the report stated that the high rate of illegitimate births calls for preventive measures. Ontario Board of Health, *Annual Report, 1885* (Toronto, 1886), p. 132.

[17]Ontario, Legislative Assembly, *An Act for the Protection of Infant Children*, Revised Statutes, 1887, Chapter 209.

[18]"Opening of the Rescue Home," *War Cry* (Toronto), 12 May 1888, p. 5; "A Refuge for Girls," *The Globe*, 1 November 1888.

[19]The Salvation Army's work in this area set the way for later expansion in the establishment of the Grace Maternity Hospitals. R. G. Moyles, *Blood and Fire in Canada: A History of the Salvation Army in the Dominion 1882-1976* (Toronto: P. Martin Associates, 1977), pp. 134-8.

[20]Ontario, Legislative Assembly, *An Act to Regulate Maternity Boarding Houses and for the Protection of Infant Children*, Statutes, 1897, Chapter 52.
[21]Letter to J. J. Kelso, Superintendent of Neglected and Dependent Children, from Charles Sheard, M.D., 4 January 1899. Ontario, Legislative Assembly, Sessional Papers, *The Sixth Report of Work Under the Children's Protection Act*, 17 (Toronto, 1899).
[22]Women's College Hospital, *History of Women's College Hospital* (Toronto: Women's College Hospital, 1974); G. Maloney, *Women's College Hospital as a Teaching Institution* (Toronto: Women's College Hospital, 1973).
[23]See C. Lesley Biggs, "The Case of the Missing Midwives: A History of Midwifery in Ontario from 1795-1900," in this volume, pp. 20-35.
[24]Ontario, Registrar-General, *Report Relating to the Registration of Births, Marriages and Deaths, 1899* (Toronto, 1900), p. 15.
[25]Ontario, Board of Health, *Annual Report 1882* (Toronto, 1883), p. vi.
[26]*Ibid.*, p. xi.
[27]Ontario, Board of Health, *Annual Report 1897* (Toronto, 1898).
[28]Ontario, Registrar-General, *Report Relating to the Registration of Births, Marriages and Deaths, 1898* (Toronto, 1899), p. 16. This paper makes extensive use of the mortality data collected and published by the Registrar-General of Ontario in the late nineteenth century. The reliability of that data has been questioned in recent years by historians. See the article on death and mortality records by Bruce Bowden and Roger Hall, "Impact of Death: An Historical and Archival Reconnaissance into Victorian Ontario," *Archivaria* 14 (Summer 1982), 93-105; and specifically George Emery, "Ontario's Civil Registration of Vital Statistics, 1869-1926: The Evolution of an Administrative System," *Canadian Historical Review* 64, 4 (December 1983), 468-93. The present author is aware of the possible limitations of this data and employs these statistics here, first, because they are the only available aggregate data, and, second, because the figures--correct or not-- were extensively employed in contemporary debates and literature.
[29]Charles Hodgetts, *Review of Vital Statistics of the Year 1904*, in Ontario, Board of Health, *Annual Report 1906* (Toronto, 1907), pp. 99-102.
[30]Ontario, Legislative Assembly, *An Act Respecting the Production and Sale of Milk for Human Consumption*, Statutes, 1911, Chapter 69.
[31]Canada, *Report of the Bureau of Child Welfare*, cited in Ontario, Board of Health *Annual Report 1917* (Toronto, 1918).
[32]Ontario, Board of Health, *The Baby* (Toronto, 1919).
[33]Archives of Ontario, Provincial Board of Health, Office of the Chief Medical Officer of Health, RG 62, B-1-b, folder 438.5, Memorandum for the Provincial Secretary, 27 June 1918.

[34]Ontario, Board of Health, "Report of the Division of Maternal and Child Hygiene," *Annual Report 1921* (Toronto, 1922), p. 179.

[35]See Figure II.

[36]W. J. Bell, "Maternal Mortality," in Ontario, Board of Health, *Annual Report 1921* (Toronto, 1922), pp. 184-91.

[37]*Ibid.*

[38]In 1924 the Department of Health was created. It assumed much of the work previously done by the Board of Health.

[39]Ontario, Department of Health, *Health Almanac* (Toronto, 1926).

[40]Ontario, Department of Health, *Annual Report 1927* (Toronto, 1928), p. 42.

[41]*Ibid.*, pp. 74, 101.

[42]*Ibid.*

[43]*Ibid.*

[44]Ontario, Department of Health, *Annual Report 1929* (Toronto, 1930), p. 39.

[45]*Ibid.*

[46]Ontario, Department of Health, *Annual Report 1930* (Toronto, 1931), p. 47.

[47]Ontario, Department of Health, *Annual Report 1931* (Toronto, 1932), p. 52.

[48]Ontario, Department of Health, *Annual Report 1932* (Toronto, 1933), p. 44.

[49]Ontario, Department of Health, *Health Almanac* (Toronto, 1940).

[50]Ontario, Department of Health, *The Baby* (Toronto, 1940).

[51]Ontario, Department of Health, *Annual Report 1934* (Toronto, 1935), pp. 59-60.

[52]See Figure VI.

[53]It is particularly interesting to note that in 1979 a similar controversy to that of 1929 arose. Dr. George Moss, Medical Officer of Health in Toronto, was dismissed from his post when it was discovered that he refused to accept a minority report of the Hospital Council of Metropolitan Toronto - University Teaching Hospitals Association (HCMT-UTHA) Joint Committee on High Risk Pregnancy. The minority report recommended a $1 million per annum pre-natal care education programme and opposed the majority report, which Moss supported, that called for a $6 million per annum increased technology programme. See "Board demands birth report," *Toronto Star*, 1 December 1979, p. A3.

[54]The Home Birth Task Force was organized early in 1978 to provide pre-natal instruction with a particular emphasis on home birth preparation and labour coach assistance for doctor-assisted home births. In 1980 the Ontario Association of Midwives was formed by approximately 20 women, many of whom had been associated with the Home Birth Task Force, to extend the work of the Task Force to include midwife-assisted home births. There are currently 50 women members in the O.A.M.

[55]The College of Physicians and Surgeons of Ontario, "Nurse-Midwives," *College Notices*, January 1982.

[56]David Stewart and Lee Stewart, eds., *Safe Alternatives in Childbirth* (Chapel Hill, North Carolina: National Association of Parents and Professionals for Safe Alternatives in Childbirth [NAPSAC], Inc., 1976); David Stewart and Lee Stewart, eds., *21st Century Obstetrics*, Vols. 1 and 2 (Marble Hill, Missouri: NAPSAC, Inc., 1977); Lewis Mehl, Gail Peterson, Michael Whitt and Warren Hawes, "Outcomes of Elective Home Births: A Series of 1,146 Cases," *Journal of Reproductive Medicine* 19, 5 (November 1977), 281-90; M. Tew, "The Case Against Hospital Deliveries: The Statistical Evidence," in Sheila Kitzinger and John Davies, eds., *The Place of Birth: A Study of the Environment in which Birth Takes Place with Special Reference to Home Confinements* (Oxford: Oxford University Press, 1977); David Stewart and Lee Stewart, eds., *Compulsory Hospitalization or Freedom of Choice in Childbirth*, Vols. 1-3 (Marble Hill, Missouri: NAPSAC, Inc., 1979); Claude Burnett, James Jones, Judith Rooks, Chong Hwa Chen, Carl Tyler, and Arden Miller, "Home Delivery and Neonatal Mortality in North Carolina," *Journal of the American Medical Association* 244, 24 (19 December 1980), 2741-5; David Stewart, *The Five Standards of Safe Childbearing* (Marble Hill, Missouri: NAPSAC, Inc., 1981; Ontario Association of Midwives, "Response to the College of Physicians and Surgeons of Ontario Position Statement on Out-of-Hospital Births," unpublished letter available from O.A.M., P. O. Box 85, Postal Station C, Toronto, Ontario; Susan Meyer, "The Home Birth Working Group," submission to the Task Force on the Implementation of Midwifery in Ontario, Toronto, October 1986. All the submissions to the Task Force are available by writing to: Midwifery Task Force, P. O. Box 489, Postal Station P, Toronto, M6B 5C2. The "Report of the Task Force on the Implementation of Midwifery in Ontario 1987" is available, free of charge, from the Ontario Government Publications Division.

[57]The College of Physicians and Surgeons of Ontario, "Out-of-Hospital Births," *College Notices*, March 1983; May 1987.

Chapter Five

THE CONFINEMENT OF WOMEN: CHILDBIRTH AND
HOSPITALIZATION IN VANCOUVER, 1919-1939[*]

Veronica Strong-Boag and Kathryn McPherson

Only relatively recently have large numbers of women been confined
to institutions for the delivery of their children. The
institutionalization of childbirth has radically transformed a major
human experience, and the impact of this transformation has been
a subject of debate among mothers, childbirth reformers, medical
professionals and social scientists.[1] For its defenders, the hospital
has served as an important vehicle for wider distribution of
obstetrical supervision and treatment with a concomitant reduction
of maternal morbidity and mortality. Critics have responded that
delivering these services within the confines of a hierarchical,
bureaucratized institution has contributed to the medicalization of
childbirth, depriving women of control over the bodies and creating
new psychological and physiological disorders.

As this contemporary debate rages, historians have begun to
examine the historical process whereby doctors appropriated, and to
some degree women relinquished, control over childbirth.[2] This
study contributes to that ongoing investigation by examining the
medicalization of childbirth in Vancouver during the 1920s and
1930s. It begins with a discussion of the general trends in maternal
care and then turns to the specific obstetrical treatment provided by
the Vancouver General Hospital (VGH). Within this institutional
setting medical professionals found new opportunities to set the
terms on which the city's women experienced childbirth.

Although the issue of maternity has attracted recent
attention from historians of British Columbia and Canada as a
whole, the focus of their work has been on pre-natal and post-natal

[*]Reprinted by permission from *BC Studies* 69/70 (Spring/Summer 1986), 142-74.
We would like to thank Lynn Bueckert, Anita Clair Fellman, Robin Fisher, Linda
Hale, Andrée Lévesque, Indiana Matters, Angus McLaren, Arlene Tigar McLaren
and the anonymous referee from *BC Studies* for their comments on earlier drafts of
this article. We would also like to acknowledge the support of the S.S.H.R.C.
Strategic Grant 498-83-0014.

75

care of reproductive women.[3] Few works concern themselves more directly with issues related to the delivery process. The McLarens' examination of the effect of abortion deaths on maternal mortality in B.C. makes some useful mention of the treatment by medical practitioners of unwillingly pregnant women, but their treatment is not the focus of the authors' study.[4] Of greater relevance are two works dealing with the shift from home to hospital deliveries in twentieth-century Ontario. That transition is closely identified with fears about levels of maternal and infant mortality and the campaign of the medical profession to control health care. Both authors conclude that hospitalization itself did little to improve women's chances for survival before World War II. What was improved in the hospital was doctors' opportunity to monopolize the provision of services during confinement.[5] A less critical view is presented in an article examining attempts to reduce maternal mortality in British Columbia. That author sees hospitalization as a substantial advance which parturient women recognized and utilized. The author's conclusion, however, that institutionalization of the delivery process was the logical follow-up to good pre-natal care and just as essential to the reduction of maternal mortality stops short of considering either the nature of hospital obstetrical therapy itself or possible alternative methods and facilities for distributing obstetrical services.[6]

Improved maternal care was desperately needed in post-World War I Vancouver. During the 1920s, B.C., with the lowest birth rate of the provinces, also had one of the highest rates of maternal mortality. As Table 1 indicates,[7] maternal mortality rates per 1,000 births in B.C. ranged from 4.7 to 6.7 between 1926 and 1935, then dropped permanently below the 5.0 mark in 1936 and slid steadily to 3.1 in 1940. While in 1926 B.C. had been significantly above the Canadian average of 5.7 maternal deaths, it had improved substantially upon the national figure of 4.0 fourteen years later. In comparison to rural areas of the province, Vancouver was a slightly more dangerous place for mothers, but the discrepancy in favour of the countryside remained about the same as it was nationally and much less striking than it was in Ontario and Nova Scotia.[8] Figures from a 1942 report cite 26 deaths or 6.9 per 1,000 live births in the city for the 1926-30 period, 15 deaths or 4.5 per 1,000 live births between 1931 and 1935 (a decrease of 34.8 per cent), and 14 maternal deaths or 3.5 per 1,000 live births for the 1936-40 years (a decrease of 22.2 per cent). While the precise pattern of this downward trend is not discernible, it is clear that a major decrease in Vancouver's maternal mortality occurred in the 1930s.

Meanwhile, B.C. led the nation in the institutionalization of its parturient women. In 1942 the House of Commons' Special Committee on Social Security discovered that B.C. had dramatically increased its rate of hospitalization from 48.3 per cent to 84.4 per cent of live births between 1926 and 1940. These figures were

TABLE 1

Maternal Mortality Rates per 1,000 Live Births in Canada, by Provinces, 1926-1940

Year	Canada	P.E.I.	N.S.	N.B.	Que.	Ont.	Man.	Sask.	Alta.	B.C.
1926	5.7	4.6	4.6	6.4	5.2	5.6	5.9	7.1	5.9	6.5
1927	5.6	2.4	6.8	6.2	4.9	6.0	5.1	5.4	6.4	6.7
1928	5.6	6.1	5.2	5.8	5.3	5.8	5.1	5.8	6.8	5.9
1929	5.7	7.8	4.2	7.3	5.3	5.4	6.8	6.2	7.3	5.6
1930	5.8	2.9	6.7	5.4	5.5	6.2	5.2	5.1	6.5	5.8
1931	5.1	6.9	4.7	5.6	4.8	5.4	4.8	4.4	5.0	6.3
1932	5.0	6.4	4.6	5.8	5.1	5.1	4.8	4.9	3.8	5.3
1933	5.0	4.1	4.7	6.0	5.0	5.4	4.1	4.6	4.5	4.7
1934	5.3	5.1	6.2	5.1	5.5	5.6	3.8	4.4	5.0	5.1
1935	4.9	4.0	5.3	4.6	5.4	5.0	4.2	4.1	4.3	5.2
1936	5.6	5.6	4.3	6.6	6.0	5.7	5.4	4.5	5.8	4.7
1937	4.9	5.7	3.0	3.7	5.2	5.2	4.3	4.6	4.8	4.5
1938	4.2	2.5	4.2	4.5	5.2	3.8	2.9	2.5	4.3	3.8
1939	4.2	7.5	4.1	4.8	4.6	4.3	3.5	3.3	3.6	3.1
1940	4.0	2.9	4.2	4.8	4.5	3.7	3.9	3.2	4.0	3.1

TABLE 2

Percentage and Number of Live Births in Vancouver Institutions, 1928-1929

1928	67.9%	2,589
1929	70.6%	2.731
1930	76.8%	3,076
1931	77.8%	2,902
1932	78.5%	2,708
1933	79.8%	2,543
1934	75.7%	2,407
1935	77.9%	2,529
1936	80.2%	2,733
1937	83.8%	3,166
1938	86.0%	3,522
1939	89.0%	3,657

extremely high when compared with the lowest figures in the country, reported for P.E.I. and Quebec, which ranged respectively from 2.7 per cent to 26.2 per cent and from 4.8 per cent to 15.6 per cent over the same years. Even Ontario, with its shift from 24.9 per cent to 62.1 per cent, far from matched the west coast. The only province to come at all close to B.C.'s rates was Alberta, but even in 1940 it reported only 72.9 per cent of live births in its hospitals.[9] As the most highly urbanized of all the provinces, B.C.'s figures are not surprising, particularly in light of Vancouver's preference for hospital births, which began early in the century[10] and continued almost unabated during the 1930s (Table 2).[11]

Overall, these trends indicate a percentage drop in maternal mortality substantially greater than the percentage increase in hospital births in the late 1920s and the 1930s. In addition, relatively high levels of hospitalization appear to have preceded any substantial reduction in maternal mortality. This lack of correlation suggests that there was no necessary causal relationship between increased hospitalization and mothers' survival rates in Vancouver.[12] But if pregnant women were not obviously spared death by hospital confinement, another group reaped evident benefits. For the medical profession, struggling to maintain its dominant position in health care, institutions in which it could regulate medical practice, eliminate non-medical competition and in time develop an effective therapy were promising indeed.[13] The spread of hospital care correlates very positively with doctors' drive for professional dominance in the health care delivery field. Vancouver's expectant mothers, like other patients, were the presumed beneficiaries of doctors' enhanced authority. The nature of that advantage is examined below.

It was an overwhelmingly male profession which in the 1920s and 1930s presided over women in their experience of childbirth. Not only were there very few female doctors in the city, but obstetrics as a field was, ironically enough, especially difficult for women to enter. In 1939 VGH typically allowed only one female interne and St. Paul's Hospital none.[14] In contrast to this exclusion from the profession, women supplied a critical part of the patient load. Targeted for special attention by local and national health agencies, pregnant women readily became consumers of medical advice which promised relief from the threat of disaster. For general practitioners such patients were essential in establishing a clientele.[15]

Yet, for all its significance in persuading Canadians of the value of medical superintendence and in providing doctors with entrée to the treatment of entire families, obstetrics was very late emerging as a specialty and remained a lowly cousin of more glamorous fields such as surgery. Just as inauspicious was its special affinity for surgical and later chemical and endocrinological solutions to labour problems.[16] For students, inadequate training in obstetrics remained a continuing problem. VGH, for example, only offered its internes two months on the maternity wards; if any individual wanted more experience, he had to arrange to trade assignments with a colleague.[17] In his address to the Toronto convention in 1928, the president of the American Association of Obstetricians, Gynaecologists and Abdominal Surgeons damned existing medical programmes in his field in both Canada and the United States. He pointed out that McGill and Toronto, among many other schools, allocated surgery much more time, despite the fact that obstetrics was the backbone of most general practices.[18]

Owing in large part to the absence of a medical school, Vancouver was later than Montreal, Toronto and London, Ontario, in developing a body of recognized and certified obstetrical experts. By 1940 the American College of Surgeons had approved only Toronto General Hospital and Royal Victoria in Montreal for graduate training in obstetrics and gynaecology. Canadians, usually associated with the university medical faculties of McGill, the University of Toronto, or the University of Western Ontario, were regular contributors to the premier publication, the *American Journal of Obstetrics and Gynaecology (AJOG)*, from its inception, but between 1920 and 1945 no B.C.-based doctor published so much as a research note. In contrast, Alberta with its medical school in Edmonton produced several submissions. The pages of the *Canadian Medical Association Journal (CMAJ)* were equally dominated by eastern contributors, with only the very occasional appearance by a B.C. writer.

There were attempts to remedy this situation. Although it did not establish a Committee on Maternal Welfare until October 1938, the Vancouver Medical Association (VMA) was an eager proponent of a more educated and specialized body of doctors in the province.[19] Its sponsorship of summer schools brought leading specialists from all across North America to lecture to B.C.'s doctors on the newest developments in their areas, and obstetrics was a regular part of the programmes.[20] The inauguration in 1924 of a monthly publication, the *VMA Bulletin*, spread further news of changes in medical practice and procedure. The *Bulletin* produced a number of obstetrical articles from 1924 through to 1945, but most appear to have echoed, often by some years, concerns voiced by the more prestigious journals.

Such limited publishing credentials were accompanied by relatively little interest in acquiring specialist certification. The American Board of Obstetricians and Gynecologists, organized in 1930, for example, held regular examinations after March 1931, but the first Vancouverite was not successful until 1938; the second until 1939. No others were certified before 1945.[21] While some Vancouver practitioners undoubtedly oriented more toward professional developments in Britain and Europe,[22] their training seemed to be overwhelmingly North American in origin. The near-absence of specialist credentials from the American Board further confirms relatively low levels of obstetrical training on the part of the city's doctors.

79

This was the case, for example, with the first two heads of obstetrics and gynaecology at VGH, Doctors William B. Burnett and Walter Turnbull, who received their early medical education in Canada. Burnett, chief throughout the 1920s and much of the 1930s, was an 1899 McGill graduate who never took any specialized obstetrical training. He was, however, a member of the Pacific North West Obstetrical and Gynaecological Association and the American Gynaecological Association. Turnbull graduated from Toronto in 1903 and some twenty years later took post-graduate studies in "obs & gyn" in Europe, New York, Boston and Buffalo.[23] Both men published in their chosen field in the *VMA Bulletin* but in neither the *AJOG* nor the *CMAJ*. On balance, Vancouver then does not appear to have been a centre of obstetrical expertise in anything but a regional sense.

Although the city lacked a elite corps of obstetricians, doctors' training, reinforced regularly by that of immigrant professionals, combined with the directives of the medical press and powerful health institutions, such as Vancouver General Hospital, to ensure that the great majority of physicians and their treatments differed little from those found in Canadian or American cities of a similar size. Given the shortcomings in training and licensing, there is no reason to believe that Vancouver was exempt from the "meddlesome midwifery" on the part of obstetrician and GP alike of which medical literature regularly complained.[24] "Meddling" could take many forms, from the use of x-rays, to administration of anaesthetics and substances such as pituitrin to produce more rapid contractions, to artificial induction of labour, to versions (turning the child manually in the womb), to episiotomies (cutting several inches through skin and muscles of the perineum, the area between the vagina and anus), to the use of low, mid and high forceps, to Caesarian sections and the use of manual or chemical means to extract the placenta. Such substances and techniques all presented problems even to the relatively skilled practitioner. And yet, for a number of reasons, they were tempting and their use tended to increase throughout the decades. On the one hand, they promised to save time for the "busy practitioner"[25] and to assert his authority over the timing and experience of delivery. On the other hand, as doctors pointed out, they often responded "to the pleadings of the patient and the relatives to 'do something'."[26] Mortality and morbidity rates associated with intervention worried contemporaries, some of whom, like those in Montreal at Royal Victoria Maternity Hospital, became eager to label themselves "conservatives."[27] Unfortunately, it is impossible to tell how much such intervention contributed to rates of maternal death and disability. Many procedures, for example, added to the possibility of haemorrhage, but this in turn might be countered by new blood transfusion techniques. The actual human cost of medical intervention, like that of abortion, remains a matter of speculation.[28]

This question of excessive obstetrical intervention unsettled collegial relations within the medical profession. Lacking authority over the actions of doctors in private practice, hospital administrators and specialists across the continent sought to influence medical practice through their control over hospitals. As part of its certification standards which identified a modern North American institution, the American College of Surgeons informally set in 1928, and soon required for approved hospitals, a "Minimum Standard for Obstetric Departments in Hospitals." This included a "properly organized and equipped department of obstetrics, providing exclusive and adequate accommodation for mothers and the newborn," "segregation or isolation of infected mothers," "adequate clinical laboratory, x-ray and other facilities, under competent supervision," the administration of a "competent, registered nurse, who has executive ability and assistance," adequate supervision by a chief or head of service or department, adequate and complete records, major obstetrical procedures to be performed only after consultations, the adoption of a standard for morbidity, minimum monthly review/analysis of obstetrics, and the opportunity for theoretical instruction and practical experience for student nurses.[29] Such external directives for standardized care were powerful inducements to change, and Vancouver's major hospitals--St. Paul's, Grace and VGH--all struggled to maintain certification standards.[30]

Crucial to the effort to standardize procedures was the formation in 1918 of the B.C. Hospitals' Association, which annually brought together the senior medical and administrative personnel of the province's health institutions. Repeated constantly was the message that the application of more "scientific" and bureaucratic methods would save the mothers of the province and guarantee the authority of medically trained professionals. VGH's decision in the late 1920s to restrict its public wards to staff physicians typified efforts to assert control over the delivery of health care and indicate by example the standards which private practitioners were expected to imitate. Yet, ironically, in spite of complaints that unsupervised GPs attempted dangerous procedures in private practice, by promoting hospitalized care administrators and specialists brought women into an environment where the staff and the equipment, and thus the opportunity and temptation, for greater intervention were more readily available. For example, elaborate preparation procedures, such as shaving, enemas and lysol washes, and the insistence on stirrups, arm straps and a lithotomy position in which a woman lay on her back with her legs in the air were taken for granted as part of the normal environment of the modern hospital.[31]

The advantages for general practitioners and hospital medical staff of institutionalized confinement are clear. Women's motives for utilizing hospital services are less amenable to study, in part because few women recorded their thoughts or feelings on their experiences in childbirth and in part because they were rarely consulted by those who claimed to serve them. There is little doubt, however, that fear of childbirth loomed large in many women's lives.[32] One city social worker acknowledged this in observing that "women are very, very frightened of this coming child and their health is undermined on account of that."[33] The prospect of death or lifelong disability[34] undermined pleasure taken in intercourse, encouraged a certain fatalism or denial, as with mothers' resistance to telling daughters the "whole" story,[35] and, more positively, inspired the search for better birth control and obstetrical assistance.[36] Finally, women's acquiescence to medical directives was ensured by repeated assurances from public health authorities and the popular media that experts know best and that doctors alone could guarantee the happy termination of pregnancy.[37] In general, while the safety of mother and child was presented as a legitimate concern, a woman's right to some say over the course of childbirth was not. As the Chairman of the Maternal Welfare Committee of the Canadian Medical Association concluded, "cooperation is more to be desired than self-reliance" in the nation's mothers.[38]

Yet traditionally, women had often looked to collective solutions to the rigours of childbirth. Female relatives, neighbours and friends regularly pooled resources and knowledge in efforts at mutual aid.[39] This familiar female culture was undermined by the transiency which was so much a feature of expanding cities like Vancouver, but perhaps still more by concerted attacks from modern health and child care professionals. Women's would-be advisors shored up their own claims to authority by ridiculing customary exchanges of information as "old wives'" tales.[40] As consumers in a society where scientific and technical knowledge was increasingly the property of professionals, prospective mothers were far from being the sole arbiters of their own destiny. The economics of a class and patriarchal society, in which material resources were distributed unevenly in general and within the family in particular, also placed major restraints on real choice in labour.[41]

To be sure, midwives or nurses were possible alternatives to male domination, although the unsupervised work of both was rigorously opposed by doctors. Just as forceps had been monopolized by male practitioners earlier,[42] their twentieth-century successors were no more eager to share the results of obstetrical advances. The determination to maintain control over the use of anaesthetics was typical.[43] The result was often, as a former nursing superintendent at VGH knew when she cited a senior VON authority, that "nurses are given a very inadequate maternity training so far as the technique of delivery is concerned. We are warned on no account to take a case without a doctor, and with our training we are not likely to do so. We make an attractive setting for a good obstetrician and an unwilling and critical collaborator with a poor one." She bluntly concluded, "The medical profession is responsible for this condition. They do not fear the competition of the nurse in any other department of medicine."[44]

Meanwhile, the medical establishment remained as opposed to midwives as it had been in previous decades.[45] True, the persistent lack of care and assistance for Canada's mothers and mothers-to-be, and the knowledge of low maternal mortality rates achieved by northern European countries which promoted midwife-assisted childbirth, led some medical commentators to support the reintroduction of midwives or obstetrical nurses.[46] Charlotte Hanington, superintendent of the Victorian Order of Nurses (VON) for Canada from 1917-23, placed her career on the line over her unsuccessful attempts to import midwives to Canada.[47] However, the disruption during urbanization of community and neighbourhood networks in which midwives traditionally had worked, combined with the absence of provision for their training or licensing, meant that creating a corps of skilled midwives would have required a major reallocation of resources and priorities. Most members of the medical establishment were unable or unwilling to envision such a move and held fast to the belief that "we have committed ourselves for generations to the policy of physician-accouchers. We cannot turn back now even if we should wish to."[48]

Policy aside, there did occur for many years a significant, albeit declining number of non-institutional births in the city, and not all were under medical supervision. Between 1925 and 1929, for instance, Vancouver recorded at least 1,743 deliveries by midwives out of a total of 19,730.[49] Such lay help persisted despite critics. One of the latter, more sympathetic than most, described such competitors as "women, good-hearted souls and all that sort of thing, practising maternity work and calling themselves maternity nurses, and they have absolutely no such qualifications; they know absolutely nothing about the work. They don't know about sterilizing; they don't know the first rules of procedure. . . .They happen to drop in at a neighbour's house when a case is coming off." The critic conceded that "when it is an easy birth, they get through all right, but when there are complications it works out different."[50] Lacking legal status, these attendants must have hesitated to call in medical authorities when complications did arise, but so long as the pregnancy was normal and hospitals remained centres of infection and intervention, domestic surroundings and experienced, if unlicensed, care might be a very sensible solution.[51] Whatever their professional qualifications, such women were cheap, potentially extremely helpful with domestic duties and reassuringly familiar when compared with their more scientific and impersonal rivals. Complaints regarding women's difficulty in finding unlicensed attendants indicate the role non-medical care continued to play for some expectant mothers in these years.[52]

For less affluent women wishing institutional services, the options actually available in Vancouver in the 1920s and 1930s were very much limited by class and ethnicity. Oriental and native patients found that segregated facilities and/or different standards awaited them whenever they applied to hospitals.[53] Even when race was no barrier to access, poverty, which growing numbers faced throughout these decades, meant reliance on the VON, hospital out-patient services and public wards. The pre-natal clinic established at VGH in 1932 saw women lining up along 12th Avenue. As the Women's Auxiliary noted, many outpatients "had a scanty breakfast--or, if coming for a blood test, none at all--leaky shoes on and no rubbers, the one cotton housedress a year issued by Central Clothing, and a raincoat." After walking or waiting for a streetcar, they then waited for an hour or two "on a hard wooden bench" for a doctor to see them.[54] Costs of confinement itself, reckoned in 1921 as $35 for a normal delivery, $50 with haemorrhage, $45 with instrumental labour and $35 if a miscarriage occurred, were far beyond the budgets of many families.[55] Not unexpectedly, the first thing a woman often asked herself when she failed to menstruate was "How am I going to foot the bill?"[56] It is hard to be surprised that abortion tempted many.[57] Others resigned themselves to charity, and such cases made up a majority of VGH's public wards.[58] In fact, the pressure on VGH facilities became so serious in the early years of the Depression that no normal obstetrical cases were admitted to public wards without the consent of the medical superintendent.[59] It was arranged with the City Relief Office to provide $10 to the VON and $20 to a doctor to provide for charity patients at home.[60]

During these years some unmarried mothers, especially younger ones, turned to a variety of rescue homes operated by the city's churches. Some of these, as with the homes maintained by the Catholic Church and the Salvation Army, were associated with hospitals where girls often became patients in the public wards before returning to religious chaperonage.[61] Their special anxieties about the future of themselves and their babies must have only too often made the birthing process itself all the more intimidating and alienating.

Middle- and upper-class women, with greater financial resources, might choose to deliver at home, but for them the most specialized and certified of assistance was available. They might elect a licensed private maternity hospital or home, although these almost disappeared over the twenty years.[62] Probably more important were the services of the small group of specialists appearing in the city who increasingly limited private practice to obstetrics and sometimes to obstetrics and gynaecology.[63] Such privileged treatment continued into VGH, where home-like private rooms with meals on a silver service promised the best of results. Here too the perennial servant problem of the middle class was solved, at least in the short term, and prospective mothers could benefit from the compulsive standards of cleanliness which advertising's hard-sell told them should also characterize their own homes.[64] By 1920 the days were over when "no self-respecting woman, however much she dreaded the coming ordeal or the upsetting of her household, resultant upon its advent, would entertain for a moment the suggestion of going to the hospital. The hospital was only for the outcast and the unfortunate."[65] The belated passage in December 1926 of the municipal money bylaw to finance a new maternity building, eventually completed in 1929, made VGH all the more attractive a choice for those who could afford $5 and more a day, plus physicians' fees, for privacy.

For all the differences which distinguished female experience, the fact or the possibility of childbirth encouraged bonds of sympathy between races and classes. The creation, for instance, of such national institutions as the federal Division of Child Welfare and the VON, which were instrumental in developing effective pre- and post-natal maternal and child care, owed a great deal to first-wave feminism's proclivity for women helping women.[66] Provincially, the campaigns of women's organizations for maternity insurance benefits and mothers' allowances, like the activities of the VGH Women's Auxilliary and the auxiliaries to the other hospitals, were very much predicated on a sympathetic appreciation of the difficulties of motherhood shared by all women.[67]

Submissions by the city's women's groups to the provincial Royal Commissions on Health Insurance and Maternity Benefits of 1919-21 and then of 1929-32 reflect both the consensus within the women's community over the problems of inadequate maternity assistance and the changing beliefs as to how these problems could be solved. The 1919-21 Commission recommended that a maternity benefit be paid to women, or wives of men, who earned less than $1,200 per year. These women would be given $35 per child and $25 per additional child in the case of multiple births, if proof was presented that the mother was attended by a qualified doctor or, if no doctor was available, a qualified nurse.[68] Although there was some difference of opinion as to how and to whom benefits would be administered, the concept of a cash benefit was approved by the sixty-nine women's groups represented. There was also the strong sense that women, whatever their situation, should be insured as a group. A speaker for women in the Vancouver Trades and Labor Council endorsed universal coverage, arguing "all mothers should be covered because there are a number of people who would look upon it otherwise as a charity." A representative from the Women's Forum also advocated the inclusion of married and unmarried mothers, urging women "let us stick together."[69]

Three points are especially significant in these hearings: first is the unanimous support for benefits by women of different classes; second is the support for a cash payment directly to parturient women, which would increase women's consumer power in the obstetrical care market; and third is the discussion of maternity benefits as distinct from other types of health insurance. It is noteworthy that the general superintendent of VGH reserved his opinion on maternity benefits until advantages to the province's institutions could be demonstrated. In his mind, evidently, concern for the hospital outweighed the need to provide women with choice in the health care market.[70]

By the time of the 1929-32 Commission, the degree of concern over maternal health had heightened, but with new solutions that VGH's general superintendent would have found very congenial. As J. H. McVety of the B.C. Hospital Association advised, "have the maternity benefit part of the general scheme, recognizing it just as though it were a sickness" paid directly to the institution or individual providing the service so the money will be spent as intended, not "diverted."[71] Women's testimony now also advocated direct financing of institutions and organizations. Unlike hospital representatives, however, women appeared less defenders of the institutions than cognizant of the shortcomings of the private health care market. As one woman concluded, "It is impossible for the majority of families today to pay $35 a week for a trained nurse. And so few families can afford to put down $25 before the mother can go to a hospital."[72]

This social concern over high levels of maternal mortality, pressure within their profession for doctors to perform obstetrical interventions within an approved hospital and the limited choice of assistance for home deliveries combined to promote the growth of institutional births in post-World War I Vancouver. By 1940 safer confinements meant utilizing professional staff and enhanced equipment within updated specialty wards and out-patients' services such as provided by VGH, the publicly funded institution which accommodated more than one-half the city's hospital deliveries during these two decades.[73]

Conditions in the province's largest hospital were, however, far from satisfactory during these years. Major investigations of VGH in 1912, 1930 and 1936 all described concerns with overcrowding, underfinancing, questionable procedures and limited facilities.[74] Maternity patients suffered along with others. In 1920 VGH's maternity wards, not untypically, experienced "a very pressing lack of accommodation, and such a large number of cases had to be handled constantly that at times. . .facilities were not capable of coping with the work."[75] Not unexpectedly, the maintenance of isolation and the restriction of infection were very difficult to guarantee. Although the need for a separate maternity facility was evident from the first study, the 1920 defeat in every ward in the city of a money bylaw requesting $500,000 to build a new maternity building and a new nurses' residence retarded improvements until the end of the decade. Even with its construction in 1929 there were problems, as one head maternity nurse remembered: "That maternity building. . .my goodness, you ran your feet off. It was a headache! It was very cheaply built, you know. The plumbing was dreadful. You could hear every sound. You could be in a private room and hear every cough and sneeze

above you and below you. . . .The plumbing made so much noise and the hot water pipes cracked in the night. . .but the doctors thought it was alright. . ."[76]
Nor was accommodation the only cause for discomfort. The 1930 Commission, which included as chairman Dr. A. K. Haywood, VGH's future general superintendent, and Dr. Malcolm MacEachern, former general superintendent, condemned routine examinations of maternity patients "which are not in accord with the teachings of the leading obstetricians who warn against certain practices in normal cases."[77] This critical assessment flew in the face of the earlier assertion by VGH's head of obstetrics that "every doctor. . .is a good maternity doctor because of the practical training he received in this department as a student, and by dint of the two cases he handled all by himself while 'Interne' in the surgical ward afterwards."[78] The Commission's further complaints about record-keeping and the refusal of some physicians to accept the discipline of up-to-date procedures suggested how far VGH and at least some of its medical chiefs had strayed from MacEachern's earlier standards.

As general superintendent of VGH between 1913 and 1923 and founder of the B.C. Hospitals' Association, MacEachern was instrumental in establishing standards which won VGH accreditation by the American College of Surgeons soon after the war. An energetic administrator, his talents soon took him far from Vancouver, eventually to become Associate Director of the American College of Surgeons and its Director of Hospital Activities. His *Hospital Organization and Management*, originally published in 1935 and reprinted many times, became a classic in the field. MacEachern himself donated a first edition to VGH's Internes' Library. The inclusion of a substantial section on obstetrical care was close to the heart of an author who was also the inventor of the MacEachern Obstetrical Table and former Surgeon and Medical Superintendent of the Montreal Maternity Hospital. MacEachern's influence in Vancouver was reaffirmed throughout the 1920s and 1930s by regular visits back to his former home and such official duties as membership on the Vancouver Hospital Survey Commission in 1930.[79]

The appointment of the Commission's chairman as general superintendent that same year was an obvious attempt to bring about reform. Dr. Haywood, M. B. (Tor.), M.R.C.S., L.R.C.P., who took the superintendency over from 1930 to 1947,[80] shared MacEachern's enthusiasm for raising hospital standards, but his dedication to making VGH a fully up-to-date and efficient operation ran full tilt into the municipal and provincial cutbacks to hospital funding in the Depression.[81] Wards W and X, for example, had to remain in the basement of the old main building. Despite being badly ventilated, without proper conditions for segregating patients, and containing inadequate provision for nursing and food service, they supplied the only accommodation "for a decent woman patient who might have become septic during childbirth or abortion."[82] There, because the Maternity Building itself lacked provision for isolating infected patients, she would join prostitutes and others needing treatment for VD. On the other hand, Haywood's era did see the revival of the Women's Auxiliary, which had collapsed in 1926 under the weight of its responsibilities for managing much of the Out-Patient Department and supplying the hospital with many of its regular supplies. Renewal of the Auxiliary's assistance with layettes, food and practical advice to maternity patients entering the public wards was a significant benefit, for all the accompanying assumptions of superiority and authority.[83]

Such sympathetic support was especially important when, as one Vancouver practitioner acknowledged, it was too easy for doctors to be insensitive when dealing with obstetrical patients. Noting that pregnancy bordered "on the pathological," a growing belief within the profession, he urged his colleagues to postpone internal examinations during the first consultation with nervous patients and to make every effort to be helpful and supportive.[84] Such admonitions may well have been taken to heart, but after 1929, when public ward patients were denied the services of private practitioners and assigned routinely to the staff service, the reassurance of whatever prior contacts had been made with a sympathetic doctor disappeared, at least for the poor. The barring of family members from delivery rooms, in contrast to the likelihood of their presence at home births, still further depersonalized an institutional environment which might promise safety but also readily imposed alienation. It would be hard for an already overworked nursing staff--predominantly student nurses being taught the gospel of cleanliness, neatness and routine procedure--to compensate for the emotional and personal deficiencies of such a system.[85]

The procedures recommended upon the onset of labour continued the objectification of the patient. Her hair was arranged in "two tight braids"; the area around the vagina was shaved and bathed with soap, water and lysol. She was given only a liquid diet, "even though she does not ask for it" and was to excrete every hour. In the meantime, the prospective mother was checked regularly for her own and the baby's pulse rate.[86] In the delivery room itself she was surrounded by doctors, nurses and students, commonly strangers, hidden in gowns, caps and masks. She herself was similarly disguised with elaborate draping. At this point the woman and her physician faced a number of options which varied not only with her condition but with shifting fashions in obstetrics and the relative skill and knowledge of those in attendance.

Unfortunately, given available records, dating the introduction at VGH of particular drugs and techniques is difficult. Between 1922 and 1929 the hospital's annual reports did include appendices citing statistics for the various areas of medical and surgical treatment. However, few surgical or manual and no

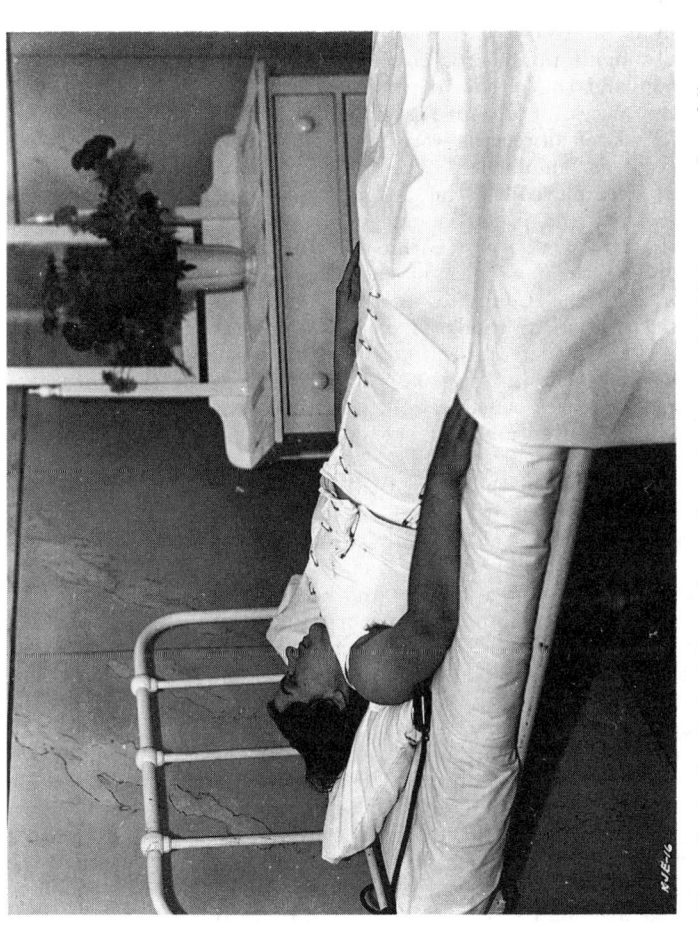

"Immediately after the birth the mother can be made more comfortable by means of carefully applied binders." Ernest Couture, *The Canadian Mother and Child* (Ottawa: Department of National Health, Division of Child and Maternal Hygiene, 1940), p. 63. Photograph by Eugene Michael Finn, C.G.M.P.B. (NFB), December 1939.

Source: National Archives of Canada. PA-803153

chemical procedures are specified for obstetrical cases, and while the type, frequency, outcome and average stay of obstetrical cases are indicated, no information regarding the relationship between particular therapies and patient health is offered. It is nearly impossible to gain insights from these reports into the efficacy of hospital obstetrical practices. Individual practitioners may have recorded this information, and hospital medical staff may have included it on record cards for public patients, but if so only a relatively small number of doctors benefited. The city's medical profession and the public in general were left largely in the dark about the success of various obstetrical practices.

New kinds of records were created by VGH from at least 1933. These records emphasized the type and frequency of medical procedures employed by the hospital on maternity patients and provided staff and practitioners generally with empirical evidence with which to evaluate scientifically current obstetrical practices. The appearance of articles in the *Vancouver Medical Association Bulletin* and the *Canadian Medical Association Journal* which presented statistical analyses of VGH's obstetrical interventions indicated the wider dissemination of this evidence within the medical profession in the 1930s.[87] This shift in the nature of published statistics reflected the mounting preoccupation with the promise of intervention and the desire to confirm the 'scientific' basis of medical action.

Just as with the statistical record, chemical treatments appear to have been in a state of some flux during these years. Chloroform and ether, old stand-bys from the 1840s, continued to be used into the 1920s. Their use was, however, more restricted since the possibility of damage to liver and kidneys was now recognized.[88] Twilight sleep, a combination of morphine to deaden the pain and various amnesiac drugs, notably scopalomine, had been used in Canada since its development in Germany in the early twentieth century, but its potential for causing vertigo and delirium in the mother and narcoticizing the baby limited its popularity severely.[89] Also available to doctors were rectal anaesthesia, although this demanded considerable control by the patient,[90] and a combination of nitrous oxide and oxygen.[91] The latter seems to have become especially popular. It did, for all the usefulness and success noted by a prominent Vancouver doctor, however, definitely require the presence of an anaesthetist.[92] This added not only to the numbers of strange attendants surrounding the patient but also to her final bill at VGH as elsewhere.[93] Only with the introduction of spinal anaesthetics in the 1940s would choices change substantially, and even then the additional expense remained.

The extent of medical intervention also varied from private to public wards. There is some indication that staff doctors were rather more conservative than private practitioners. One report, examining VGH records for 1934, 1935 and 1936, made this point about induction, arguing that "when one is dealing with a private patient. . .there is a real urge to make it truly successful, to get it over with. Patients are not much impressed with the idea of going home and coming back and, as a result, the doctor gets the blame; it is rather poor advertising." This staff doctor believed that patients should not in fact be induced solely because they were at term, but he noted that VGH's chief of obstetrics disagreed with him.[94] This self-proclaimed conservatism changed markedly once it came to a discussion of the use of low forceps, admittedly much less serious than the mid or high variations. Usually done "for the benefit of the interne on the service," their employment was supervised by a resident or staff member. The author thought that more patients might be delivered this way since "it wouldn't hurt. . .and it would be a great help to the interne who is soon to embark in private practice." With his own primipara cases he preferred "prophylactic low forceps and median episiotomy" as a matter of course.[95] Despite this predilection, he observed that instrumental deliveries are far more common on the private than on the staff side." Even then they made up a small part of the caseload in these years since 1,253 of 1,519 confinements, or 82.49 per cent, were assessed as normal, with 129 cases of low forceps, 27 of mid-forceps, 20 of version, 45 of Caesarian section and 45 breech deliveries.[96]

This staff doctor's preference for instrumental intervention, however 'moderate', helped change the percentage of so-called 'normal', deliveries over the longer period 1933-1941, when only 13,359 of 18,539 or 72.2 per cent were so identified at Vancouver General.[97] This trend occurred despite the retirement in 1937 of Dr. Burnett, head of obstetrics, who had been a devotee of elective versions and whose patients made up a majority of these interventions.[98] Table 3[99] reveals some significant trends.

What stands out here is the difference, not always large but almost always present, between private and public patients. The fact that 44 per cent of false labours over the 1933-41 period occurred in the public ward, which accounted for only 26 per cent of VGH's deliveries in those years, indicates a willingness on the part of staff doctors and their charity patients to wait for natural labour rather than attempt induction.[100] In almost every case the degree of medical intervention, including all types of forceps and the very dangerous, if 'glamorous', C-section,[101] was greater on private wards. Explanations for this phenomenon vary. Patients anticipating difficulty may have made additional efforts to raise funds to pay for confinement and doctors' fees. Certainly more and more women were turning to private or semi-private accommodation over these years. What cannot be ignored, however, is the fact that interventions such as versions or C-sections added to medical fees and incomes while simultaneously asserting the supremacy of the professional. They also commonly shortened the length of the delivery, a boon perhaps to a weary mother but always to a busy practitioner. Nor is the fact that the majority of cases were delivered by GPs without significance.[102] Obstetricians regularly

91

condemned this group for attempting treatments beyond their experience or understanding. Their interventions were characterized as frequently providing later employment for gynaecologists.[103]

TABLE 3

Maternity Statistics, VGH, 1933-1941

		1933	1934	1935	1936	1937	1938	1939	1940	1941	Total
Deliveries	To*	1773	1605	1647	1728	1991	2191	2343	2490	2771	18,359
	Pr	1001	1104	1171	1231	1463	1592	1748	1970	2426	13,706
	Pu	772	501	476	497	528	599	595	520	345	4,833
False	To	117	63	55	57	54	59	80	76	62	623
Labour	Pr	44	37	29	16	37	33	45	55	51	347
	Pu	73	26	26	41	17	26	35	21	11	276
Normal	To	1363	1111	1245	1265	1447	1547	1684	1763	1934	13,359
deliveries	Pr	680	704	830	834	969	1042	1168	1306	1634	9,167
	Pu	683	407	415	431	478	505	516	457	300	4,192
Caesarians	To	45	48	69	48	61	70	74	87	110	612
	Pr	29	38	49	33	52	58	68	82	101	510
	Pu	16	10	20	15	9	12	6	5	9	102
% or	To	2.5	2.3	4.1	2.7	3.0	3.1	3.1	3.4	3.9	3.3
Caesarians	Pr	2.9	3.4	4.2	3.6	3.6	3.6	3.9	4.2	4.2	3.7
	Pu	2.1	2.0	4.2	1.7	1.7	2.0	1.0	.96	2.6	2.1
Versions	To	52	63	26	31	22	13	11	8	3	229
	Pr	49	51	22	27	17	9	11	5	3	194
	Pu	3	12	4	4	5	4	-	3	-	35
High	To	3	2	-	-	2	5	2	7	5	26
forceps	Pr	3	2	-	-	1	2	2	7	5	22
	Pu	-	-	-	-	1	3	-	-	-	4
Mid	To	61	69	67	59	62	102	121	121	149	811
forceps	Pr	38	59	58	51	59	85	102	111	146	709
	Pu	23	10	9	8	3	17	19	10	3	102
Low	To	249	312	240	325	397	454	451	504	570	3,502
forceps	Pr	202	250	212	286	265	395	397	459	537	3,103
	Pu	47	62	28	39	32	59	54	45	33	399

*To = Total: Pr = Private: Pu = Public

The trends in maternal morbidity and mortality, as evident in tables 4[104] and 5,[105] also reveal differences between private and public wards but are somewhat inconclusive about the exact effect of differential treatment over the nine years surveyed. At the very least, however, it is fair to say that the benefits of private care in terms of these two major variables are uncertain. The erratic pattern of morbidity over the years 1933-41 also suggests that the hospital experienced considerable difficulty in controlling infection. The introduction of sulfonamide drugs in the late 1930s, as acknowledged by one 1943 observer, appeared to have been critical in lowering pregnancy's dreaded cost.[106]

In keeping with its effort to maintain institutional standards, Vancouver General Hospital made some attempt to regulate doctors' regimes. The increase in the incidence of C-sections, for example, prompted a rule requiring the prior consent of the general superintendent or one of his assistants.[107] In other developments the institution concurred. The steady increase in episiotomies revealed in table 6[108] reflects a trend which was becoming normative in North American hospitals.[109]

Again there is a significant difference between private and public wards. In every year but one the patient under the care of her own physician faced a substantially higher chance of experiencing this form of intervention. It is also quite clear, however, that episiotomies were being 'democratized' over this period as well.

Once the baby arrived, and if the hospital were not overcrowded, the woman might rest in the delivery room under observation for an hour. Should there be bleeding, pituitrin and ergometrine would be given; haemorrhage, and its threat of shock, brought the administration of intravenous fluids by a specialist.[110] After her pulse returned to safe levels and there were no signs of distress, the woman would be returned to her room, where the extent of comfort and nursing care depended on a private or public location. The increasing employment of registered nurses, still assisted by students, in these decades, especially the 1930s, also brought changes to patient care.[111] That transformation, with its promise of more knowledgeable staff, undoubtedly helped convince expectant mothers to choose hospitals for their confinements. What it actually meant in terms of real contact is more difficult to say.

In her own bed the patient could not expect unregulated access to her new baby. The modern hospital of VGH's ambition imposed a strict regimen based on the most up-to-date strictures about successful child care. Breastfeeding was a central dictum, but some procedures, such as MacEachern's recommendation that it was "most important" not to nurse the baby for at least six to eight hours after delivery,[112] very likely made it more difficult. The attempt to inculcate regular habits right from the onset may have had the same effect, as with the "Standing Orders" for an efficient obstetrical department which recommended feedings at precise four-hour intervals for three days and "only fifteen minutes" at a time with the mother. Later, twenty minutes would be allowed on the same schedule.[113] The baby herself or himself was carefully tagged and distinctively stencilled with the family surname by exposure to a sunlamp.[114]

TABLE 4

Percentage of Maternal Morbidity, VGH, 1933-1941

	Total	Private	Public
1933	4.6%	3.5%	6.1%
1934	5.4%	3.6%	9.5%
1935	4.4%	3.0%	7.6%
1936	6.1%	4.1%	11.9%
1937	5.4%	3.5%	10.0%
1938	7.5%	7.5%	7.5%
1939	7.4%	9.7%	5.2%
1940	6.8%	7.3%	5.0%
1941	5.3%	5.4%	4.9%

TABLE 5

Percentage of Maternal Mortality, VGH, 1933-1941

	Total	Private	Public
1933	0.5%	.8%	.3%
1934	0.5%	.5%	.6%
1935	0.3%	.3%	.2%
1936	0.3%	.4%	.2%
1937	0.05%	.05%	-
1938	0.1%	.1%	-
1939	0.04%	.04%	-
1940	0.2%	.2%	-
1941	0.03%	.03%	-

Mothers' activities were also closely regulated. They were to recline in bed until the fifth or sixth day, only then to sit up if all went well. Not until five or so days passed were they allowed out of

TABLE 6

Percentage of Episiotomies, VGH, 1933-1941

	Total	Private	Public
1933	8.7%	14.4%	1.7%
1934	13.2%	17.7%	3.6%
1935	13.5%	17.2%	6.5%
1936	17.6%	22.2%	9.9%
1937	23.3%	27.1%	13.1%
1938	28.4%	31.3%	20.7%
1939	32.3%	34.2%	27.1%
1940	35.3%	35.1%	35.8%
1941	36.6%	38.3%	25.2%

bed for limited periods. They were not to leave the hospital for twelve to fourteen days.[115] VGH seems to have observed this rule throughout these years, despite the circulation problems it might have caused for the patient, the added risk of infection and the contribution such stays made to the hospital's chronic problem with overcrowding.[116] On the other hand, it may be that mothers without urgent domestic responsibilities awaiting their arrival looked forward to such respites from household chores.[117]

Throughout this course of treatment women and their relatives undoubtedly demanded the full range of up-to-date procedures which might in any way ease childbirth's pains and dangers. For them, like the professionals they consulted, there were trends and fads. Nevertheless, however much they might 'shop around', prospective mothers were finally expected to deliver themselves into the hands of their doctors. Joint decision making was not encouraged. MacEachern's influential recommendation that "No information regarding baby other than 'favorable' is to be given mother by the nurse"[118] represented a common enough attempt to control the flow of information and thus to determine the process.

Once home, the model patient was to continue consultations with her doctor and public health nurse. The reality for many women, however, was an immediate return to postponed duties and tasks.[119] Domestic labour and family budgets made medical visits a low priority for many families in the days before medicare. The highly centralized services of the hospital did not easily follow the patient upon release, and it was only too likely that poverty in the case of the clients of the public wards would undo whatever good had been achieved.[120] The conditions of poor nutrition and abysmal housing which undermined women's health in the city at large remained for the most part untouched.[121]

Within the confines of the hospital women encountered a highly bureaucratized set of procedures presided over by male medical professionals. In this setting, where pregnancy was so readily defined as an illness, doctors found ample opportunity to assert their overriding authority and an equal temptation to employ techniques of intervention which dramatically influenced the pace and quality of childbirth. As a group women found themselves more highly regulated. Patients' status in the world beyond the walls of the institution was also reaffirmed by individual assignment to private rooms or public wards. Differences in treatment appear to have continued into the delivery room itself, where private patients were more likely to encounter intrusive procedures such as C-sections and forcep delivery. Over time, however, the common denominator of sex was powerful and the experience of public patients came to match that of the more well-to-do.

Just as it is hard to credit hospitalization with responsibility for a significant reduction in maternal mortality in these years, it is difficult to judge the effectiveness of new medical regimes in improving women's experience of confinement. Given an allocation of public resources which favoured institutions and doctors rather than home care and domestic assistants, choices for pregnant women were limited. The absence of real alternatives and the medical profession's ability to campaign for its own interpretations of the road to good health directed women to the relief that hospitals could provide. Some patients benefited from advances in medical procedure such as blood transfusions and anaesthetics which were most safely performed in a hospital setting. Relief, however, did not include provision for allowing women to make an informed choice about their experience of confinement nor address factors in the community which made pregnancy and illness in general the special burden of the poor. The overall result in these two decades was to leave decision making firmly in the hands of professionals, who alone were deemed capable of understanding the physiology of women and the relative benefits of intervention. In time, however, disillusionment would set in. This would provide fertile ground for women's rebellion against the tyranny of the medical expert and their demand for informed choice and effective therapy in childbirth.

Notes

[1]See Ann Oakley, *Women Confined: Towards a Sociology of Childbirth* (London: Billing & Sons Ltd., 1980); Shelly Romalis, ed., *Childbirth: Alternatives to Medical Control* (Austin: University of Texas Press, 1981); and Tim Chard and Martin Richards, eds., *Benefits and Hazards of the New Obstetrics* (Philadelphia: J. B. Lippincott Co., 1977). See in particular Oakley's "Crosscultural Practices," pp. 18-33, in which she distinguishes between the medical treatment women received and the broader issue of the "medicalization" of pregnancy and childbirth, that is "people's dependence on medicine and...the control of health and sickness by the medical profession," p. 19.

[2]See Barbara Ehrenreich and Deirdre English, *For Her Own Good: 150 Years of the Experts' Advice to Women* (London: Pluto Press, 1979); E. Shorter, *A History of Women's Bodies* (New York: Basic Books, Inc., 1982); and Nancy Schrom Dye, "History of Childbirth in America," *Signs* 6, 1 (Autumn 1980), 97-108.

[3]See, for example, Norah Lewis, "Advising the Parents: Child Rearing in British Columbia During the Inter-War Years," unpublished Ed.D. thesis, University of British Columbia, 1980; Suzann Buckley, "Ladies or Midwives? Efforts to Reduce Infant and Maternal Mortality," in Linda Kealey, ed., *A Not Unreasonable Claim: Women and Reform in Canada 1880s-1920s* (Toronto: Women's Press, 1979); and Veronica Strong-Boag, "Intruders in the Nursery: Childcare Professionals Reshape the Years One to Five, 1920-1940," in Joy Parr, ed., *Childhood and Family in Canadian History* (Toronto: McClelland and Stewart, 1982).

[4]Angus McLaren and Arlene Tigar McLaren, "Discoveries and Dissimulations: The Impact of Abortion Deaths on Maternal Mortality in British Columbia," in this volume, pp. 126-59.

[5]Jo Oppenheimer, "Childbirth in Ontario: The Transition from Home to Hospital in the Early Twentieth Century," in this volume, pp. 51-74, and Catherine Lesley Biggs, "The Response to Maternal Mortality in Ontario, 1920-1940," unpublished M.Sc. thesis, University of Toronto, 1983. Biggs argues that only the introduction of sulpha drugs in 1937 made hospital birthing as safe as home delivery.

[6]Norah Lewis, "Reducing Maternal Mortality in British Columbia: An Educational Process," in Barbara K. Latham and Roberta J. Pazdro, eds., *Not Just Pin Money: Selected Essays On the History of Women's Work in British Columbia* (Victoria: Camosun College, 1984), pp. 337-55.

[7]Canada, House of Commons, Special Committee on Social Security, *Health Insurance*, Report of the Advisory Committee on Health Insurance Appointed by Order-in-Council, P.C. 836, 5 February 1942, p. 266.

[8]*Ibid.*, pp. 257-8, "from 1926 to 1930 [Vancouver] had an annual average of 26 deaths or a rate of 6.9 per 1,000 live births,

but by 1936 to 1940 the average annual rate had dropped to 3.5 or 14 deaths." In 1939, 17 rural women died in childbirth compared to 21 urban women. Dr. Helen MacMurchy, *Maternal Mortality in Canada* (Ottawa, 1927) cites mortality figures for the early 1920s, but they are based on a survey of physicians' cases rather than on the more complete statistics of the 1942 *Health Insurance* report.

[9]*Health Insurance*, p. 309.

[10]See L. O. Stone, *Urban Development in Canada* (Ottawa: Dominion Bureau of Statistics, 1967), p. 39, for statistics on rates of urbanization. See Margaret Andrews, "Medical Attendance in Vancouver: 1886-1920," in S. E.D. Shortt, ed., *Medicine in Canadian Society: Historical Perspectives* (Montreal: McGill-Queen's, 1981), pp. 431-4, for an assessment of one doctor's obstetrical patients who, beginning in the 1890s, turned slowly to hospital deliveries.

[11]Compiled from *B.C. Sessional Papers*, Reports of the Provincial Board of Health, 1929-1941/2. These figures are for registered births. Neil Sutherland claims that in the early 1930s unregistered births in B.C. were over 5 per cent of the total registered births. Neil Sutherland, "Social Policy, 'Deviant' Children, and the Public Health Apparatus in British Columbia Between the Wars," *Journal of Educational Thought* 14, 2 (August 1980), 80-91.

[12]In "Cross-cultural Practices" Oakley places the "home-hospital" debate in an international framework. Comparing Britain, with high rates of hospitalization, to the Netherlands, which supports midwife-assisted home confinements, Oakley concludes that the "correlation between the rise in hospital delivery and falling maternal and perinatal mortality rates cannot be taken as cause-and-effect" (p. 25), and that home birth has been a central feature of improved maternal health in many societies.

[13]For an instructive analysis of the role institutions played in the development of the Maritime medical profession see Colin Howell, "Reform and the Monopolistic Impulse: The Professionalization of Medicine in the Maritimes," *Acadiensis* 10, 1 (1981), 3-22.

[14]See "Hospitals Approved for Interneships," *Canadian Medical Association Journal* (henceforth *CMAJ*) (September 1939), 304-5.

[15]Lewis, "Reducing Maternal Mortality," p. 342.

[16]On these associations see Richard W. Wertz and Dorothy C. Wertz, *Lying-In: A History of Childbirth in America* (N. Y. and London: The Free Press and Collier MacMillan, 1977).

[17]Provincial Archives of British Columbia (PABC), Sound and Moving Image Division, West Coast Medical History Collection, Interview with Dr. Emile Therrien, 2,370: tape 1, track 1.

[18]Dr. Palmer Findley, "The Teaching of Obstetrics," *American Journal of Obstetrics and Gynaecology* (henceforth *AJOG*) (November 1928), 611-24. For more details on the training of Canadian GPs

and its shortcomings, see S. E.D. Shortt, "'Before the Age of Miracles': The Rise, Fall, and Rebirth of General Practice in Canada, 1890-1940," in Charles G. Roland, ed., *Health, Disease and Medicine* (Toronto: Hannah Institute for the History of Medicine, 1982).

[19]C. T. Hilton, "Maternal Welfare," *Vancouver Medical Association Bulletin* (henceforth *VMAB*) (September 1939), 352-3.

[20]See, for example, Dr. B. P. Watson, "Antepartum Haemorrhage," *VMAB* (August 1927), 339. Dr. Watson was a professor of medicine at Columbia University.

[21]The first was A. C. Frost, the second Edward M. Blair. See first biannual and then annual examination reports, *AJOG*, 1931-45.

[22]The *Register* of the B. C. Medical Association during these years suggests that doctors with European or British training remained a minority of Vancouver practitioners. In 1920, 40 of 275 doctors (14.55 per cent) living in Vancouver had trained or been licensed in England, Scotland or Ireland. By 1930 this figure had declined to 12.94 per cent (44 of 340). In 1939, 12.71 per cent (53 of 409) of Vancouver's doctors had credentials from Great Britain. BCMA *Register* 1920, 1930, 1939.

[23]See Vancouver Academy of Medicine, BCMA Biographical Files.

[24]See, for example, M. R. Bow, "Maternal Mortality as a Public Health Problem," *CMAJ* (August 1930), 169-73; Robert Ferguson, "A Plea for Better Obstetrics," *CMAJ* (October 1920), 901-4; J. R. Goodall, "Maternal Mortality," *CMAJ* (October 1929), 447-50; E. D. Plass, "The Relation of Forceps and Caesarian Section to Maternal and Infant Morbidity and Mortality," *AJOG* (August 1931), 176-99; and Ethel Johns, "The Practice of Midwifery," *Canadian Nurse* (January 1925), 11.

[25]*CMAJ* (July 1920), 678.

[26]Ross Mitchell, "The Prevention of Maternal Mortality in Manitoba," *CMAJ* (September 1928), 293. See also D. Bjornson, "An Obstetrical Retrospect," *CMAJ* (December 1925), 1236-9, and W. K. Burwell, "Report from Staff (Gynaecological Division) of Vancouver General Hospital," *VMAB* (June 1937), 192-7. In 1919 the Ontario Medical Society was addressed by a representative of the Labour Party of Toronto, "who declared that, more particularly in obstetrics, labour felt itself at the disadvantage of being unable to secure for the wives of their class, those advantages that wealth could command." It is not, however, clear what those advantages were--whether mechanical, manual or chemical intervention or social and economic benefits of supervision and assistance during the after pregnancy. *CMAJ* (April 1920), 305.

[27]Wesley Bourne, M.D., "Anaesthesia in Obstetrics," *CMAJ* (August 1924), 702-3, concerning obstetrical anaesthesia at the Montreal Maternity Hospital. Bourne claims "it may be seen at once that we are conservative; we think advisedly so."

W. W. Chipman makes similar claims for conservatism at the Montreal Maternity Hospital. *CMAJ* (June 1926), 681-2. Others proclaimed themselves "moderates"; see, for example, J. W. Duncan, "The 'Radical' in Obstetrics," *AJOG* (August 1930), 225.

[28]In the years 1931-40, for example, pueperal haemorrhage was "the third largest contributing factor to maternal mortality in Canada. . .the percentage of deaths from haemorrhage to the total maternal deaths has ranged from 11.3 in 1931 to 16.5 in 1939." *Health Insurance*, p. 260. See also M. Blair, "The Role of Haemorrhage in Mortality Rates in Pregnancy and Childbirth," *CMAJ* (February 1945), 168.

[29]M. T. MacEachern, "The Program of the American College of Surgeons for Maternal Care in General Hospitals," *AJOG* (March 1938), 535-40.

[30]*American College of Surgeons Bulletin 3A* (October 1935), 80.

[31]See M. MacEachern, *Hospital Organization and Management* (Chicago: Physicians' Record Co., 1935).

[32]For a sensitive discussion of women's anxieties see Judith Walzer Leavitt, "'Science' Enters the Birthing Room: Obstetrics in America since the Eighteenth Century," *Journal of American History* 70, 2 (September 1983), 281-304.

[33]PABC, GR707, B. C. Royal Commission on State Health Insurance and Maternity Benefits, 1929-32, Transcript, Mrs. Fischer, p. 318.

[34]See Robert E. McKechnie II, *Strong Medicine: History of Healing on the Northwest Coast* (Vancouver: J. J. Douglas Ltd., 1972), pp. 155-6, for his description of physical damage to women.

[35]See, for example, the reticence of the mother in the account by "Violet Teti Benedetti," in Daphne Marlatt and Carole Itter, eds. *Opening Doors: Vancouver's East End*, Sound Heritage Series, VIII, 1 and 2 (Victoria, 1979).

[36]See Angus McLaren, "Birth Control and Abortion in Canada, 1870-1920," in Alison Prentice and Susan Mann Trofimenkoff, eds., *The Neglected Majority: Essays in Canadian Women's History*, Vol. II (Toronto: McClelland and Stewart, 1985), pp. 84-101.

[37]See Strong-Boag, "Intruders in the Nursery" for its discussion of the authority of medical professionals.

[38]W. B. Hendry, "Maternal Welfare," *CMAJ* (November 1934), 520.

[39]Hilda Chaulk Murray, *More Than Fifty Percent: Woman's Life in a Newfoundland Outport 1900-1950* (St. John's: Breakwater Books Limited, 1979) describes a female culture which survived well into the twentieth century in a stable Newfoundland community.

[40]See, for example, Jane Lewis, *The Politics of Motherhood: Child and Maternal Welfare in England, 1900-1939* (London: Croom Helm, 1980) and Strong-Boag, "Intruders in the Nursery."

[41]See the discussion of the unequal distribution of family

income in Marjorie Griffin Cohen, "The Decline of Women in Canadian Dairying," in Alison Prentice and Susan Mann Trofimenkoff, eds., *The Neglected Majority*, Vol. II, pp. 61-83; and Veronica Strong-Boag, "Pulling in Double Harness or Hauling a Double Load: Women, Work and Feminism on the Canadian Prairie," *Journal of Canadian Studies* 21, 3 (Fall 1986), 32-52.

[42]See Wertz and Wertz, *Lying-In*, pp. 34-5.

[43]See, for example, Dr. Wesley Bourne of McGill, "The Administration of Chloroform in Obstetrics by Nurses," *Canadian Nurse* (November 1930), 585-7.

[44]C. Hannington, cited in Ethel Johns, "The Practice of Midwifery in Canada."

[45]Buckley, "Ladies or Midwives?"; Kathy Kuusisto, "Midwives, Medical Men and Obstetrical Care in Nineteenth Century Nova Scotia," unpublished M.A. thesis, University of Essex, 1980, argues that by 1900 midwives in Nova Scotia had been marginalized, and eliminated as serious competition to doctors. In "Traditions and Neighbourhoods: The Folklife of a Newfoundland Fishing Outpost," unpublished M.A. thesis, Memorial University of Newfoundland, 1971, G. J. Casey states that, in the community he studied, at least one midwife practised. She "had received no formal training except advice and the experience from some older midwife, and occasionally the advice of a medical person," p. 119. Nancy Schrom Dye in "History of Childbirth in America" argues that the modern period in the history of childbirth in America began in the 1920s when physicians emerged as the unchallenged birth attendants. Authors such as Buckley and Kuusisto suggest that in Canada this periodization is applicable, though Casey's work is an important reminder of the different pace of developments in some rural areas.

[46]See H. M. Little, "What's the Matter with Obstetrics?," *CMAJ* (May 1929), 647, who concluded "there is crying need for specially trained obstetric nurses, call them midwives if you will."

[47]Buckley, "Ladies or Midwives?", pp. 144-7.

[48]J. R. Goodall, "Maternal Mortality," 449. For a discussion of community disruption which accompanied Vancouver's rapid rate of urban growth, see D. L. Matters, "A Report on Health Insurance: 1919," *BC Studies* 21 (Spring 1974), 28-32.

[49]W. N. Kemp, "The Stillbirth Problem in Relation to Iodine Insufficiency," *VMAB* (December 1933), 58.

[50]PABC, GR707, B.C. Royal Commission on State Health Insurance and Maternity Benefits, 1929-32, Transcript, Mrs. Sadie Moore, p. 314.

[51]A May 1929 *CMAJ* editorial by H. M. Little of the Montreal Maternity Hospital criticized the contemporary obstetrical surgical procedures and claimed, "Obstetrics is still in the large majority of cases a matter for the home," "What's the Matter With Obstetrics?", 646. This opinion was supported by the international statistics for midwife deliveries often reported in the journal. For

example, McGill professor of obstetrics and gynaecology J. R. Goodall's article, "Maternal Mortality," cites an Aberdeen, Scotland, inquiry into maternal mortality which discovered the maternal mortality rate of institutions to be five times greater and doctors' rate two times greater than that of midwives. *CMAJ* (October 1929), 447-50.

[52]Mrs. McLachlan's testimony before the 1929-32 Commission on State Health Insurance and Maternity Benefits, "You can pick up all kinds of help to do housework when you cannot pick up a trained nurse," is representative of such complaints. PABC, GR707, Royal Commission, Transcript, p. 324.

[53]For instance, for some years, oriental maternity patients were regularly released some days sooner after childbirth than their sisters of European origin. See PABC, GR749, B.C. Provincial Secretary, Health Insurance Research, "Report on Information Collected and Compiled in Reference to Certain Phases of Hospital Work in British Columbia," 1934, p. 17.

[54]"Report of the Social Service Committee of the Women's Auxiliary," *Annual Report* of VGH, 1935, p. 37.

[55]PABC, GR706, B.C. Royal Commission on Health Insurance and Maternity Benefits 1919-21, File 2/5, "Report on Health Insurance, 1921," p. 55.

[56]PABC, GR707, B.C. Royal Commission on State Health Insurance and Maternity Benefits 1929-32, "Transcript of Evidence," Appendix H, Vol. II, testimony of Mrs. Manifold of the Women's Navy League, p. 317.

[57]See McLaren and McLaren, "Discoveries and Dissimulations" in this volume, pp. 126-49.

[58]See, for example, PABC, GR706, Royal Commission on Health Insurance and Maternity Benefits 1919-21, File 4/5, "Proceedings," testimony of Dr. MacEachern, p. 668.

[59]In 1933, 772 of 1,773 or 43.5 per cent of deliveries at VGH were in the public wards. While the number of deliveries in the VGH Maternity Building increased between 1934 and 1940 from 1,605 to 2,490, the percentage of public ward deliveries decreased from 31.2 per cent to 20.9 per cent.

[60]"Report of the Out-Patients' Department," *Annual Report* of VGH, 1933, p. 61.

[61]See Andrée Lévesque, "Deviants Anonymous: Single Mothers at the Hôpital de la Miséricorde in Montreal, 1929-1939," in this volume, pp. 108-25 for her useful discussion of the distinctive treatment received by women bearing children out-of-wedlock. Unfortunately, it is not clear whether this extended to differences on the obstetrical table itself, although one suspects this may indeed have been the case.

[62]See listings under "Hospitals" in *Wrigley's B.C. Directory* for Vancouver 1919-1939. See also Margaret W. Andrews, "St. Luke's Home, Vancouver, 1888-1936," *Journal of the Canadian Church Historical Society* 24, 2 (1982), 90-8, for an example of an Anglican

initiative in this area which succumbed to the superior obstetrical resources of the large hospitals.

[63]Vancouver physicians such as Harold Caple and Isabel Day travelled east in the 1930s for six to twelve months' post-graduate work in obstetrics and gynaecology, though according to the Vancouver Medical Association records the number of doctors specializing in this way were few. Vancouver Academy of Medicine, VMA Biographical Files.

[64]For a very useful discussion of middle-class responsiveness see Wertz and Wertz, *Lying-In*, Ch. 5.

[65]Dr. A. S. Munro, "The Hospital--Past, Present and Future," *Proceedings* of the First Convention of the Hospitals of B.C., 1918, p. 11.

[66]See Lewis, "Advising the Parents" and "Reducing Maternal Mortality," and Strong-Boag, "Intruders in the Nursery."

[67]See Linda Hale, "The British Columbia Woman Suffrage Movement, 1890-1917," unpublished M.A. thesis, University of British Columbia, 1977; Gillian Weiss, "As Women and as Citizens: Clubwomen in Vancouver, 1910-1928," unpublished Ph.D. thesis, University of British Columbia, 1984; and Susan Walsh, "Equality, Emancipation and a More Just World: Leading Women in the B.C. CCF," unpublished M.A. thesis, Simon Fraser University, 1984.

[68]PABC, GR706, B.C. Royal Commission on Health Insurance and Maternity Benefits 1919-1921, Box 1, File 1, "Report on Maternity Insurance, 1921," p. 9.

[69]*Ibid.*, File 4, "Proceedings," pp. 522-8.

[70]*Ibid.*, p. 698.

[71]PABC, GR707, Royal Commission on State Health Insurance and Maternity Benefits 1929-32, "Transcript of Evidence," Appendix H, Vol. II, p. 357.

[72]*Ibid.*, p. 316.

[73]At present the available documentation on the major alternatives to confinement within VGH--St. Paul's Hospital, run by the Sisters of Providence since 1892; Grace Hospital, managed by the Salvation Army beginning in 1927; and St. Vincent's, run by the Sisters of Charity from 1939--is scanty. Still less is known about the operations of such small, privately owned, licensed and unlicensed institutions as Tolmie Maternity Home and Impey Maternity Hospital, both operating in the 1920s. VGH remained the largest maternity facility throughout the period. In 1935, for instance, VGH reported 1,585 births while St. Paul's reported only 683 and Grace another 370. See *Vancouver Sun*, 31 December 1935.

[74]B. C. Royal Commission on Vancouver General Hospital, *Report*, 1912; Vancouver Hospital Survey Commission, *Report upon the Hospital Situation of Greater Vancouver*, 1930; W. H. Welsh, M.D., with comments by A. K. Haywood, M.D., *A Study of the Vancouver General Hospital*, March 1936.

[75]"Report of the Medical Departments of the Hospital," *Annual Report* of VGH, 1920, pp. 44-5.

[76]PABC, Sound and Moving Image Division, Vancouver General Hospital Collection, Interview with Helen King, 520, tape 2, track 2, transciption, p. 2.

[77]Vancouver Hospital Survey Commission, *Report*, 1930, p. 88.

[78]Burnett, "Maternity Work in the Small Hospital," *Proceedings* of the First Convention of the Hospitals of B.C., 1918, p. 81.

[79]On these visits see the B.C. News section of the *CMAJ*. On MacEachern himself see *The Canadian Who's Who*, Vol. VI, 1952-4, pp. 648-9. See also Margaret Andrews, "Medical Services in Vancouver, 1886-1920; A Study in the Interplay of Attitudes, Medical Knowledge, and Administrative Structures," unpublished Ph.D. thesis, University of British Columbia, 1979, especially Ch. 3.

[80]J. C. Schwartz, ed., *Who's Who Among Physicians and Surgeons*, I (New York: 1938), p. 747. Also Anne S. Cavers, *Our School of Nursing, 1899-1949* (Vancouver: School of Nursing, VGH, n.d.), p. 87.

[81]For a useful discussion of these funding problems see Harry M. Cassidy, *Public Health and Welfare Organization* (Toronto: Ryerson Press, 1945).

[82]Haywood in Walsh, *A Study of the VHG*, n.p.

[83]See the work and reports of the Women's Auxiliary in the *Annual Reports* of VGH.

[84]Dr. C. F. Covernton, "Problems of Primipara," *VMAB* (May 1931), 179-83.

[85]Like other Canadians hospitals, the VGH staffed its wards with student nurses enrolled in the VGH School of Nursing. For a discussion of the content of nursing training see Kathryn McPherson, "Nurses and Nursing in Early Twentieth Century Halifax," unpublished M.A. thesis, Dalhousie University, 1982, Ch. 2.

[86]MacEachern, *Hospital Organization*, pp. 866-75.

[87]W. K. Burwell, "Report from Staff (Gynaecological Division) of Vancouver General Hospital," *VMAB* 13 (1937), 193-7, and F. Sidney Hobbs, "Maternity Statistics," *CMAJ* (January 1943), 48-51. Obstetrical statistics for the 1920s can be found in VGH *Annual Reports*. According to Frederick J. Fish, VGH's director of medical records, the VGH changed its record-keeping system in 1932. This "effort at standardization which, although purely local, will have, it is hoped, an effect for good," included adopting the Massachusetts General Hospital interpretation of disease nomenclature and discarding "the classification books, in which all diagnoses were recorded heretofore.. . .in favour of the more handy and efficient 'Kardex' cabinet." See F. J. Fish, "The Medical Records System of the Vancouver General Hospital, Vancouver, B. C." *Bulletin of the American College of Surgeons* 18, 2 (June 1933), 52-8.

[88]Dr. G. M. Feldert, "Alleviating the Pains of Childbirth," *Canadian Nurse* (August 1920), 470.

[89]For more negative views see U. E. Bateson, "Twilight Sleep in Obstetrical Practice in Reports of Cases," *CMAJ* (June 1925), 639-40; W. Bourne, "Anesthesia in Obstetrics," *CMAJ* (August 1924), 702-3. For a more positive assessment see Ross Mitchell, "The Use of Pituitary Extract and Scopalomin-Morphine in Obstetrics," *CMAJ* (May 1921), 351-5. See also the critical editorial which follows Mitchell's article. This condemned the "tendency in certain countries and localities" to make use of drugs recommended by Mitchell "as an incentive to the patient to choose certain centres as her temporary place of abode. To promise a patient the application particularly of the latter [i.e., twilight sleep]. . .has led without question to its abuse, and in large extent its discredit." *CMAJ* (May 1921), 366. In another article D. Bjornson, "An Obstetrical Retrospect," *CMAJ* (December 1925), 1236-9, asserts that modern women knew about, and demanded, twilight sleep, ether, etc., leaving young practitioners in a quandary. A later editorial claimed that one of the causes of maternal mortality in Canada was "the insistence of mothers and their relatives and friends on the speedy termination of labour;" see "Maternal Mortality and the Practice of Obstetrics," *CMAJ* (February 1929), 180-1. There is some non-medical evidence that individual women did actively seek out chemical assistance in labour; for example, see Laura Salverson, *Confessions of an Immigrant's Daughter* (Toronto: University of Toronto Press, 1981). However, Canadian women did not collectively demand greater availability of twilight sleep to the same extent as their American sisters, who publicly campaigned for such intervention to ease the lot of their sex. For the U.S., see Wertz and Wertz, *Lying-In*, pp. 150-4, and Judith Waltzer Leavitt, "Birthing and Anesthesia: The Debate Over Twilight Sleep," *Signs* 6, 1 (Autumn 1980), 147-64.

[90]See R. N. Ritchie, "Rectal Anaesthesia in Obstretics," *Canadian Nurse* (July 1924), 352-4, and J. D. Graham, "Rectal Anesthesia in Obstetrics," *CMAJ* (September 1925), 935-9.

[91]W. Bourne, "Nitrous Oxide-Oxygen Analgesia and Anaesthesia in Obstretics," *CMAJ* (November 1921), 818-22.

[92]Bergland, "The Relief of Pain in Labour," 57-9. See also MacEachern, *Hospital Organization*, p. 282.

[93]See Haywood, *Hospital Survey Commission* 1930, pp. 89-90.

[94]Burwell, "Report from Staff," p. 193.

[95]*Ibid.*, p. 195.

[96]*Ibid.*, p. 196.

[97]F. Sidney Hobbs, "Maternity Statistics," *CMAJ* (January 1943), 49.

[98]*Ibid.* See also Burnett, "Versions," *VMAB* (November 1928), 42; "It is essential for every obstetrician to be able to do a version."

[99]Calculated from Hobbs, "Maternity Statistics," table I, p. 49.

[100]*Ibid.* Burwell states that in public wards "one may not

hesitate to let the patient return home after one or two unsuccessful inductions of labour where no obstetrical abnormality is present," "Report from Staff," p. 193.

[101]Burwell, "Report from Staff," p. 196.

[102]Hobbs, "Maternity Statistics," p. 48.

[103]Robert Ferguson, "A Plea for Better Obstetrics," *CMAJ* (October 1920), 901-4. Ferguson claimed that 30 per cent of the work of gynaecologists was created by bad obstetrics. John Osborn Polak of Brooklyn, New York, claimed that 60 per cent of gynaecological cases were direct results of poor obstetrical practice, "Effect of Popular Gynaecological Procedures on the Future Child-Bearing Women," *CMAJ* (September 1924), 797-803.

[104]Calculated from Hobbs, "Maternity Statistics," table II, p. 50.

[105]*Ibid.*

[106]*Ibid.*, p. 51. See also Biggs, "The Response to Maternal Mortality in Ontario," for a discussion of the role sulfanomide drugs played in that province's maternal health.

[107]See G. McKee, "A Review of Caesarian Sections in the Vancouver General Hospital, 1941," *VMAB* (April 1943), 206-10.

[108]Calculated from Hobbs, "Maternal Statistics," table II, p. 50.

[109]Wertz and Wertz, *Lying-In*, pp. 141-3.

[110]M. Blair, "The Role of Haemorrhage," pp. 166-9.

[111]1931 B. C. Hospital statistics report a 1:2 nurse-patient ratio, with 455 nurses (181 graduate nurses and 274 students) responsible for up to 1,153 patients. PABC, GR707, Box 5, Appendix D "Hospital Statistics, B. C., 1931." However, these figures do not reflect the fact that nurses worked in shifts and were not all on the wards at one time. Nor was their distribution in the hospital even. Some wards and wings required higher levels of staffing, while the staffs of private wings were augmented by graduate nurses hired by individual patients. As staff requirements grew, so too did the number of students accepted into the school, but by the mid-1920s shortage in student residence space began limiting enrolment. Staff shortages and unhealthy working and living conditions for students became so acute in the 1930s that the hospital was forced to hire Graduate or Registered Nurses on its staff, a move which most Canadian hospitals did not have to resort to until the 1940s and 1950s. These graduate nurses faced the same long hours and heavy work load as student nurses, and in 1940 the superintendent of nursing was still claiming that "in our desperate effort to keep expenses down to what we think the city 'will stand for,' we have been placing an all too great burden on our staff, which has necessitated the unpleasant closing of our eyes to continuous long overtime." *Annual Report* of VHG, 1940, p. 22. Thus the employment of graduate nurses did not necessarily improve the availability of nurses to patients, though graduate nurses could be relied on for swifter, calmer responses in

emergencies and more experienced execution of therapeutic techniques. For a comparison of VGH nursing staff size to those across the country see J. M. Gibbon and Mary S. Mathewson, *Three Centuries of Canadian Nursing* (Toronto: Macmillan Company of Canada Limited, 1947), pp. 489-91.

[112]MacEachern, *Hospital Organization*, p. 283.

[113]*Ibid.*, pp. 870-1.

[114]Vancouver City Archives, *Sun* and *Province* Clipping File, "VGH," "General Hospital is Mother to 27,395 Babies," 2 November 1935.

[115]MacEachern, *Hospital Organization*, p. 283.

[116]In the early 1930s white maternity patients between the ages of 16 and 45 in the VGH, St. Paul's and Grace were hospitalized on average between 12.32 and 12.70 days each. PABC, GR749, "Report on Information Collected and Compiled in Reference to Certain Phases of Hospital Work in British Columbia," 1934. Given the shortage of space at the VGH in these years, it is not surprising that "The gynaecological and obstetrical section of the staff keeps constant watch upon the efficacy of their treatment and their efforts towards reducing the length of stay in hospital." Frederick J. Fish, "The Medical Records System of the Vancouver General Hospital, Vancouver, B. C.," *American College of Surgeons Bulletin* (June 1933), 56.

[117]Wertz and Wertz, *Lying-In*, Ch. 5.

[118]MacEachern, *Hospital Organization*, p. 869.

[119]See Veronica Strong-Boag, "Keeping House in God's Country: Canadian Women at Work in the Home," in Craig Heron and Robert Storey, eds., *On the Job: Confronting the Labour Process in Canada* (Toronto: McGill-Queen's, 1986), pp. 124-51, for its discussion of the extent of home-based work.

[120]In 1920 Dr. MacEachern acknowledged this problem, stating that many poor women, whose health had improved during their stay at VGH, return home and "drift back into poverty condition." His solution, "more care of the financial condition," was beyond the mandate or resources of the hospital. PABC, GR706, B.C. Royal Commission on State Health Care and Maternity Benefits 1919-21, Proceedings, Letter from Dr. MacEachern, p. 7.

[121]See W. Peter Ward and Patricia C. Ward, "Infant Birth Weight and Nutrition in Industrializing Montreal," *American Historical Review* 89 (February 1984), 324-45, for an insightful discussion of the effects of maternal malnutrition on infant health.

Chapter Six

DEVIANTS ANONYMOUS: SINGLE MOTHERS AT THE
HÔPITAL DE LA MISÉRICORDE IN MONTREAL,
1929-1939*

Andrée Lévesque

Historians and sociologists have stressed the prominence of the
Catholic patriarchal family in Quebec society, women's role within
that institution and the paramount importance of motherhood
within marriage. Few scholars have so far studied the experience of
women who did not fit the conventional model of married mothers
at home. Childbearing was particularly honoured in Catholic
society; yet women who were reproductive outside the bounds of
marriage had no visible place in Quebec. The *revanche des berceaux*,
so valued by the Church and by Catholic nationalists, was to take
place within the family. Illegitimacy[1] violated the moral and
cultural ideal of the family defined by church and society.
Consequently women who transgressed societal and familial norms
disrupted the stability of the family and brought shame upon
themselves, their immediate family and their kinship network. This
shame had to be hidden, and single pregnant women who could not
go to private maternity homes or be sent to distant friends or
relatives concealed their condition amongst other women, nuns, who
had themselves renounced family life, sexuality and motherhood for
the higher calling of religious life. The hospitals provided by the
nuns give us a microcosm of the world of the single mother: the
handling of the pregnancy, the conditions of stay, the submission
and rebellion of the woman and the contradictory demands of
society regarding her child.

*Reprinted by permission of the Canadian Historical Association from *Historical
Papers/communications historiques* (1984), 168-84. I would like to thank Bettina
Bradury, Barbara Brooks, Geoffrey Ewen, Paul Lachance, Jane Lewis and Susan
Mann Trofimenkoff for their helpful comments and suggestions. I, of course, claim
full responsibility for errors of facts or interpretation. I am also very grateful to
Odette Vincent Domey and Jacques Domey for their invaluable help in unravelling
the intricacies of word processing. I am forever in debt with Nicole Laferte for
having granted me access to the archives of the Hôpital de la Miséricorde and
without whose help this study would not have been possible.

Each year, from 1929 to 1939, there were officially between 2,335 (1934) to 2,668 (1939) children born out of wedlock in Quebec.[2] Roughly 20 per cent of these (an annual average of 560), were born at the Hôpital de la Miséricorde in Montreal.[3] There are no statistics for pregnancies out-of-wedlock, but they were surely more numerous given the number of miscarriages and abortions. The reported illegitimacy rate in Quebec was slightly lower than the national average by .3 to .7 per cent. According to federal statistics, from 2.9 to 3.4 per cent of total live births were to single mothers in Quebec.[4]

The Hôpital de la Miséricorde had been performing a service to single mothers and illegitimate children since the mid-nineteenth century. In 1840, Mgr. Bourget asked widow Rosalie Jetté, née Cadron, to take a young single pregnant woman into her home. This request was followed by others until he asked her to leave her own children, rent a house and manage it as a home for unmarried pregnant women. This was the beginning of the Refuge Ste-Pélagie in 1845. Three years later, Rosalie Cadron Jetté and seven other women founded the Congregation of the *Soeurs de Miséricorde* to look after women who "needed to hide."[5] The babies were then looked after by the Grey Nuns. This arrangement lasted until 1889 when the *Soeurs de Miséricorde* set up their own crèches. By 1920 the hospital had a school of nursing and was used by the students of the school of medicine at the University of Montreal for their training in obstetrics.[6]

As long as some women had to conceal their pregnancies, the hospital fulfilled a genuine need. Single pregnant women's imperative to hide their condition highlighted society's orthodox view of the role of women, a role they had failed to follow. In the inter-war period the clergy, the politicians and the doctors all entertained a rigidly polarized view of lay women: they were either mothers-at-home, or their antithesis, prostitutes.[7] The woman who found herself a prospective mother, after exercising her sexuality outside the bounds of matrimony, literally had no place in this dichotomized representation. She was an outcast from the time her condition was obvious; her chance of regaining a place in her milieu was linked to the success with which her fault could be concealed from those around her.

The woman who registered at the Dorchester Street hospital was usually French Canadian and Catholic; only exceptionally was an Italian, an Irish or a Lithuanian woman admitted. A close female relative, her mother, aunt or cousin, was likely to accompany her to the admission. Often an orphan, since 27.7 per cent of single mothers had lost their own mothers and 25.8 per cent their fathers,[8] she was usually a young domestic servant. Statistics show that 60 per cent of the women were between 18 and 22. Before their admission, 47 per cent were domestic servants and 31 per cent lived with their family. Only 5.7 per cent worked in factories or in offices. Occasionally a schoolgirl, a nurse or a teacher sought admission.[9]

The occupations entered in the register may give us a false impression regarding the number of domestic servants: the women may have come to Montreal to work as servants once they became pregnant, or they may already have been domestics when they became pregnant. Similar problems concern the place of residence: of all the women who gave Montreal as their last address, some had been there only a short time. The medical records contain information concerning the patients' health. The figure for weight is meaningless because it was taken when the women were pregnant and we are not given their usual weight. A large number had bad teeth that necessitated extraction in the hospital. During the whole decade, an average of 30 per cent had gonorrhoea and 3.7 per cent a positive Wasserman test indicating syphilis. For 16 per cent of the women this was not their first pregnancy.[10] Undoubtedly, the stay at the hospital gave many inmates an opportunity for obtaining diagnosis and some treatment.

During the period of isolation at Miséricorde, a period which could last as long as a year, the new boarder was to assume a new identity. The first step, upon registration, was to receive an "imposed name" from an existing bank of names.[11] These were not ordinary names but rather highly unusual ones, sometimes conveying an intended meaning, such as Humiliane or Fructueuse! The names were assigned in alphabetical order and when the list was exhausted, after many months, the process started over again. Along with her new name, the boarder acquired, at the cost of $2, a uniform. In exceptional cases, some paying boarders occupying a private room would be veiled for the length of their stay to ensure greater secrecy. From the moment of registration until her departure, the *repentante*, or penitent, as she was to be known, was shut off from the world and could trust that the nuns would ensure complete discretion. Except during Lent or Advent, she could receive visitors at the parlour once a week, but those visitors had to be close relatives who were given a card with the boarder's "imposed name" on it. Without this card no visit was permitted, as in the case of one out-of-town mother who could ill-afford the transportation costs and had left her card at home.[12] Discretion was assured even in the case of a mother enquiring whether her thirty-four-year old daughter was a patient. Sister Tharcisius, in charge of the women, answered: "If the young girl was always good, why fear or doubt?"[13]

The anonymity extended to the child from the moment of her/his birth. It seems that the mother had little say in the name given her child. The surname was the same for all babies born each month; it might be that of a nurse or an intern on duty. As for the first names, they were assigned in alphabetical order. To a mother who asked for a note in order to see her child in the crèche in Trois-Rivières and who inquired about the godparents' names, Sister Tharcisius wrote that their names were not required: "Anyway, they are pure strangers, a nurse and one of our interns."[14]

La Miséricorde was a peculiar institution in that boarders usually entered voluntarily--if we ignore social pressures for the moment--but once inside they lived in a state of sequestration. They were not free to leave at will and they were subject to strict discipline. A short, one-page prospectus described the terms of admission, the cost for single or double rooms or wards ($90, $60 or $8 a month) and $155, $130 or $120 for adoption fees and the cost of the delivery.[15] The new boarder was told that she would have to spend six months of service at the hospital after the birth of the child and after her two-week period of recuperation. Only thus could she refund the costs of her delivery and treatment and the adoption fees. Any time spent working at the hospital before the delivery could be deducted from the six months term of service. Death of the child at birth or later did not change the conditions of admission; indeed a burial charge of $25 was added to the amount owing.[16] Even though the terms were explained at admission, the length of time to be served surprised many, particularly if the baby died.

Although 47 per cent of the women were under the age of 21, all boarders whatever their age were considered minors. Visits were controlled and mail was censured. Letters could be written only on Sunday and not during Lent or Advent. If a patient tried to escape she was brought back by a detective. In fact, the status of pregnant single women was similar not only to that of children but also to that of criminals: the father of the child was referred to as "the accomplice" by the nuns.[17] Deemed to have committed an offence, some of the women were themselves the victims of crime. In about 3 per cent of the cases when the young woman was under sixteen, "and of previously chaste character," according to section 301 of the Criminal Code, the baby's father was guilty of seduction and subject to five years imprisonment. If the woman was 16 or 17 years old, as 11 per cent were, "and of previously chaste character," he could receive a maximum of two years in prison. If the man were over 21 and the woman under 21 and he promised to marry her, he was nonetheless guilty of seduction punishable by one year in prison under Section 210 of the Criminal Code.[18] Very few of the cases of seduction which were brought to court each year resulted in a conviction.[19] It was also a crime to seduce a feeble-minded woman or an employee, but one can only guess at the number of single mothers who were victims of these crimes or of incest.

Whatever the circumstances surrounding the pregnancy of the single woman, great care was taken to shield the outside world from her presence. Some patients' mothers begged the hospital to let their daughters go before their six months were up because people would start talking if their daughters were missing for too long. In another case, the mother argued that if the father came down from the shanties and realized that his daughter had been gone for so long, he might guess the cause of her absence.[20] Younger siblings had to be protected from the truth since their

111

PROSPECTUS

Hopital Catholique de la Maternité
de Montréal

Sous la direction
des Soeurs de Miséricorde
Fondée en 1845.

⇐⊃⇒

Le but de cette Institution est de fournir un asile aux femmes qui sont sur le point de devenir mères, et de leur offrir, avec les soins corporels requis, le moyen de sauver leur honneur et celui de leur famille.

Les religieuses qui ont l'administration de cet hôpital se dévouent pour le bien moral et spirituel des hospitalisées, tandis que d'habiles gardes malades sont chargées de leur donner les soins que réclame leur position.

Dans l'admission des patientes aucune distinction n'est faite à cause de la religion, de la nationalité ou de la résidence de celles qui font application, et aucune n'est refusée à cause de sa pauvreté. Seulement, celles atteintes de quelque maladie contagieuse sont exclues.

Les patientes privées sont libres d'appeler un médecin autre que celui de l'Hôpital, si elles le désirent.

Les patientes doivent fournir leur propre linge et tous leurs objets de toilette.

Les conditions de l'admission sont comme suit:

SALLE COMMUNE.

Pension par mois	$8.00
Adoption de l'enfant et frais de maladie	$120.00

PENSION PRIVEE.

Chambres doubles, par mois	$60.00
Adoption de l'enfant et frais de maladie	$130.00
Chambre strictement privée, par mois	$90.00
Adoption de l'enfant et frais de maladie	$155.00

Les remèdes sont chargés au compte de la patiente.

La pension est payable chaque mois et les autres charges sont exigibles à l'entrée.

Le décès de l'enfant à la naissance ou plus tard ne modifie en rien les conditions ci-dessus mentionnées.

Porte d'entrée pour patientes, 440, rue Dorchester Est.

Pour conditions et informations, adressez.

SECRETAIRE DES PENSIONNAIRES,
440, rue Dorchester Est,
Montréal, P. Q.

sister was an object of scandal.[21] A father wrote that he could not telephone the hospital and did not want the nuns to contact him to announce the birth of his grandchild since people listened on the party line he shared with twenty families. He also requested that letters not bear the hospital's return address as the staff at the post office would then "find out."[22] One patient is known to have left the hospital immediately when she recognized a new boarder.[23]

While the world was protected from her presence, the single mother went through a state of infantilization or "minorization." Depending on her behaviour she could earn good marks which could shorten her stay by as much as two weeks, or bad marks, which had the opposite effect. Attempts to smuggle letters out of the hospital resulted in bad grades.[24] One patient was kept an extra month for having hit a child and having kept a pacifier for her own child.[25] The parents of another inmate came from out-of-town only to find that their daughter was being kept an extra fortnight.[26] Marks were earned by giving a blood transfusion to one's own child, or by breastfeeding several babies.[27] Good behaviour was also rewarded with responsibilities such as supervising a ward. Such activity could in turn be translated into good points toward an early release.

The image of the single mother justified this treatment. She was considered weak and ignorant, strong-minded and wicked, or simple-minded. Perhaps because mentally handicapped women were more vulnerable to abuse, single mothers were often believed to be of inferior intelligence. A doctor writing in a Quebec medical journal in 1932 stated that "natural [i.e., illegitimate] children seem particularly exposed to madness. . .It is probable, in fact, that the parents of a natural child are often abnormal."[28] In the register, one finds such comments as "stupid" or "idiot" written in by the nuns. The nuns may have been exaggerating at times, but one cannot rule out passive resistance from the women who wanted to be expelled before their term was up or, if brought in forcibly by their parents, before their delivery.

Even if it was recognized that many of the women had been abused, sometimes by a relative--while recommending a patient, the parish priest would occasionally make a point of writing that she came from a very poor but good family and had been taken advantage of--most were deemed to have fallen and hence needed to repent. This feeling was sometimes shared by the inmates' mothers. One wrote that she hoped that her daughter's stay of one year and three months would be a good lesson for her.[29] In a few cases, the parents or the parish priest requested that a young woman be kept after her six months until the age of 21, or even later, working in return for room and board as well as protection from the outside world and her own weakness.[30] These cases were referred to the *Soeurs du Bon Pasteur d'Angers* who had a home for young delinquent women. Some of them were taken there most reluctantly.[31]

The women were confined not only to avoid causing scandal

but also to reform. Attendance at chapel was required three times a day. The whole atmosphere was designed to induce humility, repentance and penance. Sr. Tharcisius, for instance, wrote to a woman coming back for the second time: "Poor lamb wounded on the thorns along the path, you will be above reproach if you show yourself to be repentant, submissive and humble."[32]

The work the single mothers performed at La Miséricorde was both a means of atonement for sin and an economic necessity. The avowed purpose of the six months of service was to refund the cost of the delivery and medicine and to pay for the child who was *abandonné*. If the baby were placed and adopted, the service was reduced to three months. If the baby died, six months work remained owing to pay for the cost of burial. If the child were kept in the crèche, the daily board was $1. The work was assessed at $20 a month, but days of sickness were not counted.[33] Clearly it was not simply economic considerations that dictated the length of service; the good or bad marks also affected the time spent in the institution. In 1933, when a large number of beds were needed, some inmates were given a month's grace. According to the correspondence found in the files, there was much confusion regarding the counting of the days of service. Inmates wrote notes to Sr. Tharcisius asking how long they still had to serve, relatives were uncertain as to the date of discharge and there was much pleading to let a daughter out either because she was needed to help her mother or because there was sickness at home. There were cases of members of the family trying to raise sufficient funds so that a sister or a daughter could be let out early. One woman implored the nuns to let her sister go and asked if the government could not help: "I understand," she wrote, "that it is not your fault nor that of the government" and offered to pay $75 a month. Sr. Tharcisius answered that the patient could go only when her account was reduced to the last $75 and that "one should not forget that this child is hers and not the government's nor ours although we will keep him for six years."[34] A letter from the parish priest, if it could be obtained, proved the surest way of getting an early dismissal. Women who had nowhere to go went on serving the nuns for many months, sometimes years, in return for room and board. They thus had the spiritual and material benefits of living in a religious community without being committed to vows.

There were other instances, however, when women had to work against their will to pay off a non-existent debt. Someone who cared for the patient, in some cases a priest, or another nun from her home town, sent money but asked that the inmate not be told "so that she can prolong her time for a complete recovery if possible."[35] Recovery here seems to mean moral recovery. When the father of an eighteen-year-old patient successfully sued the baby's father, the hospital got $300, but the family was not reimbursed the $126.50 for the woman's board before delivery, $50 for abandoning the child, and $44 for the doctor's fees and treatment.[36]

Whether for penance or to refund a debt, service in the hospital consisted of general housework, such as washing furniture; kitchen work, like peeling potatoes; laundry work, diapers being the most arduous; and work in the nursery or crèche, feeding, supervising and changing the babies or children. One mother breastfed three to four babies and exhausted herself to the point of anaemia and then was discharged because she was incapable of doing her work. A few days before delivering, a boarder wrote: "I spend all day ironing."[37] The doctor asked that an inmate who had developed a skin irritation washing furniture should stop work for forty days. She was then given damp clothes to fold and the doctor told her to stop if she felt weak and to take a tonic three times a day.[38] It is difficult to argue that this kind of work was solely for moral reform when women in private rooms were exempt from all work before their delivery (nor did they work afterwards since they paid the fees) except for "*des ouvrages de fantaisie pour elles-mêmes, des lectures. . .*"[39] And yet, one Protestant woman was discharged after three months of service because "*puisque protestante ne peut tirer aucun profit spirituel.*"[40]

The penitents were also the objects of rescue work. The most devout could join the Madelon, named after St. Mary Magdalene, and become Oblates. The condition of admission, according to Sr. Tharcisius, was good health and good will. After spending a few months as a Daughter of St. Marguerite, the candidate was issued a uniform and given a new name; she then entered the order on 22 July, feast day of St. Mary Magdalene. The Oblates did not have the strict discipline of the ordained nuns: they did not have to fast, but they could not go out and had parlour only once a month. They worked for the nuns, the stronger ones in the kitchen, the others sewing or performing housework.[41] Thus they would atone for their sins for the rest of their life. At least one mother wrote advising her daughter to expiate her fault by renouncing her life and entering the order.[42]

A very small number entered the Madelon. Those who did not hear a religious calling had to deal with the immediate responsibility for their offspring. Single mothers were generally encouraged to keep their child. Already in 1915, the Women's Directory of Montreal, engaged in reform work for single mothers, aimed at keeping mother and child together to encourage breastfeeding, partly in order to cut down on infant mortality.[43] In 1931, the feminist Idola Saint-Jean recommended to the Royal Commission on Social Services (the Monpetit Commission), that the single mother keep her child "as a safeguard for her." She also argued that it would not only be beneficial for the mother but would also allow children to enjoy the warmth and maternal care that no institution could provide.[44] While the experts recommended that mothers keep their child either for their own or for the child's welfare, only 14.6 per cent of patients actually did leave the hospital with their child. Legally, the so-called illegitimate child

115

was the mother's responsibility; it was a crime for her to neglect or abandon her offspring. She was bound to support it, though the law allowed her to avail herself of adoption.[45]

By leaving her child at La Miséricorde a mother indicated that she wished it to be adopted. The mother would pay a lump sum of at least $50 for the upkeep of the child at the crèche until adopted. If, instead of leaving the child to be adopted, she could afford the daily fee of $1, she could keep her child at the crèche and retain visiting rights on the first Thursday of the month.[46] A number of women intended to look after their child when their financial situation improved or if they married. They would send money for months, sometimes years, although they usually stopped gradually when personal circumstances changed. In some cases, the child was indeed claimed after the mother married. In other cases, the babies left the hospital with their grandmother, but a larger number were destined to spend their childhood in institutions.

The nuns exercised great power over the relations between the mother and her child. The hospital's desire to avoid a new infant charge led the nuns to trace a patient who had deserted, placing the baby in her arms and sending both on their way after extracting a promise from the mother to send the payments.[47] Another woman came back to get her child, but she was refused on the advice of a priest and the Children's Aid Bureau.[48] Mothers who left their children at the crèche often wrote to enquire about their health and wellbeing: "Let her take fresh air outside. I would so much like her to enjoy good health."[49] Many sent money for photographs to be taken and one mother, noticing that her child had bandy legs, sent money for a pair of boots.[50] Even three years after she had left the hospital, one mother was encouraged to come and pick up her child. An anglophone patient wrote: "If your answer to me would be that my baby had died and God had taken him to Heaven, I would be so much happier. I am so lonesome for him."[51]

For over a third of the mothers, long-term responsibilities for the care of their child did not pose a problem since it died during its first year. At the beginning of the decade, Montreal had the unfortunate reputation of having one of the highest infant mortality rates in Canada if not in the western world: it fell from 125 per thousand in 1931 to 72 per thousand in 1938.[52] At La Miséricorde, 37.7 per cent of the infants born between 1929 and 1939 died in their first year, mostly from preventable diseases such as gastroenteritis or pulmonary infections.[53] For the sisters and some mothers, the death of a child was almost a cause for rejoicing since the infant would be spared a life of misery. To a mother who wrote that she could not forget her child and wanted to know its complete name, Sr. Tharcisius answered: "Our good Mother in Heaven has taken care herself of little Adrien. She came and got him last May. It is a little angel who is up there watching over his maman." This was written in November, six months after Adrien's death.[54] In the same vein, the sister wrote to a grandfather: "Dear Sir: We regret to say that the baby born to E.C. is dead. Thank God for this great favour."[55] To concerned mothers, the sisters gave news regarding the child's weight and behaviour. Sometimes this information appears to have referred to the wrong child. One mother asked whether her child was dead so she could stop worrying. In April, she was informed that "elle va bien et est toujours gracieuse;" shortly after this, she was notified that the child had died the previous December.[56]

While Sr. Tharcisius personally encouraged mothers to keep their children, most of them could not do so and a large number left the hospital to take up positions as domestics. It was a special favour to be chosen by a doctor to serve his family.[57] Many left for another city, as far away as Ottawa, to make a new start and forget their past. Others tried to save money in order to claim their child one day and kept in touch even when they had signed the "abandonment" form.

There are difficulties in assessing the changes that took place during the period under study. The number of admissions was limited by the number of beds; yet we know that the total number of births from single women in Quebec rose from 2.9 per cent of live births in 1931 to 3.4 per cent in 1939, which is a 17 per cent increase.[58] In 1933, both the Miséricorde in Montreal and the one in Quebec City were full and turning women away. In Montreal, La Miséricorde began to restrict admission to women from the city in their seventh month of pregnancy or later. Was there an increase in illicit sex? The illegitimacy rate did go up from 3 per cent in 1932 to 3.2 per cent in 1933, but the main reason for the rise in demand for admission was that, in both cities, private maternity homes were closing because of the Depression and the overflow was going to the Miséricorde hospitals.[59]

What did decrease during the period were the rates of syphilis and of infant mortality. The rate of positive Wasserman tests which was 8 per cent in 1930, never went above 6 per cent after January 1936.[60] An active anti-venereal diseases campaign had been launched in the early twenties, but Prime Minister Bennett's government had cut the federal funds in 1931. More refined studies are needed to provide a satisfactory explanation for the decreasing rate of syphilis.[61] The drop in infant mortality, from 43 per cent in 1930 to 27 per cent in 1939,[62] follows the trend in Quebec and Canada. As physical conditions inside the institutions did not change noticeably, the decrease can only be attributed to traditional causes which have been identified by other historians: better nutrition and a better understanding and application of measures of hygiene.[63]

*   *   *

The treatment of single mothers at the Hôpital de la
Miséricorde raises a number of questions. The letters intercepted
and kept in the dossiers may give us a biased picture of the living
conditions since the majority were written by dissatisfied boarders.
There were, however, some letters from grateful ex-patients to Sr.
Tharcisius. Besides the correspondence, comments written in the
patients' records by the supervisors provide some insights into the
reaction of the boarders, the extent of submissiveness or rebellion.
While the nuns commented on the patients' stubbornness or
insubordination, inmates' letters repeatedly mention tears,
tiredness, suicidal thoughts and general depression. Unhappiness
was expected by the authorities and interpreted as a sign of
repentance. Sr. Tharcisius wrote to an ex-boarder with whom she
kept up a warm correspondence and who planned to come to
Montreal for a visit: *"Il vous sera sans doute agréable de revoir la
chapelle où vous avez tant de fois prié et pleuré."*[64]

Except for women who had nowhere to go, with no family or
friends, and for whom the hospital was indeed a haven from a
corrupt world,[65] we can assume that most women were anxious to
leave as soon as possible. The majority appeared to be resigned,
some trying to get good marks in order to be let out early, others
begging their parents, relatives or boyfriend to find some money to
pay off their debt.

Comments by the nuns would lead us to believe that some
silent sabotage and passive resistance occurred. One patient was
deemed not to be very bright because she took so long getting her
work done. Yet her intercepted letters are very coherent and show
no signs of dimness of wit. Out of desperation, some women threw
letters out of windows, attempted to smuggle them out with visitors
or entrusted them to companions leaving the institution. We only
know of those who got caught.[66] The supervisors reported
misdemeanors, but were all cases detected and reported? We know
that some 4 per cent of the women were discharged for being
insubordinate, stubborn or vulgar.[67] The best way to get expelled
quickly was to be an object of scandal, to use foul language and hold
conversations on scandalous subjects.[68] At least one young woman
may have tried to injure herself voluntarily since she needed an
operation on a finger "infected by guilty negligence."[69] A small
minority managed to escape without being brought back. Others
attempted to escape but were captured by the detective called by the
authorities. In the case of minors, the nuns presumably had the
help of the police because they acted in loco parentis. In other
instances, they were on shaky grounds, as in the case of an inmate
who was discharged under orders from her lawyer.[70] Closely
guarded, often strangers to the city, perhaps without sympathetic
relatives nearby and threatened with capture by a detective and an
extended stay if caught, rebellious women were discouraged from
actively reacting to their situation.

Open rebellion, at great risk, was only the most overt manifestation of resistance. In most cases, even passive resistance was out of the question. Depressed women, often coping with the trauma of having been deserted by their lover and being cast out from their familiar surroundings, busy all day and bearing the discomforts of pregnancy, had little energy left for rebellion. Like their mothers, most would have internalized the religious, traditional and patriarchal values which justified their punishment. Society's rules had been transgressed by them and their child's father. They, and later their child, were to pay the price.

Women had to come to terms with the social consequences of out-of-wedlock pregnancies. Given the contradictory demands made on single mothers--to hide their shame and to keep their child--anonymity provided an escape route if the child died or if, transgressing the usual prescription, the mother left it with the nuns. This dissimulation, during and after pregnancy, could only be accomplished with the complicity of other women, nuns or mothers. Nuns offered shelter, discretion, correction and rehabilitation. Mothers had to protect their daughters from the danger of losing their honour. Yet in many cases mothers were not there since over a quarter of single mothers had lost their own mothers. As this seems higher than for the majority of women their age, their mothers' absence may have been in part responsible for their situation. Mothers of single mothers showed their concern for their daughters, suffered great grief and often blamed themselves for their children's faults. This feeling of guilt was reinforced by some popular writings of the time. In a collection of morality tales, the chaplain of the Hôpital de la Miséricorde in Quebec City, Father Victorin Germain, maintained that if a single woman became pregnant it was usually a sign that her own mother had previously sinned either by having an illicit love affair before her marriage, or by practising birth control.[71] Not only did the inmates' mothers take moral responsibility for their daughters but, within their means, they also showed concern for their material well-being. They sewed clothes for their daughters, wrote them letters and covered up for them. Of the patients who had a mother--this applied to 72 per cent--5 per cent took charge of their grandchildren, usually adopting them.[72]

Confronted with an unwanted pregnancy many women attempted some form of abortive procedure, from taking hot mustard baths to inserting an instrument into the cervix. Presumably not all of them admitted this to the examining doctor at the hospital, but this information appears on 5.1 per cent of medical records.[73] Short of aborting, the surest way of escaping the social consequences of single motherhood was to marry the father. Canada and Quebec do not keep statistics on births occurring within six months of marriage and, except by consulting parish records, we cannot estimate the incidence of pre-marital pregnancies. The correspondence found in the hospital reveals that some fathers claimed that they intended to marry the mother when their financial situation allowed it, when they found a job for instance. Some kept their word and the child was claimed later on. Some parents forbade their daughter to keep in contact with her lover and their mail was intercepted even when the woman was 21 years of age.[74] The nuns took note of at least one woman who married a drunk she did not love only to give their child a name.[75] A few times a year women married in the chapel of the hospital, either before the birth or, more often, upon leaving with her child.[76] If the father were acceptable, both the parents and the nuns viewed marriage as the best solution short of entering the convent.[77] Thus the woman could reenter society in the role prescribed for her, that of a married mother.

Starting anew as if nothing happened was the other route back into "the world." The woman faced a paradox here: the best way to hide her past was to hide her child. Yet the law, the experts and the nuns all made the mother responsible for her child. This contradiction could only engender feelings of guilt and inadequacy.[78]

In order to survive economically and socially, the single mother had little choice but to abandon her child. Jobs were difficult to get during the Depression and domestic service was the main occupation for single women. Few employers were willing to hire a woman with her child. In 1937, single mothers who tried to subsist on welfare were denied this means of survival in Montreal when the city, to comply with orders from the Quebec government, cut single mothers off the relief lists.[79] Economic conditions forced many mothers to institutionalize their children and make them available for adoption. An institutionalized illegitimate child had a minimal chance of being adopted during these years of Depression when adoption rates were dwindling.[80] The social stigma attached to illegitimacy would pursue such a child for the rest of her/his life. The label was in the parish registers and some religious orders did not accept bastards, hence denying them the highest aspiration of a Catholic. A mother could well feel guilty for condemning her child to a life of discrimination by putting her own welfare first. In this context, the expressions of relief at the death of the child are not surprising. As one grandmother wrote Sr. Tharcisius, "we are satisfied. The baby is dead, the past erased."[81] But the past was erased only after the single mother had undergone a period of anonymity, in isolation, in penance, as atonement for her sin and just retribution for her delinquent behaviour.

Notes

[1]Throughout this article I have used the expression 'illegitimate' to refer to births to single mothers. I understand that this term is obsolete and even insulting, but for the sake of convenience I have used it in its historical context.

Andrée Lévesque

²Province de Québec, *Rapport annuel du ministère de la Santé et du Bien-être social pour les années 1935 à 1941* (Québec, 1944), p. 204.

³Compiled from the registers of the Hôpital de la Miséricorde, in Archives de l'Hôpital de la Miséricorde, Montreal (hereafter AHM).

⁴*Recensement du Canada*, 1931, Vol. 12; M. E. Fleming and M. MacGillivray, *Fécondité de la femme canadienne* (Ottawa: King's Printer, 1936), p. 262.

⁵Sr. Saint-Jean-Vianney, s.m., M.S.S., "Un peu d'histoire," paper presented at the Journée d'étude tenue à l'occasion du 10ᵉ anniversaire de l'incorporation du service social de la Miséricorde, le 17 novembre, 1955, pp. 4-5.

⁶J. E. Dubé, "Nos hôpitaux. Leur passé, leur évolution, le présent," *L'Union médicale*, 61, 2 (février 1932), 179-80. In Quebec City, the Hôpital de la Miséricorde, under the direction of the Soeurs du Bon Pasteur, performed the same function as its homologue in Montreal and recorded an average of 457 deliveries a year between 1929 and 1933; see Albert Jobin, "Hôpitaux de la Miséricorde et de la Crèche St. Vincent de Paul," *Bulletin de la Société Médicale des Hôpitaux Universitaires de Québec* 35 (août 1934), 304.

⁷For the medical discourse and prescriptions on women, see Andrée Lévesque, "Mères ou malades." *Revue d'histoire de l'Amérique française* 38, 1 (été 1984), 23-37.

⁸Statistics compiled from AHM registers, 1929-39.

⁹*Ibid.* Given the small percentage of women who entered La Miséricorde, it does not seem that illegitimacy was linked to industrial work. It is not the purpose of this article to add one more footnote to the modernization debate. Edward Shorter's hypothesis has been answered by Joan W. Scott and Louise A. Tilly, and John R. Gillis has analyzed the pregnancy of servants in London. E. Shorter, "Illegitmacy, Sexual Revolution and Social Change in Modern Europe," in Theodore K. Rabb and Robert I. Rotberg, eds., *The Family in History. Interdisciplinary Essays* (New York: Harper Torchbooks, 1973), pp. 48-84; J. W. Scott and L. A. Tilly, "Women's Work and the Family in Nineteenth Century Europe," *Comparative Studies in Society and History* 17, 1 (January 1975), 36-64; J. R. Gillis, "Servants, Sexual Relations and the Risks of Illegitimacy in London, 1908-1900," *Feminist Studies* 5, 1 (Spring 1979), 142-73.

¹⁰*Ibid.* While no conclusion regarding the health of the mother can be drawn from her weight statistics, neither can any be drawn from the infant weight since it was seldom recorded. Lack of adequate data prevents us from making a comparison with Patricia Ward and Peter Ward's findings in "Infant Birth Weight and Nutrition in Industrializing Montreal," *American Historical Review* 89, 2 (April 1984), 324-45.

¹¹AHM. Here are just a few of these unusual names: Heraïs, Calithène, Potamie, Rogata, Macédonie, Gemelle, Nymphodore, Extasie, or Symphorose.

121

[12]Information taken from the correspondence found in a patients' files will be identified by the date or the registration number.
[13]AHM, 1932.
[14]AHM, Sr. Tharcisius to A., 12637.
[15]AHM, _Prospectus_, Hôpital Catholique de la Maternité de Montréal, sous la direction des Soeurs de la Miséricorde.
[16]AHM, Sr. Tharcisius, 30 September 1935; 21 October 1935; 7 November 1935.
[17]AHM, 32653, 32771.
[18]Public Archives of Canada, Charlotte Whitton Papers, MG 30, E 256, Vol. 20, John Kerry,"The Legal Status of the Unmarried Mother and Her Child in the Province of Quebec," (1926).
[19]Montréal, Archives judiciaires, Cours des Sessions, Cour du Banc du Roi, 1929-39.
[20]AHM, Sr. Tharcisius refused the request, 24 July 1937.
[21]AHM, 1933.
[22]20 June 1936. A mother also wrote, "nous avons des parents de prêtre, des cousines religieuses dans plusieurs communautés à Montréal aussi ne donnez de réponse à personne, ni prêtre, ni religieuse." 2 March 1933.
[23]AHM, 35181, 10 May 1937.
[24]When caught, a patient had to serve an extra month; altogether she worked seven months after her delivery; AHM, 34502, 30 March 1936.
[25]AHM, 32542, 1933.
[26]As a mother from St. Hyacinthe put it, "je ne voudrait pas voyager pour rien le temps est trop dur [sic]." AHM, 32000, 1933.
[27]The blood transfusion was assessed at $20 or one month of service. AHM, 32537.
[28]C. A. Décary, "Maladies mentales," _Annales Médico-chirurgicales de l'Hôpital Ste-Justine_ 1, 3 (mai 1932), 126.
[29]AHM, 1939
[30]A curé wrote Sr. Tharcisius, "que je serais content pour les parents et leur fille Y., si vous pouviez décider cette dernière à demeurer chez-vous comme une autre des soeurs, parmi les filles repentantes. Là seul elle serait sauvegardée contre de nouveaux malheurs qui la guettent chez elle, j'en ai la ferme conviction." AHM, 17 October 1933, 32760. Similar requests from the patients' mothers are in 32357, 17 October 1933, and 32578, 19 November 1933.
[31]AHM, 32509, May 1937; a 17 year old "fait une scène pour ne pas rester, prétend être amenée de force."
[32]AHM, Sr. Tharcisius, 10 August 1938.
[33]AHM, Sr. Tharcisius, 30 September 1935, 21 October 1935, 15 October 1937.
[34]AHM, 22 July 1938.
[35]AHM, 3 November 1937. Even women over the age of 21 were sometimes kept against their will. To a hotel keeper who had

122

Andrée Lévesque

brought his 27-year old employee, an orphan, to the hospital, Sr. Tharcisius wrote: "she wants to leave the hospital at all costs. . .she believes she is in prison. . .If we keep her here it is only in answer to your desire which you have expressed so clearly already." 12 April 1932, 31557.

[36]AHM, 32460 and 35175, May 1937. The woman still owed $97.

[37]AHM, 32662, 1932. In 1938, a twenty-year-old anglophone of Lithuanian origin was "acquitted" after four months as a wetnurse. In a note to Sr. Tharcisius, she wrote, "my mother thinks I only do 6 babies, she doesn't know I have been doing 13 babies for 3 months, washing them, feeding them and scrubbing." How many was she breastfeeding? 35436, 1938.

[38]AHM, 1932

[39]AHM, Sr. Tharcisius to the curé of Ste-Justine-de-Dorchester, 18 April 1939.

[40]AHM, 33660, 2 October 1935.

[41]AHM, St. Tharcisius to E.P., 15 July 1937.

[42]AHM, 2 March 1933.

[43]First Annual Report of the Women's Directory of Montreal (Montreal, 1915).

[44]La Presse, 13 January 1931.

[45]Kerry, pp. 9-10.

[46]Parlour on a week day was very inconvenient for working mothers, especially if they lived out of town. AHM, 4 July 1940.

[47]AHM, 30590, 4 October 1930. Also 33919, 2 September 1935.

[48]AHM, 33296, July 1934.

[49]AHM, 1935.

[50]AHM, 1937.

[51]AHM, 27 June 1940, written when the child was one year old.

[52]Province de Québec. Ministère des Affaires Municipales, de l'Industrie et du Commerce. Annuaire statistique du Québec, 1930-40. (Québec: Imprimeur de Sa Majesté le Roi, 1931-1941).

[53]Statistics compiled from AHM, the registers, 1929-39.

[54]AHM, 27 November 1939.

[55]AHM, 1934. A 19 year-old who left the hospital just two weeks after her child's birth, wrote Sr. Tharcisius, "Si le bon Dieu venait la chercher pour faire un petit ange au ciel à que je serais heureuse car qui dit plus tard qu'elle n'aura pas de misère, je sais qu'elle me maudira peut-être un jour, mais il me faut subir mon sort que j'ai voulue [sic]." She need not have feared being damned one day, as the baby died at nineteen days. 35065.

[56]AHM, 32634, April 1934 and 9 September 1934.

[57]AHM, 32192, April 1933.

[58]Province de Québec. Rapport annuel du ministère de la Santé et du Bien-être social pour les années 1935 à 1941 (Québec, 1935-1944), p. 204.

123

[59]*Ibid.* AHM, C. Joncas to Sr. Tharcisius, 20 February 1933; Sr. Tharcisius to the curé B., January 1933.

[60]Statistics compiled from AHM, the registers, 1929-39.

[61]Suzann Buckley and Janice Dickin McGinnis, "Venereal Disease and Public Health Reform in Canada," *Canadian Historical Review* 63, 3 (September 1982), 337-54. See Jay Cassel, *The Secret Plague: Venereal Disease in Canada, 1838-1939* (Toronto: University of Toronto Press, 1987).

[62]Mortality rate of infants born at the Hôpital de la Miséricorde: 1929: 39.6 per cent; 1930: 43 per cent; 1931: 44 per cent; 1932: 51 per cent: 1933: 59 per cent: 1934: 37 per cent; 1935: 34 per cent; 1936: 35 per cent; 1937: 29 per cent; 1938: 17 per cent; 1939: 27 per cent. Statistics from AHM, the registers, 1929-39.

[63]See Terry Copp, "The Health of the People: Montreal in the Depression Years," in David A. E. Shepard and Andrée Lévesque, eds., *Norman Bethune, his time and his legacy/son époque et son message* (Ottawa: Canadian Public Health Association, 1982), pp. 129-31.

[64]AHM, 34378 stayed a year and a half.

[65]AHM, 24 June 1937.

[66]Having tried to send a letter "en cachette," 34502 had to work an extra month in the nursery; altogether she had already served seven months after her delivery. AHM, 32771; 35217, 29 May 1937; 35840, 14 May 1938, were also caught and punished.

[67]Statistics compiled from AHM, the registers, 1929-39.

[68]AHM, 33275, 1934.

[69]AHM, May 1939.

[70]According to the register, she still owed the institution $97. AHM, 35173, May 1937. In October of 1935, the police were called to put 34168 to bed. When 30621 threatened to desert in August of 1930, a detective escorted her to the sisters' other crèche in Sault-Aux-Récollets, a Montreal suburb.

[71]Victorin Germain, *Contes de la crèche* (Québec, 1939).

[72]Statistics compiled from AHM, the registers, 1929-39.

[73]*Ibid.*

[74]AHM, 36523, 9 October 1939. Gillis has already shown that, in nineteenth-century London, men who might have considered caring for their girlfriends and their children were often prevented by circumstances from doing so. Gillis, 157-63.

[75]AHM, 30377.

[76]Statistics compiled from AHM, the registers, 1929-39.

[77]To a patient's mother who asked for some advice as to whether her daughter should correspond with the young man who promised to marry her, Sr. Tharcisius answered, "le meilleur conseil est de la laisser marier puisque le jeune homme le désire. . .c'est son désir aussi. . .Ce serait la meilleure solution car elle ne montre pas d'attrait pour le couvent. Et le travail est très difficile à trouver." AHM, 32578, 19 November 1933.

[78]Seventeen years later, parents wrote enquiring about their

child, adding: "plus nous vieillissons, plus nous y pensons, sa ne se pase pas [sic]." AHM, 36571, 17 December 1956.

[79]*Le Devoir*, 18 May 1937.

[80]AHM, C. Joncas to Sr. Tharcisius, 20 February 1933.

[81]AHM, 31541, April 1932.

Chapter Seven

DISCOVERIES AND DISSIMULATIONS: THE IMPACT OF ABORTION DEATHS ON MATERNAL MORTALITY IN BRITISH COLUMBIA[*]

Angus McLaren and Arlene Tigar McLaren

One of the most striking improvements in the health of Canadian women was brought about by the lowering of the risk of maternal mortality. Between the 1930s and 1960s the chances of dying in pregnancy fell from about 1 in 150 to 1 in 3,000. Maternal deaths, which in the early 1930s had accounted for 10 to 15 per cent of all deaths among women in the childbearing years, fell in three decades to 2 to 3 per cent.[1] This dramatic breakthrough was so welcomed that few have asked why it occurred so late. In the early nineteenth century about one-quarter of the deaths of women aged between 15 and 50 were related to pregnancy and its complications. With the onrush of medical improvements associated with Joseph Lister's discovery of antisepsis in 1867 there was the real possibility of eliminating many of the traditional causes of maternal death.[2] Conditions did improve somewhat, but if one were to judge by the statistical data the gains made in the first decades of the twentieth century were still disappointingly modest. Whereas the infant mortality rate fell from 120 deaths per 1,000 live births at the beginning of the century to 68 per 1,000 by 1936, the maternal mortality rate continued to hover at about 5 per 1,000 and actually rose to a century high of 5.8 per 1,000 in 1930.[3]

The fact that Canadian families were becoming smaller and that as a result a higher percentage of all births were the more dangerous first births contributed to the sustaining of the high maternal mortality rate. But even with the larger percentage of primaparous births, the lower age of mothers and the improvement in medical care should have led to a decline in deaths associated

[*]Reprinted by permission of *B. C. Studies* 64 (Winter 1984/85), 3-26. This paper could not have been written if it had not been for the skilful and diligent work of our research assistant, Debra Ireland. We would like to thank her for her help, Ellen Gee, Chad Gaffield and Rennie Warburton for the comments, and the staff of the Provincial Archives of British Columbia for their assistance.

with pregnancy. In a 1934 study of 334 maternal deaths in one year in Ontario an important finding was unearthed. Researchers found that fifty-nine, or 17 per cent, of all maternal deaths were due to abortion. These abortion deaths were "artificially" inflating the number of deaths attributed to normal pregnancies.[4] This chapter has two purposes. The first is to employ the statistics available on maternal and abortion deaths in British Columbia to demonstrate that what the Ontario researchers discovered was not an isolated phenomenon.[5] We will show that abortion played an increasingly important role in keeping maternal mortality figures high right through the inter-war period. The second purpose of this paper is to reveal how an analysis of the relationship of abortion deaths to all maternal deaths raises methodological issues that must interest those who use quantitative evidence. How a maternal death was classified depended ultimately on the differing judgments and sometimes conflicting concerns of doctors, coroners, and magistrates. We will attempt to determine both the magnitude of the discrepancies in classification that resulted and the professional preoccupations that underlay such conflicts.

* * *

Abortion Deaths

Social amnesia--the failure of one generation to remember the experiences of an earlier one--is a not uncommon occurrence.[6] It is a weakness to which some of the current commentators on the abortion debate seem prone. Since the 1969 reform of the law relating to abortion and contraception, deaths due to abortion have become a rarity in Canada. In the decade 1970-79 there were in the entire nation only thirty-one such deaths reported, and one-half (fourteen) occurred in 1970 before many hospitals had established therapeutic abortion committees. In 1978 and 1979 no abortion deaths whatsoever were recorded in Canada.[7] It has thus become easy to forget that, in the past, deaths were frequently associated with abortion.[8] We have found, for example, that in British Columbia alone there were in the 1930s at least 139 abortion deaths. We use the term "at least" advisedly because of the impossibility of determining the real rate of abortion deaths. The difficulties encountered when determining the number of abortion deaths and establishing the impact they had on the overall rate of maternal mortality in British Columbia are the main topics broached in the first part of this chapter.

The estimation of the frequency of abortion-related deaths is at best a hazardous task and cannot be tackled in a straightforward fashion. In this study we used three separate sources: 1) a survey of medical practitioners; 2) British Columbia vital statistics; and 3) the records of the Attorney-General's office. Each of these sources reports on the number of abortion deaths that occurred in British Columbia over extended periods of time. The survey of doctors covers the years 1955 to 1968, British Columbia vital statistics provide data on the period from 1922 to 1968, and the records of the Attorney-General's office were searched for the years 1896 to 1937. Though these records tended to show some of the same overall patterns regarding the changing trends in the frequency of abortion deaths, they often differed remarkably in the number of deaths they reported for each year. No single source provided an entirely satisfactory account; each had its particular strengths and weaknesses.

Medical Reports

Unfortunately we have only one medical account devoted to determining the changing pattern of British Columbia abortion deaths. In 1970 Dr. W. D. S. Thomas reviewed the forty-four cases of maternal death attributable to abortion for the years 1955 to 1968.[9] They represented 22.4 per cent of the total of 197 maternal deaths. For the purposes of our study Dr. Thomas' findings for the years 1955 to 1959 are of special interest inasmuch as they allow us to compare medical reportage of abortion deaths--based on hospital records, coroners' reports and "personal communications with medical examiners"--with those of the division of vital statistics. For that five-year period the estimate of British Columbia abortion deaths ranged from the nineteen reported by doctors to the fourteen cited by Vital Statistics. (See table 1.)

TABLE 1

Reported B. C. Abortion Deaths

Year	Doctors' Report	Vital Statistics
1955	2	0
1956	3	3
1957	6	6
1958	3	3
1959	5	2
	—	—
	19	14

Sources: *B. C. Medical Journal*, 12 (May 1970), 111-12; B. C. Vital Statistics.

FIGURE 1

Reportage of Abortion Deaths

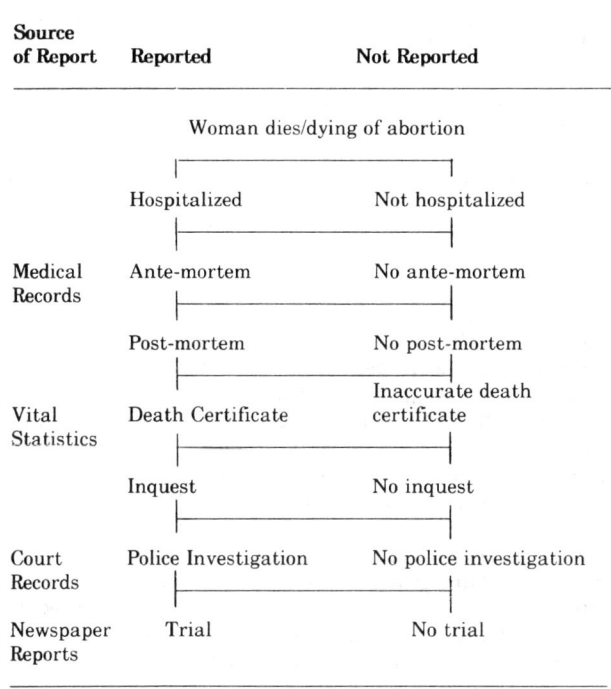

Source of Report	Reported	Not Reported
	Woman dies/dying of abortion	
	Hospitalized	Not hospitalized
Medical Records	Ante-mortem	No ante-mortem
	Post-mortem	No post-mortem
Vital Statistics	Death Certificate	Inaccurate death certificate
	Inquest	No inquest
Court Records	Police Investigation	No police investigation
Newspaper Reports	Trial	No trial

This comparison suggests that only two of every three abortion deaths was reported by Vital Statistics and presumably even a lower ratio of deaths known to medical authorities may have come to the attention of legal authorities. Why was this the case? The first reason was the fact that for a report of an abortion death to be made by Vital Statistics and by the judiciary (and perhaps beyond that by the newspaper press) it had to be first passed on by medical authorities. Whether intentionally or not, this process was not always carried out. An ante mortem or deathbed statement might not have been taken, a death certificate might have been inaccurately drawn up, a post mortem might not have been held. Figure 1 indicates the various stages at which a report of an abortion death might go astray and thereby fail to show up in the classifications of the next reporting agency, be it Vital Statistics, the judiciary or the newspaper press.

The second reason for the failure of the medical records to

tally with those of Vital Statistics and the Attorney-General is that some doctors simply did not want to report abortion deaths. We will be returning to this issue in the second part of the chapter; here it is only necessary to note that because of the illegal nature and moral stigma attached to abortions, many doctors may have concealed them to protect the reputations of their colleagues and patients.

That so few abortion deaths reached the notice of the courts is perhaps dramatic witness to the ambivalence that the medical profession felt regarding the status of abortion. British Columbia statistics on abortion were accordingly flawed for the same reasons suggested by an American writer in an 1934 issue of *New Republic*.

It is natural to wonder why, with scores of statistical tables being published year after year, the true state of affairs has not been revealed before. But it is not hard to understand when you know how the statistics are obtained. For example, Anna J. Brown comes into a hospital with a high temperature, and a story of falling down the cellar stairs in the third month of pregnancy. The hospital authorities may or may not believe the cellar-stairs explanation, but their function is to treat her for a dangerous septic condition, not to do police work. If she dies, the death is correctly certified as puerperal septicemia, and that's that, so far as the hospital is concerned. This grain of fact is deposited in the county health records. Eventually it is turned over to the federal Census Bureau. And Anna J. Brown, now relegated to the limbo of statistics, becomes one of six thousand infinitely shadowy women who die in this country each year of puerperal septicemia--a disease known to centuries of women as childbed fever.[10]

The result was that enormous discrepancies appeared between what doctors and legal officials knew regarding the numbers having recourse to abortion.

Medical authorities clearly knew better than any other officials the extent of abortion-related deaths; the problem is that we have very little information on the process of classification they employed. Much more work should be done in this area, but, given the medical profession's concern for self-policing, it is likely that only an 'insider' who enjoyed the confidence of his colleagues--as does Dr. Thomas--could provide an accurate picture of their perceptions. It also has to be remembered, however, that even doctors missed some cases of abortion--one researcher commented on the "unbelievable gullibility and stupidity of doctors" who misdiagnosed causes of miscarriage-related deaths--and medical statistics have to be presumed to be minimal estimations.[11]

TABLE 2

British Columbia Maternal Deaths: 1922-1968

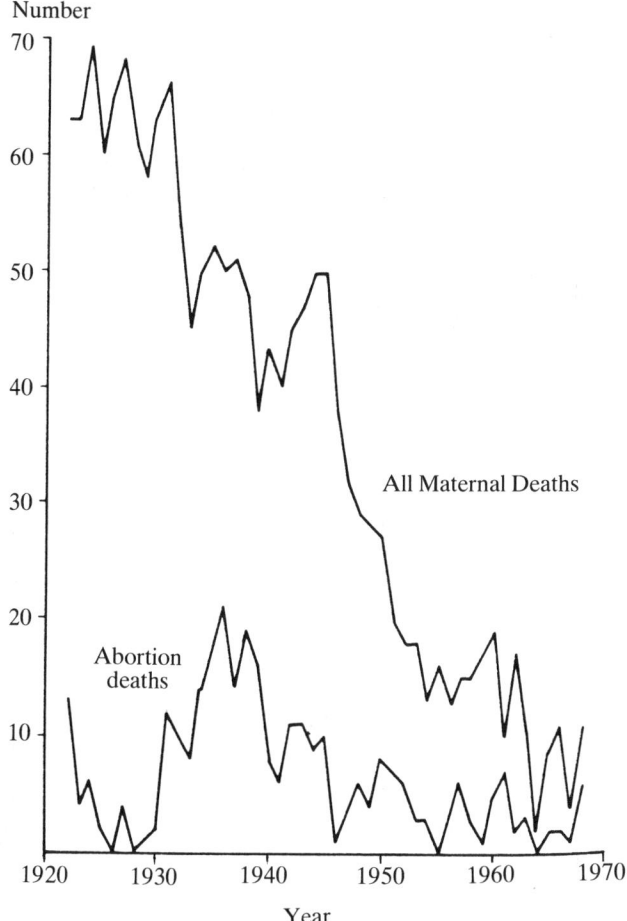

Source: B. C. Vital Statistics.

Vital Statistics

The information concerning abortion deaths reported by British Columbia Vital Statistics was based on the death certificates completed by doctors.[12] As already indicated, these figures were certainly lower than those known to doctors for the period after 1955. A similar under-reporting of abortion deaths by

131

Vital Statistics must have occurred in earlier decades as well, but its full extent cannot be determined.[13] This source, therefore, has certain inherent weaknesses. Its great strength is that it allows us to gain an impression of the frequency of *reported* abortion deaths, of changes in their frequency over time and of the extent to which such deaths varied in relation to other causes of maternal mortality.

TABLE 3

Maternal Death Rates in B.C.   **Crude Birth Rates in B.C.**
(rates per 1,000 live births)   **(rates per 1,000 population)**

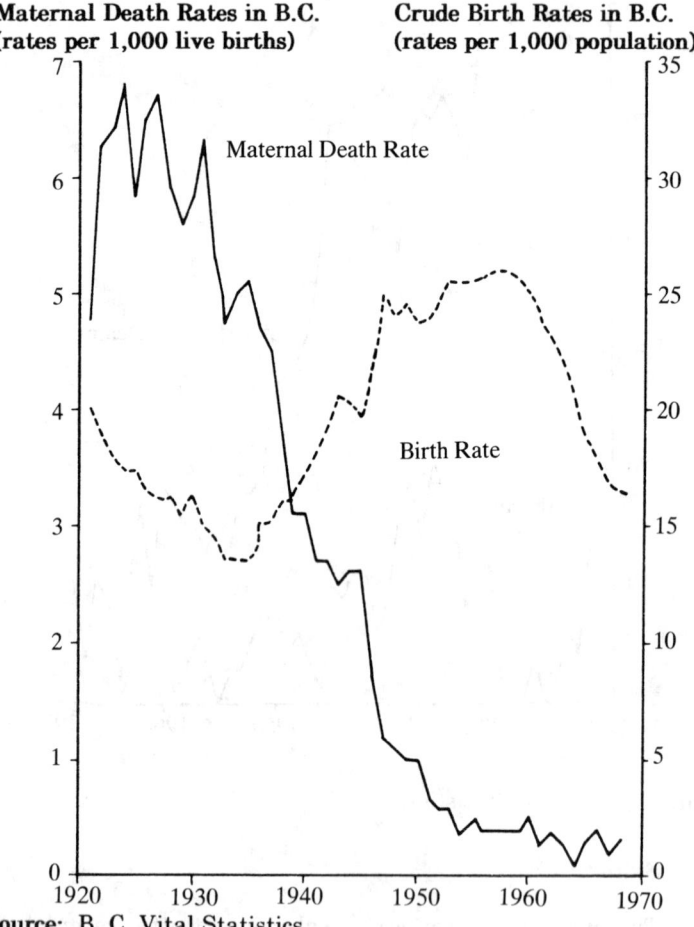

Source: B. C. Vital Statistics.

What was the general twentieth-century pattern of deaths due to abortion in British Columbia? In the vital statistics maternal deaths were classified as due to sepsis (infection), toxaemias (eclampsia or poisoning), haemorrhage, abortion without sepsis or toxaemias, abortion with sepsis, and other complications. The average number of annual deaths attributed to abortion in the 1930s was 13.3; in the 1940s the number declined to an average of 6.9; and in the 1950s it further declined to an average of 4.1. (The years 1925-30 were reported to have an average of only one abortion death per year; the reasons why we feel this figure is suspiciously low are given below.) As table 2 shows in more detail, the number of annual abortion deaths peaked in 1936 at twenty-one. The decline was very gradual, and only in the 1950s did abortion deaths become unusual.

Table 2 also shows the number of maternal deaths during these four decades. Abortion deaths in almost every year contributed to the level of maternal mortality, but the proportion which they contributed varied substantially over time. In the 1920s maternal mortality in British Columbia peaked and then began to decline. In 1924 sixty-nine maternal deaths were reported. By the mid-1930s the figure had dropped to about fifty deaths a year. From 1934 onward the maternal mortality rate began to drop dramatically and consistently. (See table 3.)

Ironically, just as maternal mortality rates were in the 1930s reaching ever lower levels, abortion deaths appear to have been reaching unprecedented heights. As table 4 indicates, from the 1930s to the 1950s abortion deaths continued to claim a large proportion of the maternal deaths. In 1927, according to Vital Statistics, abortions accounted for only about 6 per cent of all maternal deaths; in 1936 they were responsible for a staggering 42 per cent of all maternal deaths. Even through the 1950s, abortion remained a major contributor to the overall maternal death rate. Why was the rate of abortion deaths, especially during the 1930s and early 1940s, so high? The first reason was that women seeking abortion shared some of the same risks as those bearing children: complications of pregnancy, childbirth, and puerperium or sepsis. But since abortion deaths were rising substantially just as the rate of maternal mortality was declining, other factors besides the risks of childbearing had to be at work. The rate of maternal mortality was pulled down by the increased percentage of term deliveries in hospitals, the employment of antibiotics to control infection, the better use of blood and blood substitutes to control haemorrhaging, the identification of high risk patients, the judicious use of Caesarian section and more use of pre-natal and postpartum care.[14] It is obvious that while hospital practices relating to childbirth improved significantly during the 1930s and 1940s, they improved much less rapidly among women who sought the aid of abortionists or attempted to induce their own abortion. Because women were forced to work within an illegal system, they were at a much greater

TABLE 4

British Columbia Maternal Deaths:
Complications of Pregnancy Including Abortion

Year	Total Maternal Deaths	Abortion Deaths	Abortion Deaths as a % of Total Deaths
1922	63	13	20.6
1923	63	4	6.3
1924	69	6	8.6
1925	60	2	3.2
1926	65	0	0.0
1927	68	4	6.1
1928	61	0	0.0
1929	58	1	1.8
1930	63	2	2.9
1931	66	12	18.1
1932	54	10	18.5
1933	45	8	17.7
1934	50	14	28.0
1935	52	17	32.7
1936	50	21	42.0
1937	51	14	27.4
1938	48	19	39.5
1939	38	16	42.1
1940	43	8	18.5
1941	40	6	15.0
1942	45	11	24.4
1943	47	11	23.4
1944	50	9	18.0
1945	50	10	20.0
1946	38	1	2.6
1947	32	3	9.3
1948	29	6	20.6
1949	28	4	14.2
1950	27	8	29.6
1951	20	7	35.0

1952	18	6	33.3
1953	18	3	16.6
1954	13	3	23.0
1955	16	0	0.0
1956	13	3	23.0
1957	15	6	40.0
1958	15	3	20.0
1959	17	2	11.7
1960	19	5	26.3
1961	10	7	70.0
1962	17	2	11.7
1963	11	3	27.2
1964	2	0	0.0
1965	9	2	22.2
1966	11	2	18.1
1967	4	1	25.0
1968	11	5	45.4

Source: B. C. Vital Statistics

risk of exposure to unsanitary conditions and methods that were dangerous and undependable. The rate of abortion deaths was high and in fact rising through the 1930s relative to other causes of maternal mortality largely because of the illegal nature of the operation, not because of the backwardness of medicine.

But abortion deaths were, according to the vital statistics, not simply increasing relative to the rate of maternal deaths. In the 1930s and 1940s they increased in absolute numbers. Such a rise in abortion deaths suggests that despite the illegality of the procedure more and more women were seeking to terminate their pregnancies. This was the second reason for the high rate of abortion deaths. Certainly many commentators believed that they were witnessing an abortion epidemic. It should be stressed, however, that the rate of abortion deaths as reported by Vital Statistics is not to be taken as an indicator of the actual number of women who sought abortions. It has been estimated that in industrial countries in the first half of the twentieth century the rate of pregnancies ending in both spontaneous and induced abortions probably rose from 10 to 15 per cent. Despite the obvious risks posed by abortion, its mortality rate was low: it has been deduced that only 1/10 of 1 per cent of all abortions resulted in death.[15] It was because so many women were seeking to terminate their pregnancies in the 1930s and the 1940s that the absolute number of abortion deaths was so frighteningly high.

Attorney-General Records

Doctors knew that there were more abortion deaths in British Columbia than those reported by Vital Statistics; Vital Statistics in turn classified far more abortion deaths than those dealt with by the provincial Attorney-General. Since abortion was a crime, it would be natural to assume that legal records would provide a good indicator of the incidence of such practices. In fact, when one turns to the papers of the Attorney-General's office, one immediately discovers how difficult it is to trace systematically the pattern of abortion prosecutions. Some cases of abortion reported in the press could not be located in the court records. Some files had been removed. Some abortion death cases were treated as murder or manslaughter.[16]

Three series of reports emanating from the provincial Attorney-General's office were searched: A.-G. (B.C.) Correspondence-Inquiries which related to preliminary investigations into suspected abortion deaths which sometimes were followed by an inquisition; A.-G. (B.C.) Inquisitions which provide records of the formal inquisitions; and A.-G. (B.C.) Court Records which documented the cases that proceeded to court. Because of the lacunae noted above only the papers for the 1920s and 1930s provided a fairly satisfactory but certainly not complete account, as indicated by the fact that in 1936, when Vital Statistics listed twenty-one deaths as attributable to abortion, the provincial legal authorities' papers reported only five cases. Of our three sources the Attorney-General's files clearly provide the most inadequate account of the rate of abortion deaths. Nevertheless, this source is of immense interest because it provides detailed accounts of individual cases stretching right back into the nineteenth century. It offers insights into the relative shifts in the number of abortions of concern to the judiciary and reveals how the police and courts functioned. The greatest value of this source is that it contains a rich mine of information concerning the interplay of doctors, lawyers, abortionists and women. An exploitation of such material allows one to flesh out the dry, quantitative accounts presented by Vital Statistics and have some sense of the personal dramas posed by abortion.

The fact that a low level of abortion deaths was reported by the Attorney-General's office should occasion no surprise. The Attorney-General would presumably have dealt only with cases where there was a possibility of criminal prosecution. A certain proportion of attempted abortions would have been self-induced, and these amateur attempts might have been more likely to bring about sepsis, but there would be no point in laying a charge in such cases. Other women might have been admitted to hospital in such a state that they were not able to explain who performed the abortion. It is thus easy to imagine that although a woman was listed on her death certificate as having died as a result of an abortion, legal proceedings might, for a variety of reasons, not be pursued. As a result one would expect the number of abortion deaths cited in the Attorney-General's papers to be lower than those reported by Vital Statistics. Table 5 indicates that this was generally the case. Between 1931 and 1940, for example, Vital Statistics reported 139 abortion deaths for an annual average of 13.9, while the Attorney-General's office reported 34 for an annual average of 3.4. Vital Statistics was therefore reporting four to five times more abortion deaths than were dealt with by the legal authorities. For some reason, however, the situation was reversed between 1926 and 1930. As noted earlier, Vital Statistics reported a suspiciously low number of abortion deaths in those years. A comparison of these figures with those of the Attorney-General's office reveals that, in fact, Vital Statistics reported only seven deaths caused by abortion in those five years whereas the Attorney-General's office dealt with eighteen. Such a discrepancy might have been caused by Vital Statistics listing as abortions those deaths directly caused by abortion but not those that occurred as a result of abortion complications such as puerperal septicaemia. It would appear, however, that some reform in the classification system took place in the early 1930s. This would explain why according to Vital Statistics abortion deaths as a percentage of maternal deaths suddenly leapt from 2.9 per cent in 1930 to 18.1 per cent in 1931. The reported surge must have been at least in part a product of new methods of reportage and recording.

Other evidence from the Attorney-General's papers can also be drawn on to support the assertion that abortion must have been more prevalent in the 1920s than the Vital Statistics figures suggest. Indeed, the legal accounts list almost as many deaths from abortion in the 1920s (thirty-three) as in the 1930s (thirty-six). It is difficult to determine which decade had the highest level of abortion deaths. It would be reasonable to suppose that in the 1920s less sophisticated medical techniques might have resulted in more deaths. A stronger argument can be made, however, that the social and economic dislocations caused by the Depression led more women to terminate their pregnancies and accordingly produced a higher level of mortality in the 1930s.

The discrepancies between the two sources could, of course, be the result of shifts in record keeping and changes in the efforts of the Attorney-General's office to track down cases of abortion. These questions raised by the data cannot be easily answered. The Attorney-General's papers do impress upon us, however, the fact that abortion deaths did not suddenly crop up in the 1930s; they were a tragically familiar phenomenon in British Columbia from at least the time of the First World War.

If Vital Statistics gave an inaccurate account of the number of abortion deaths reported in the 1920s, their figures from that decade on at least appear to be fairly reliable. In any event, for the later decades it is necessary to rely primarily upon them, because the Attorney-General's files for the 1940s and subsequent decades are closed. The Attorney-General's records that are accessible indicate that the vast majority of abortion cases that were brought to the attention of the Attorney-General were pursued because they involved the death of a woman. (See table 6.) These records make it abundantly clear that, though abortion and attempted abortion were criminal acts, the higher levels of the judiciary only pursued prosecutions when death or serious complications ensued. Between 1930 and 1939 as many as thirty-six out of thirty-nine abortion cases drawn to the attention of the Attorney-General involved deaths. The court records of the period from 1896 to 1937 help give us some idea of what women were up against in their desire to control their reproduction. Because abortions were against the law, women were forced to resort to whatever methods they could devise and to seek the often inadequate help of those willing to take the risk of aiding or performing an illegal act. If complications arose as a result of the attempt to abort, the woman had to face the opprobrium of the medical and legal systems and of much of the community in which she lived, as well as the real risk of death. The court records show the extent to which women were determined to control their births even when forced to work within a hostile legal environment.

In the second section of this chapter we will further employ the papers of the Attorney-General's office to illustrate the ways in which abortion deaths might either be reported or covered up. In concluding the first part of this chapter it is only necessary to reiterate that each of the three sources we have exploited in seeking to determine the rate of abortion deaths has its advantages and disadvantages. The medical survey, though presumably the most accurate source, covers a limited time span. Vital Statistics deals with a longer period but does appear to under-report--especially for the 1920s--the incidence of abortion deaths. The papers of the Attorney-General's office are quantitatively the least adequate of our sources, but they do provide invaluable qualitative material. Each source reveals the fact that the categorization, classification and recording of social events are complex processes subject to a variety of constraints.

By drawing on the strengths of each source it is possible to conclude that, though the actual number of abortion deaths for any one year cannot be precisely determined, there can be no doubt that they contributed significantly from the 1920s to the 1950s in keeping maternal mortality rates high. If we add the number of abortion deaths cited by the Attorney-General's office for the 1920s to those reported by Vital Statistics for the 1930s and 1940s, we arrive at a total of 241 deaths in three decades. We have noted, however, that in the 1950s only two out of every three abortion deaths were correctly reported by Vital Statistics and only one out of every ten may have come to the notice of the Attorney-General. If we assume that a similar under-reporting occurred between the

TABLE 5

B. C. Abortion Deaths 1922-1959

---   Reported by Vital Statistics
___   Cited in Attorney-General's Papers

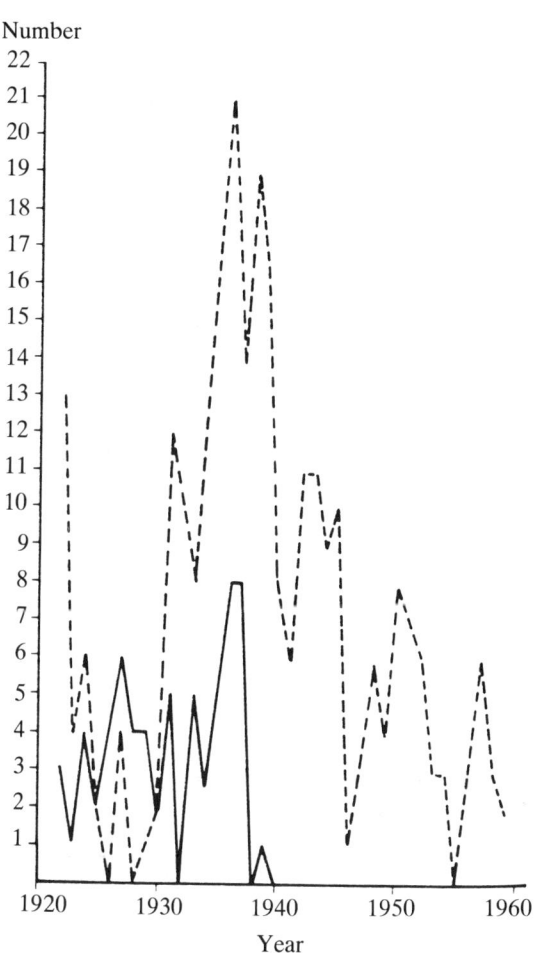

Number

Year

TABLE 6

Abortion Cases in the Attorney-General's Files

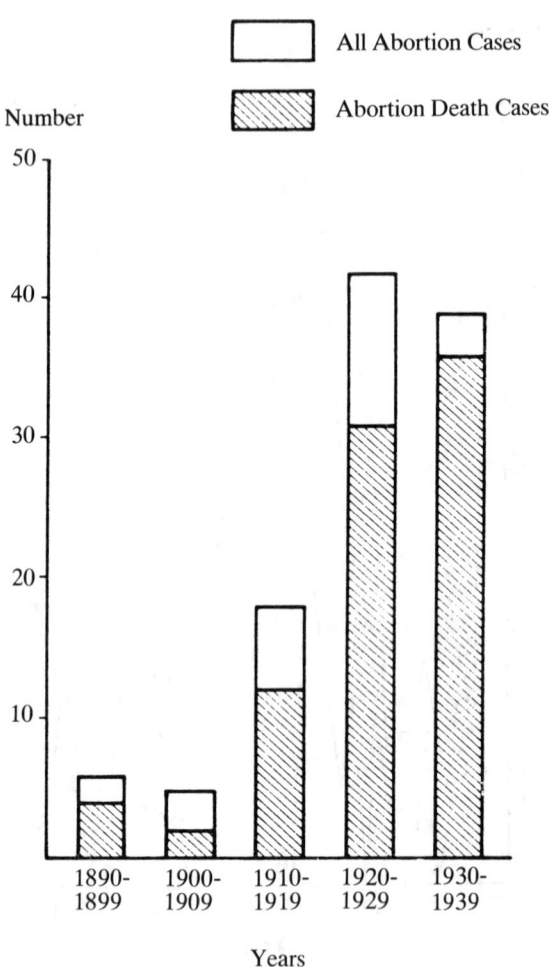

Years

1920s and the 1940s and multiply the Attorney-General's only by six and those of Vital Statistics by one and one-third we arrive at a corrected abortion death total of 476, which would account for approximately 30 per cent of all maternal deaths. This would appear to be about right since Dr. W. D. S. Thomas found that in the 1950s abortion deaths were responsible for 27.5 per cent of all maternal deaths.[17]

Discrepancies in Reportage

Enormous difficulties are met with when one attempts to determine the rate of illegal acts such as abortion. The overwhelming majority of successful abortions would never come to public attention for the simple reason that no one involved would have any interest in revealing such information. We usually only have evidence of the unsuccessful, most often the rare cases, in which death resulted. In testifying at a 1921 abortion trial Dr. Archibald Dunbar was asked by the prosecuting attorney, W. M. McKay, about the incidence of abortion:

208   Q. In fact the numbers are very large, aren't they Doctor?
       A. Quite large.
209   Q. In every large city?
       A. Yes.
210   Q. It amounts, I am told, to some hundreds per month even in this city of Vancouver. Would you go so far as to say that?
       A. I could not say the exact number. . .because I have no way of telling.
211   Q. And the number of deaths that result from them is insignificant in number?
       A. Yes, the deaths are not very prevalent.[18]

When deaths did result, this still did not guarantee that they would be classified and reported as abortion deaths. Relatives would frequently seek to conceal the cause of death because abortion--like suicide--was considered by many to be evidence of the immorality of the victim. Doctors might be sympathetic to such concerns and could also have their own reasons for failing to report abortion deaths. From the quantitative point of view the main issue was whether or not a doctor who knew of an abortion death passed this information on to the appropriate authorities. If he did, it would be reported in the Vital Statistics and possibly be followed by legal enquiries. If he did not, the information would be lost.

A good deal of evidence can be drawn from the papers of the Attorney-General's office to demonstrate how doctors and lawyers could clash over the question of the reporting of abortions. The inquest held to investigate the death in July 1919 of Mrs. S _____ R _____ provides a good example. In the inquest held by the

141

Vancouver coroner, Dr. Thomas W. Jeffs, evidence was first given by William Bailie, the accountant of the Vancouver General Hospital. He testified that, to protect the hospital officials from possibly being incriminated in an abortion, they had received from Mrs. R _____ the following deathbed declaration:

> My trouble started with going to a doctor in Vancouver, Dr. T _____ V _____, Lonsdale Ave., North Vancouver. . . .I was told of him by Mrs. P_____, Denman Street, West End, Vancouver. I saw him last Friday week. I told him I was six weeks overdue in menstruation. I asked him if he could do any thing for me and if there was any risk. He asked me who my husband was, and said he charged $100 and there was no great risk as he did eight and ten a day. I went home and my husband implored me not to go. I went the next day with $75 and told him that was all I could afford. He told me he would not do it. I cried to him and eventually he did. I was ill on the Saturday night and the Sunday and the Monday I phoned him. He said he did not remember me. When I asked him what to do for the pain in the abdomen, he said "Better get used to it," said "Take a hot soap-sud douche" which I did. Continued sick as ever. I went to see him on Wednesday. He felt my pulse and said I would get along alright. On Thursday at 4 o'clock in the morning my husband phoned him and demanded him out at once. My husband met the six o'clock boat. He came and curetted me and douched me without anaesthetic.[19]

Near death Mrs. R _____ was taken to Vancouver General Hospital where she was attended by Dr. George Ernest Gillis. Gillis admitted that in order to protect himself and the hospital, Mrs. R _____ was stimulated with drugs so that she would be in a fit state to make an ante mortem statement. The case was not reported to the coroner. Charles Reid, the justice of the peace who took the ante mortem statement, asserted in court that the hospital officials were negligent in not notifying the authorities of the abortion death until Mrs. R_____ was buried. As a result the body had to be exhumed to permit an inquest to be carried out.

Dr. V _____, who R _____ claimed had performed the abortion, was in fact the North Vancouver coroner. He did not appear at the inquest, but was defended by his colleague, Dr. Ernest Phillip Fewster. Dr. Fewster handled all of Dr. V _____'s cases in Vancouver when V_____ was not available and had seen Mrs. R._____ before she entered hospital. According to Dr. Fewster the deceased had told him:

> I have been doing a number of things to myself and taking a lot of drugs for a long time. I was flooding badly and I

went over to Dr. V_____ of North Vancouver. He examined me and took a piece of tissue from me which was hanging out of my womb. He said he thought I would be alright but I was to go home and if I did not feel better he would come over to Vancouver and curette me.[20]

In other words, Dr. Fewster suggested that Dr. V_____ had only tried to give some comfort to a woman who had already induced her own abortion. Mr. R_____ retorted that Dr. Fewster's statement was an absolute lie; that the doctor had been informed of the nature of the operation Dr. V_____ had carried out on his wife.

The inquest verdict was straightforward: "Mrs. S _____ R _____ came to her death at the General Hospital, Vancouver, B. C., July 9, 1919, from septic poisoning resulting from an operation for abortion." What was not cleared up was the question of who performed the abortion. The very fact that an abortion death had even occurred had required a good deal of effort to establish. The coroner was obviously outraged by what appeared to him to be the efforts of doctors and the hospital management to protect themselves. In charging the jury he stated:

It is a very serious matter, you know, this abortion business--criminal abortion--anybody that advises it or tries to cover it up in any way is guilty, and medical men may run themselves into trouble, because if they grant a certificate in a case that should be reported to the coroner it is an offense and a criminal offense.[21]

He referred in particular to the unsatisfactory testimony of Dr. Fewster, which he noted was contradicted in toto by that of Mrs. R_____'s husband and sister-in-law. It was, Dr. Jeffs concluded, the dirtiest type of tactic to try to cast all the blame for an abortion onto the deceased woman.

For the purpose of this chapter, the R_____ case is of importance inasmuch as it shows how both hospitals and doctors might try to circumvent the regulations pertaining to the reportage of abortions. In the R_____ case there was the very strong impression given that it was the doctors' desire to protect themselves from possible criminal prosecution that primarily preoccupied them. In other cases it was the concern of the doctor to protect the reputation of the victim that led to a coverup of abortive practices. After the death of a woman in St. Paul's hospital in 1921 the coroner asked one doctor:

Q. Dr. Fuller, is it not really customary to report these cases when they get better?
A. I don't know. As a matter of fact I guess not. Many are reported but I thank the Lord I have so few of them I don't know from my experience. I think if a doctor could

find any information that would do any good, most of them would be willing and glad to give information, but what is the good of going to a whole lot of expense when you cannot do anything.[22]

A similar situation was found when doctors did not seek to obtain an ante mortem but simply let a woman die in relative peace. In 1922 Dr. Alexander Stewart Munro and the Vancouver General Hospital Medical Superintendent were criticized by the coroner for failing to notify the police of the condition of a woman dying as a result of an abortion. The coroner informed the jury:

Hospital authorities were negligent in not reporting the criminal abortion to police immediately instead of several hours after the woman's death. Certainly hospital authorities were not giving any help in the detection of crime. This made an ante-mortem statement impossible.[23]

The coroner played a key role in mediating the relationship between the medical profession and the courts. In turn, the personality and efficiency of the coroner clearly had a good deal of influence on the process of reporting abortions. If the official was especially zealous--as seemed to be the case with Dr. Thomas Jeffs--noncomplying doctors would find themselves subjected to hostile questioning in front of inquest juries. After receiving Dr. Jeff's direction a 1916 jury brought down the verdict: "We recommended that the law be inforced or improved to force medical men to give information whenever a case of this nature [abortion] comes to their notice."[24] Jeffs, who was Vancouver coroner from 1910 to the early 1920s, never missed an opportunity to berate medical authorities for their failure to track down cases of abortion. It is not clear why he was so preoccupied by the subject, but there can be little doubt that, if a less conscientious official had been in charge, the reportage of abortions would have been lowered. It is, of course, difficult to provide evidence of non-reportage, but a 1923 case is instructive. When a twenty-one-year-old woman died in St. Paul's Hospital of toxemia caused by a suspected abortion, the new coroner, W. D. Brydone-Jack, decided that an inquest would not be held. He informed the Attorney-General's office:

As she [the woman] refused to give any information, I felt that it was unnecessary to institute any further inquiry, especially as there seemed no possibility under the circumstances of incriminating any person.[25]

The case would not have come to light had not a Vancouver lawyer written the Attorney-General to protest that the woman according to the newspapers died suddenly of pneumonia. As a matter of fact, you will observe that she died of septicaemia consequent on an attempted abortion. It strikes me that the coroner's excuse for no inquest. . .is altogether absurd.[26]

It seems that the coroner's desire for discretion was in this case shared by the Attorney-General's office. The deputy attorney-general informed the Attorney-General:

It appears to me that the Provincial Police should be directed to inquire into this matter with a view to discovering who performed the abortion or administered the drug which caused the abortion. Possibly the girl herself procured the drug. In any case inquiry should be made with such secrecy that in case it leads to nothing the public will be none the wiser and the reputation of the dead girl will be spared publicity.[27]

Apparently nothing was found, because no other references to the case were made. Had Jeffs still been Vancouver coroner, one suspects that a far more vigorous investigation would have been undertaken and as a result the statistics on abortion deaths necessarily altered.[28]

Conclusion

This chapter set out to determine the impact of abortion deaths on maternal mortality rates in British Columbia and to explain why there were discrepancies in the reportage of abortion deaths. In part one we established that abortion deaths did significantly contribute to maternal mortality, in some years accounting for a large percentage of all maternal deaths. Two conclusions can be drawn from this finding. The first is that abortion was a method of fertility control far more widely employed in past decades than is often realized. The ratio of reported abortion deaths to the total number of abortions presumably varied from year to year and is impossible to determine. But whether the ratio was 1:100 or 1:1000 it still means that enormous numbers of women were seeking by risky and illegal methods to terminate their pregnancies. The second conclusion which emerges from this reappraisal of the causes of maternal death is that any discussion of the general health of women in the first half of the twentieth century must take into account the extent to which abortion deaths inflated the maternal mortality rate. The number of maternal deaths began to fall in the 1930s. The number of annual abortion-related deaths was only lowered a decade later--presumably as a result of the belated employment by abortionists of more sophisticated methods--but the percentage of all maternal deaths attributed to abortion was consistently high. Changes in the law relating to abortion in addition to medical improvements were necessary to abolish the frightening spectre of maternal death.[29]

In the second part of this chapter we examined some of the reasons why there were discrepancies in the reporting of abortion and abortion deaths. We encountered problems similar to those met with by researchers investigating cases of rape and suicide.[30] Statistics on such subjects are inevitably suspect because of the problems of definition of the act, of variations over time in the use of such definitions, and the inconsistent application by reporting agencies of the definitions. Because of the nature of abortion deaths many cases were not discovered, or not reported, or not recorded. In some cases the victim herself or the victim's family might have applied pressure to have the facts classified as other than an abortion death. Doctors, because they were, or were afraid of being, implicated in abortion deaths might fail to report cases. The courts, in their turn, were inconsistent in their investigation and prosecution of abortion. Abortion death statistics therefore have to be seen not as neutral numbers but as social products.[31] This leads to our final conclusion. The under-reporting of abortion deaths, in our view, raises both methodological and political issues. Although the various agencies we investigated did not, in under-reporting abortion, set out deliberately to deceive or mystify, that was their final effect. The statistics that resulted therefore had an ideological colouring; the importance of the need for safe, legal abortions could not be fully appreciated while the numbers of women who died as a result of illegal abortions were concealed.[32]

Notes

[1]M. C. Urquhart and K. A. H. Buckley, *Historical Statistics of Canada* (Cambridge: Cambridge University Press, 1965), p. 40; Sam Shapiro and Edward C. Schlesinger, *Infant, Perinatal, Maternal and Childhood Mortality in the United States* (Cambridge, Mass.: Harvard University Press, 1968), pp. 143-9; Suzann Buckley, "Ladies or Midwives: Efforts to Reduce Infant and Maternal Mortality," in Linda Kealey, ed., *A Not Unreasonable Claim: Women and Reform in Canada, 1880s-1920s* (Toronto: Women's Press, 1979), pp. 131-50.

[2]Edward Shorter, *History of Women's Bodies* (New York: Basic Books, 1982), p. 98.

[3]Canadian demographers and sociologists, while paying a good deal of attention to the decline in infant mortality, have virtually ignored shifts in maternal mortality. See, for example, Roderick Beaujot and Kevin McQuillan, *Growth and Dualism: The Demographic Development of Canadian Society* (Toronto: Gage, 1982); Carl F. Grindstaff, *Population and Society: A Sociological Perspective* (West Hanover, Mass.: Christopher Publishing, 1981); Warren E. Kalbach and Wayne McVey, *The Demographic Basis of*

Canadian Society (Toronto: McGraw-Hill Ryerson, 1977); Johannes Overbeek, *Population and Canadian Society* (Toronto: Butterworths, 1980). One French-Canadian study actually appears to lament the fact that whereas before the Second World War the chances of survival of men between the ages of 15 and 35 were better than that of women, such is no longer the case. For this curious insistence on describing a decline in female mortality as really a case of "la surmortalité masculine" see Desmond Dufour and Yves Péron, *Vingts ans de mortalité du Québec: les causes de décès, 1951-1971* (Montréal: Les Presses de l'Université de Montréal, 1979), pp. 58-9.

[4]J. T. Phair and A. H. Sellers, "A Study of Maternal Deaths in the Province of Ontario," *Canadian Public Health Journal* 25 (1934), 563-79; see also F. W. Jackson and R. D. Jeffries, "A Five Year Study of Maternal Mortality in Manitoba, 1928-1932," *Canadian Public Health Journal* 25 (1934), 97. On parity see Linda G. Berry, "Age and Parity Influence on Maternal Mortality: United States, 1919-1969," *Demography* 14 (1977), 297-310 and Steve Selvin and Joseph Garfinkel, "Paternal Age, Maternal Age and Birth Order and the Risk of Foetal Loss," *Human Biology* 48 (1976), 223-30.

[5]On the relation of abortion deaths to maternal deaths in Britain in the 1930s see Jane Lewis, *The Politics of Motherhood* (London: Croom Helm, 1980), pp. 36-8, 209-11. In the United States the Children's Bureau reported in the 1930s that a survey of 7,500 maternal deaths revealed a fourth were abortion related; the New York Academy of Medicine set the figure at 17.5 per cent. See Helena Huntington Smith, "Wasting Women's Lives: The Frightful Toll of Abortion," *New Republic* (28 March 1934), 178.

[6]See Russell Jacoby, *Social Amnesia: A Critique of Conformist Psychology from Adler to Laing* (Boston: Beacon Press, 1975).

[7]Canada, Statistics Canada: Health Division, *Therapeutic Abortion, 1981* (Ottawa: Minister of Supply and Services, 1983), p. 126; Robin F. Badgley, *Report of the Committee on the Operation of the Abortion Laws* (Ottawa: Minister of Supply and Services, 1977), pp. 29, 66.

[8]No references are made to maternal deaths in works opposed to abortion such as Alphonse de Valk, *Morality and Law in Canadian Politics: The Abortion Controversy* (Dorval: Palm, 1974) and E. J. Kremer and E. A. Synan, eds., *Death Before Birth: Canada and the Abortion Question* (Toronto: Griffin House, 1974). Even pro-abortionists give only vague impressions of the risks that were associated with illegal abortion. See, for example, Eleanor Wright Pelrine, *Abortion in Canada* (Toronto: New Press, 1971), p. 56 and Wendell W. Watters, *Compulsory Parenthood: The Truth About Abortion* (Toronto: McClelland and Stewart, 1976), pp. 169-71.

[9]W. D. S. Thomas, "Abortion Deaths in British Columbia, 1955-1968," *B. C. Medical Journal* 12 (May 1970), 111-12. In a

later study of 132 maternal deaths Thomas found that 60 were due to direct obstetric causes and 27 per cent of these were abortion related. See J. L. Benedet, W. D. S. Thomas and B. Ho Yuen, "An Analysis of Maternal Deaths in British Columbia, 1963 to 1970," *Canadian Medical Association Journal* 110 (1974), 783-7.

[10]Smith, "Wasting Women's Lives," p. 179.

[11]H. R. M. Johnson, "The Incidence of Unnatural Deaths Which Have Been Presumed to be Natural in Coroners' Autopsies," *Medicine, Science, and Law* 9 (1969), 102 cited in Malcolm Potts, Peter Diggory and John Peel, *Abortion* (Cambridge: Cambridge University Press, 1977), pp. 24-5.

[12]British Columbia, Provincial Board of Health, *Report of Vital Statistics, 1922-1946*; Department of Health Services, *Vital Statistics of the Province of B.C., 1947-1968*.

[13]On the problems posed to the collectors of statistics see J. T. Marshall, *Vital Statistics in British Columbia* (Victoria: B. C. Provincial Board of Health, 1932).

[14]See Shorter, *A History of Women's Bodies*, pp. 139-76; Jo Oppenheimer, "Childbirth in Ontario: The Transition from Home to Hospital in the Early Twentieth Century," in this volume, pp. 51-74; Anne S. Lee, "Maternal Mortality in the United States," *Phylon* 38 (1977), 259-66. It is important to note that recent studies indicate that antibiotics were not in widespread use in Canada until the 1940s, antenatal care was limited, and home births were safer than hospital births. See C. Lesley Biggs, "The Response to Maternal Mortality in Ontario, 1920-1940," unpublished M.Sc. thesis, University of Toronto, 1983; Biggs, "The Toronto Maternal Welfare Program, 1933-1947," paper delivered to the Canadian Society for the History of Medicine, 1983; Suzann Buckley, "From Prescriptions to Misconceptions: How to Reduce Maternal Mortality in Canada," unpublished paper.

[15]Potts, *Abortion*, pp. 270-1; Shorter, *A History of Women's Bodies*, p. 195.

[16]On the actual number of abortion cases prosecuted in British Columbia (which would, of course, be larger than the number relating to abortion deaths) see Canada, Statistics Canada, *Statistics of Criminal and Other Offences* (Ottawa: Statistics Canada, 1973), Ref. HA 743 85 201. On the national figures see Badgley, *Report*, p. 68.

[17]It should be noted that there were marked contrasts in the causes of maternal death for the Indian and non-Indian population in British Columbia. Indians, who accounted for only 2 per cent of the population between 1955 and 1965, were responsible for 5.7 per cent of all births and 16.1 per cent of maternal mortality. But whereas abortion accounted for 27.5 per cent of non-Indian maternal deaths, it accounted for only 11.5 per cent of Indian maternal deaths. Postpartum haemorrhaging was the great killer of native Indian women, whose maternal death rate was three times that of non-Indians. See W. D. S. Thomas, "Maternal Mortality in

Native British Columbia Indians: A High Risk Group," in Carl F. Grindstaff, Craig L. Boydell and Paul C. Whitehead, eds., *Population Issues in Canada* (Toronto: Holt, Rinehart and Winston, 1971), pp. 54-9.

[18] Attorney-General (B.C.), Court Records, Vol. 239 (1921), 31.

[19] The information that follows on the R_____ case is drawn from Attorney-General (B.C.), Inquisitions, Vol. 33 (1919), 138; *Vancouver Daily Province*, 10 July 1919, p. 16; *Vancouver Sun*, 11 July 1919, p. 10; 18 July 1919, p. 3; 19 July 1919, p. 11.

[20] *Ibid.*

[21] *Ibid.*

[22] Attorney-General (B.C.), Inquisitions, Reel 38 (1921), 249.

[23] Attorney-General (B.C.), Inquisitions, Reel 40 (1922), 208. See also *Vancouver Sun*, 5 August 1922, p. 28.

[24] Attorney-General (B.C.), Inquisitions, Reel 28 (1916), 261. For similar concerns expressed by the Victoria coroner at doctors' ignorance of the law see Attorney-General (B.C.), Inquisitions, Reel 36 (1920), 330.

[25] Attorney-General (B.C.), Correspondence, Reel 107 (1924), C 49-6.

[26] *Ibid.*

[27] *Ibid.*

[28] On the way in which coroners can construct images of sudden death, see J. Maxwell Atkinson, "Societal Reactions to Suicide: The Role of Coroners' Definitions," in Stanley Cohen, ed., *Images of Deviance* (London: Penguin, 1971), pp. 165-91.

[29] On the elimination of maternal mortality after the law reforms of the 1960s see Potts, *Abortion*, pp. 142-3; Watters, *Compulsory Parenthood*, pp. 169-71; Betty Sarvis and Hyman Rodman, *The Abortion Controversy* (New York: Columbia University Press, 1973), pp. 154-64.

[30] See, for example, Charles W. Dean, *The Crime and Consequences of Rape* (Springfield, Illinois: Thomas, 1982); Lorenne Clark and Debra J. Lewis, *Rape: The Price of Coercive Sexuality* (Toronto: Women's Press, 1977); Jack Douglas, *The Social Meaning of Suicide* (Princeton: Princeton University Press, 1967).

[31] B. Hindess, *The Use of Official Statistics in Sociology* (London: Macmillan, 1973); John Irvine, Ian Miles and Jeff Evans, eds., *Demystifying Social Statistics* (London: Pluto Press, 1979).

[32] In 1947 Mrs. Strum pointed out to the House of Commons that, although every Canadian knew that 41,000 servicemen were killed in the Second World War, few were aware that since 1926 21,000 women had died in childbirth. But Mrs. Strum was herself either unaware of or reluctant to mention the extent to which abortion deaths sustained the high level of maternal mortality. There was similarly no reference to abortion in the many newspaper accounts of the problems posed by childbearing. See Canada, House of Commons, *Debates*, 1947, V, 4054; *Daily Colonist* (Victoria) 23 January 1935, p. 8; *Daily Times* (Victoria) 30 September 1937, p. 4; *Daily Times* (Victoria) 27 February 1947, p. 7.

Chapter Eight

WOMEN'S INVOLVEMENT IN THE CANADIAN BIRTH
CONTROL MOVEMENT OF THE 1930s: THE HAMILTON
BIRTH CONTROL CLINIC[*]

Dianne Dodd

In the Depression years of the 1930s, the movement to legalize the
distribution of birth control information and the sale of birth
control devices to Canadians gained respectability as middle-class
reformers of various stripes took up the cause. As recent research
into the Canadian birth control movement by Angus McLaren and
Arlene Tigar McLaren has shown, there was an active movement in
British Columbia beginning in 1923 with the formation of the
Canadian Birth Control League.[1] As the McLarens point out, the
birth control movement in Canada, as elsewhere, was initiated by
the left, with socialist feminists in the forefront, and it was only the
desperate Depression conditions which forced some middle-class
'maternal' feminists tentatively to promote birth control.[2] The
middle-class movement was dominated by eugenicists, primarily
interested in using birth control as a tool of social control rather
than as a means to personal freedom or women's emancipation.
The distinction which the McLarens make between conservative
middle-class 'maternal' feminists and socialist feminists, based on
the latter's more radical critique of women's reproductive role and
their class analysis,[3] should not, however, be allowed to obscure real
gender differences both within the left and within the more
conservative middle-class groups. Just as socialist women were
more likely to emphasize women's emancipation in their advocacy of
birth control, while socialist men stressed birth control's

[*]Reprinted by permission of the Ontario Historical Society from *Ontario History*
75, 1 (March 1983), 71-86. For their comments and suggestions on this revision of
an earlier paper entitled the "Hamilton Birth Control Clinic of the 1930s", the
author would like to thank Dr. Ruth Pierson of OISE, and Dr. Marilyn Barber of
Carleton University. For their patience in allowing me to use the then
uncatalogued papers of the Hamilton clinic, my thanks to the staff of the Hamilton
Planned Parenthood Association; and finally my gratitude to Mrs. Thelma Will for
sharing her experiences with me.

contribution to a healthy labour movement,[4] so middle-class women differed from their male counterparts in placing greater emphasis on women's emancipation and showed less concern with eugenics. This chapter is an examination of birth control organizations of the 1930s, centred in Ontario, which were dominated by middle-class reformers.[5] Although all of these reformers shared certain 'middle-class' values, there were significant differences, both in motivations and methods, between the male activists who dominated the movement and women's organizations active in birth control work.

Whether using birth control clinics, door-to-door methods or a combination of the two, birth controllers focussed their message on the poor. All sought to make birth control respectable, that is, both legally and socially acceptable, in order to grant the poor access to a privilege long enjoyed by wealthier citizens. Birth controllers also focussed on the family as the basic unit of society. Male birth controllers who dominated the Canadian birth control movement, however, were primarily concerned with controlling the fertility of marginal groups who were perceived as a political or social threat. Birth control was a tool of eugenics which promised to reduce infant and maternal mortality, improve the health of Canadian mothers and thereby improve the racial stock. Sterilization of the unfit was another reproductive technology in the eugenicists' arsenal, used to deny reproductive rights to those deemed unsuitable as parents. Women's organizations did not stress eugenics. They showed a humanitarian concern with the quality of women's mothering experience. Better infant and maternal health was an end in itself rather than merely a means to race betterment. And, by asserting women's right to birth control, women reformers pointed out the potential threat to patriarchal authority in the home which this reproductive technology promised. Though they did not articulate a critique of the patriarchal family, they did seek to improve women's position within it.

Women's input into the birth control movement was, in most cases, subordinate to male interests. As nurses and social workers, women did the day-to-day work of distributing birth control information to Canadian women. Sometimes they worked under the direction of male-dominated organizations, and sometimes they formed their own groups, although these were usually on a local, small scale. There were several of these women's organizations in Canada,[6] including birth control clinics and/or services in Winnipeg, Windsor and Hamilton. The Hamilton Birth Control Society opened a clinic in 1932. This women's organization, while a part of the larger male-dominated birth control movement, was relatively autonomous and allows the historian a glimpse at middle-class women's motivations for birth control work.

The central figure in the Canadian birth control movement was A. R. Kaufman, a Kitchener industrialist. Kaufman established the Parents' Information Bureau[7] in Kitchener, following his 'discovery' of high fertility among the poor, unskilled workers that he had been forced to lay off in 1929. The Bureau, which expanded rapidly in the 1930s, had as its goal the distribution of low cost contraceptives to the poor and socially dependent through visiting nurses working in a number of Canadian cities. Kaufman also lobbied governments to legislate in favour of birth control and sterilization, founded two birth control clinics, arranged a number of sterilization operations, and provoked a trial in 1936-7 which helped clarify the legal position of birth control work.[8]

Along with a growing number of middle-class Canadians at this time, Kaufman saw in the unrestrained fertility of certain marginal groups a threat to social and economic stability. The distribution of birth control to the poor and sterilization of the 'unfit' (loosely defined as the 'feeble-minded', insane and diseased) were promoted as a solution to poverty, social unrest and general racial decline.[9] The Eugenics Society of Canada, to which Kaufman belonged, emerged in the 1930s as the political voice of those who hoped to cure all manner of social problems through restricting the reproduction of the 'feeble-minded' and genetically inferior.[10]

Since 1892 the advertising, sale and distribution of contraceptive devices and information were punishable under a section of the Canadian Criminal Code dealing with obscenity. There was, however, a clause allowing that, if the public good were served, no conviction was possible.[11] The trial of one of the Parents' Information Bureau nurses, Dorothea Palmer, who was charged in 1936 with disseminating contraceptive information in Eastview (now Vanier), Ontario, served as the movement's platform for arguing the benefits of birth control.[12] The defence presented birth control as a technological solution to social, economic and political problems ranging from infant and maternal mortality to poverty, juvenile delinquency and racial tension, and thus won Palmer's acquittal on the basis of the "for the public good" clause.[13] At the trial, it was only the women, Palmer herself and several middle-class birth control reformers, who stressed the right of women to control their childbearing function, while the male 'experts'--economists, sociologists, psychiatrists and social workers--stressed the social, economic and eugenic benefits of birth control.[14]

The driving force behind the Hamilton clinic was Mary Elizabeth Hawkins, a prominent and wealthy Hamilton widow. Hawkins had worked with many charitable groups, including the Family Services Bureau and the Community Chest in Hamilton, and from this experience had concluded that a service to help women avoid unwanted children was badly needed. An American-born Vassar graduate, Hawkins was influenced by Margaret Sanger, a summer neighbour in Nantucket, Massachusetts, with whom she had discussed birth control.[15] Through Gertrude Burger, who appears to have been in touch with Marie Stopes while studying in London, she also came to be influenced by Stopes' methods and philosophy.[16] Burger was a nurse and social worker, active with the Samaritan Club in Hamilton which cared for tuberculosis victims.

Burger and Hawkins investigated the legal position of birth control and found that dissemination of birth control information was a crime, punishable under the Criminal Code, but took comfort in the "public good" clause. In 1932, they visited Crown Attorney George Ballard at the Wentworth County Court House in Hamilton, who told the women to continue their work as he was solidly behind the aims of the society.[17] Mrs. Hawkins wrote her M. P., C. W. Bell, suggesting an amendment to the Criminal Code. He took this up with the Minister of Justice, Hugh Guthrie, receiving the polite but firm reply that legislation on this very important but controversial subject was not forthcoming. This lobbying activity got her nowhere and her lawyer informed her that such an amendment was unfeasible due to the expected opposition from the Province of Quebec.[18]

Despite a few setbacks, a birth control clinic was opened in Hamilton in 1932. Dr. Elizabeth Bagshaw, one of the few female physicians in Hamilton, was persuaded to work as the clinic's medical director after the early resignation of Dr. Rowena Hume of Toronto, who had found the commuting distance too great.[19] Dr. Bagshaw was to remain with the clinic for more than 30 years, retiring at age 84.[20] Bagshaw attended the Sanger Clinic in New York for instruction in birth control techniques, as medical doctors received no training in contraception.[21] Supplies of diaphragms, jelly and condoms were provided by Kitchener capitalist A. R. Kaufman at cost, and workers claimed that no woman was ever turned away because she could not pay for supplies, although patients were expected to pay what they could.

Clinic workers received a small fee, "enough to keep us there," as Thelma Will, the registered nurse who worked with the clinic from 1937 to 1970, described it. Her starting salary was fifty cents per half day.[22] Dr. Bagshaw received an honorarium for the two to four hours she donated to the clinic each week, examining and instructing patients and fitting diaphragms. Gertrude Burger donated her Friday afternoons to the clinic, interviewing women and keeping records. She referred many patients from the TB sanitorium as well, patients who were well enough to go home on weekends, but who could not handle an unwanted pregnancy. This was certainly a more humane alternative than the eugenicists' suggestion that TB victims be sterilized.

Since discussion of birth control was considered an obscenity in Canada, the clinic had to work quietly and unobtrusively. Most of the clinic's advertisement was word-of-mouth.[23] In fact, it worked so quietly that Thelma Will had not even heard of it until she was approached to work there.[24] The clinic had been in operation for five years by that time.

The clinic was financed by membership fees, an annual tea

which was attended by prominent Hamilton women, and the donations of its founder, Mrs. Hawkins.[25] A number of community services, including the Samaritan Club, the Local Council of Women which encompassed most of the women's groups in the city, many of the Protestant churches, and some members of the medical profession, supported the clinic.[26]

While Hawkins, with her connections among Hamilton's elite, helped win support for the clinic among medical, legal and religious leaders, it appears that many communities in the 1930s showed similar tolerance. In fact, it is at the local level that the birth control movement was most active. Remembering that municipalities were responsible for doling out relief to the unemployed, one should not find it surprising that they showed an interest in birth control in the 1930s. That interest was tentative and cautious, however, given birth control's association with vice and obscenity. Many local governments, some under pressure from eugenicists, considered resolutions in favour of birth control and sterilization.[27] In Brantford, for instance, where the President of the Eugenics Society of Canada, Dr. William Hutton, was medical officer of health, birth control dissemination was carried out with official endorsement.[28] In Calgary, Toronto, Niagara Falls, York County and Essex County, however, efforts to place birth control dissemination in the hands of municipal authorities met with failure probably for a combination of political and financial reasons.[29]

Most municipalities found it politically expedient to carry on the work quietly and unofficially, thus minimizing opposition. In many cases, although the official attitude toward birth control was one of indifference, or even hostility, the social workers themselves actually supported the cause. Kaufman's nurses obtained referrals from a growing number of clergymen and social welfare agencies, including very often municipal relief officials.[30]

The Palmer acquittal gave birth control advocates the legal assurances they needed to carry on their work with reasonable freedom from judicial interference. In the Hamilton case, public health nurses were forbidden to discuss birth control with clients until 1937, when the municipality began to pass on to the birth control clinic the names of people who relief officials felt needed birth control.[31]

Like birth control reformers elsewhere, the Hamilton group was not introducing a new practice but rather new, more effective methods of birth control and offering older methods at a considerable cost saving.[32] The clinic relied primarily upon the combination of diaphragm and jelly, as it was the latest and most effective method of birth control then available. Contraceptive jelly and condoms, however, were also available at considerably lower prices than drug stores offered. If either of these two methods were unsuitable for one reason or another, a tampon or sponge soaked in a contraceptive substance such as vinegar could be used. Women were given a choice, although it seems that most women preferred the diaphragm.[33]

Like Kaufman, the Hamilton women focussed their message on the poor, who they believed needed birth control the most, assuming that birth control was already known among the well-off. There was a tendency to equate poverty with huge families and exaggerate the helplessness of the poor. Birth controllers tended to emphasize ignorance rather than cost as a barrier to birth control use among the poor. The condoms and vaginal suppositories available in the drug stores,[34] which middle-class women knew about, were too expensive for working-class women, especially during the Depression.

Birth controllers also ignored and/or denounced traditional methods of birth control, which, although less effective, offered some protection.[35] When Thelma Will was asked what birth control methods the women whose homes she visited were using, she mentioned douching and withdrawal. Will said of these two popular methods, "they're a good way to get pregnant."[36] Abortion was not mentioned by the women, as most women were reluctant to admit to it, even though there is evidence that it was a widespread practice. Hawkins complained of receiving requests for abortions.[37]

How many women were able to obtain a pessary (diaphragm) from their doctors is unknown. Very few of the doctors in Hamilton would openly endorse birth control--so much so that the clinic had trouble finding a replacement when Dr. Bagshaw went on holidays.[38] There may have been many more who were willing privately to fit diaphragms, although the lack of medical training in contraception must have been a handicap. The clinic itself corrected this omission by providing instruction to a number of doctors over the years. Probably the use of condoms, suppositories, sponges and douches was more common among middle-class women than the use of the diaphragm. Thelma Will herself obtained a diaphragm only after working at the clinic. Until that time she and her husband had used condoms, apparently a common practice.[39] The view expressed by many birth controllers, that middle-class women could easily get birth control from their doctors, while the poor were denied such access, may have been an exaggeration. It seems that middle-class couples got their birth control from the corner drug store.

The most extreme and desperate cases were always written up in the Society's pamphlets and reports to reinforce the association of poverty with uncontrolled fertility. This literature appealed to middle-class fears and prejudices though evidence from the Toronto clinic suggests some misrepresentation.[40]

Hamilton clinic case, Mrs. S., 9 living children, 2 dead children (2 sets of twins in 12 months). Married 13 years. On city relief.
Mrs. N., (Tubercular) 2 years in Sanitorium, 7 living

children, 3 dead children, 6 abortions, 16 pregnancies in 26 years married life. On city relief.[41]

Birth controllers also complained that too few of their target population took advantage of their services. Thelma Will claimed the clinic didn't reach as many women as it should have, although it was successful. There was a steady increase in patients and after seven years of work, the clinic could boast that 2,000 patients had been helped, and that many patients had made return visits and referred friends and relatives.[42] Moreover, the clinic had to expand its hours of operation from one to two days a week. Yet despite this, the women felt more still could be done. This perceived lack of enthusiasm among the poor caused Kaufman to abandon the clinic method, closing down his Toronto and Windsor clinics.

Hawkins and Kaufman also showed a tendency to blame the 'failures'--those who got pregnant despite all the good intentions of clinic workers--on the patient rather than the method. They showed a general insensitivity to factors of motivation and incentive among the poor. And, like most middle-class reformers, they sometimes indulged the temptation to preach to their social inferiors on the value of self-sufficiency. The poor were supposed to recognize that they, and not society as a whole, were responsible for their poverty,[43] lest anyone get the wrong impression that what they received was their right and not a charitable act of generosity.

Support for family values was also evident throughout the movement although there is a difference in emphasis between this women's organization and Kaufman's involvement in birth control dissemination. Women asserted a limited autonomy for women within the family, sought to improve conditions of labour for women, and spoke of birth control as a right, while men avoided the issue of birth control's impact on sexual relations altogether.

Several pamphlets, issued by the Hamilton clinic during the Depression years, highlight the social welfare approach of the clinic toward birth control. Like the eugenicists these women reformers saw birth control as a means of reducing the evil of abortion and of ensuring healthier mothers and children. But their goal was improving women's domestic experience, not racial purity. One pamphlet states, for example, that "birth control is based on the love of children, more and more children who are well cared for, and planned for, fewer and fewer the offspring of exhausted mothers, overburdened fathers and overcrowded homes."[44] Elsewhere, the view was expressed that "the scourge of abortion is nothing more than the necessary consequence of a lack of birth control."[45] Hawkins stated that she believed no child should be brought into the world who "hasn't a reasonable hope of a healthy body, a sound mind, decent surroundings and a fair chance."[46] Her stated aim was to "control the health and well-being of women, children and families in her community."[47]

Hawkins was not adverse to pointing out the economic costs

involved in uncontrolled fertility, especially when appealing for funds. Like the female suffragists of an earlier era who used the 'maternal' feminist argument in order to achieve their primary goal of enfranchisement,[48] Hawkins used the economic and eugenic arguments as a means to her goal of making birth control respectable, and therefore available to all women. Unwanted babies, the clinic advised potential supporters, not only strained homes, but became a drain on the city's welfare and relief funds, adding that many of the clinic's patients were on relief.[49] The clinic, Hawkins argued, was not only alleviating the suffering of women and children, and of families, but also reducing the load of the overburdened taxpayer. Arguments of this sort were important in swaying public opinion in favour of birth control. The Depression was clearly a catalyst in legitimizing birth control practices.

The eugenic and economic benefits of birth control, however, were given a lower priority in the clinic's literature than arguments which placed a high value on the health and welfare of women and children. In contrast to the eugenicists' condescension and contempt for the poor, Hawkins called for sympathy and understanding in dealing with the destitute, whom she described as demoralized and dispirited by the impact of unemployment and relief. She referred to poor women as heroines facing adverse conditions with courage and strength.[50] Thelma Will tells us that, despite her wealth, Hawkins identified with the women the clinic helped[51] and she took an active role in the clinic's day-to-day work. At the Eastview birth control trial, Hawkins protested against the Catholic Church's view that a woman's life must be sacrificed before that of her child. She also spoke to women's groups in Hamilton about birth control and was probably responsible for the Sanger visit to Hamilton in 1933.[52] Her distaste for abortion was motivated by a sympathy with the risks it presented for women and a belief that birth control offered a saner, safer alternative. Prior to its quasi-legalization in the 1970s, abortion was a dangerous procedure associated with self-induced injuries, dangerous drugs and 'backstreet' abortionists. Some women did not survive the attempt to abort an unwanted foetus.[53]

Dr. Bagshaw was not a woman to worry much over moral dilemmas and does not appear to have developed a political position on birth control. She was, however, very conscious of herself as a woman in a male-dominated profession and she showed considerable courage in supporting the clinic against the snubs of her male colleagues.[54] Thelma Will, during her 33 years at the clinic, also braved the sneers of public opinion. Although she, like Bagshaw, would not become entangled in moral debates about birth control, she believed it should be available to any married woman who wanted it and was not afraid publicly to endorse a practice, which she and others of her class practised privately.[55]

The clinic's methods of birth control dissemination and its relative indifference to eugenic sterilization[56] say much about its respect for women. Hawkins believed that the clinic method, employing fully certified medical practitioners to fit diaphragms and spot any gynaecological problems, was the best approach to birth control. She was, at least in the beginning, "dead against" Kaufman's visiting nurses.[57] She felt that the medical profession must be involved in the dissemination of information about birth control in order to "do the greatest good and least harm."[58] By including the medical profession in birth control dissemination or, more accurately, forcing them to participate by taking the lead in a field they considered their preserve,[59] she hoped to minimize opposition to birth control within the profession. She also hoped to win support among the general public by associating birth control with the prestigious medical profession. She was careful to limit clinic patients to married women with at least two children and stated emphatically her opposition to abortion[60] in an effort to dissociate that practice from the work of the clinic. Hawkins wanted to see birth control made respectable and thus available to all women, but she also wanted to offer women the best quality contraceptive then available--the diaphragm and contraceptive jelly--which required a medical fitting.

Mary Elizabeth Hawkins   Albert R. Kaufman

Source: Thomas Melville Bailey, *For the Public Good: A History of the Birth Control Clinic and the Planned Parenthood Society of Hamilton, Ontario, Canada* (Hamilton: The Planned Parenthood Society of Hamilton, 1974), pp. 2, 4.

In contrast to Hawkins, Kaufman employed visiting nurses and used the mails to distribute cheaper and simpler methods, such as jelly or foam used alone or with condoms (even though he claimed working-class men were too irresponsible to use condoms).[61] He closed clinics in Toronto and Windsor, concluding that the poor would not attend clinics in large enough numbers to warrant the cost of operation, and that working-class women were too ignorant to learn to use the diaphragm effectively.[62]

The findings of Lucy Ingram Morgan who conducted a very thorough study of 2,126 cases at Kaufman's Toronto clinic do not confirm Kaufman's prejudices about the poor. While the majority of clinic patients were poor--half were on relief--they were not the excessively fecund, marginal group Kaufman wanted to reach.[63] Neither were they incapable of using the more effective methods. Of the 36 per cent confirmed successful cases, the study found an 89.37 per cent success rate with the vaginal pessary and 91.07 per cent success rate with cervical pessary. Jelly and nozzle effectiveness rates were 83.78 per cent.[64]

The clinic also enjoyed substantial community support, with 12 per cent of patients referred by visiting nurses, 23 per cent by social agencies, 19 per cent by doctors, nurses or hospitals, 1 per cent by clergymen and 13 per cent by interested individuals.[65] Kaufman complained, however, that, of the 10,000 women the clinic served in 5 years, only 5 per cent were referred by welfare agencies or relief officials.[66] Not only were not enough poor coming to the clinics, but the wrong type were attending. He had hoped to reach more of the socially dependent and 'feeble-minded'. In order to reach this group he relied on simpler methods, distributed through the Parents' Information Bureau. His aim was to reach the largest number of the poor as possible and he believed that simpler methods had greater acceptance among this group.[67] Kaufman's simpler methods philosophy did not address the issue of motivation in contraceptive practice. Those oppressed with poverty had no incentive to curtail their fertility, and it was only with hope of a better standard of living that the very poor would be motivated to use birth control.[68]

Both the Hamilton clinic and the Toronto clinic demonstrated, however, that, with adequate instruction and motivation, most women could use the more effective means of birth control. In the Winnipeg case as well as in Hamilton where extensive follow up was done, women reported success in using the diaphragm.[69] The clinic women refused to sacrifice the quality of service they offered to women for the sake of reaching greater numbers.

The McLarens argue that, despite Kaufman's contempt for the poor, and "neo-Malthusian" motivations, he ironically provided better service to the poor through his 'innovative' technique of by-passing the medical profession and taking culturally acceptable methods to the poor.[70] Kaufman claimed to have reached 250,000 Canadians over the years through the Parents' Information

Bureau.[71] In 1937, he claimed, the Parents' Information Bureau reached 23,000, while the Toronto clinic reached only 2,000, one tenth that number.[72] Likewise the Hamilton clinic averaged fewer than 200 patients per year.[73] Figures on the Parents' Information Bureau cannot be verified as Kaufman used statistics in a casual and cavalier fashion to vindicate his methods and bolster arguments with the Hamilton women. The only study done on effectiveness rates with the Parents' Information Bureau patients was careless in the extreme. His claims to 99 per cent effectiveness[74] cannot be taken seriously as other groups using similar methods achieved much lower rates. The study also showed that a significant number of people ordered supplies through the Parents' Information Bureau, but did not reorder.[75] Some of the women at the Eastview trial testified to taking the supplies out of curiosity.[76] It is likely that Kaufman's 250,000 patients included those who ordered supplies only once. Because of the nature of his programme, which left little room for patient follow up, it is also impossible qualitatively to assess the success of the programme.

Consistent with Kaufman's eugenic concerns, the Parents' Information Bureau was a national organization seeking to make an impact on Canadian fertility rates and it is to be expected that it reached larger numbers than the locally based Hamilton or Toronto clinics. Whether it reached a greater percentage of its national target population than the Hamilton group reached of its local target population is impossible to tell. One cannot, however, measure a group's success by numbers alone. Not only do Kaufman's figures give no indication of effectiveness rates, but intangible benefits also cannot be measured quantitatively. The Hamilton clinic's training of local doctors in contraceptive techniques and its low-key, continuous efforts to make birth control 'respectable' may have made birth control available to many more women than those who actually visited the clinic.

Clearly the Bureau provided a service to isolated Canadians, those afraid or unable to go to clinics or doctors, and those too poor to afford contraception during the Depression. In the long run, however, the clinic method, which combined medical care with contraceptive services, ultimately formed the basis for contraceptive dissemination.

The implications of the philosophy and motivations of these two groups must be considered, as well as their numerical impact. Kaufman's philosophy led him in the direction of population control, while the clinic women moved toward social reform amid a quasi-feminist support for women's reproductive freedom. This is clear from their post-Depression activities. The Hamilton clinic continued to operate long after the Depression-induced eugenics hysteria subsided, later merging with the Family Planning movement of the 1960s. Kaufman handed over the day-to-day operation to his nurse, Anna Weber (the Bureau folded in the early 1970s) and turned his attention to third world population control programmes where he could continue to experiment with simpler methods to gain greater results.[77]

While the Hamilton women clearly supported the family--birth control was only offered to married women with two children or more--they sought to give women reproductive control within that institution. Hawkins' programme in some ways parallels the domestic science reformers in that it combined a conservative, pro-family position with a set of demands to improve women's position within the home.[78] Domestic science, like birth control, promised to bring the benefits of twentieth-century science and technology to women who laboured in the home, improving their working conditions and implicitly their status. To recognize mothering and domestic labour as 'real' work, worthy of simplifying and enhancing through technological and/or scientific means, was to elevate it to a status equal to labour force participation. Although there is as yet little research done on women's organizational activities in the inter-war period, recent studies point to a practical, domestic-centred concern among women.[79] Hawkins' group certainly fits this mould.

With the Depression-induced 'back-to-the-kitchen' hysteria also came a concern with domesticity among middle-class women. While the popular view that married women should give up their jobs to men with families to support may not have kept many working women at home if their pay cheque meant family survival,[80] professional opportunities for middle-class women were severely restricted. Domestic responsibilities for women, whether working in the labour force or not, increased due to unemployment and economic uncertainty for all family members. Unwanted babies added considerably to the strain. In the opinion of Thelma Will, who visited many poor Hamilton women in the 1930s, it was largely on women that the burden of feeding and clothing children fell. When asked if husbands were concerned about restricting family size for economic reasons during difficult times, she replied that men seemed relatively indifferent even to this consideration. "Well, that's mankind," she said.[81] Most men were indifferent to the clinic's work because they saw birth control as a woman's problem and let their wives deal with it in their own way, she thought.[82]

But these women were doing more than improving working conditions and helping women survive. By asserting married women's right to birth control, they undermined patriarchal authority in the home. However much birth controllers tried to camouflage the threat, the issue surfaced nonetheless. At the Eastview trial, for example, the only claim that the prosecution could make which unnerved the confident defence, led by Kaufman and his male 'experts', was that birth control undermined male authority in the home. The Crown prosecutor asked all the defence witnesses, especially the 'experts', what they thought would happen if there were a disagreement between husband and wife on whether to use birth control, or to have another child. As most of the defence witnesses were active promoters of the cause, they generally answered that the wife should have the veto power, although some did so reluctantly.[83] Often the question was left to the end of the cross-examination in order to create effect. The prosecutor played on the fear that birth control could alter power relations within the home, and thus pointed out an important contradiction within the birth control movement. In terms of expediency, one had to focus on the woman, addressing the birth control message to her, yet in doing so male authority in the home was threatened. Kaufman was asked whether the contraceptives the Parents' Information Bureau distributed could be used without the husband's knowledge and consent. Kaufman's answers stressed that such methods (i.e., condom and contraceptive jelly) would be difficult to use without the husband's knowledge but evaded the underlying question of whether male authority would be undermined.[84] While Hawkins and many of the women who testified stated strongly that married women had a right to birth control, most of the male 'experts' tried to sidestep or downplay the issue.[85]

But fear of female autonomy could take uglier forms. During the trial, Palmer almost became victim to the hostility of a husband whose wife she had visited with birth control information. He threatened her with sexual assault, reportedly wanting to show her "what it's like without birth control."[86] A few of the Hamilton husbands expressed fears that birth control would give women the means to marital infidelity.[87] Also Kaufman's nurses, who did the 'dirty work' in disseminating birth control information, were at times subjected to harassment and violence.[88]

There was, of course, much open opposition to the Hamilton clinic. While birth controllers such as Kaufman and Hawkins attributed all opposition to Roman Catholics and socialists, their analysis of their opponents' positions amounted to caricatures. Hawkins, with her upper middle-class background, sometimes turned on the left, condemning what she termed "the socialist insistence that the poor should be able to have as many children as they wished, whatever the cost."[89] Hawkins clearly distorted the left's position on birth control, which was ambivalent at best. In fact, the left, as the McLarens point out in their book, were among the first advocates of birth control.[90] That position ranged from an uneasy support for birth control by male socialists, as a means of restricting labour supply and thus enhancing labour's bargaining position, to an unqualified support by women within the movement based on humanitarian considerations and birth control's potential for women's emancipation. But by the 1930s the left had grown understandably suspicious of recent middle-class converts to the cause, primarily interested in using birth control as a means of avoiding economic reform and of blaming poverty on its victims.[91]

Dr. Bagshaw, not a woman to worry over moral dilemmas, found the lofty, theoretical condemnations of Hamilton's Roman Catholic Bishop J. T. McNally mildly amusing and liked to express the view that they served to advertise the clinic to Catholic women.[92] Kaufman particularly loved to blame the Catholics for opposition to birth control. He gloated over the statistics showing the number of Catholic patients he helped, and voiced paranoid fears of the papacy's attempts to impose its canon law on the state.[93] Probably the most vocal opposition to the Hamilton clinic came from the Roman Catholic Church. Here we see a reaction against birth control's potential to undermine male authority in the home, as Bishop McNally regularly and vehemently denounced the clinic from his pulpit.[94] When Margaret Sanger spoke on birth control in Hamilton in 1933, saying, among other things, that birth control would allow women more leisure for higher culture, the Bishop retorted that such "higher culture" would probably consist of sleeping until noon, playing golf in the afternoon, and bridge at night.[95] He also ridiculed women's emancipation, saying that, "although the woman stayed at home, and sewed, cooked or mended, she was monarch of all she surveyed, especially in a house filled with children."[96] He thought women already enjoyed greater freedom than men and denounced the clinic women as harlots, calling their philosophy degrading, blasphemous, depraved and atheistic.[97] Clearly the Bishop saw birth control as a feminist demand and, in fact, Hawkins's attack on Catholicism centred on the Church's devaluing of maternal life.

The Bishop's comments show that he believed birth control to be immoral and excessively materialistic and it can hardly be denied that birth control gained widespread acceptance only with the rise in consumerism of the twentieth century. As the nation's advertisers pushed their new messages urging people to consume rather than conserve, to indulge rather than restrain, sexual enjoyment with the sobering restraint of parenthood became more acceptable. Most of the Protestant clergy who testified at the trial condoned sexuality as a healthy form of expression of marital love.[98] The Bishop, however, felt that people who wanted fewer children should abstain from sexual relations, altogether failing to recognize the difficulty most women faced in marriage of imposing abstinence on husbands. Birth control allowed people to have sexual pleasure without facing its necessary consequence, procreation, and to the Bishop that was irresponsible, immoral, unnatural and contrary to God's will.[99]

The Church's condemnation of eugenics was rarely addressed by the birth control reformers. It was easier to ridicule the Church for its outdated authoritarianism. Ironically, its critique of eugenics bears similarity with the position of the left. The Bishop argued that Christian principles dictated society should care for its weaker members, rather than discard them in order to breed a race of supermen,[100] as the eugenicists would have it. He suggested that society should redistribute its wealth so that the poor could raise their children in peace and that 'feeble-mindedness' and other conditions which eugenicists continually pronounced upon were not inherited, but actually the product of "the exaggerated artificiality and worry of modern life."[101] While the left would have diagnosed the problem as capitalist exploitation of workers, the solution, redistribution of wealth, was the same.

Catholic women's groups shared with their Catholic men an opposition to birth control because it separated sexuality from procreation, but they also shared with the Hamilton Birth Control Society a desire to preserve the family and a respect for women as mothers.

The Catholic Women's League of Hamilton withdrew its membership from the Local Council of Women in 1933 in protest against a resolution the Council passed approving sterilization of the 'unfit'.[102] The Hamilton Birth Control Society may have been the initiator of the resolution, although similar statements of support for birth control and sterilization were being made by women's groups all over the country in the 1930s.[103] Catholic women were given an opportunity to abstain from the resolution while remaining in the Council--they refused. The Local Council of Women was not willing to expel the Hamilton Birth Control Society in order to accommodate the Catholic Women's League.[104]

Like earlier voluntary motherhood proponents,[105] these Catholic women saw artificial birth control as an assault on the dignity of motherhood and the vital institution of the family.[106] Catholic women felt that their special role as wives and mothers would be threatened by the sexual freedom which birth control offered.

In a letter to the editor of the *Toronto Daily Star*, one Catholic woman responded to Hawkins' plea that Catholic women be supplied with birth control as compensation for their Church's doctrine of sacrificing women's lives to procreation. She replied that Catholic women knew what their church expected of them and gladly sacrificed their lives for the privilege of creating new life:

> I know. . .that the purpose of marriage is fulfilled in giving birth. I know that the God who gave me life, may see fit to see that life as the price of another life. I also know that God has a definite plan, has had from eternity, for each soul that is conceived and I know that just as surely as I interfere with the life of an unborn child I am as miserably guilty of murder, in the eyes of God who ordained the life of that child, as I should be if I deliberately shot or poisoned a fellow man.[107]

This woman opposed efforts to bring motherhood onto the same plane as other forms of labour, preferring to see it as a divine mission.

While both groups of women saw motherhood as a central facet of women's role in society, Catholic women saw birth control as a threat to women, opting for abstinence as the only justifiable means of fertility control. Birth controllers sought to improve domestic working conditions and to enhance women's personal autonomy by embracing artificial means of fertility control. They felt this would strengthen the family and improve women's lot within it.

Clearly many Catholic women did not follow their Church's teaching in private life, although there was at least one case of a Catholic woman in Hamilton who came to the clinic, but never returned due to the interference of her priest, at least as reported by the clinic worker.[108]   Of course, Catholics were not alone in privately practising a measure which neither they, nor their organizations, could openly endorse. As was shown with the relief authorities, it is clear that Protestants were also capable of a two-faced approach to birth control. Most women, regardless of religious persuasion, paid less attention to religious and moral pronouncements on birth control than to practical considerations. They were attempting to survive as best they could, to care for themselves and their children, and the moralizing of social reformers and bishops understandably meant little to them.

There is scant information about the women who availed themselves of the clinic because the clinic's medical records were destroyed. Many birth control workers expected desperate women to come in droves to hear the birth control message, yet in Hamilton that was not the case, even though the clinic was usually busy. After the legal clarification of birth control work in 1937, Thelma Will was hired to go door-to-door in a campaign to bring more women to the clinic. She described the usual response as polite indifference.[109] Women would tell her whatever they thought she wanted to hear in order to get rid of her, but they never came to the clinic.[110] In short, they treated her like any salesperson who might show up at their door. The stigma attached to birth control was so strong, claimed Will, that clinic patients generally preferred to go all the way downtown to pick up supplies, rather than go to the convenient "jelly stations" which were set up in board members' homes to be closer to patients.[111] No doubt there was also considerable suspicion regarding a middle-class woman, a nurse who mysteriously appeared at the door and refused to reveal where the referral had been obtained. In point of fact, a large part of her list came from the relief authorities, conditional upon that source not being disclosed.

Those women who did come were very appreciative of the service, Will said.[112] The letter of one woman which remains in the files is a touching testament. In it she submits one dollar to help pay for contraceptive supplies which she had received free because her husband was unemployed. Now, after two years of unemployment, he was working again, and she had struggled to scrape together that dollar. She said she had thought of not sending the money, but decided that, if too many people did that, well, there'd be no more clinic; so she sent the money. She did not know how she would have managed with a husband out of work and two children to look after, if it were not for the clinic.[113] Clearly the Hamilton clinic was providing a valuable service for those women who wanted it badly enough to venture out.

Looking at the Hamilton Birth Control Society, as part of the larger middle-class, male-dominated birth control movement of the 1930s, allows the historian a glimpse at how a women's organization approached the dissemination of a technology which affects women's work and autonomy, as well as political issues such as population control, labour supply and eugenics. While middle-class men and women birth controllers alike focussed their message on the poor, showed hostility to the left and Catholicism, tried to impose middle-class standards on all, and supported the institution of the family, there are nonetheless significant differences. The Hamilton group's choice of the most effective method of birth control, and its lesser interest in reaching large numbers, and in sterilization of the 'unfit', indicate an interest in birth control as a means to women's autonomy within the home rather than race betterment. Just as within the birth control movement class differences clearly emerged, with the socialist emphasis on labour relations and women's emancipation in the 1920s giving way to a middle-class, eugenicist takeover in the 1930s, it is also true that within both classes, gender differences emerge. Neither an exclusively class nor gender based analysis is sufficient to study this social movement.

Neither can the 'maternal' feminist defence of the family be seen entirely as a reactionary bolstering of the established order. While middle-class women birth controllers did not demand birth control in the name of emancipation from the family as did a few socialist feminists, they did seek to improve conditions for women working in the home by alleviating poverty, decreasing maternal and infant mortality, reducing family size, eliminating abortion, and increasing family stability. For them, simple justice dictated that married women should control their own fertility and that neither the church nor husbands had any right to interfere. They allied with the conservative medical profession in order to enhance the respectability of birth control, and used the economic and eugenic arguments to garner support for their cause.

Birth control is an important technology not only for such 'male' concerns as population control, labour relations and eugenics but for women's sexual and reproductive autonomy. Women's contribution to the Canadian birth control movement of the 1930s should not be forgotten, or dismissed as auxiliary to the male-dominated movement. Women had a distinct and unique input motivated by a desire to ameliorate domestic working conditions and increase women's autonomy in the home. It is important for feminist scholars to give equal weight to family-centred, or private sphere reform activities on the part of women, whether or not they can be classified as feminist. Women's history must have as one of its central concerns a study of women in the family, because so much of women's labour and women's consciousness has resided in that realm.

Notes

[1]Angus McLaren and Arlene Tigar McLaren, *The Bedroom and the State: The Changing Practices and Politics of Contraception and Abortion in Canada, 1880-1980* (Toronto: McClelland and Stewart, 1986), Chapter Three: "Socialist Feminists, Maternal Feminists, and Family Limitation," pp. 54-70.

[2]*Ibid.*, pp. 55, 67-70.

[3]*Ibid.*, p. 67.

[4]For example, Alexander Maitland Stephen, the leading advocate of birth control in Vancouver in the 1920s, argued that, besides ending the slavery of women, birth control would "make the working class home a pleasant place to which the husband would happily return; it would check the reckless breeding of the diseased and the criminal; it would lead to a healthier, stronger labour movement. . ." As the McLarens put it, "this curious amalgam of ideas called for the emancipation of women, while assuming that they would remain in the home, and demanded freedom of individuals to determine their own family size, while bemoaning the uncontrolled reproduction of the criminal and the alcoholic." *Ibid*, pp. 63, 64.

[5]For a discussion of the movement in British Columbia, see McLaren and McLaren, *The Bedroom and the State*, and Mary F. Bishop, "Vivian Dowding: Birth Control Activist, 1892-," in Barbara K. Latham and Roberta J. Pazdro, eds., *Not Just Pin Money* (Victoria, B. C.: Camosun College, 1984), pp. 327-35.

[6]One group was established in Winnipeg in 1934 by a woman prominent in that city, while the Essex County Maternal Health League took over Kaufman's abandoned Windsor birth control clinic. Winnipeg Family Planning Association, Annual Reports, 1939-1965; Essex County Maternal Health League, n.d., uncatalogued papers, Hamilton Planned Parenthood, Hamilton, Ontario (hereafter the Hamilton Papers). At the time of the original research for this paper, this collection of clippings, correspondence and miscellaneous material from the Hamilton Birth Control Clinic, approximately 1930 to 1960, was not catalogued. It is, however, now deposited in the Hamilton Public Library.

[7]A. R. Kaufman, "The Parents' Information Bureau," *The Journal of Contraception* (March 1938), 54-5.

[8]Gerald Stortz and Murray E. Eaton, "'Pro Bono Publico': The Eastview Birth Control Trial," *Atlantis* 8, 2 (Spring 1983), 51-60; Dianne Dodd, "The Birth Control Movement on Trial, 1936-1937," *Histoire sociale/Social History* 16, 32 (November 1983), 411-28.

[9]Letter to H. L. Mencken from A. R. Kaufman, 10 August 1937, Gamble Papers, Francis A. Countway Library of Medicine, Boston, Massachusetts.

[10]"The Aims and Objects of the Eugenic Society of Canada," File 43, Palmer Papers, University of Waterloo Library, Waterloo, Ontario.

[11]Canada, Revised Statutes, 1892, *The Criminal Code*, Sec. 179, ch. 29, p. 80.

[12]Stortz and Eaton, 2.

[13]Dodd, "The Birth Control Movement on Trial."

[14]*Ibid.*

[15]"Survives Despite Opposition," *Hamilton Spectator*, 1 March 1962, Hamilton Papers.

[16]McLaren and McLaren, p. 99.

[17]Thomas Melville Bailey, *For the Public Good: A History of the Hamilton Birth Control Society* (Hamilton: Hamilton Planned Parenthood, 1974), p. 14.

[18]*Ibid.*

[19]Letter to Mary Elizabeth Hawkins from Dr. Hume, 30 March 1932, Hamilton Papers.

[20]Bailey, pp. 10-12. Dr. Bagshaw died in 1982 at the age of 100.

[21]*Ibid.*, p. 10.

[22]*Ibid.*, pp. 15, 16.

[23]*Ibid.*

[24]Thelma Will, interview with the author, Hamilton, 22 January 1982.

[25]Bailey, p. 19.

[26]*Ibid.*, p. 7.

[27]"Suggested Resolutions to be Passed or Rejected by Municipal Council," Hamilton Papers. In Orillia, such a resolution was passed concerning the sterilization of the 'unfit' to be released from the Orillia School for the Mentally Retarded, Hamilton Papers.

[28]*Toronto Mail and Empire*, 12 December 1932.

[29]*Calgary Herald*, 1 December 1938; *Toronto Mail and Empire*, 12 December 1932; *Essex County Maternal Health League* (pamphlet published by Essex County Maternal Health League, ca. 1937).

[30]"No Rush of Clinics Seen From Birth Control Trial," (Interview with A. R. Kaufman following the trial), *Toronto Star*, 20 March 1937, p. 1.

[31]Thelma Will, interview with the author, Hamilton, 22 January 1982.

[32]Dianne Dodd, "The Canadian Birth Control Movement, 1929-1939," unpublished M.A. thesis, University of Toronto, 1982, ch. 3.

[33]Thelma Will, interview with the author, Hamilton, 22 January 1982.

[34]*Ibid.*

[35]James Reed, *From Private Vice to Public Virtue* (New York: Basic Books, 1977), p. 11. For instance, the actual use effectiveness of withdrawal is 75-80 per cent, according to *Contraceptive Technology* (1973-74), cited by *Our Bodies Our Selves* (New York: Boston Women's Health Collective Inc., 1971), p. 185.

[36]Thelma Will, interview with the author, Hamilton, 22 January 1982.

[37]"Interim Report, Hamilton Birth Control Society, 1931," Hamilton Papers.

[38]Thelma Will, interview with the author, Hamilton, 22 January 1982.

[39]*Ibid.*

[40]Lucy Ingram Morgan, "An Analysis of 2,126 Cases Registered at the Toronto Birth Control Clinic Between October 3, 1933 and December 20, 1934," Gamble Papers.

[41]"An Outline of the Work and Aims of the Hamilton Birth Control Society," Hamilton Papers, 4-5.

[42]Bailey, p. 25.

[43]McLaren and McLaren, pp. 102-3.

[44]*An Outline of the Work and Aims of the Birth Control Society of Hamilton, Indicating the Social, Economic, Political and Religious Aspects of the Subject* (Hamilton: Hamilton Birth Control Society, n.d.), Hamilton Papers.

[45]*Ibid.*, p. 11.

[46]Bailey, p. 21.

[47]"Declares Aim is to Control Family Health," *Hamilton Spectator*, n.d., Newspaper Clippings, Hamilton Papers.

[48]Ernest Forbes, "The Ideas of Carol Bacchi and The Suffragists of Halifax: A Review Essay on *Liberation Deferred? The Ideas of the English Canadian Suffragists, 1877-1918*," *Atlantis* 10, 2 (Spring 1985), 119-26.

[49]Bailey, p. 22.

[50]*Ibid.*, p. 4.

[51]Thelma Will, interview with the author, Hamilton, 22 January 1982.

[52]Bailey, pp. 22-3. Also *Toronto Mail and Empire*, 5 August 1936; *Hamilton Spectator*, 6 April 1933; *Hamilton Herald*, 7 June 1933; and "Minute Book," Hamilton Birth Control Society, 1933, Hamilton Papers.

[53]McLaren and McLaren, pp. 32-51.

[54]Mark McCurdy (director), *Doctor Woman: The Life and Times of Dr. Elizabeth Bagshaw* (Montreal: National Film Board of Canada, 1978).

[55]Thelma Will, interview with the author, Hamilton, 22 January 1982.

[56]The Hamilton women were not opposed to eugenic sterilization; they did not, however, give it the same priority as the eugenicists did.

[57]Letter to Mary Hawkins from Janet B. Whitenack,

American Birth Control League, New York, 12 November 1936, Palmer Papers, Box 1, File 33, University of Waterloo Library, Waterloo, Ontario.

[58]"President's Address," 15 January 1934, Hamilton Papers.

[59]Hawkins offered Hamilton doctors the chance to take over the clinic, which they declined. This effectively silenced the criticism that the clinic was competing with the medical profession. McLaren and McLaren, p. 101.

[60]"Interim Report," Hamilton Birth Control Society, 1931, Hamilton Papers.

[61]A. R. Kaufman to Dr. Gamble, 21 July 1937, Gamble Papers.

[62]A. R. Kaufman, "The Parents' Information Bureau of Canada," *The Journal of Contraception* (March 1938), 54, 55.

[63]Because many did not bother to return to the clinic for follow-up visits, the clinic could confirm only 36 per cent of their cases as successful. Morgan, p. 61.

[64]*Ibid.*, 67.

[65]*Ibid.*, 10.

[66]A. R. Kaufman to Mrs. L. T. Morgan, 22 December 1938, Gamble Papers.

[67]Reed, pp. 248-308.

[68]*Ibid.*

[69]Winnipeg Family Planning Association, Annual Reports, 1939-1965.

[70]McLaren and McLaren, pp. 105-16.

[71]Kaufman, 55.

[72]McLaren and McLaren, p. 103.

[73]Kaufman, 55.

[74]A. R. Kaufman to Dr. Gamble, 12 March 1936, Gamble Papers.

[75]*Ibid.*

[76]Dodd, "The Birth Control Movement on Trial," 416.

[77]Gamble Papers.

[78]Diana Pederson, "The Scientific Training of Mothers: The Campaign for Domestic Science in Ontario Schools, 1890-1913," in R. Jarrell and A. Roos, eds., *Critical Issues in the History of Canadian Science, Technology and Medicine* (Ottawa: HSTC Publications, 1983), pp. 178-94; Patricia Saidak, "Home Economics as an Academic Science," *Resources for Feminist Research* 15, 3 (November 1986), 49-51.

[79]Marilyn Barber, "Help for Farm Homes: The Campaign to End Housework Drudgery in Rural Saskatchewan in the 1920s," *Scientia Canadensis* 9, 1 (June 1985), 3-26; Veronica Strong-Boag, "Pulling in Double Harness or Hauling a Double Load: Women, Work and Feminism on the Canadian Prairie," *Journal of Canadian Studies* 21, 3 (Fall 1986), 32-52.

[80]For a discussion of the effect of the Depression on women's work, see Alice Kessler-Harris, *Women Have Always Worked* (New York: The Feminist Press, 1981), pp. 138-44.

[81]Thelma Will, interview with the author, Hamilton, 22 January 1982.

[82]*Ibid.*

[83]Dodd, "The Birth Control Movement on Trial," 419.

[84]*Ibid.*

[85]*Ibid.*

[86]Jean Hollobon, "Did Dirty Work For Men At Trial, Pioneer of Birth Control Says," *Globe and Mail*, 30 November 1978. (Interview with Dorothea Palmer Ferguson.) Palmer was quickly dismissed by Kaufman after the trial due to some doubts about her 'character' and marital status.

[87]Thelma Will, interview with the author, Hamilton, 22 January 1982.

[88]Letter from Mary Bishop to the author, 10 December 1981.

[89]*Hamilton Spectator*, ca. 1934, Newspaper Clippings, Hamilton Papers.

[90]McLaren and McLaren, ch. 4.

[91]*Ibid.*

[92]*Doctor Woman: The Life and Times of Dr. Elizabeth Bagshaw.*

[93]Morgan; Dodd, "The Birth Control Movement on Trial."

[94]Bailey, pp. 18-19.

[95]"Launches Attack on Birth Control," *Hamilton Spectator*, 11 October 1933, Newspaper Clippings, Hamilton Papers.

[96]*Ibid.*

[97]Bailey, p. 35.

[98]Dodd, "The Birth Control Movement on Trial."

[99]*Hamilton Spectator*, 11 October 1933, Newspaper Clippings, Hamilton Papers.

[100]*Ibid.*

[101]*Ibid.*

[102]*Hamilton Spectator* 5 March 1934, Newspaper Clippings, Hamilton Papers.

[103]Bailey, pp. 7-8; Helen MacMurchy, *Birth Control? Sterilization? A Book for Family Welfare and Safety* (Toronto: Macmillan, 1934). See also Angus McLaren, "The Creation of a Haven for 'Human Thoroughbreds': The Sterilization of the Feeble-Minded and the Mentally Ill in British Columbia," *Canadian Historical Review* 67, 2 (June 1986), 127-50.

[104]*Hamilton Herald*, 5 March 1934, Newspaper Clippings, Hamilton Papers.

[105]Linda Gordon, *Woman's Body, Woman's Right* (Harmondsworth: Penguin, 1977).

[106]The following statement came from the Catholic Women's League of Canada: "Whereas the Catholic Women's League of Canada, believing in the divine institution of marriage and its sacramental dignity, views with alarm the rise of false and perverse morality in the advocacy of birth control, and believes that the spiritual welfare of the state as well as the temporal happiness of

its citizens, cannot remain safe and sound when the unit of society--
the family--is threatened with destruction, by the actions of certain
organizations who ask governments to establish clinics and facilities
for birth control." *Hamilton Herald*, 5 March 1934, Newspaper
Clippings, Hamilton Papers.

[107]"The Responsibility of Motherhood," *Toronto Daily Star*, 14
November 1936.

[108]Thelma Will, interview with the author, Hamilton, 22
January 1982.

[109]*Ibid.*

[110]*Ibid.*

[111]*Ibid.*

[112]*Ibid.*

[113]Letter to Hamilton clinic from Mrs. R. W. Dyet, R.R.#1,
Selkirk, Hamilton Papers.

Chapter Nine

MOTHERING IN A NEWFOUNDLAND COMMUNITY:
1900-1940

Cecilia Benoit

Introduction

In much of the prolific literature on women published in the past
two decades, there has been a tendency to focus on the home as a
sphere of production instead of merely an enclave of retreat from
the "world of 'work'."[1] In addition, feminist historians have begun
to re-examine historical records in an attempt to discover women's
hitherto hidden history.[2] Attention has also been drawn to the
position of women in societies undergoing modernization and to the
individual and collective political behaviour of women--within and
outside the household.[3] Much of the literature on women, however,
has remained abstract and theoretical. We still lack substantive
evidence, for example, for a theory of gender hierarchies, in part
perhaps because we have only begun to become familiar with the
socio-economic and cultural circumstances of the lives of rural
women. Only such substantive evidence can lead to a fuller
understanding of the paradoxical position of women throughout
history.[4]

I will describe below one historical case of women's
subordination in a Newfoundland community immediately prior to
modernization at the onset of World War II. In particular, I will
examine the political economy of mothering and attempt to
demonstrate that women's unequal status in family and community
was associated with social and economic processes which excluded
women from most forms of wage labour. While males found
employment in the market economy, their female kin remained
within the bounds of the community as 'procreators' and
'homemakers', statuses closely regulated by economic structures and
religious institutions. Nevertheless, these women managed to
survive and find satisfaction in informal networks of production and
friendship.

My focus in this paper is the problem of mothering (as an

institution and as a personal encounter)[5] in one historical instance, as experienced by the women themselves. The time span is the period from 1900 to 1940, still within the lived experience of older people in the community, and just prior to the opening of an American air force base at the beginning of World War II, an event which changed the community virtually overnight into a modern town. By use of the snowball technique, informal tape-recorded interviews were conducted with approximately twenty women and ten men (age 65-95). Typical of the general population as a whole, many of my female interviewees were widows, living either alone or with one of their adult children. Whenever husbands and wives were interviewed, separate time was alloted for each, since the women and men were generally reluctant to discuss 'private matters' (e.g., sexuality, birth control, pregnancy) in the company of the other sex. The interviews ranged from one to two hours, and a few were repeated. Census data and other archival materials, in addition to local and cross-cultural studies on the topic, were consulted in order to substantiate the interview data.

The Setting

> I was born ten years before the new century came in--not yesterday, hey? We had a lovely house back off the pond, around two miles from the church and the merchant's store. In 1900 there wasn't much very big around here. No way for a woman to earn a cent really. No doctor, just the midwife to take care of the folks. The road was really not much more than a cow path and unless you were a man or grown boy, you didn't get to see what the other side of the Bay was like.
>
> (Housewife, born 1890)

The situation of women in Stephenville, Newfoundland, between 1900 and 1940 illustrates some of the dilemmas of motherhood. Although in some ways this small community was unlike other outport communities in Newfoundland during this period,[6] most of its structural features can be found in cultural settings elsewhere.[7] In this Catholic community of Scots, Acadians and Micmac Indians, mothers and daughters rarely left their community while husbands and sons were absent for long periods each year. This situation resulted in an extremely sharp division of labour between women and men and, in consequence of the prolonged periods of separation, in a ruptured bond between many husbands and wives. The sexes were indeed "worlds apart":[8]

> Women from Stephenville were born to work and stay put and so we lived with it. Work was your story and so you bit your lip and got on with it. We women had what it took to make a good frame. And then we helped each

other. Sometimes I wonder, though, as I sit here getting
old, how we conquered it all.

(Housewife, born 1898)

Stephenville men were commonly known as "Jacks-of-all-
trades." They tried their hands at farming, fishing, lumbering and
hunting, often at a combination of several of these. Nevertheless,
they were always "in the red" with the local shop owners, and hence
in constant search of paid work. After 1925,[9] men were
increasingly able to sell their labour on the open market in return
for a low wage, a bunk bed in a lumber camp, and perhaps three
meals a day. After the fall harvest they usually left their
community and did not return before Christmas. Soon thereafter
they would be gone again until spring planting time. Despite their
hard work, the men earned a few dollars at most for a twelve-hour
day. Bad weather or a poor tree crop sometimes meant that they
returned home with nothing more than "the shirts on their backs."
They would help the women with the garden, cut firewood, perhaps
hunt or fish, and soon start the cycle once again. The women
watched their male kin come and go with the seasons, never quite
sure where they were, always fearful that they would return
without enough money to settle accounts with the merchant.

Which forces, we may ask, kept the women bound to their
community? And what economic contribution did they make to the
survival of their families? As I will argue below, their non-wage
labour often meant the difference between minimal comfort and
destitution. Women frequently bartered their crafts for food at the
merchant store. They also performed the tasks necessary for the
upkeep of the Church and the priest. Their many other productive
activities, too, were essential for the well-being of their families:

One thing was sure, the people here were not ill-fed or ill-
clothed. All the women worked together like a team. At
least we could plant our basic food and gather enough
berries for winter preserves. Then we had hens and lots of
fresh milk. No, we didn't get through the rough times on
salt fish alone.

(Housewife, born 1898)

Community Women

Stephenville women conceived life as a cyclical process and
such notions as individual freedom (or 'women's rights') were foreign
to them. They were daughters and usually mothers, always tied to
some household, whether married, spinstered or widowed. Their
lives were tightly interwoven with significant others. They lived on
the edge of the modern world familiar only to their male kin. All
this is not to say that these women did not experience change. In
fact, their lives were continuously in flux. There was the

175

Margaret Kelly and one-year-old child, Gambo, Newfoundland, circa 1945.

A mother and her daughter, Stephenville, Newfoundland.

precariousness of the community economy, and there were the rhythms of the seasons, of birth, puberty, marriage, menopause and old age. They lived each day at a time, investing their hopes for change in their children and getting by on the friendship and support they freely gave each other.

> You were a respected woman if you worked hard and tended to the family and had a brood of youngsters. It was your assigned lot in life as a woman. Work and having babies after marriage was all we had, except [for] each other.
>
> (Housewife, born 1898)

While the Newfoundland census for the period under examination records a variety of males "gainfully occupied" (farmers, fishermen, mechanics, loggers, sawmill operators, miners, factory workers and fish curers, as well as "professionals" such as civil servants and teachers),[10] the only recorded "gainfully occupied" females are a small number of fish curers (forty-eight in 1911, eighteen in 1921). The sole profession mentioned is teaching, "gainfully occupying" one to three females. No women are recorded as otherwise employed, although my interviewees frequently mentioned the midwife, who sometimes received money for her services. They also spoke of a woman apprenticed by the government to the local priest, eventually performing the duties of post office mistress (while doubling as the priest's domestic help). All other women, according to the census, were "homemakers," without salary or wage. This societal definition of women as "homemakers" included all single women keeping house for their male kin, single mothers living within their fathers' households, re-adopted widowed daughters and so forth--in addition, of course, to the married women. It is important to note that throughout this period the yield of agricultural and animal products was consistently high. In attempting to understand women's subordination to men two interconnected spheres must be examined in which women lacked effective control: sexuality and procreation, as well as the institution of marriage.

Sexuality and Marriage

The Stephenville Catholic hierarchy strongly believed that a woman should be "protected" by a man--either by a father, a husband, a male relative, or at least by the local priest. Marriage was the highest goal for woman, other than entering the convent. Since prior to World War II, few labouring families had sufficient financial resources to send a daughter to a convent (or a male to a seminary), the option of "spiritual marriage" to the Church was closed to Stephenville women.

My female interviewees point out that, according to the

religious orthodoxy of the time, "good women" were supposed to be asexual and virtuous and to suffer through the sex act without moving as much as a muscle. While enjoying sex was seen as a vice in the case of women, it was regarded as a "natural" male urge assigned to men by nature. Not surprisingly, sex was frequently regarded as yet another form of labour expected of married females, along with domestic work, church work, garden work, and so forth. When a woman married and set up house with a man, she often did so not out of love but in order to achieve the status of a legitimate mother.

> Women were told that "once you find some man to take you to be his wife, you made your bed and now you lay in it." Well, let me tell you this much, the women from around here didn't have any soft beds to choose from. As a single girl, sex and your period were dirty and evil, not proper discussion for 'virgin' ears. I was fourteen when I started comin' around, you know, when a girl starts changing. I recall my mother saying that the best years of any woman's life were before the change.
>
> (Housewife, born 1900)

Stephenville women, during this period, had virtually no way of disassociating pregnancy from sexuality. Unexpected pregnancy was a constant worry for both married and non-married women. If a single woman's lover were a Catholic boy willing to marry her, then her status remained intact. But if he were not Catholic, perhaps someone she had met through her lumberjack brothers at the fall harvest or a traveller en route elsewhere, marriage was virtually impossible, even if he were willing.

> I had my only child when I was seventeen. I wasn't married, you know. My little child, she only lived a month and two days. It was probably the best for the both of us. Now I really wanted to marry that fellow. But I was scared to death 'cause he was a 'black' Protestant. Father and the priest went wild. I got the strap for my sin and then had to do nine months of penance at Sunday mass. It was a mortal sin, my dear, the blackest sin of all. For the rest of my life I had to live with it. After that, I just kept away from men.
>
> (Single mother, born 1916)

In brief, whichever direction these women turned, their hands were tied. Since mixed marriages were unheard of then, such a pregnant woman was marked for life.[11] However, because marriage was economically crucial for achieving the social status 'woman', and also because it was difficult to meet a non-kin male since a woman was usually tied to the community, she was forced to take her chances--at a time when there was no effective birth control. Nor was medically safe abortion available. This situation placed single women in a very vulnerable position:

> Sometimes my brothers would come back home with a bunch of lumberjacks they met in the woods and have a lot to drink and brag about. When a fellow comes out of the lumberwoods after living in bunk houses with perhaps five hundred to a thousand men and blackarding[12] and gambling their spare time away, you can well imagine the state their minds and body was in when we laid eyes on them. All they wanted to do is drink and party and have someone to run after them. And, imagine, they were about the only fellows you had to choose from for a husband. A girl had to be real careful, 'cause once she got in trouble, her life was done for.
>
> (Spinster, born 1910)

A young girl finding herself pregnant, with an extremely strict father to deal with and the priest to face (if her lover were a Catholic and not a close relative), experienced a genuine trauma. Nevertheless, there was community pressure on the man to marry her. If he chose to support the child financially, however, no further social pressure was applied.

> Fellows used to say, "If you don't give in to me, I'll leave you 'cause there's lots more of your kind dying to grab hold to a husband around here." These fellows were just out for themselves and a bit of fun. Well, it wasn't much to laugh about being left in trouble with a bad name and a bastard child on the way. Sometimes the fellow would sincerely promise to marry you if you let him get close and then, after he had his bit, he'd clear out to the woods or God knows where. They were always trying to corner you.
>
> (Housewife, born 1903)

Some women caught in such circumstances without a 'legitimate' male partner tried drastic and occasionally fatal measures.

> I sometimes heard tell of some girls taking stomach salts or jumping from the loft and things like that. Poor things, they didn't have it very easy. I heard talk of one who took the scissors to herself. It's no wonder, 'cause back in those times you got punished some bad for your misdeed. You had to go up to the front of the altar at Sunday mass and to penance before the entire congregation. You were an utter disgrace and your poor child, after all that, had to suffer. For without a real

father, it had to go without being baptized, and the
government would make note in the books that it was not
normal, and for the rest of its days it was labelled. For
sure, this wasn't right. I think that the Church and most
of the old men were too strict with the womenfolk.

(Midwife, born 1889)

Stephenville women who 'chose' to avoid men entirely were at
least able to avoid the trauma associated with unwed motherhood.
"Spinsterhood," however, as one woman put it, "was no bed of roses
either." A society which measured women's status according to the
frequency of her pregnancies within marriage gave little praise to a
woman who did not make her biology her destiny. Such a woman
was labelled an "old maid" and remained a servant and perpetual
minor in her parents' house, despite her age, life experience and
productive labour. Even the married women tended to view her as
somehow "abnormal" since she did not mother children.

As mentioned above, the unavailability of eligible partners
was a problem for both sexes. The lack of opportunity for women to
leave their community, however, made their situation even more
desperate than it was for their male counterparts. By the late
1930s, according to one respondent:

There was no one in Stephenville for a girl to marry.
Before the war came, things were so bad that a girl
couldn't get married unless she ended up marrying her
first or second cousin. We were all really blood relatives.
But what were we all to do? Everyone was a streak of
relations.

(Widow, born 1909)

Marriage, then, while wanted by most women, also meant
sacrifice. As an institution, it was full of contradictions. But the
women who 'escaped' marriage had trials of their own to endure.
And neither could avoid productive labour without monetary
reward.

Women's Productive Labour

Work--both inside the household and on the family farm--was
the common experience of all women. Childhood freedom frequently
ended as early as age eight or nine. Young girls, like their male
siblings, might leave school after the second or third grade.[13] Prior
to World War II, few finished high school. As one female
interviewee put it, "by the time you were up to your mother's apron
pocket, you were ready for hard work." While boys were off with
their male kin, every morning at dawn mothers and daughters were
already working, no matter what season.

A young girl was like an apprentice or helper to her mother or big sister. I suppose it was a good practice for when we got married and had babies of our own. I had to stand on a chair to do the first batch of dishes I washed. We made butter with a hand churn, baked lovely biscuits and molasses buns for the crowd and washed with a scrubbing board. All this before you were perhaps nine years of age.

(Spinster, born 1910)

Without male support, the women took over the 'hard' work, in addition to the other activities of their sex. They planted seeds, weeded, doctored animals, put the cattle out to pasture, gathered driftwood at the shore, thus keeping the entire family and farm operating until the men returned.

We knew all about the winds and the sea. We could tell the time by the sun and the weather by the moon. We knew just where to find the best berries and wild plants. Two women could break forty gallons of tame strawberries in a hard day's work. We were not easy. There was no slacking about.

(Housewife, born 1900)

Inside the household there was constant activity: a diaper to change, a cup of tea for grandpa, a bandage for an injured soul, and so on. It was only after the children and old folks had gone to bed and the dishes were washed that these women took out their looms and spinning wheels to begin their other activities, such as making clothes and quilts:

My dear, we made it all. We'd soften up brinebags and make them into diapers. I was at the loom by the age of twelve. My mother was some marvelous spinner. We also used a sewing machine, the kind with the pedal. We would rip out a worn pair of trousers for a pattern. It was all rough, but real warm. We used to make lovely crochet and needlework and knit sweaters with our own homespun wool. Some of it we donated to the Church. The merchant would trade for staples only when we were in dire straits.

(Midwife, born 1889)

The women called these occasions of communal craft production "frolics" or "bees" (the male equivalents were the communal construction of a barn or house). Their productive labour during these spare moments in their daily cycle, as well as the food they collected and harvested, provided many of the basic necessities of survival. The use value of the things they produced or

Margaret Kelly, husband and three children, Gambo, Newfoundland, circa 1945.

Family picnic, Stephenville, Newfoundland.

collected cannot be overemphasized, even if the merchant assigned little exchange value to them. As one woman put it, "we had no commodities back then. What we made by hand wasn't worth a dime outside the family. Still, without all of it, we wouldn't be here today." In brief, these women's reproductive and productive lives consisted of endless series of tasks during each day, year, their lifetime. From childhood onwards they were tied to the soil, the household, the laws of the community, and ultimately to the biological rhythms of their bodies.

Yet this is not to say that their male kin did not face hardships as well. Wage labour forced the men to live for long periods outside their community. This sharp sexual division of labour often had devastating effects on family life.[14] Under the impact of the dual stresses of separation and poverty, marriage and families were seldom sustained by bonds of intimacy or love. When the men returned to their families, they usually desired a rest from the hardships of communal living. And their still relatively traditional society, based as it was on the laws of the Church, which justified women's subordination, was a welcome break from the alien world where they were periodically forced to sell their labour. The community and the extended family provided these men with emotional security and a means of livelihood during periods of unemployment. At home they had some real power: power over women. Within the family they could set down rules and demand to be served. And the community elders, especially the priest and the aging family patriarchs, sanctioned such dominance of men over women.

My female informants were rather sober in their assessment of their relationships with men. They have few romantic reminiscences, and are usually quick to state that they would never wish their kind of marriage or their own father-daughter relationship on anyone else. Many felt "runned to death" as the servants of men rather than seeing themselves as their equals.

There were, nevertheless, ways for women to find at least some limited degree of satisfaction or even happiness. Since their primary role was to reproduce and to maintain the kin group, and since their husbands, brothers and fathers were mostly working-class men spending much of their time away from home, these Stephenville women sought out the company of other women. It is, therefore, important to examine this hidden side of their lives, left out of the records of the past, for it was precisely in their own restricted sphere that these women made sense of the forces they could not change. In their 'separate' world of frolics, spinning bees, childbirth, doctoring and death, they were a "power to be reckoned with."

The Safety Net of Women's Experience

In Stephenville prior to 1940, it was virtually impossible to obtain medical attention. One doctor periodically visited rural people and examined them for signs of an epidemic, or he came upon the request of a merchant family who could afford to pay for his services. The closest hospital (after 1933) was more than twenty miles away and connected by an often impassable gravel road. Consequently, few women left home during childbirth. The members of the community made do with herbal medicines and the aid of the local midwife, who was important to every person's health and who was well respected, sometimes even loved.

> We usen't to bother with the company doctor. I had the midwife, Auntie Elizabeth, for all my babies. There was no limit to the things she used to handle--curing measles and yellow jaundice with a brew made from sheep dung; sour-duck seeds for anybody with hay fever; and yellow root for the cramps. She was so kind and sweet to us all.
>
> (Housewife, born 1910)

These women had never heard of invalidism. Nor had they heard of gynaecology and obstetrics. Urban women, especially of the upper classes, might have been told by (male) medical professionals that "the uterus was the real heart of woman, from which all her other parts sprung," that "women by *nature* were essentially frail, weak and nervous creatures whose main purpose in life was to have sons as heirs," or that they would continuously experience "bouts of illness caused by their wombs."[15] Stephenville women, in contrast, were "layin-in" nearly every year for eleven days or so under the watchful eye of the midwife, returning to their work as soon as humanly possible.

> Don't worry, we were some tough. We would be down at the beach or in the garden until we went into labour. Having babies was only one part of it. It never kept me bedridden for long.
>
> (Widow, born 1901)

These women did not for long remain confined within the narrow walls of their homes. They saw family as interrelated spheres of production, reproduction, and consumption, as a part of the non-market economy in which they exchanged the goods they had made and the medical skills they had learned from each other. They cared for each other's children during sickness and childbirth, and they provided friendship during difficult times.

> I first learned to doctor the women and others in the village from my dear mother. I learned to give a newborn

a steeped brew from weeds--caraway seeds perhaps. I was always present during birth, consoling and guiding my expectant mother. All the women used to help out: some cooked; others kept house; others washed and fed the kids. Together we were a strong team.

(Midwife, born 1889)

The midwife or "granny," as she was called, like all the other women, had little contact with medical professionals. She possessed her own common sense knowledge about the human body. She saw childbirth as one among many changes in a woman's life, as part of a continuous life process of reproductive moments. Pregnancy and menopause were not diseases but natural and inevitable events in the lives of women. Knowledge about the granny's own body rhythms complemented the advice she had received from the midwife whom she had succeeded. She had no ambition to become a professional health care worker but merely aspired to guide the community members along a path of well-being.

I always made my expectant mothers stay confined for ten days. That was my only rule. After childbirth, I often gave them boiled juniper or senna tea. A warm drink did wonders. I did lose some babies, but not very many, and few mothers. The women used to trust me. Of course, I didn't have any fancy doctor instruments for plucking out babies. But my homemade remedies served the purpose most of time.

(Midwife, born 1889)

Although ignorant of modern obstetrics and without access to medical back-up services, the grannies nevertheless succeeded in gaining the respect of most community members, not least because they were in many ways companions who shared their knowledge rather than professionals in positions of power vis-à-vis their clients. During the evenings, sitting in the kitchen of an expectant mother while spinning, weaving, or knitting with a group of neighbouring women, the granny tended the woman in labour without dominating her or speeding up the birth process. She was not, like professionals,[16] "a cut above the average folk;" she received no government payment, and often even her nominal five to ten dollar fee was replaced by a piece of woven cloth or some vegetables, or payment was postponed to some later date. She performed other health care activities in a similar manner: pulling teeth, mending broken bones, nursing colds, and even doctoring the villagers' animals. During this period, Stephenville would have indeed hardly managed without her non-wage labour.

Many other productive activities--such as weaving, spinning, carding or gathering--were performed by these women in a similarly informal manner, frequently out of sheer economic necessity.

During their frolics at home, along the seashore or in the garden, they could talk about their problems, share intimacies and laugh a little, while teaching their daughters future skills.

> At our matting and spinning bees we used to talk about it all. We would complain about the merchant and often about the priest as well. We also had our little laughs. One woman swore that every time her husband hung his pants on the bed post, she ended up pregnant again. It eased the hardships, having each other.
>
> (Housewife, born 1902)

In both the productive and reproductive areas of women's lives, the joys were frequently closely tied to the pains. Poverty and family life were burdens which nevertheless did not prevent frequent moments of enjoyment. Little pleasures, such as seeing the first plants break the soil in the early summer, giving their kinfolk a handmade quilt and, of course, giving birth, *were* concrete satisfactions, even if these women were forced to contend with a subordinate position in the presence of their male relatives and of the religious authorities. However, even where women achieved independence in some spheres of work (for example, as midwife, gardener or weaver), this neither led to equality within the family during the off-seasons when the sexes mixed nor to their right to reformulate the rules of the Church or of the traditional law which formally subordinated them to men.

Conclusion

I have tried to show that the lives of rural women are worth examining. Studies of the relationship between the sexes in Western pre-modern societies may well contribute to the badly needed substantiation of present generalizations concerning gender hierarchies.

The concept of 'motherhood' has had a long, though hidden, career. Women, as procreators, have often been rendered subordinate, both by their biology and by patriarchal social systems. This is well demonstrated by the community in which I conducted my interviews. There, as elsewhere, mothering has involved ambiguous and even contradictory features: on the one hand, we confront a relatively isolated community with a limited degree of economic development, in which most people led an existence of toil, in which women had to survive for long periods without the presence and support of their male kin, and certainly without the amenities now taken for granted in welfare states. On the other hand, poverty and a sharp sexual division of labour paradoxically also permitted a kind of independence which women now frequently lack in modern suburban communities. Furthermore, the knowledge shared by the midwife and the other women was of crucial importance for their physical and emotional well-being (and indeed for the health of all community members), constituting a means of coping with daily life and contributing to a network of skills and intimacies from which men were excluded. In brief, pre-modern motherhood, while clearly involving economic exploitation and patriarchal domination, was rarely just misery; for rural mothers their sorrows were balanced by genuine joys, both of which joined them together in sisterhood.

Notes

[1]For an examination of the "domestic labour debate," see Jean Gardiner, "Women's Domestic Labour," *New Left Review* 89 (January/February 1975), 47-58; Margaret Coulson, Bianka Magas and Hilary Wainwright, "The Housewife and Her Labour Under Capitalism--A Critique," *New Left Review* 89 (January/February 1975), 59-71. Also see Margrit Eichler, "Women's Unpaid Labour," *Atlantis* 3, 29, pt. II (Spring 1978), 52-61, and Bonnie Fox, ed., *Hidden in the Household: Women's Domestic Labour Under Capitalism* (Toronto: The Women's Press, 1980).

[2]For an account of women's history "in the cracks," as Elise Boulding puts it, see her *The Underside of History* (Boulder, Colorado: Westview Press, 1976); see also Gerda Lerner, "Placing Women in History: A 1975 Perspective," in Berenice Carroll, ed., *Liberating Women's History: Theoretical and Critical Essays* (Urbana: University of Illinois Press, 1975), pp. 357-67.

[3]Concerning economic and industrial change and its impact on working women, see, in particular, Louise A. Tilly and Joan W. Scott, *Women, Work and Family* (New York: Holt, Rinehart and Winston, 1978). Concerning women's power positions, see Mary Beard, *Woman as Force in History* (New York: The Macmillan Company, 1946) and Michèle Barrett, *Women's Oppression Today* (London: Verso, 1980).

[4]Ruth Pierson and Alison Prentice argue that:

> The critical task of feminism. . .is to examine the structures of women's inequality. When and where has systematic subordination of women existed? What have been the social, economic and political mechanisms of women's oppression? [However], because an exclusive preoccupation with these mechanisms could lead to a distorting and purely negative picture of women as victims, it is equally a task of feminism to reclaim, elucidate and re-evaluate the positive aspects of women's experience in the present and the past.

See Ruth Pierson and Alison Prentice, "Feminism and the Writing and Teaching of History," *Atlantis* 7, 2 (Spring 1982), 38.

[5]For an analysis of giving birth and rearing children, see

Adrienne Rich, *Of Woman Born* (New York: W. W. Norton & Company, 1976) and Jessie Bernard, *Women, Wives and Mothers: Values and Options* (Chicago: Aldine Publishing Co., 1975).

[6]For a general history of social and economic conditions in other areas of Newfoundland, see James Faris, *Cat Harbour: A Newfoundland Fishing Settlement* (St. John's: Institute of Social and Economic Research, Memorial University, 1966); David Alexander, "Development and Dependence in Newfoundland, 1880-1970," *Acadiensis* 4, 1 (1974). There have been several recent attempts to correct and broaden our understanding of women's lives in Newfoundland, especially Ellen Antler, "Women's Work in Newfoundland Fishing Families," *Atlantis* 2, 2, pt. II (Spring 1977), 106-13. See also Hilda Chalk Murray, *More Than 50%: Woman's Life in a Newfoundland Outport 1900-1950* (St. John's: Breakwater Books, 1979).

[7]See John Berger and Jean Mohr, *Seventh Man* (London: Writers and Readers, 1972); Marilyn Porter, "Worlds Apart: The Class Consciousness of Working Class Women," *Women's Studies International Quarterly* 1, 1 (1978); Carol Stack, *All Our Kin* (New York: Harper and Row, 1974).

[8]As Carroll Smith-Rosenberg notes, however, such a division of women and men is hardly atypical:

> In hundreds of cultures around the world and across time, women have lived in highly sex-segregated communities; spending their time with other women; developing female rituals and networks. . . .This is true among Tiwi aborigines, Victorian ladies, Nazi women, and working-class women in London in the 1960s.

Carroll Smith-Rosenberg, "Politics and Culture in Women's History," *Feminist Studies* 6, 1 (Spring 1980), 61.

[9]At this time, a pulp and paper mill opened in the nearby town of Corner Brook, employing males from the surrounding areas to cut logs to supply the mill. This work was seasonal in nature, generally occurring in the late fall and winter months. The men had to supply their own transportation and tools, and their room, board and doctor bills were subtracted from their earnings. Payment was made by the cord of wood cut (between 1-2 dollars per cord was the norm). According to my interviewees, the average worker was lucky to make a dollar a day and often less when cutting in areas of slow tree growth or when the demand for logs was low.

[10]*Census of Newfoundland*, 1901, 1911, 1921, 1935. The population of Stephenville showed a gradual increase during this period, from 643 to 926 persons. It was roughly equally divided by sex. Most families owned their own dwellings, which housed on the average six persons. Twice as many females were widowed as males, although the percentage was low for both sexes. While in

1901 approximately one-fifth of the adult population over 20 years remained single, in 1911 and 1921 the figure was approximately one-third and by 1935 it had risen to nearly fifty per cent. Given that the community during this period was virtually totally Catholic, it is not surprising that divorce and separation appear in the census only once--in 1921 when two such persons were recorded.

[11]Stephenville males did not have to confront such a problem, even when they fathered a child with a non-Catholic woman, since they did not reside in the same community as the mother-to-be. In fact, the religious elite and family patriarchs of their own community were often totally unaware of such 'illegitimate offspring'.

[12]In the Newfoundland dialect of the French Shore (west coast of the island), "blackarding" means cursing or using 'dirty' words.

[13]Between 1900 and 1920, almost two-thirds of the population between ages five and fifteen were *not* in school, while after this time up to 1940 the reverse was the norm. See *Census of Newfoundland*, 1901-11, 1921, 1935.

[14]Ethnographics of blue-collar marriages highlight similar relationships between spouses as a result of a sharp sexual division of labour. See M. Komarovsky, *Blue Collar Marriage* (New York: Vintage Books, 1962); Lillian Breslow Rubin, *Worlds of Pain: Life in the Working-Class Family* (New York: Basic Books, 1976). For a fictionalized account of the strong negative emotions within a Newfoundland family, see P. Janes, *House of Hate* (Toronto: McClelland and Stewart, 1970).

[15]See Barbara Ehrenreich and Deirdre English, *For Her Own Good: 150 Years of the Experts' Advice to Women* (Garden City, New York: Anchor Press/Doubleday, 1978); C. Smith-Rosenberg, "Puberty to Menopause: The Cycle of Femininity in Nineteenth-Century America," *Feminist Studies* 1, 3-4 (Winter/Spring 1973), 58-72.

[16]The same kind of non-professional approach was also taken by the midwife and by the village women in regard to other reproductive moments in their lives, such as menstruation and menopause. For a cogent description of the non-medical understanding of menopause in another Newfoundland community, see Dona Lee Davis, *Blood and Nerves: An Ethnographic Focus on Menopause* (St. John's: Memorial University of Newfoundland, Institute of Social and Economic Research, 1983). For a discussion of communal and professional types of control, see T. Johnson, *Professions and Power* (London: Macmillan Press, 1972).

Chapter Ten

EDUCATING MOTHERS: GOVERNMENT ADVICE FOR
WOMEN IN THE INTER-WAR YEARS*

Katherine Arnup

As any woman who has recently given birth can testify, a new
mother is confronted by a virtual flood of information on aspects of
motherhood ranging from natural childbirth and breastfeeding to
toilet training and temper tantrums. An examination of the
historical record reveals, however, that this 'information explosion'
is by no means a recent development. In Canada, departments of
health have been producing and distributing pamphlets for mothers
since the early decades of this century. In this chapter, I will
examine advice literature developed for mothers by various levels of
government during the inter-war years, situating these texts within
their historical context, analyzing their content, and suggesting the
implications which they may have had for the daily lives of women.

Between 1900 and 1920, concern developed in Canada, as in
Britain, the United States and elsewhere, regarding the question of
infant mortality. Despite an improvement in the health of the
general population as a result of developments in medical
technology and sanitation, and discoveries in the fields of
bacteriology and immunology, infant mortality rates continued to
soar. In 1901, in the city of Toronto, for example, 160 of every
thousand babies died before reaching the age of one.[1] Montreal
claimed the highest infant mortality rate in North America, as one
in every three babies died before reaching its first birthday.[2]
Alarmed at these statistics, government officials throughout the
western world turned their attention to the health of their nations'
children.

In Britain, the issue of infant mortality came to the fore when
recruitment for the Boer War revealed the poor quality of the

*I wish to thank Susan Genge, Ruth Pierson, and my Women's History Group
for their comments on this paper. An earlier version of this paper was presented
at the Annual Meeting of the Canadian Sociology and Anthropology Association in
Winnipeg, June 1986.

nation's health. As many as a third of the possible recruits were rejected as unfit for military service, thus exposing, in Anna Davin's words, "the poor health of the working class in Britain, from which were drawn both soldiers and sailors to defend the empire, and workers to produce goods with which to dominate the world economically." Furthermore, Britain's poor showing in that war "had dramatized fears of national inadequacy."[3]

Officials in Canada developed a similar appreciation of the significance of the soaring rates of infant deaths. Dr. Helen MacMurchy,[4] a key figure in the infant welfare movement in Canada, explained:

> We are only now discovering that Empires and States are built up of babies. Cities are dependent for their continuance on babies. Armies are recruited only if and when we have cared for our babies.[5]

Recruitment for military service during World War I had revealed the poor quality of the health of Canadian men, as a substantial proportion of potential recruits were rejected on the basis of ill health. That fact, compounded by the staggering losses of the Great War, the steadily declining birth rate among the population of British stock, and high rates of immigration, led to widespread fears of "race suicide."[6] Many reformers and government officials believed that, without drastic measures, the future of the nation--the white Imperial Nation--was at risk. To counteract these trends, they "sought the production of healthy Canadian babies."[7]

Although a variety of voluntary organizations became involved in the issue of infant mortality in Canada, the major impetus was provided by the rapidly developing public health bureaucracy. Between 1900 and 1920, an elaborate system of institutionalized health care developed at all levels of government.[8] Departments of health, each with its own division responsible for child welfare, were set up to confront the problems of poor national health. In Toronto, the Division of Public Health Nurses was created in February 1914. The Division of Child Hygiene was formed in June of that year. In Ontario, the Bureau of Child Welfare was established in October 1916 under the jurisdiction of the Provincial Board of Health. In 1919, that board was transferred to the Minister of Labour and Health and several new divisions were created, including Public Health Education, Maternal and Child Hygiene, and Public Health Nursing. Finally, in 1919, under pressure from reform elements including the National Council of Women, the Federal Department of Health was formed. The Division of Child Welfare was the first division to be established, with its chief, Dr. Helen MacMurchy, being appointed on 10 April 1920.

Within each of these new divisions, experts in the field of

public health were prominent. These doctors, nurses, and reformers believed fervently in the value of preventive medicine, arguing that most infant deaths could be prevented.[9] Infant welfare workers acknowledged that many factors, including poverty, overcrowding, and malnutrition, contributed to the problem of infant mortality. In looking for solutions, however, they focussed almost exclusively upon mothers, arguing, as MacMurchy did, that "It is through the mother that infant mortality can be prevented."[10]

The reason for this emphasis lay in the special role that infant welfare experts assigned to breastfeeding. MacMurchy, for example, stated:

> One thing we know about Infant Mortality. If the baby is nursed by its mother, the chances are great that it will live. If the baby is fed in any other way, the chances are great that it will die.[11]

"Mother's milk," she concluded, "is the only really safe food for baby."[12] In an age before pasteurization of milk and the widespread availability of sterilized baby formula, breastfeeding was undoubtedly the safest method of infant feeding. The problem was not the encouragement of breastfeeding as such but the focus on this solution to the exclusion of all other alternatives.[13] Women were to be taught the value of nursing and to be encouraged to set aside anything--be it work in the paid labour force or other family responsibilities--that interfered with that enterprise.

To improve the quality of child health, child welfare workers believed that women had to be educated to the tasks of motherhood. As Jane Lewis has documented for Britain, "Infant welfare services were strictly educational; health visitors and infant welfare clinics were not permitted to offer medical treatment and confined themselves to instructing mothers in infant hygiene."[14] In a parallel development in Canada, governments and voluntary organizations alike concentrated on educational campaigns designed to teach women to be 'proper' mothers.[15]

In justifying the need for maternal education, Helen MacMurchy herself argued that women could not fairly be blamed for their 'ignorance'. She explained:

> We expect the ideal mother to know everything by instinct, without giving her any chance to learn. We might much better expect her to read by instinct, for the alphabet can always be found not far away. We teach reading, and we leave parenthood to come by chance. It does not so come, and there is great need that our people, most of whom are to be parents, should be educated with this great privilege and responsibility and power in view.[16]

Educating women for motherhood became the theme of much of the work in child welfare in Canada during the early decades of this century.[17] Through films, radio talks, lectures, and advice clinics, and especially through the production of pamphlets at a staggering rate, officials at all levels of government sought to teach women the skills of 'mothercraft'.[18]

Government agencies produced a tremendous volume of literature during the twenties and thirties.[19] The initial publication produced by the federal government's Division of Child Welfare was *The Canadian Mother's Book*, received from the printer on 3 March 1921, and reaching a distribution figure of 150,000 by the end of its first year. A publication that began at some 50 pages and eventually expanded to nearly 250, *The Canadian Mother's Book* went into six editions, and approximately 800,000 copies had been distributed to mothers across Canada by the time the Division was disbanded in 1933.[20]

The Division of Child Welfare was only one of several branches of government producing advice literature during this period. In March, 1917, the Ontario Board of Health published *The Baby*. Within two years, nearly 25,000 copies of that pamphlet had been distributed to mothers across the province.[21] Toronto's Division of Child Hygiene also prepared pamphlets on pre-natal and infant care,[22] which were available at no cost and could be obtained at well baby clinics or from the visiting public health nurse.

These publications on infant and pre-natal care were in high demand throughout the early decades of this century. As MacMurchy was to remark in an article she wrote about the Division's work: "No one will ever convince the Division of Child Welfare that mothers do not want to learn. Thousands of mothers' letters are on file to prove the contrary."[23] Women (and their husbands, friends, mothers, and sisters) wrote to all levels of government requesting copies of the publications. In light of the staggering rates of infant and child death it is not surprising that mothers did want to learn. The question is, what were they being taught? And what implications might these lessons have had for their daily lives as mothers?

Pre-natal Care and the Medical Profession

Throughout all the publications of the period, one finds evidence of the increasing medicalization of pregnancy, childbirth, and child rearing. From the moment a woman first thought that she might be pregnant, and throughout her pregnancy, confinement, and her child's early years, a mother was to consult her doctor and follow his advice. Women were cautioned to ignore traditional sources of information and support, such as family members or friends, and to follow instead the 'modern' methods of 'scientific' child rearing advocated in the government health publications.

"The husband should accompany his wife on her visit to the doctor, at the beginning of her pregnancy, and obtain first-hand information." Ernest Couture, *The Canadian Mother and Child* (Ottawa: Department of Pensions and National Health, Division of Child and Maternal Hygiene, 1940), p. 35. Photograph by Eugene Michael Finn, C.G.M.P.B. (NFB), December

Source: National Archives of Canada, PA-163733

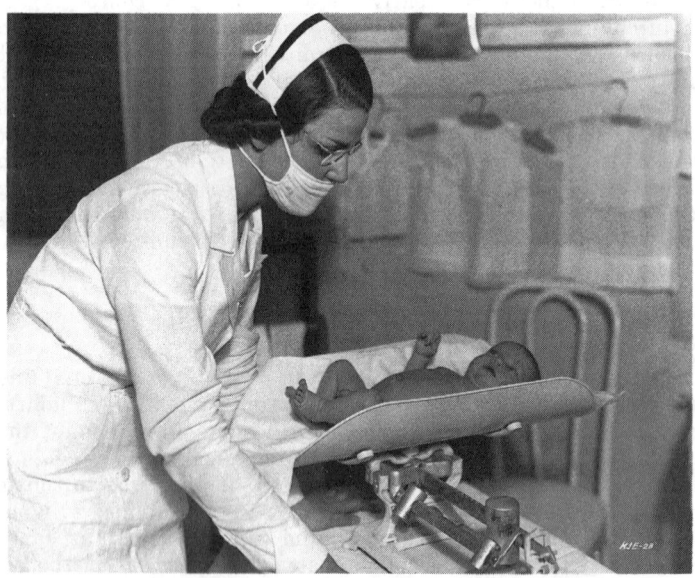

"Nurse weighing unidentified baby," Ottawa, Ontario, December 1939, photography by Eugene Michael Finn, C.G.M.P.B. (NFB), for possible use in *The Canadian Mother and Child*.

Source: National Archives of Canada, PA-163913

One of the key recommendations to emerge from the infant welfare movement was that pregnant women should be provided with early and sustained pre-natal care from a doctor. All of the government publications insisted that the mother obtain the services of a physician as early as possible during her pregnancy. *The Baby* advised that "The mother should, on the slightest suspicion of pregnancy, consult the best physician available, put herself under his direction and be guided by his advice."[24]

Although the publications offered a variety of instructions concerning pre-natal care, including the importance of diet, sleep (eight to ten hours a day plus two rests during the day!), and freedom from worry ("don't be down-hearted--there is no reason you should be. Don't be frightened. Cheer up."),[25] the single most important (and most oft repeated) 'order' was to consult the doctor. "If there is anything wrong with you at all . . . ask the Doctor about it at once," MacMurchy advised, reassuring the mother that "there is always something the Doctor can do to make you better. That is what a Doctor is for."[26]

If a woman did not already have a family doctor, then MacMurchy advised her to ask friends--"sensible, trustworthy people"[27]--to recommend a physician. "Consider this matter of choosing a doctor carefully,"[28] she cautioned. "Having found a good Doctor, you will then have good medical advice and supervision all through your pregnancy."[29] Such a promise could only be fulfilled, of course, if the doctor's orders were strictly observed. Therefore, MacMurchy admonished women: "Do what the Doctor tells you."[30]

Lest anyone fear that the proliferation of government publications might encroach upon the doctor's domain, the authors of Toronto's publication were quick to set the record straight. They wrote, "The advice given in this book is intended for all expectant mothers. It cannot replace the advice of the physician, which must vary with the conditions found upon examination."[31] Women were to derive their daily instructions from the health publications, but they were to consult their doctors to insure that they were implementing these rules in exactly the right way. The central role afforded to doctors in the literature of the period clearly reflects what Buckley has termed "doctors' determination to professionalize the practice of medicine by strengthening their pecuniary positions and their controls of medical care."[32] Through the supervision of pre-natal care and childbirth, doctors could be assured of a point of entry to families' future medical care.[33]

Although women were encouraged to consult their friends regarding the choice of a suitable doctor, the pamphlets contained explicit admonitions against taking the counsel of relatives or friends on other matters. When a woman experienced any of the so-called 'danger signs' of pregnancy, she was advised to consult her doctor at once. "Do not attempt to carry the responsibility yourself, and under no circumstances take the extreme risk of following the advice of a neighbour or friend."[34] Another pamphlet explained:

Neighbours and relatives may tell you much gossip in regard to the bearing of children which will tend to alarm you or misguide you. While in most cases the intention is good, the advice or alarming story is generally quite unsafe to follow or believe. Follow the advice of your physician and it will save you much worry.[35]

The doctor's role was to continue long after the period of confinement, as his terrain extended into matters of infant and child care ranging from breastfeeding and weaning to habit formation and temper tantrums. Indeed, by the 1930s a significant proportion of the doctor's time was taken up with care of the "normal child"[36] rather than with the treatment of disease at all![37]

Scientific Child Care

The way in which child health was to be preserved was through the implementation of the methods of what was termed 'scientific' child care. During the 1920s and 30s, the authors of advice literature attempted to transform the rearing of infants and young children from an affective, tradition-based relationship into a scientifically controlled and managed experiment. Whether they were successful is not at issue in this chapter.[38] That they did seek to promote a radically different style of child rearing--a style that broke with traditions previously passed from generation to generation--is clearly reflected in the advice literature.[39] Child rearing booklets in this period advocated regimentation and regularity in all dimensions of the child's development in an endeavour apparently to help the mother to turn her baby into what noted pediatrician Alan Brown approvingly termed "a 'little machine'."[40]

The key to scientific child rearing was the establishment of fixed times for every activity. From the minute the baby arrived home from the hospital (and indeed from the moment she or he[41] was born) a rigid timetable was to be set up. Charts indicating the correct time for feeding, sleeping, elimination, bathing, and even sunbathing were included in almost every pamphlet. Everything was to take place "by the clock."[42] Only then would the baby learn what was expected of her/him. MacMurchy explained the importance of this regimen as follows:

Keep Right to the Time-Table. It gives the baby a good start in life, with good habits of eating, sleeping, bathing, toilet and recreation. Watch him Live and Thrive. Regular habits are Best for the Baby.[43]

Training in habit formation was to begin early, as the following publication of the city of Toronto advised:

It is in the first few days that the baby's habits are formed. He is born without habits, and it is just as easy to form good ones as bad ones. He should be fed regularly, should be made comfortable and left in his bed to sleep.[44]

The authors stressed that the task of ensuring the development of good habits rested "largely with the mother or attendant."[45] In the 1933 edition of this publication, the authors delineated the lines of responsibility more sharply:

The responsibility for the formation of habits of conduct in the child of normal mentality rests entirely with the parents, both parents sharing equally in this responsibility. Neither the primary school, the playground, nor the Sunday school can be anything but contributing factors.[46]

Once acquired, bad habits could be extinguished, but that process would be a trying one for both baby and mother. One author warned, "If the baby has been allowed to form a bad habit, breaking it may mean several prolonged crying spells, or in some cases two or three wakeful nights."[47] This ordeal would be well worth the trouble, however, for the result would be a well-trained baby--one who "will acquire the habit of taking its food at regular intervals, by day and by night, and will go to sleep and waken at regular hours."[48] Such a baby "will thrive and be easy to care for,"[49] mothers were assured.

Every activity was to be carefully regimented and monitored. Toilet training, for example, was to begin by the second week in order to establish "regularity."[50] One author provided the following instructions for the mother:

To do this hold a small (warmed) basin or mug firmly in the lap. Place the baby above this with feet extended in the hands, back resting against the mother's breast. This should be done at regular times for stools, morning and afternoon. Place the baby on the basin at regular intervals when awake or before feeding for urination. Such a procedure will reduce the number of diapers.[51]

A later edition of *The Baby* postponed the onset of toilet training to three months. Nonetheless, the authors advised that the mother insert a soap stick into the rectum for the first two or three days of toilet training to insure that the baby perform at the appropriate moment.[52] Similar advice is provided in both the Toronto and federal publications.[53]

Getting the child to sleep was held to be no problem for the parents of the properly trained baby. One publication explained that "A well-trained infant will go to sleep when put in bed without

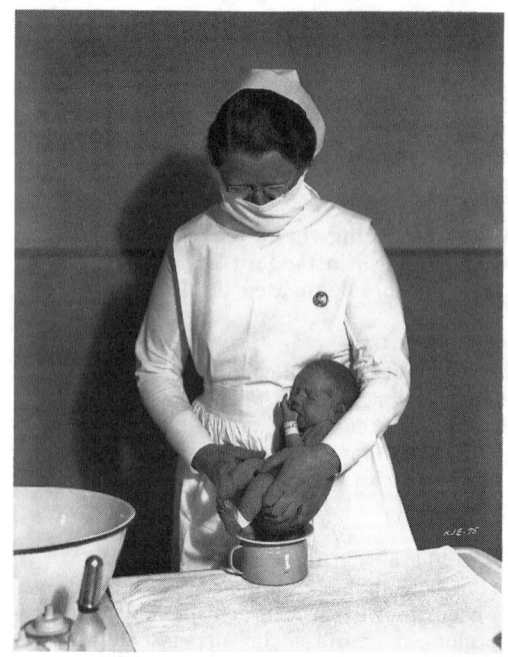

"With patience, a baby can be trained at an early age to regular toilet habits." Ernest Couture, *The Canadian Mother and Child* (Ottawa: Department of Pensions and National Health, Child and Maternal Hygiene Divison, 1940), p. 97. Photograph by Eugene Michael Finn, C.G.M.P.B. (NFB).

Source: National Archives of Canada, PA-803178

"Another good precaution is 'Never kiss the baby on the mouth'." Ernest Couture, *The Canadian Mother and Child* (Ottawa, Department of Pensions and National Health, Child and Maternal Hygiene Division, 1940), p. 186. Photograph by Eugene Michael Finn, C.G.M.P.B. (NFB).

Source: National Archives of Canada, PA-163914

being rocked, patted or sung to sleep. If a well child is fed, diapered and made comfortable, he will go to sleep at a regular hour."[54] Similarly, "the fear of going to bed in the dark" was considered to be not a common stage of childhood but "the result of bad training." Mothers were advised that "this habit should be corrected at the earliest possible moment,"[55] lest the child develop more serious sleeping problems.

The preferred method of extinguishing "bad" habits was to "let the baby cry it out." Crying was, in fact, lauded by some experts as a necessary and healthy "part of his daily exercise,"[56] so the mother did not need to worry about any harmful effects as a result of prolonged crying spells. Furthermore, some babies might cry in order to get attention.[57] Such cries were to be ignored to prevent the baby from acquiring "that most undesirable habit of temper tantrums the breaking of which taxes the strength and patience of the mother."[58]

As with sleeping, eliminating, and crying, feeding was to be strictly regimented. "Nursing times should be regular by the clock; regular feeding insures regular sleep," the Ontario Board of Health advised in the 1920 edition of *The Baby*.[59] To ensure that the baby kept to a strict schedule the mother was told to "Awaken the baby at nursing time and soon he will form the habit of waking regularly."[60] In almost the identical words, the Toronto publication offered the following advice:

> Feed regularly by the clock, even if the baby must be wakened. You will soon train him to awaken at the proper time. Regularity in habits not only makes the baby comfortable and keeps the milk secretion uniform, but lays an early foundation for regularity in other habits.[61]

Once weaned (and the advice on this subject could fill volumes) an equally rigid regimen was to be adopted. *The Baby* advised the mother that:

> strict rules regarding what it may and may not eat should be laid down when it first is weaned, and . . . these rules should never be broken, for only by unswerving adherence to such rules will children learn to eat what is put before them without begging and whining for those things which adults indulge in.[62]

There can be no doubt that the infant, once properly trained, was a much easier charge for her/his caretaker to manage. If training went as directed by these publications, the child ought to have become predictable, well behaved, and even tempered, requiring fewer diapers, fewer feedings, more sleep. Mothers were given licence to leave an obstreperous youngster to cry, knowing it was 'for its own good'.[63] At face value, perhaps, the 'scientific' child rearing advice may have benefited both mother and child. Two questions remain unanswered: did mothers follow this scientific advice? And if they did, at what cost? I will briefly consider these issues at the end of this chapter.

The Modern Mother

Once these publications had been written and distributed to homes across the nation, a crucial problem remained--how to ensure that the advice contained within them would be followed. The approach taken by most authors was two-pronged--the elevation of mothering to a national duty and the equation of motherhood with 'normal' womanhood. Once again, Helen MacMurchy waxed eloquent as she spoke of the glory of motherhood. MacMurchy likened mother's work to that of the soldiers during World War I, maintaining that mother, too, "is making the home where the love of Peace, Honour and Freedom grew."[64] "Children," she argued, "are the security of the home and the nation."[65] In bearing and rearing children, then, women were performing a "National Service."[66] Home for MacMurchy was to be a very special place:

> Mother's house is her castle, where all she loves are safe and happy. The Preacher has his Pulpit and the King has his Throne, but Mother does not envy them. In her own Kingdom she is all-powerful. Neither Church nor State could stand without the kind of home that Mother makes and manages.[67]

To encourage women to take up this challenge, authors of government advice literature articulated a version of the ideology of motherhood.[68] Not only was motherhood an important occupation, they argued, but it was one for which women were uniquely suited. Motherhood was, in the words of one author, "the greatest duty allotted to womankind."[69] It was, in essence, synonymous with 'normal womanhood'. In an early pamphlet MacMurchy proclaimed that "a woman's life is in her love. Love is her Native Air. The heart of the Mother is the innermost centre of the charmed circle of home."[70] Woman, then, was naturally suited to the self-sacrifice which motherhood necessarily entailed. In this final passage, MacMurchy stressed both the importance of this job and the life-long commitment it required:

> Being a mother is the highest of all professions and the most extensive of all undertakings. Nothing that she can know is useless to a mother. She can use it all. The mother reports for special duty about 250 days before the baby is born and she is never demobilised until she meets the Bearer of the Great Invitation. Mother, at ninety years, is still Mother.[71]

MacMurchy and her contemporaries did not, of course, create this conception of motherhood. Rather, they relied upon, and reinforced, the notion of separate spheres for men and women in order to ensure that women would take up and study the task of motherhood for which they were believed to be so perfectly inclined.[72]

Implications for Mothers

What did this literature mean for women trying to raise their children during the twenties and thirties? Because I have relied entirely upon the publications themselves, I am not in a position to state whether women did in fact follow this advice.[73] What I will do in this last section of the chapter is to suggest the impact which this advice *might* have had on women who attempted to put these ideas into practice.

One of the strongest warnings one encounters in this literature concerns the danger of worry. Time and time again, mother was exhorted to "cheer up."[74] A Toronto publication warned that "Worry and anxiety are always harmful, and especially so during pregnancy."[75] After the birth, worry was equally dangerous. MacMurchy warned that "Passion or temper or any other bad feeling should never enter the mother's room. Great emotion spoils the nursing milk and the milk secreted under such conditions makes the child ill."[76] Worry, then, was to be avoided at all costs, for it represented "one of the greatest enemies of health and happiness,"[77] a danger to mother and child alike.

But how were women to avoid worrying? For many women, deprived of their husbands' income through death or unemployment, supplying their families with the basic necessities of life was an incredible struggle. How was a mother-to-be to avoid worrying when she could scarcely afford to feed the children she already had? How could she help but worry abut where the food would come from to feed one more mouth? As one mother noted, in a letter to Prime Minister R. B. Bennett, "The worry of all these things is driving me mad."[78] Another mother, struggling to live on relief, told Bennett, "in the month of January they gave me $3.00 to live 6 persons I don't know how I could give my children three meals a day with so Small quantity. I tell you we are suffering . . ."[79]

Faced with drastically reduced levels of income, many women were forced to do without, rather than deprive their children of what little food remained. Mrs. R. Paddy described one such situation in her letter to R. B. Bennett:

> We are just one of many on relief and trying to keep our place without been starved out. Have a good 1/2 section not bad buildings and trying to get a start without any money and 5 children all small. Have been trying to send 3 to school and live on $10.00 a month relief for everything, medicine meat flour butter scribblers.

> Haven't had any milk for 3 months but will have 2 cows
> fresh in March some time. Am nursing a 10 month old
> baby and doing all the work cooking washing mending on
> bread and potatoes some days.[80]

In the face of such desperate poverty, a simple exhortation to 'relax' would merely have added a burden of guilt to the problems women already bore.

Other pieces of advice contained within these publications further compounded the situation. In the sections on pre-natal and post-natal care, women were told to rest at least once a day and to sleep a minimum of nine or ten hours a night.[81] Pregnant women were warned not to do any heavy work around the house--"Do not lift anything heavy nor do the washing, except a few little things. . . . Don't let me see you stretching up to hang out the clothes on the line. Somebody else must do that."[82]

Following the birth, women were ordered to remain in bed for at least two weeks. The new mother was to "Avoid all excitement and visitors for the first month after birth of baby" in order that she might "regain [her] strength more quickly and have a better chance to nourish [her] child."[83] "Household duties should be resumed gradually if this is at all possible, so that the full work of the house is not undertaken until about six weeks after the birth of the baby."[84] In light of the warning against visitors, and the widespread poverty that existed in Canada during the period when much of this literature was produced, it is difficult to imagine how women would have been able to put off doing the household chores until the sixth week post partum, if, in fact, they were able to postpone them at all!

The problem with much of this advice, then, is not so much that it was 'wrong' but rather that it was highly impractical for women living in Canada during the 1920s and 30s. This is revealed perhaps most clearly in MacMurchy's recommendations regarding household arrangements. In one publication, MacMurchy remarked in an almost off-handed manner: "You are not living in a flat are you? A flat is not a good place for a baby."[85] Elsewhere she consoled: "You haven't a bath-room? Never mind, you can do without until you can get it," adding parenthetically, "(get it as soon as you can.)"[86] No such sympathy is offered for the mother who intended to share a bed with her new baby. MacMurchy ordered the mother, "Never let the baby sleep with anybody!"[87] How was a mother to feel if she could not provide her baby with a room of its own, if poverty forced her to resume household chores as soon as the baby arrived, or worse, forced her to work outside the home? MacMurchy and the others warned her that she might kill her child. But what choice did she have?

Perhaps she might take some consolation from the words of Helen MacMurchy, which appeared directly after a long list of items one needed for baby:

Now don't feel badly for one minute if you cannot give
your baby all these things. If you nurse him and keep him
warm and clean and dry and happy you are a Good
Mother to him. You are doing fine.[88]

While these remarks might seem reassuring, they would appear to
be incompatible with virtually *all* the previous advice contained in
MacMurchy's publications. This last quotation illustrates what I consider to be a
fundamental contradiction which permeates all the literature I have
examined in this chapter--the contradiction between science and
nature. Throughout the texts, women were urged to view
pregnancy and birth as "natural" and "normal" processes.[89]
MacMurchy exhorted women to "Be Brave," reminding them that,

This is not some strange thing which is going to happen
to you. It is the right, natural and healthy thing for you,
just as it was for your own mother when you were born.[90]

Although women were deemed to be uniquely suited to
motherhood, they were warned against relying upon their "maternal
instincts" to guide them in the performance of their duties. Instead,
women were told to rely upon the medical profession, who would
teach them the rules of 'scientific' child rearing. Did it not create a
conflict for women to be told to rely on their instincts to lead them
into motherhood and to reject all such impulses once the child was
born? In this light, Veronica Strong-Boag has argued that child
care experts attacked "women's competence as nurturers of infants
and small children," thereby, perhaps, undermining "one customary
basis for public and self-esteem" for women. She concludes that,
while the experts were able to offer women the possibility of better
health for their children, "In exchange . . . women had to surrender
power over themselves and their offspring."[91] While MacMurchy
and the other authors of government literature may have exalted
motherhood in its ideal state, they may also have reduced women to
slavish followers of their detailed advice.[92]

The emphasis on 'scientific' child rearing may have posed a
further problem for women. The dictates of science demanded that
women reject the traditional ways of their family and friends in
favour of the 'modern' ideas of psychologists and doctors. In
previous times, women had relied upon the support network of
friends and family both to learn the skills involved in infant care
and to help with the household chores and with the older children
following a birth. Cut off from such assistance, to whom could
women turn for support or help in times of difficulty? What
conflicts might the reliance upon 'science' have created in families
that had traditionally sustained their members through life's major
transitions? Finally, what impact might this advice have had on women's

relationships with their children? Raised in an era that had encouraged affection and nurturance, women were now being told to avoid physical contact with their children. The young baby "should not be handled any more than is absolutely necessary."[93]

Kissing of young children was strictly forbidden, as it was believed to spread deadly germs.[94] Feeding "by the clock" frequently meant waiting an hour or more while baby "cried it out." John and Elizabeth Newson, among others, argue that "innumerable women made valiant efforts to stifle their natural desire to cuddle their babies and to feed them when they were hungry, or were racked with guilt and shame when they 'mawkishly' rocked the child or sentimentally eased his stomach pangs in the small hours with a contraband couple of ounces."[95] What did this do to women and to their babies--to ignore or stifle the intense bond between them? These questions can only be answered by turning to the mothers themselves.[96]

*   *   *   *

Faced with what they perceived to be a national health crisis, officials at all levels of government produced an unprecedented volume of pre-natal and child care literature during the 1920s and 30s. Most of this literature was directed towards the mother, for these authors recognized that it was women who assumed primary responsibility for the care of infants and small children. Whether these experts were successful in their endeavour to persuade women of the merits of scientific child rearing must be the subject of further research. We do know, however, that women *did* actively seek out this literature. If, in fact, they attempted to put these ideas into practice, they may have faced many conflicts and difficulties as they carried out the day-to-day tasks of mothering.

Notes

[1]Michael Piva, *The Condition of the Working Class in Toronto--1900-1921* (Ottawa: University of Ottawa Press, 1979), p. 114. In her first report on infant mortality, Helen MacMurchy noted that the rate for the province of Ontario in 1898 stood at 128.22 deaths under one year to 1000 live births and in 1907 at 150.06 per 1000 live births. Helen MacMurchy, *Infant Mortality: Special Report* (Toronto: King's Printer, 1910), p. 6.

[2]In his study of Montreal, Terry Copp states that, "Between 1897 and 1911, approximately one out of three babies died before reaching the age of twelve months. As late as 1926, the rate was still 14 per cent, a figure almost double the average for New York or Toronto." Terry Copp, *The Anatomy of Poverty* (Toronto: McClelland and Stewart Ltd., 1974), p. 93. The authors of "The Mother and Child Exhibit," Ontario Science Centre, 11 December

1986 to 30 April 1987, claim that Montreal's infant mortality rate was the highest in the Western World.

[3]Anna Davin, "Imperialism and Motherhood," *History Workshop Journal* 5 (1978), 12.

[4]For a full discussion of her life and career, see Kathleen McConnachie, "Methodology in the Study of Women in History: A Case History of Helen MacMurchy, M.D.," *Ontario History* 75, 1 (March 1983), 61-70, and "Science and Ideology: The Mental Hygiene and Eugenics Movements in the Inter-War Years, 1919-1939," unpublished Ph.D. thesis, University of Toronto, 1987.

[5]MacMurchy, *Infant Mortality*, p. 3.

[6]See Angus McLaren and Arlene Tigar McLaren, *The Bedroom and the State: The Changing Practices and Politics of Contraception and Abortion in Canada, 1880-1980* (Toronto: McClelland and Stewart, 1986).

[7]Suzann Buckley, "Ladies or Midwives? Efforts to Reduce Infant and Maternal Mortality," in Linda Kealey, ed., *A Not Unreasonable Claim: Women and Reform in Canada, 1880s-1920s* (Toronto: Women's Press, 1979), p. 135.

[8]For information on Toronto's public health nursing activities, see Marion Royce, *Eunice Dyke: Health Care Pioneer* (Toronto: Dundurn Press, 1983). For the establishment of the Bureau of Child Welfare in Ontario, see Ontario, Board of Health, "Annual Report (1916)," *Sessional Papers* (1917), ch. 21, p. 11. The Board of Health was transferred to the Minister of Labour and Health under the authority of O/C 98/255. The Federal Department of Health was established by Canada, Statutes, *An Act respecting the Department of Health*, 9-10 George V (1919), ch. 24.

[9]MacMurchy argued that "At least 50 per cent, and probably 60 per cent or even 80 per cent, of Infant Mortality, is preventable." MacMurchy, *Infant Mortality*, p. 18. To determine the best means of preventing infant deaths, the government of Ontario commissioned Helen MacMurchy, later Chief of the Federal Division of Child Welfare, to conduct a study on infant mortality. Her reports, published in 1910, 1911, and 1912, helped to shape the infant welfare movement in Ontario and indeed throughout North America.

[10]*Ibid.*, p. 15.

[11]*Ibid.*, p. 5.

[12]*Ibid.*

[13]MacMurchy emphasized that "The way above all others to save the baby and reduce Infant Mortality is to see that the child is being nursed by the mother, and any occupation that prevents this or makes it hard, is a direct cause of Infant Mortality." *Ibid.*, p. 17.

[14]Jane Lewis, *The Politics of Motherhood: Child and Maternal Welfare in England, 1900-1939* (London: Croom Helm, 1980), p. 14.

[15]Buckley, p. 141.

[16]MacMurchy, p. 31.

[17]The government of Ontario, for example, offered the following explanation for the publication of their first child welfare pamphlet. "Ignorance is conceded by all authorities to play an important part in the problem of infant mortality, and as printed instruction is an essential feature of propaganda, the Board published 'The Baby'." Ontario, Board of Health, "Report of the Bureau of Child Welfare (1917)," *Sessional Papers* (1918), no. 21, p. 25.

[18]In her book, *The Mothercraft Manual*, Mary L. Read claims that she "coined" the term "mothercraft" to describe that "comprehensive scope of the training" provided at the School of Mothercraft, a school for mothers established in New York City in December, 1911. Mary L. Read, *The Mothercraft Manual* (Boston: Little, Brown and Company, 1916), p. xii. The author notes that "the word has since come into use in England in a narrower sense, including merely infant care." The Mothercraft Society, an organization designed to reduce infant mortality through the encouragement of breastfeeding and proper methods of infant care, was established in New Zealand by Dr. Truby King. The Truby King method quickly spread to England, where a Mothercraft School was established in Highgate in 1917. The Canadian Mothercraft Society was founded in Toronto in 1931. For a discussion of Truby King's methods, see Christina Hardyment, *Dream Babies: Child Care from Locke to Spock* (London: Oxford University Press, 1984), pp. 176-82. In her article, "Imperialism and Motherhood," Anna Davin notes that Dr. Sykes, Medical Officer of Health for St. Pancras and one of the founders of the St. Pancras School for Mothers, is "said to have invented the word 'mothercraft'." Davin, 39. In a footnote, Davin adds that the earliest mention of the word she was able to locate was in 1911, by Lady Meyer, an active participant in the School for Mothers.

[19]A number of voluntary organizations and commercial enterprises including the Victorian Order of Nurses, the Metropolitan Life Insurance Company, and the Canadian Council on Child and Family Welfare (CCCFW) produced pamphlets and brochures on child care. The CCCFW, for example, produced several series of letters designed to promote maternal and child health. In this chapter, I will deal only with those publications produced by government agencies.

[20]In addition to *The Canadian Mother's Book*, the Division of Child Welfare also produced a series of pamphlets which soon became known to the general public and government alike as "The Little Blue Books," a term first used by mothers in their letters to the Division of Child Welfare. See MacMurchy, "The Division of Child Welfare," *Canadian Journal of Public Health* 17 (1928), 517. By the end of its first full year of existence, the Division had distributed a total of 365,503 copies of their advice publications. Canada, House of Commons, *Sessional Papers* (1923), p. 37. Similar

figures are available for succeeding years: e.g., 338,467 for 1924-5; and 313,717 for 1925-6, from *Sessional Papers.*

[21]Ontario, Board of Health, "Report of the Bureau of Child Welfare (1919)," *Sessional Papers* (1920), no. 21, p. 33.

[22]The Division of Public Health Nursing of the Department of Public Health of the city of Toronto produced educational literature, beginning in 1922, when the publication, *Pre-Natal Care--Advice to the Expectant Mother,* first appeared. This material was later expanded into two publications termed "The Red Books" because of their red covers. The second of these publications, *The Care of the Infant and Young Child* had been reprinted 17 times by 1931. Marion Royce notes that "Both pamphlets were prepared under the direction of the Division's Supervisor of Child Welfare and approved by the Medical Director of The Hospital for Sick Children. *The Expectant Mother,* which had been approved by a professor of Obstetrics and Gynaecology in the University of Toronto, was published separately in 1927." See Marion Royce, pp. 93-4. Samples of these pamphlets are held at the City of Toronto Archives, RG 11, F1, Box 7, file "Advice for the Expectant Mother."

[23]Helen MacMurchy, "The Division of Child Welfare," 517. For an excellent study based on mothers' letters to the U.S. Children's Bureau, see Molly Ladd-Taylor, *Raising a Baby the Government Way: Mothers' Letters to the Children's Bureau, 1915-1932* (New Brunswick, New Jersey: Rutgers University Press, 1986).

[24]Ontario, Board of Health, *The Baby* (1924), p. 4.

[25]*The Canadian Mother's Book* (1923), p. 29.

[26]*Ibid.,* pp. 11-12.

[27]*Ibid.,* p. 10.

[28]*Ibid.*

[29]*Ibid.,* p. 11.

[30]Helen MacMurchy, *How to Take Care of the Baby,* 1922, p. 4.

[31]City of Toronto, Department of Public Health, *The Expectant Mother* (1927), p. 5.

[32]Buckley, p. 133.

[33]*Ibid.* In her article in the same collection, Veronica Strong-Boag notes that "Childbirth was often the occasion which initiated a doctor's association with a family and its illnesses." Veronica Strong-Boag, "Canada's Women Doctors: Feminism Constrained," in *A Not Unreasonable Claim,* pp. 111-12.

[34]*The Baby* (1924), p. 9.

[35]City of Toronto, Department of Public Health, *Pre-Natal Care: Advice for the Expectant Mother* (1922), p. 7.

[36]Alan Brown, *The Normal Child: Its Care and Feeding* (Toronto: McClelland and Stewart, 1932).

[37]"Doctoring the Family: Part 3," radio programme, "Ideas," *CBC Radio,* April 1985.

[38]For a provocative discussion of the role of advice literature

in historical research, see Jay Mechling, "Advice to Historians on Advice to Mothers," *Journal of Social History* 9, 1 (Fall 1973), 44-63. Mechling argues that child rearing texts can be used solely for the purposes of examining the ideas and values of their authors and can tell us very little about maternal practices or about the values of the society as a whole. For a compelling counter-argument for the importance of examining child rearing texts, see Nancy Pottishman Weiss, "The Mother-Child Dyad Revisited: Perceptions of Mothers and Children in Twentieth Century Child-Rearing Manuals," *Journal of Social Issues* 34, 2 (1978), 29-45.

[39]For a discussion of the work of the child care professionals in the inter-war years, see Veronica Strong-Boag, "Intruders in the Nursery: Childcare Professionals Reshape the Years One to Five, 1920-1940," in Joy Parr, ed., *Childhood and Family in Canadian History* (Toronto: McClelland and Stewart, 1982), pp. 160-78. For a more uncritical examination of child rearing advice, see Norah L. Lewis, "Advising the Parents: Child Rearing in British Columbia During the Inter-War Yars," unpublished Ed.D. thesis, University of British Columbia, 1980.

[40]In *The Normal Child*, Brown noted that: "If properly trained, and the training must begin at birth, a baby will acquire the habit of taking his food at regular intervals by day and by night, and he will also acquire the habit of going to sleep and waking at regular intervals. As a result of a careful regime regarding feeding, sleep, bathing, and airing, and the performance of its various functions at stated times every day, the baby will soon develop into a 'little machine', as one mother called her babe. Such a child causes no trouble and thrives far better than one who is fed every time he cries, day or night." Brown, p. 223.

[41]In the advice pamphlets of the period babies are uniformly referred to as "he."

[42]*The Care of the Infant and Young Child* (1931), p 7.

[43]Helen MacMurchy, *How to Take Care of the Baby* (1923), p. 13.

[44]*The Expectant Mother* (1931), p. 11.

[45]*The Baby* (1920), p. 37.

[46]*The Baby* (1933), p. 54. This reference to the equal participation of men and women in the tasks of child rearing was unusual in the literature of the period. For the most part, the roles of men and women were strictly delineated. MacMurchy, for example, explains that "If you take care of the Mother then she can take care of the Baby. The Father is the only one who can really take care of the Mother and the Mother is the only one who can really take care of the Baby." *How to Take Care of the Baby* (1923), p. 7.

[47]*The Care of the Infant and Young Child* (1931), p. 43.

[48]*Ibid.*

[49]*Ibid.*

[50]*The Baby* (1920), p. 46.

[51]*Ibid.*, pp. 45-6.

[52]*The Baby* (1933), p. 30.

[53]See, e.g., *The Care of the Infant and Young Child* (1931), p. 44; *Canadian Mother's Book* (1932), p. 160.

[54]*The Care of the Infant and Young Child* (1931), p. 27.

[55]*The Baby* (1933), p. 46.

[56]*Ibid.*, p. 30.

[57]*Ibid.*

[58]*The Care of the Infant and Young Child* (1931), p. 44.

[59]*The Baby* (1920), p. 10.

[60]*Ibid.*

[61]*The Care of the Infant and Young Child* (1931), p. 7.

[62]*The Baby* (1933), p. 48.

[63]For a thought-provoking discussion of the consequences of such child rearing practices, see Alice Miller, *For Your Own Good: Hidden Cruelty in Child-Rearing and the Roots of Violence*, trans. by Hildegard and Hunter Hannum (New York: Farrar-Straus-Giroux, 1983).

[64]Helen MacMurchy, *How to Take Care of Mother* (1922), p. 11.

[65]*The Canadian Mother's Book* (1923), p. 7.

[66]*Ibid.*, p. 5.

[67]Helen MacMurchy, *How to Manage Housework in Canada* (1923), p. 5.

[68]For a discussion of the ideology of motherhood, see, for example, Anna Davin; Jane Lewis; Sheila M. Rothman, *Woman's Proper Place* (New York: Basic Books, 1978); and the classic work by Adrienne Rich, *Of Woman Born: Motherhood as Experience and Institution* (New York: W. W. Norton and Company, Inc., 1976).

[69]*The Care of the Infant and Young Child* (1931), p. 5.

[70]Helen MacMurchy, *How to Take Care of Mother* (1922), p. 14.

[71]Helen MacMurchy, *How to Take Care of the Children* (1922), p. 4.

[72]See the literature cited at note 68 above.

[73]It is worth noting, however, that many of the authors employed what amounted to 'scare' tactics in order to persuade women to follow their advice. For example, women were told that risks of infant mortality were far greater for bottle-fed babies. Similarly, babies who were fed table scraps might die. It is probable that mothers, anxious to save their babies' lives, might well have heeded these dire warnings. In my Ph.D. thesis, I will examine this issue in greater depth, using interviews with women who reared their children during the period 1920-1960 and letters to government officials to help me assess the impact of this literature on women's daily lives.

[74]See, for example, MacMurchy's advice to the pregnant woman. "Don't be down-hearted-- there is no reason you should be. Don't be frightened. Cheer up. We are all standing by you." *The Canadian Mother's Book* (1923), p. 29.

[75]*The Expectant Mother* (1927), p. 13.

[76]*The Canadian Mother's Book* (1923), p. 32.

[77]*How to Take Care of the Mother* (1923), p. 24.

[78]Dorothy Franklin, Kent, Ontario, letter to R. B. Bennett, 15 December 1931, in L. M. Grayson and Michael Bliss, eds., *The Wretched of Canada: Letters to R. B. Bennett 1930-1935* (Toronto: University of Toronto Press, 1971), p. 16.

[79]Mrs. Daria Collinet, Widow, Upsalquitch, N. B., letter to R. B. Bennett, 2 February 1934, in Grayson and Bliss, p. 73.

[80]Mrs. R. Paddy, Burton, Alberta, letter to R. B. Bennett, 19 February 1935, in Grayson and Bliss, p. 117.

[81]MacMurchy ordered pregnant women to "lie down a few minutes and take a rest" following the noon meal. *How to Take Care of Mother* (1922), p. 13. The Toronto publication informed her that "A rest of an hour or two should follow the noon meal." *The Expectant Mother* (1927), p. 8.

[82]*The Canadian Mother's Book* (1933), p. 25.

[83]*Pre-Natal Care: Advice for the Expectant Mother* (1922), p. 11.

[84]*The Expectant Mother* (1927), p. 17.

[85]*The Canadian Mother's Book* (1933), p. 25.

[86]*How to Take Care of Mother* (1922), p. 7.

[87]*How To Take Care of the Baby* (1922), p. 10.

[88]*How to Take Care of the Baby* (1923), p. 17.

[89]"Motherhood is a natural and should be a normal process," *The Expectant Mother* (1927), p. 8.

[90]*The Canadian Mother's Book* (1923), p. 8.

[91]Veronica Strong-Boag, "Intruders in the Nursery," p. 161.

[92]See Barbara Ehrenreich and Deirdre English, *For Her Own Good: 150 Years of the Experts' Advice to Women* (Garden City, New York: Anchor Press/Doubleday, 1978).

[93]*The Expectant Mother* (1931), p. 11.

[94]"There is a sensible way of treating children. Treat them as though they were young adults . . . Never hug and kiss them, never let them sit in your lap. If you must, kiss them once on the forehead when they say good night. Shake hands with them in the morning." John B. Watson, *The Psychological Care of the Infant and Child* (London: George Allen and Unwin Ltd., 1928), p. 73.

[95]John and Elizabeth Newson, "Cultural aspects of childrearing in the English-speaking world," in Martin Richards, ed., *The Integration of a Child into a Social World* (London: Cambridge University Press, 1974), p. 61.

[96]See Katherine Arnup, "Education for Motherhood: Women and the Family in Twentieth Century English Canada," unpublished Ph.D. thesis, University of Toronto, in progress.

Chapter Eleven

SCHOOLS FOR HAPPINESS: INSTITUTS FAMILIAUX
AND THE EDUCATION OF IDEAL WIVES AND
MOTHERS*

Sherene Razack

Most domestic science schools of the twentieth century have been
vocational institutions dedicated to the teaching of domestic science
as professional training. The existence in Quebec up to the late
1960s of domestic science schools, almost exclusively concerned with
education for marriage and motherhood, appears, then, to be a
striking anomaly. Despite their singularity, the *instituts familiaux*
until recently have inspired little curiosity.[1] At least a part of the
neglect has to do with the belief that such schools require little
explanation in a province where the family and motherhood enjoyed
a prominent place in nationalist ideology. In fact, the *instituts
familiaux* merit attention because they are an illustration of how a
traditional feminine ideal is energetically promoted through
education.

The *instituts familiaux* were the last schools of a tradition of
domestic education institutions or *écoles ménagères* in the province
of Quebec. While they shared the most important attribute of
schools of this kind, namely their loyalty to an ultramontane
nationalist ideal of woman, the *instituts familiaux* were unique in
their own right. Unlike the *écoles ménagères* they did not claim to
serve the daughters of the rural poor. Furthermore, they
accommodated Catholic and nationalist values within a
sophisticated curriculum that was by far the most ambitious
attempt in Quebec to foster a traditional feminine ideal through
education. Add to this their emergence and relative success in a
decade when changes in education and woman's role in society
seemed to threaten their very existence, and one is faced with an
intriguing example of the strength of an ideal and the tenacity and

*I would like to thank Larry Brookwell, Yves Frenette, Vivian McCaffery and
Susan Mann Trofimenkoff. Their comments and criticisms added a great deal to
this work while their emotional support made it possible.

211

skill of those who promoted it. These two themes form the basis of this chapter.

In Quebec, woman's role in nationalism began to be articulated by ultramontane thinkers of the mid-nineteenth century. In 1856, Abbé Laflèche published a small volume outlining the relation of the family to church and nation.[2] Laflèche saw the family as a patriarchy, a divinely-ordained system of authority. Within this construct, woman had a vital role to play. Endowed with special feminine qualities which made her at once man's complement and his inferior, she confirmed his power in the family and, by extension, the power of pope over king and king over man.[3] Woman played, however, a more direct role in sustaining the hierarchical construct. As the educator of her children, a position once again inherited by virtue of the innate feminine qualities of *dévouement* and *intelligence du coeur*,[4] she ensured the endurance of religious values over generations. To this base of ultramontanism, Laflèche added a few *québécois* elements. Woman was expressly linked to the survival of French Canada, assuring *la survivance de la race* by teaching her children the French language and cultural traditions, and of course, by preserving the numerical strength of French Canadians.[5]

Laflèche had little to say on the topic of female education, but several of his contemporaries recognized an important connection between the education of girls and their success in fulfilling religious and cultural obligations. For instance, Bishop Bourget stressed that girls had to be educated for their role in the family and in the preservation of the social hierarchy. Hence he recommended that, for girls of the poorer classes, education should have as its objective the training of good housekeepers and farm wives. (Girls of the upper classes, on the other hand, needed a more sophisticated training commensurate with their position as wives of the elite.)[6] In 1882, when the first *école ménagère* was founded, it conformed directly to this educational ideal: as its founders put it, *pour assurer la grande entreprise colonisatrice il faudrait des femmes, des épouses, des ménagères capables de comprendre, d'aider et de compléter le travail de l'homme, colon et agriculteur.*[7] Thus linked to the agricultural classes, domestic education acquired a rural and conservative character that it was not to lose for several decades.

For the first few decades of the twentieth century, urbanization and industrialization served to deepen the conviction of many Catholic educators that it was more necessary than ever to carefully prepare girls for their familial obligations. Henri Bourassa and Lionel Groulx stand out as indefatigable propagandists for the proper moral and domestic education for girls. Feminism and women's work outside the home were signs to both men that women not only were unprepared for marriage and motherhood but, more fundamentally, were unwilling to limit themselves to their traditional roles. With this in mind, Bourassa proposed for girls

*un régime de vie simple et saine, une forte éducation
morale, également simple et saine, où elles apprendraient à
bien lire et à bien écrire, à compter exactement, à coudre et
raccommoder leur linge; où elles prendraient également des
notions vécues et habituelles de savoir vivre, de bonne terre,
de modestie . . .*[8]

For his part, Groulx warned teachers to discourage any belief in the equality of the sexes or in the similarity of their spheres of activity. He roundly condemned education for girls which overwhelmed the brain with knowledge, proposing instead education directly linked to domestic life.[9]

Their supporters notwithstanding, by 1929, the first *écoles ménagères* were confronting a dilemma they would never completely resolve: how to modernize and compete successfully with more academic schools, yet preserve their religious and familial orientation. The six existing schools, under the jurisdiction of the Ministry of Agriculture, were transferred to the Ministry of Education, a change which brought with it closer regulation of the curriculum.[10] By 1930, under their new name *écoles ménagères régionales*, they began to offer the traditional religious, domestic and agricultural training along with a standard academic education from the seventh to the ninth grades. Graduates could now acquire the qualifications necessary to teach domestic science to students of grades one to six.[11] These changes did little, however, to divert the schools from their dedication to *un cours de perfectionnement* for young girls destined for home and farm life.[12] One school inspector of the time took care to stress that *les écoles ménagères rurales sont une garantie d'une exploitation agricole fructueuse.*[13]

Their early flexibility in the face of changes in education and in society ultimately did not suffice to protect the *écoles ménagères* from the threat of time. By the end of the thirties, schools which were neither strictly academic nor vocational and which, furthermore, had a reputation of lower standards and a certain rural and class character, were endangered. Their *raison-d'être*, to preserve rural life and to train the agricultural classes, was incompatible with evolving educational ideals and an increasingly democratic society.

Educational reforms of 1937 heralded the dawn of a new educational system in Quebec. Curricula were revised to facilitate access to technical training schools and universities, and of course to the job market. Girls now had the choice among options that included: a general programme for "those who simply seek a solid average level of culture suitable to the middle class;" teacher training; commercial courses for future secretaries; a classical programme including Latin; and *la section ménagère*, a programme which combined some classical training with domestic science and which was now designed to prepare future domestic science teachers.[14]

213

Evidence that female education progressed along these new lines was apparent in the growth of independent Catholic schools offering vocational training and in the expansion of the female *collèges classiques* during the 1930s and 1940s. For example, vocational domestic science schools which prepared students "to play an immediate part in the world of social work and technical trades"[15] recorded 4,982 students in 1936 and over 21,000 in 1950.[16] Female institutions of classical education experienced a remarkable period of growth between 1932 and 1947 when no fewer than twenty-two new schools were opened.[17]

Promoters of domestic education for the home had some cause for anxiety in 1937. Their brand of education was increasingly anachronistic in an age of the improving of standards and new opportunities for academic and technical training. Moreover, although the majority of the new schools were urban, hence not direct competitors, they posed a threat to the rural *écoles ménagères* because they competed for funds and religious personnel. Clergymen who believed in traditional female education for the home soon reacted. In 1937, Cardinal Villeneuve is reported to have issued a directive to the new inspector of domestic science schools:

> *Servez-vous de la plume, de la presse, de la radio, du cinéma. Visitez les écoles, les collèges, les séminaires, les ministères et insistez sur cette idée que la femme est l'heureuse reine du foyer heureux mais que le métier de reine s'apprend dans la patience.*[18]

With these words, he launched a campaign to revitalize education for ideal wives and mothers. At the helm was a young priest who had a reputation as a poet, writer and film maker.

Albert Tessier was eminently qualified for the task assigned to him by Cardinal Villeneuve. Prior to and during his involvement with education, Tessier ardently preached a philosophy which went well with the plan to reform education for the home: *Faire aimer l'Eglise, faire aimer la terre!*,[19] he wrote, and French Canada would survive to fulfill *le rôle que la Providence nous confie.*[20] Women were no less important to Tessier's vision than they had been to Laflèche's. Indeed, he was prolific on the subject of *la mère canadienne*, completing by 1946 a historical work and several articles devoted to the themes *nos mères ont sauvé le pays après les malheurs de 1760*[21] and *l'idéal familial que nos mères ont élevé à un si haut degré.*[22]

The refurbishment of the *écoles ménagères* began with a structural change. In 1938 they were renamed and upgraded to include grades ten to twelve, and in 1941 grade thirteen was added for those desiring teacher training. Adding the higher grades did not automatically provide the schools with the prestige the reformers sought. In fact, since few girls received education at this level in 1940, enrolment did not pick up dramatically.[23] Moreover, popular biases against the schools persisted; the *écoles ménagères* continued to be seen as institutions for the rural poor.[24] To Tessier, changing the image of the school more than the actual programme was one way of improving the fortune of the *école ménagère*.

A concerted effort was made to render the schools more attractive to a sceptical public. Tessier arranged press coverage of exhibitions of students' work, presenting the programme as *un cours de haute culture*.[25] Advertisements appearing in *La Famille*[26] and brochures distributed by the newly created information office all portrayed the *écoles ménagères* as finishing schools for the daughters of the elite. An association of *écoles ménagères* was formed which divided its energies equally between promotion and pedagogical reform.[27] No effort was spared to increase public awareness.

Promotional activities undertook to recast traditional domestic education as one suitable for girls of all social classes. In her reports to the superintendent of education, for instance, the director of household science often took care to note that all social classes were taking part in the revival of female education for the home.[28] A description of the *écoles ménagères* (and of the boys' agricultural schools) revealed the new image:

> The object of these schools is to build up a fairly well-educated middle class of young men and women who may serve their country as able citizens and housewives, and in due course become leaders in their communities.[29]

The *Code Scolaire* was equally insistent, characterizing the *écoles ménagères* as *des maisons de formation ménagères spécialisées (qui) tendent à préparer une élite . . .*[30] Anxious to dispel the belief that only poor country girls attended the *écoles ménagères*, Tessier compiled and published intermittently statistics on the social origins of pupils,[31] an exercise that compelled him in the 1940s to admit that *les classes modestes sont encore celles qui manifestent le plus bel esprit familial.*[32]

Neither extensive publicity nor the new class image solved the crisis facing the *école ménagère*. There still remained the task of designing an educational programme that would remain faithful to religious and cultural values and possess, at the same time, the sophistication and academic rigour required of a secondary school in the 1940s. For Tessier, the answer lay in bringing a fresh approach to the teaching of traditional values. In order to do so, Tessier made use of pedagogical theories then attracting the attention of Canadian educators: the progressive movement in education.[33]

Progressive educational theory, first articulated by John Dewey, stressed the role of the school in preparing students for 'real life', an objective that led to the devaluation of abstract knowledge and to renewed emphasis on the formation of character. In Canada, this approach to education brought such innovations as report cards which measured a child's attitudes.[34]   As Catholic schools, the *écoles ménagères* had always been concerned with moral and values education, but, under Tessier, this dimension occupied two thirds of the curriculum.[35]   Henceforth, the *écoles ménagères* offered what was later described with pride as "a very thorough training in femininity,"[36] personality training that went well beyond the moral education of earlier years.   An official description of the programme in 1940 explained the new pedagogical direction:

> *La culture scolaire garde partout son importance mais, dans l'école ménagère à tous ses degrés, comme dans la vie d'ailleurs, elle vient après les qualités de fond qui conditionnent la véritable force de la personalité humaine.*[37]

It was left to Tessier to define the feminine personality and to set about outlining the pedagogical techniques which would best foster it.

The model wife and mother which Tessier sought to make of each girl was a woman of culture and refinement.   With consummate skill in every aspect of home management, *intelligence, volonté, sensibilité, imagination créatrice, aptitudes et talents manuels*,[38] she attended to the moral and material well-being of the family.   Totally committed to domestic life, the ideal woman did not, indeed would not, participate in the paid labour force.[39]   Instead, her energies went towards the creation of *un sanctuaire familial où l'âme et les mains trouveront à servir de la meilleur façon possible l'Eglise et la Patrie*.[40]   Such an ideal was traditional, to be sure, but seldom had it received as definite a form.   Moreover, the model wife and mother now shared a greater affinity with the urban middle class rather than with *les classes modestes*.

In regular bimonthly bulletins,[41] Tessier provided teachers of the *écoles ménagères* with educational guidelines.   *La gloire de la vie domestique*, he wrote in one of these, must be as tirelessly described as displayed.[42]   Schools were to resemble tasteful and pleasant family homes.   Teachers were counselled on how to invest all activities with religious and patriotic significance.   Music classes were centred on the singing of traditional *québécois* folk songs and traditional meals were prepared in cooking classes.[43]   More importantly, teachers were to remind students of their reproductive obligations: In Tessier's words, *faites tout ce qui sera possible pour donner au personnel et aux élèves un respect particulier pour cette portion de choix de la grande famille ménagère*.[44]   To encourage the students, Tessier compiled statistics on the birth rates of various rural parishes maintaining that these would impress upon the girls that *la fécondité de notre race n'est pas éteinte*.[45]

The schools that prepared the young women of Quebec for their *mission salvatrice*[46] survived the forties.   Although they still attracted less than 2 per cent of the female school population beyond grade ten, they enjoyed a constant if not spectacular expansion. Whereas in 1938 there were 18 *écoles ménagères* with a total enrollment of 579, in 1950 there were 37 and a total enrollment of 1,936.[47] Abbé Tessier had shown a remarkable ability to promote and foster a traditional ideal at a time when trends in education had pointed to its demise. In the 1950s, he was to face his greatest challenge and to reach the height of his achievements in the creation of the *instituts familiaux*, the finest incarnation to date, of schools for marriage and motherhood.

In the 1950s, promotional materials for the *écoles ménagères* began to refer to *instituts familiaux*, described as "schools for professional wives" and "schools for happiness."[48] Tessier's statistics now showed an increasing number of pupils in the categories of "bourgeois" and "professional." Whereas, at the start of the decade, Tessier contended that pupils came equally from families of farmers, the working class and the middle class (a conclusion which differed markedly from his earlier pronouncement in 1941 that *les classes modestes* dominated the *écoles ménagères*), by 1957, the statistics compiled by the *Association des instituts familiaux* showed a dramatic increase in the student population labelled as middle class. Out of a total of 2,927 students, 1,295 or 53.18 per cent were estimated to have come from "bourgeois" homes, 30 per cent from the working class and only 16.6 per cent from agricultural homes. Moreover, this description of the social composition of the school population remained the same for the years 1958 to 1962.[49]

Of course, this statistical picture of the social background of the school population must be taken with some reservations. Tessier was inclined to exaggerate his statistics in an effort to dispel the notion that the *instituts familiaux* were schools of the rural poor. On one occasion, he even suggested that 85 per cent of all pupils were of middle-class families.[50] Furthermore, the term 'middle class' was certainly one of great fluidity for him. In it, he included doctors, lawyers, merchants, civil servants and office workers thus reserving the term 'working class' specifically for factory workers and the term 'agricultural class' for farmers. Since Tessier's middle class potentially included school teachers, municipal employees of all echellons and, in fact, a large number of occupations not necessariy bourgeois, his statistics do not exactly support the conclusion that most pupils came from the middle class. Allowing for exaggeration, however, his figures do show that most pupils did not come from agricultural homes but instead from the ranks of the *petite bourgeoisie*.

Admission requirements and the pattern of school attendance tend to support the hypothesis that pupils of the *instituts familiaux* came, if not from the top strata, at least from the middle levels of the rural population. Students were required to have completed at least grade nine.[51] Between 1941 and 1961, rural Quebecers had the lowest level of formal schooling in Canada: in 1961, 85 per cent did not go beyond the ninth grade. And, as several studies have shown, prolonged schooling can be directly correlated to occupational status and social class.[52] Certainly the cost of attending an *institut familial* (over $250.00 per year) would have restricted its appeal.[53]

An *institut familial* functioned as a 'finishing' school where a girl acquired sophisticated domestic and social skills at an advanced level. Generally she did not continue on, however, to the thirteenth grade, the only level which enabled her to enter a professional or skilled occupation or to take further studies. A glance at the distribution of school certificates granted in 1951 confirms this pattern: only 106 full diplomas were awarded while 532 testimonials were granted after one year of study, 382 after 2 years and 234 after three years. As the decade progressed, this pattern of school attendance did not change markedly.[54]

For all students of an *institut familial*, opportunities for any but the least skilled occupations were rare. The programme itself was neither academic nor vocational. Furthermore, even those students who completed the full programme (grade 13) were qualified to teach only the first six grades of a domestic science school. Graduates could also seek employment as nurses aides and dieticians' assistants, and, in fact, some did, but these professions were beginning to require students with a more academic formation than the one available in an *institut familial*.[55] Few girls, then, were likely to be lured to the higher grades of a domestic science school if they intended to work outside the home. It is probable, then, that pupils entertained hopes of a future life in which domestic talents would be more relevant than marketable skills.

The best indication that an *institut familial* was perhaps an institution for the daughters of the more well-to-do of the rural population was the new curriculum of the school. As one admirer succinctly put it, the domestic training therein was not of the "broom and mop variety" but rather of the tradition of "vacuum cleaners and washing machines."[56] The 'new' psychological and philosophical insights of feminine humanism gave this sophisticated domestic science training its distinctive character.

Feminine humanism, as espoused by Tessier and his colleagues, referred to education *centrée sur le développement intégral et équilibré de la personalité féminine en vue de la mission de la femme dans l'Eglise, le foyer, la société, la patrie.* To develop feminine humanists, the education of young girls had to observe two guidelines. It had to respect the natural talents and proclivities of the female personality and it was dedicated to preparing girls for a future which biology, divine will and convention had clearly marked them. Underlying the 'new' pedagogy, was thus an old view of woman's nature: *le flux féminin, la sensibilité de l'adolescence, l'imagination exaltée et pas encore créatrice, empêchent d'avoir une vraie pensée.*[57] Girls would therefore benefit little from an intellectual training.[58] The belief that an intellectual formation was wasted on the female personality was bolstered, in Tessier's view, by yet another argument. Such an education, offered by the *collèges classiques, contribue actuellement à détruire chez la femme le culte de ce qui a fait sa grandeur et sa foi dans le passé.*[59] *Essentiellement ordonnée à la maternité,*[60] a women could therefore find fulfillment no other way but as wife and mother. An intellectual education would only stand in the way.

Ironically, although woman could only find happiness in the fulfillment of her natural obligations, not all women accepted their role with enthusiasm. Teachers were thus advised to inspire a liking for domestic tasks, which Tessier felt were often difficult and boring. Girls had to be conditioned to like the hardships of domesticity, Tessier wrote frankly, since *l'amour seul explique la continuité du don.*[61] This apparent contradiction in feminine nature had its roots in the image of woman as both Eve and Mary, "the fragile instrument of the Fall and Redemption,"[62] an image much promoted in the *instituts familiaux.* To be effective, educators had to suppress the tendencies of Eve and encourage those of Mary. Put another way, their task was to "rouse the mother and wife in every woman,"[63] and to inspire *une prise de conscience de la vraie fémininité.*[64] Thus, feminine humanism formed the basis of a complete educational programme that had as its objective the creation of the perfect feminine personality. The maxim so often cited by Tessier, *savoir, savoir-faire, vouloir-faire*[65] summed up the approach to education for girls of the *instituts familiaux.* The schools were to create women who were *instruites, bien eduquées, aimant leur tâche, habiles dans tous les travaux domestiques,* or in his phrase, *des femmes de maison dépareillées.*[66]

An *institut familial* began its ambitious training for marriage and motherhood in the *écoles ménagères.* Schools were supposed to possess a special atmosphere conducive to the development of domestic virtues.[67] In model dining rooms and well-equipped kitchens, students practiced the rituals of family life.[68] Pupils were organized into *équipes familiales* in which older pupils played mothers to younger ones.[69] Visiting priests, often Tessier and his assistant Paul Carignan, lent paternal authority to the scene and provided *"la sécurité nécessaire à un monde féminin."*[70] Students were introduced to the realities of domestic life when they were required to manage a family of junior pupils. There was also a ten-day period during which each student in the third year had under her care a baby from a nearby home.[71]

In the classroom students could absorb *la mystique familiale* in all subjects.[72] The curriculum was divided into three areas of study. *La vocation féminine* included instruction in female and child psychology and religion. The domestic arts included housekeeping, the culinary arts, sewing, weaving and the decorative arts. Finally academic subjects, taught with particular regard for feminine aptitudes and the future responsibilities of pupils, included French, English, history, sciences, and arithmetic or household accounts. Not all three areas were of equal importance. The feminine vocation made up approximately 15 per cent of the curriculum but accounted for over 35 per cent of the examination marks. The domestic arts, which were by nature extremely time-consuming, engaged over 50 per cent of the students' time. Academic study amounted to little more than 25 per cent of the programme. Physical education and singing completed the course of study.[73]

Successful marriage and motherhood required, first of all, that students understand and appreciate their feminine heritage. Next, it was necessary to learn how to become a good wife and mother. In order to fulfill her feminine obligations properly, a girl had need of a psychological understanding of herself, her husband and her children. An *institut familial* endeavoured to provide this knowledge through the teaching of religion and psychology, and to a lesser extent, through French literature, English and history.

Instruction in religion and psychology was unified by a central theme of study. In grade ten, this was the feminine personality, a general discussion of *ce que toute jeune fille doit savoir*. In fact, study of this theme entailed a light discussion of sexual mores, the principal objective of which was to remind the young girl to preserve herself for marriage.[74] In grade eleven, students were taught woman's role within the family, learning through religion and psychology the proper ways to bring up children. In the third year, these courses attempted to prepare students for the emotional difficulties of conjugal and maternal life. Finally, the fourth year entailed a synthesis of previous study.[75]

Textbooks used in the courses provide a more concrete illustration of what was taught in religion and psychology. Religious instructors relied on four books written by Abbé Llewellyn. *Ta Personne, Ton Milieu, Ton Futur* and *Ton Foyer*[76] were texts written specifically for the *instituts familiaux*; each was designed to complement one year of the programme. They were united by a single theme:

> . . .*Votre mission consiste actuellement à vous préparer à votre vie de demain, vie d'épouse, de mère, de ménagère. Elle consiste à y préparer votre corps, votre esprit, votre coeur, votre âme.*[77]

Expounded in a simple, familiar style aided by such devices as imaginary dialogues,[78] the theme of woman's mission received a detailed and tireless treatment. *Ta Personne*, the first of Llewellyn's books, sought to describe the attitudes and behaviour of an ideal woman. Chapters detailed why feminine fulfillment could come only from marriage and motherhood and not from work outside the home. Students were invited to see the justice and wisdom of true feminine behaviour, and to express it on examinations. One grade ten examination question directed towards material in *Ta Personne* asked students: . . .*comment il vous est possible dès aujourd'hui, de vous préparer à devenir une FEMME ADMIRABLE*. . .[79] If the

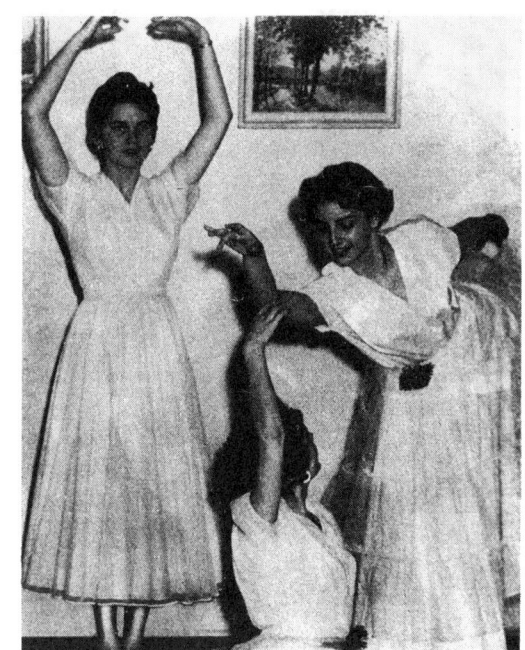

"Future wives and mothers acquire mental poise and physical grace through the elementary ballet steps."

Source: Evelyn M. Brown, *Educating Eve* (Montreal: Palm Publishers, 1957).

"In her role of homemaker in the Little Home, student 'mother' shops for provisions at the nearest stores."

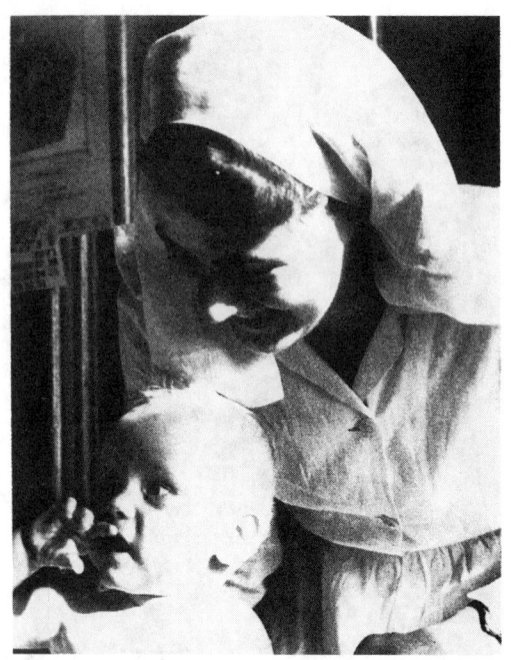

"A sweet but slippery customer. Intensive courses in child care are given to senior students in a foundling home to which they go in groups for a period of ten days."

Source: Evelyn M. Brown, *Educating Eve* (Montreal: Palm Publishers, 1957).

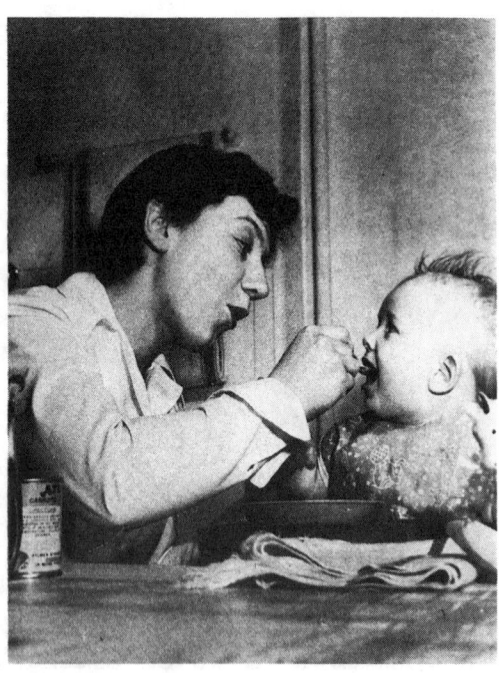

"Food tastes better with a little affection."

answer was still confined to generalities in grade ten, a study of *Ton Milieu* in the second year provided students with a more specific guide. *Ton Milieu* offered girls a clear idea of how their sphere of activity differed from that of a man. As Abbé Llewellyn phrased it,

> *l'homme gouverne le foyer. Il fournit l'argent par son travail, il porte les responsabilités, prend les decisions. . .La femme règne dans le foyer; elle humanise dans leur application constante les decisions de l'homme.*[80]

Not all of *Ton Milieu* remained on this philosophical plane, however. Good nutrition, interesting conversation and the preservation of mutual interests[81] were among some of Abbé Llewellyn's suggestions for successful home life.

By the third year of study, Llewellyn's instructions became even more precise in their application to domestic life. Most of *Ton Futur* explained why the woman was particularly suited to certain tasks of the home, such as tending the sick and listening to all complaints.[82] Occasionally, the separate spheres of activities to which the sexes were confined created difficulties. Woman's intellectual gifts and education were so vastly different from her husband's that there could well be very little communication between the sexes. To this problem, Llewellyn had a concrete solution. A wife who found herself unable to communicate with her husband because of his interest in mathematics, for example, might read the biographies of famous mathematicians rather than attempt to study the subject itself.[83] In this way, harmony in the home might be maintained without either sex having to stray too far from the assigned sphere.

Psychology texts[84] were also written specifically for the *instituts familiaux*. Marie-Paule Vinay, a writer who held a doctorate in psychology, placed the emphasis on woman's potential for evil rather than her infinite capacity to achieve marital bliss. *Qui est Jeannette?* and *La Femme et Son Coeur* often included rather dramatic illustrations of the consequences of feminine deviation. In one story, a young girl died from a mysterious fever soon after leaving home to work in the city near her boyfriend.[85] The message here, as elsewhere in the text, was clear: a woman who left her familial sphere imperilled her life both physically and spiritually. She also imperilled the lives of others. By examination time, students were expected to answer correctly such questions as *montrez les inconvénients des sorties trop fréquentes de la mère de famille.*[86]

Psychology classes were, in fact, the main avenue through which students were taught the meaning of a feminine personality. In one chapter of *La Femme et Son Coeur*, for instance, students studied thirty-three personality differences between men and women. The psychological portrait of woman was often confusing because Vinay attempted to demonstrate both the negative and

223

positive traits which she considered innate to all women. As Vinay described it, some of the principal differences between men and women were:

Elle	Lui

1. Au point du vue général:

Reçoit, enfante, conserve, multiplie, fait durer, organise.	Cherche, conquiert, produit, apporte, détruit.
Se préoccupe des siens aux dépens du bien commun.	Peut se préoccuper du bien commun aux dépens des siens.
Veut naturellement domestiquer, assujetir des libertés.	Prend instinctivement le parti des oprimés.
Elle devine.	Il raisonne.
Parle quand elle n'a rien à dire.	Se tait quand il devrait parler.
Ment facilement.	Dit les vérités qu'il faut taire.[83]

Feminine personality and female vocation were the messages of most of the academic subjects taught at the *instituts familiaux* as well. Tessier insisted that intellectual subjects be specifically tailored to the feminine personality. As a result, when students studied Molière in their French literature class, they paid particular attention to "le foyer idéal selon Molière."[87] The study of English often involved writing essays on such topics as "How does a wife create a home atmosphere?"[88] Examination questions took up the same theme. An English exam for grade twelve students in 1964 asked this question: "Mrs. Jacqueline Kennedy, a true woman in the face of life and death. Show how her beautiful Christian spirit and feminine dignity justify this statement."[89] In arithmetic and science, material was specifically tailored to have relevance to domestic life. For example, chemical experiments duplicated reactions which occurred in the cooking of food.[90] Even in physical education, Tessier stressed *il ne s'agit pas de former des femmes athlètes, mais des femmes saines aptes à remplir leur rôle dans la vie.*[91] In no subject, then, did instruction stray too far from the central function of education in the *instituts familiaux*: the preparation of mentally and technically competent wives and mothers.

One area of the programme crystallized all the aspects of woman's role as defined by Abbé Tessier--history. History taught a religious and nationalist consciousness. As the official *Programme* of 1956 frankly stated:

L'histoire nationale n'est pas une matière scolaire au même titre que l'histoire universelle, la géographie, les mathématiques, etc. Il faut que les jeunes filles d'aujourd'hui sachent que le sort moral et matériel de la Patrie est dans leurs mains.[92]

Tessier wrote the history books for the *instituts familiaux* himself. They stressed the role of the Church and the family, *les héroïsmes féminins*, and *la survivance*.[93]   History of this kind, thought Abbé Tessier, gave *aux élèves une haute idée de leur mission dans l'histoire actuelle et dans l'histoire future de notre pays*.[94]   It would also, of course, provide historical justification for some of the principles taught in the *instituts familiaux*.   For example, students were shown *trois coutumes qui marquent le caractère surnaturel de l'autorité paternelle dans la famille canadienne*.[95]   History therefore served, in general, the function of reinforcing and glorifying woman's role in the family.

Perhaps the most distinguishing feature of the philosophy of education in the curriculum of the *instituts familiaux* was the belief that marriage required a considerable amount of sacrifice and preparation on the part of the woman.   Hence, students had to learn both in and out of the classroom the knowledge and skills which would aid in what one writer termed "Eve's preparation to please Adam."[96]   In the physical sense, preparation for marriage meant cultivating the domestic skills which were necessary for pleasing men.   As Abbé Llewellyn once put it, divorce has its roots in the kitchen.[97]   Besides the culinary arts, students also learned to sew and to dress attractively.[98]   In some schools, they learned to play billiards, a skill, it was felt, which would enable them to become *d'excellentes partenaires sportives pour leur mari*.[99]   But conjugal felicity was clearly not limited to these areas.   An *institut familial* also took great care to ensure that its pupils knew how to please a man emotionally.   This aspect of preparation for marriage was left to the school paper, *Ecole de Bonheur*.

Writers in *Ecole de Bonheur* were particularly concerned that girls should understand and accommodate men.   One article described the relationship of a wife to her husband clearly:

> *Envers le mari, un amour sincère et cordial, qui fasse qu'on ait un grand soin de tout ce qui le regarde, selon le temporel et le spirituel, tâchant toujours de le gagner à Dieu par prières, bons exemples et autres moyens convenables: le respect, l'obéissance, la douceur et la patience à souffrir ses défauts et ses mauvaises humeurs.*[100]

Other writers offered additional suggestions as to how happiness in marriage might be achieved.   An article entitled *les maris sont comme ça*, ostensibly written by two parents, began: *Nous présumons, ma femme et moi, qu'un jour viendra où notre fille Alice n'aura d'autre ambition que de plaire à son mari*.   This was followed by *une série de conseils* intended to promote happiness in the home.   First, Alice was advised to encourage her future husband in male sports since *il se sentira plus viril, et par contrecoup tu auras l'impression d'être plus féminine*.   Next, it was important to praise and console a husband, taking care to attend to his every physical and emotional need. Finally, it was wise for a wife to let her husband know that *il n'a plus à lutter pour la conquérir et la garder.*[101]

An *institut familial* offered to girls a religious education compatible with a feminine personality and a feminine vocation. It also offered happiness, as the name *Ecole de Bonheur* indicated. Elusive as these goals appeared, they were nonetheless the objectives of a curriculum which aimed to provide a comprehensive training for marriage and motherhood. Because he believed that a young girl's future happiness depended on *l'épanouissement ordonné et équilibre de toutes les richesses de sa nature,*[102] Abbé Tessier designed a programme which defined the feminine personality in terms of its special talents as well as its proclivities. Made aware of her potential and also how it could be used towards the achievement of marital bliss, a young girl was then schooled in the technical and mental skills necessary for the professional management of home, husband and children. She received instruction in the decorative and functional domestic arts, and an intellectual and psychological training complementary to her role in society but not competitive with the intellectual formation of her husband.

The girl trained in an *institut familial* was intended to be cultured, 'educated' and well-versed in the domestic skills required for a middle-class rather than an agricultural home. Among other things, she was required to develop:

> *Féminité et distinction, don de soi, esprit d'invention, ton du language, droiture et simplicité, originalité intellectuelle, ordre, entrain et initiative, concentration, ponctualité, esprit d'équipe, souci de culture, esprit de discipline, esprit chrétien, goût de la 'belle ouvrage', économie, sens des responsabilités and bon goût.*[103]

It is perhaps ironic that schools which had come out of a tradition of agricultural domestic education for the rural poor should have acquired, in their fight for survival, a middle-class character. Ironic, but not incomprehensible. In that section of the rural population which sought higher education, that is beyond grade ten, a small group of resolute clergymen and some lay persons saw hope. From their ranks would be recruited *une élite d'épouses et de mamans pour la relève familiale.*[104] Upon their shoulders would fall the task of keeping the cultural and religious traditions of French Canada safe from the assaults of modern society. The rural woman, traditionally educated, would fight the materialism and familial disintegration of the cities. More importantly, such a woman would resist feminism and work outside the home. For all her differences from the student of the early *école ménagère*, she was still called upon to uphold a traditional religious social order just as she would have been had she attended a domestic science school early in the twentieth century.

The *institut familial* was therefore an institution dedicated to an ideal, one that came out of a traditional ultramontane construct in which woman's activities ensured the moral and cultural survival of the French collectivity. By seeking to save women from prevailing errors of judgement, by attempting to *leur redonner l'orgueil sain de leur féminité*[105] through education, and thus to prepare them for their feminine obligations, the *institut familial* was a traditional response to a changing society.

In the fifties and sixties, the conditions against which Abbé Tessier and others had placed the barrier of female education grew apace. Women continued to leave their familial realms for work outside the home. Education had to keep up with the changing economic and social reality; technical and academic education for women were important questions of the time.

Female education was only one problem; the reform of the entire educational system along less humanist or classical lines was another. When, during the Quiet Revolution of the sixties, all schools of secondary and higher learning became involved in the debate over classical versus scientific and commercial education, and when the shortage of funds added to the urgency, the *instituts familiaux* faced a serious threat. Neither classical nor technical, they were the target of criticism from all sides. When critics subsequently singled out for complaint the extent of religious influences in education, they dealt another ultimately fatal blow to the *instituts familiaux*. The schools which had been the culmination of a long struggle to preserve traditional moral and domestic education for girls could do little in the face of such overwhelming pressures.

Conclusion

The existence and success of the *instituts familiaux* were primarily due to the prodigious promotional and pedagogical talents of Albert Tessier and to the strength of the clergymen and individuals who believed in his vision of society. This has been the central argument of this chapter. A few final considerations will suggest that at least a part of the success of the schools must be attributed to the favorable climate of the society in which they were nurtured.

In her study of women in war industries, Ruth Roach Pierson offered the view that a "feminine mystique" did not have to be invented in Canada after the war had ended; "it had been there all along."[106] That woman found her only happiness. (and society its stability), through woman's fulfillment of her moral and familial responsibilities in the home was certainly a deeply entrenched belief. During the war years and the post-war period, this image of woman and the corresponding social vision had a special appeal. Thus, Tessier merely articulated, more strongly than others, a perception of woman shared by those who accepted his religious and nationalist vision and those who did not.

Quebecers were hardly unique in envisioning the collapse of society once woman departed from her traditional realm. Journalists across the country took up the theme when they recorded, with dismay, female participation in the work force and in the wartime amusements of dance halls and cafés.[107] In Quebec, reflections of this kind were marked by a nationalist argument made all the more pronounced by the anxieties of the war years. The St. Jean Baptiste Society well illustrated the degree to which the collective anxiety over *Survivance* expressed itself through a concern over woman's role in the family. At a congress in 1942, the Society declared that a contemptible movement was afoot to reduce the French Canadian mother to the level of her English counterpart. The war had brought conditions that afforded the enemies of French Canada a golden opportunity to destroy nationalism, and motherhood was one of the first casualties in the endeavour.[108] During the war years, writers in *L'Action Nationale*, *La Famille* and *Relations* generally agreed with the Society that the French community was endangered by war-time conditions that contrived to remove woman from her familial sphere.[109]

In the post-war period, the growing strength of a more secular, less isolationist nationalism did not immediately alter the traditional national importance attached to woman's activities in the family. Instead, the old ideal was reclothed in a more contemporary fashion. For instance, one writer in *L'Action Nationale*, turning to the question of how economic *épanouissement* might be achieved, advised the maintenance of a high birth rate. Rather than *la revanche des berceaux*, he offered an elaboration of his position in economic terms. A high birth rate was a precondition for a high standard of living. Hence, Francophones in Quebec must regain their once remarkable fertility.[110] Quebecers concerned over the fate of the French language expressed a similar view of woman's importance in the family when they suggested the problem could be solved if mothers educated their children patriotically.[111] Even during the Quiet Revolution, it seems, woman was not to abandon her post as the guardian of race and culture.

Perhaps a more revealing example of support for a traditional nationalist ideal of woman was its acceptance by the critics of the *instituts familiaux*. In their submissions to the Royal Commissions, the supporters of classical colleges and technical schools for girls asserted strongly their belief that woman had an important familial (and extra-familial) role to play in the survival of the French collectivity.

Thus, Tessier espoused an ideal of woman that was not so remarkably different to the one widely accepted in his society. That he was able to foster this ideal as comprehensively as he did may be partially explained by another characteristic of post-war society, the popularity of personality training in education.

228

Two very different educational philosophies enjoyed support during the war years. The progressive movement, developed early in the century, had its strongest influence on Canadian educators during the 1930s and 1940s. Progressive educators stressed education as socialization, a concept that led naturally to the proposition that education's central function was the training of personalities. In the view of progressivists, education had to prepare boys and girls to be well-adjusted and happy; the development of the intellect was only secondary to this goal. Intrinsically opposed to progressive ideals, Christian humanists formed, nonetheless, another group in the post-war era preaching the teaching of socially acceptable values in education. Christian humanism, revived by the Catholic educator Jacques Maritain, proposed a return to Christian values in education.[112] Maritain's call for "a return to goodness" through the proper education sounded a welcome note in a world recently torn apart by the horrors of war.[113] It would be misleading to compare Maritain's emphasis on moral education to the progressive belief in education for real life. Both philosophies, however, placed considerable value on education's role in the formation of personalities. Furthermore, educators of both persuasions believed implicitly in the link between the properly educated child and a stable society.

Whether happiness or moral responsibility was the goal, the implications for female education could, and did, result in the same kind of training for girls; preparation for marriage and motherhood. It is significant that Tessier was able to employ progressive pedagogical methods and claim, at the same time, his allegiance to Jacques Maritain. Personality training was an eminently complementary objective to education that fostered the ideal wife and mother. Dewey's emphasis on training students to be happy had much in common with the philosophical assumption of an *école de bonheur*. In the same way, some Christian humanists, accepting Maritain's tenet that education inculcate a moral and "human personality,"[114] argued that it was appropriate to educate girls solely for their familial responsibilities. In France, for example, Hélène Brûlé proposed that education stress *la dignité de la personne humaine.*[115] For a girl, this recommendation entailed learning self-abnegation, the ability to put all else after *le bonheur de son foyer.*[116] In North America, Betty Friedan has described vividly the concerns of "sex-directed" educators who proposed, in the name of humanism, "education for femininity."[117]

The *instituts familiaux* were not, therefore, as anomalous as they might have seemed. In one way, the ideal woman they promoted possessed the attraction of a universal image. Furthermore, the ideal and the corresponding education found an agreeable climate in the post-war world. Thus Albert Tessier was at once a reactionary and a man of his times. He saw, correctly, that the feminine ideal born of Catholic nationalism could be accommodated easily within the context of the times. His primary contribution to rural domestic science schools, that of changing their image from lower-class to middle-class institutions, made use of a prevailing ideal of woman. That is, as women became less involved in agricultural life, the alternative role for those who could not accept her entrance into the labour force was that of middle-class housewife. Such a woman, in the words of a Saskatchewan Royal Commission on rural life (1956), played a new role in the home; one which was "more diffuse, supportive and oriented to the gratification of other affective and emotional needs of family members."[118] In the 1950s, this role for women enjoyed an appeal that transcended rural and urban perimeters as well as cultural ones. One might even say this ideal transcended social class despite its obvious incongruence with the life of the working-class woman.

It is often propounded that *la société québécoise donne à la famille une place comme institution sociale, qui en transforme la position culturelle, et lui donne une légitimité qui n'existe pas dans les autres régions de l'Amérique du Nord.*[119] The corollary of this point of view, that the tremendous importance ascribed to motherhood and woman's activities within the family is uniquely *québécois*, is also argued.[120] An understanding of the *instituts familiaux* within the context of their time suggests these beliefs may well be unfounded. The family, and woman's role within it, undoubtedly played a role of considerable importance in Catholic nationalism in Quebec. Furthermore, Catholic educators in that province promoted, with unflagging zeal, a traditional ideal of woman in education. This ideal, however, like all mythical images, possessed "a measure of universality."[121]

Ideology relies a great deal on universal myths. And myth, writes a student of ideology, "is not really describing a situation but trying by means of this description to *bring about* what it declares to exist."[122] The story of the *instituts familiaux* demonstrates, in the realm of education, how some myths can become reality.

Notes

[1]This article was based on a Master's thesis written in 1978 entitled *The Instituts Familiaux of Quebec: Religious Nationalism and the Education of Girls for Domestic Life, 1900-1970*, and an article of the same title published in Fernand Dumond, ed. *Idéologies au Canada Français 1940-1976.* (Québec: Les presses de l'université Laval, 1981). Since this time, Nicole Thivierge has published her doctoral thesis entitled *Ecoles Ménagères et Instituts Familiaux: un modéle féminin traditionnel,* (Québec: Institut québécois de recherche sur la culture, 1982).

[2]Louis François Richer Laflèche, *Quelques Considérations sur les rapports de la Société Civile et la Religion* (Montréal: Eusèbe Sénécal, 1866).

[3]*Ibid.,* pp. 86-9.

[4]*Ibid.,* p. 99.

[5]*Ibid.*, p. 20.
[6]Nadia Eid, *Le Clergé et le Pouvoir Politique au Québec* (Montréal: Editions Hurtubise, 1978), pp. 223-6.
[7]Alphonse Désilets, "Les Ursulines de Roberval," in *L'Almanach de l'Action Sociale Catholique* 17 (1933), 70.
[8]R. P. Archambault on Henri Bourassa, "Un Grand Apôtre de la Famille," *Action Nationale* 42, 1 (janvier 1954), 159.
[9]Abbé Lionel Groulx, cited in *Bulletin Mensuel des Ecoles Ménagères* (septembre 1954), 5.
[10]Association des diététistes de Québec, *Mémoire sur l'enseignement ménager présenté à la Commission royale d'enquête sur l'enseignement par l'Association des diététistes du Québec 1962.* (Text found in Archives du Séminaire de Trois Rivières, Tessier Collection), 13.
[11]Conseil de l'Instruction Publique, *Règlements de Comité Catholique* (1930) (Québec: Conseil de l'Instruction Publiques, 1930), 227.
[12]Report of Inspectors of Urban Districts, *Annual Report of the Superintendent of Education of the Province of Quebec 1934-35* (Quebec: Printer to the King, 1935), 106.
[13]Alphonse Désilets, *Annual Report, 1934-35*, 155.
[14]Victor Doré, *Annual Report, 1939-40*, xxi.
[15]Désilets, *Annual Report, 1939-40*, 252.
[16]

Growth of Vocational Domestic Science Schools[a] 1936-1950		
Year	No. of Schools[b]	Enrollment[c]
1936-37	11	4,982
1937-38	12	5,549
1938-39	11	4,408
1939-40	10	5,107
1940-41	9	5,710
1941-42	9	3,660
1942-43	8	4,533
1943-44	10	8,110
1944-45	10	8,110
1945-46	-	-
1946-47	12	6,970
1947-48	18	10,792
1948-49	29	14,297
1949-50	39	21,593

[a]Vocational domestic science schools refer to the *écoles ménagères spéciales, municipales* and *générals.*

[b]Occasionally, some schools were re-designated as *écoles ménagères régionales*, hence not included in the statistics. This accounts for the decline in schools from 11 to 8 in 1942-43.

[c]Some exaggeration is possible since enrollment figures were occasionally compiled for all grades of the school instead of the

superior level of grades 10 to 13. This may have been the case in 1949-50.

Sources: 1. Bureau of Statistics, Province of Quebec. *Educational Statistics for the School Years 1937-1943* (Dept. of Municipal Affairs, Trade and Commerce).
2. Quebec: *Statistical Yearbooks 1944-1950* (Ottawa: Printer to the King).
3. *Annual Reports of the Superintendent of Education of the Province of Quebec 1936-1950* (Ottawa: Printer to the King).

[17]Claude Galarneau, *Les collèges classiques au Canada Français,* (Montréal: Editions Fides, 1978), pp. 146-7.
[18]Cardinal Villeneuve, cited by Abbé Paul Carignan, *Ecole de Bonheur* 1, (April 1956), 7.
[19]Abbé Albert Tessier, *Bulletin Mensuel* (April 1940), 34.
[20]Tessier, "Nos Intérêts Culturels," *Action Nationale* 9, 5 (May 1937), 263.
[21]Tessier, "La Mère Canadienne," Radio College Telecast, March 10, 1942. (Text found in the Tessier collection, Archives du Séminaire de Trois-Rivières (hereafter ASTR), Tessier Collection.) His historical work on women is entitled *Canadiennes* (Montréal: Editions Fides, 1946).
[22]Tessier, cited by Camille Caron, "L'Abbé Tessier et les Ecoles Ménagères," *Le Ralliement* (special issue), n.d. Séminaire de Trois-Rivieres, 10.
[23]

Growth of the *Ecoles Ménagères Régionales 1936-1950*

	No. of Schools			No. of Pupils		
Year	a	b	c	a	b	c
1936-37	18	-	18	3529	-	-
1937-38	18	-	16	3888	221	-
1938-39	18	19	-	579	288	-
1939-40	18	19	20	832	476	823
1940-41	20	19	20	971	681	971
1941-42	22	19	22	1159	823	1158
1942-43	24	21	24	1231	986	1231
1943-44	26	24	33	1293	1174	1293
1944-45	26	24	24	1293	1243	1690
1945-46	32	32	32	-	1621	1703
1946-47	32	32	33	1703	1705	1669
1947-48	33	32	36	1669	1730	1909
1948-49	36	36	36	1909	1900	1909
1949-50	38	36	36	1936	2013	1936

[a]Source: Bureau of Statistics, Province of Quebec, *Educational Statistics for the School Years 1937-1943* (Department of

Municipal Affairs, Trade and Commerce); Quebec: *Statistical Yearbooks 1944-50* (Ottawa: Printer to the King).

bSource: Association des Institutes Familiaux in *Mémoire à la Commission Royale d'Enquête Sur l'Enseignement*, 1962.

cSource: *Annual Reports of the Superintendent of Education of the Province of Quebec 1936-1950* (Ottawa: Printer to the King).

Statistics which appear comparatively high probably include enrollment for all grades instead of the superior level of grades 10-13. Some of the differences in figures may also be the result of different criteria for schools; e.g., vocational schools may have been included.

[24]Tessier, *Bulletin Mensuel* (février 1942), 76.

[25]*La Presse*, 12 February 1945.

[26]Advertisements of one page in length were usually taken out in every issue. See, e.g., *La Famille* 5, 2 (Oct. 1941), 213.

[27]Doré, *Annual Report*, 144-5, 207.

[28]E. Leblanc, "Rapport du service d'Enseignement ménager" *Annual Report of the Superintendent of Education of the Province of Quebec, 1944-45* (Quebec: Printer to the King, 1945), 207.

[29]The Educational Policies Committee of the Canada and Newfoundland Education Association, *Trends in Education 1944*, (Toronto: Canada and Newfoundland Education Association, October 13, 1944), 45.

[30]B. O. Filteau, *Code Scolaire de la Province de Québec 1940* (Québec: Imprimerie le Soleil Limitée, 1940), 101.

[31]Tessier's statistics were printed in the *Bulletin Mensuel*. See, for example, the issue of January, 1943, p. 109.

[32]Tessier, *Bulletin Mensuel* (janvier 1943), 168.

[33]Hilda Neatby wrote a scathing attack of this movement as it influenced Canadian educators of the 1940s in her book *So Little for the Mind* (Toronto: Clarke, Irwin and Company, Ltd., 1953).

[34]*Ibid.*, p. 220.

[35]Tessier, "Les écoles ménagères au service du foyer," *Relations*, 21, (septembre 1942), 225.

[36]Omer J. Desauliners, *Annual Report of the Superintendent of Education of the Province of Quebec* (Quebec: Printer to the King), 11.

[37]Filteau, *Code Scolaire*, 1940, p. 121.

[38]Tessier, "Les écoles ménagères au service du foyer," 236.

[39]*Ibid.*

[40]*Ibid.*

[41]Seventy-six bulletins were published between 1939 and 1949; most of these were written by Tessier himself.

[42]Tessier, *Bulletin Mensuel* (décembre 1941), 90.

[43]*Ibid.* (janvier 1939), 4.

[44]*Ibid.* (septembre 1940), 30.

[45]*Ibid.* (janvier 1944), 211.
[46]Doré, *Annual Report*, 1944-45, p. xix.
[47]

Growth of Instituts Familiaux: 1950-1960		
Year	No. of Schools	No. of Pupils
1950-51	38	1954
1951-52	39	2083
1952-53	40	2309
1953-54	41	2578
1954-55	43	2498
1955-56	43	2500
1956-57	44	2669
1957-58	44	2927
1958-59	44	3177
1959-60	45	3276

Source: Annual Reports of the Superintendent of Public Education of the Province of Quebec.

[48]Evelyn Brown, *Educating Eve* (Montreal: Palm publishers, 1957), p. 8.
[49]

Social Background of Pupils of the Instituts Familiaux					
Occupation	1957	1958	1959	1960	1961
Professional	260	315	325	318	346
Bourgeois	1215	1413	1471	1477	1690
Worker	878	921	1000	1050	1271
Farmer	486	496	494	509	563
Unspecified	8	32	13	29	13

Professional: doctors and lawyers
Bourgeois: merchants, civil servants, office workers
Worker: factory worker
Farmer: directly engaged in agriculture Source:
                     Association des Instituts Familiaux, Memoire à la Commission Royale d'Enquête Sur l'Enseignement 1962, pp. 79-80.

[50]*Ecole de Bonheur*, no. 2 (June 1956), 2.
[51]Admission requirements to the *instituts familiaux* were as follows:

To 1st year: certificate required from grade nine
To 2nd year: certificate required from grade eleven or fourth year of *Cours Lettres Sciences*.
To 3rd year: certificate required from an *école normale*.

Sister Théodore-de-la-Croix, *La Pédagogie des instituts familiaux*, 8.

[52]Donald R. White, "Rural Canada in Transition," M.A. Tremblay and Walton J. Anderson, eds., *Rural Canada in Transition* (Ottawa: Agricultural Economics Research Council of Canada, 1968), 74.

[53]Tessier, *Bulletin Mensuel* (décembre, 1955) 8.

[54]Reports of the director of household science, *Annual Reports of the Superintendent of Education of the Province of Quebec 1951-1962*.

[55]

Occupations of Graduates of the Full Programme of the Instituts Familiaux						
Occupation	1956	1957	1958	1959	1960	1961
Religion	21	13	29	18	35	20
Homemaking	35	36	39	32	49	47
Teaching	83	130	155	125	222	210
Graduate Study[a]	20	13	23	24	48	40
Nursing[b]	12	7	11	9	-	18
Other[c]	17	150	30	42	51	58

[a]Refers to the programme of the Institut de Pédagogie.
[b]Includes occupation of Nurses Aid.
[c]Refers to jobs in dietetics and sewing.

Source: Association des Instituts Familiaux, *Mémoire à la Commission Royale d'Enquête Sur l'Enseignement 1962*, pp. 84-85.

[56]Brown, *Educating Eve*, 117.

[57]Tessier, "Rapport de la réunion des aumôniers des instituts familiaux, 3-4 février, 1964 au Cap-de-la-Madeleine," ASTR, Tessier collection, File 9.

[58]*Ibid.*

[59]Tessier, *Femmes Dépareillées*, 4th ed. (Québec: Editions Pélican, 1962), p. 75.

[60]Association des Instituts Familiaux, *Mémoire à la commission royale d'enquête sur l'enseignement* (Québec: Imprimeur de la Reine, 1962), 10.

[61]Tessier, *Ecoles de Bonheur* 4 (octobre 1956), 19.

[62]Brown, *Educating Eve*, p. 19.

[63]*Ibid.*, p. 10.

[64]Département de l'Instruction Publique, *Programme des Instituts Familiaux*, 1956. (Québec: Dépt. d'éducation, 1956), 1.

[65]Tessier, cited in *Bulletin Special* 115 (décembre 1953), 4-5.

[66]Tessier, cited by Sister Théodore-de-la Croix, "La pédagogie des Instituts Familiaux," 67.

[67]Association des Instituts Familiaux, *Mémoire*, 1962, p. 59.

[68]Evelyn Brown visited Saint-Jacques-de-Montcalm and noted that the school cost two million dollars. *Educating Eve*, p. 72.

[69]Association des Instituts Familiaux, *Mémoire*, 1962, p. 63.

[70]Tessier, "Rapport de la réunion des aumôniers," 17.

[71]Association des Instituts Familiaux, *Mémoire*, 1962, p. 63.

[72]Département de l'Instruction Publique, "Les instituts familiaux," *Brochure*, 1962 (Québec: Département d'éducation), 3.

[73]Aline Eraly, "l'Action éducative des instituts familiaux," *Bulletin Spécial* 115 (décembre 1953), 8-16; Also Brown, *Educating Eve*, p. 96.

[74]Tessier, "La Pédagogie Familiale," ASTR, Tessier Collection, File, Q1.

[75]Association des Instituts Familiaux, *Mémoire*, 1962, pp. 57-8.

[76]Abbé R. E. Llewellyn, *Ta Personne*; *Ton Futur*; *Ton Milieu*; *Ton Foyer* (Trois-Rivières: Les Editions trifluviennes, 1946).

[77]Llewellyn, *Ta Personne*, p. 167.

[78]*Ibid.*, p. 8.

[79]Département de l'Instruction Publique, *Service des Examens Officiels 1963: Instituts Familiaux* (Québec: Département de l'Instruction Publique, n.d.), p. 5.

[80]Llewellyn, *Ton Milieu*, p. 38.

[81]*Ibid.*, p. 93.

[82]Llewellyn, *Ton Futur*, p. 25.

[83]*Ibid.*, p. 84.

[84]Marie-Paule Vinay, *La Femme et Son Coeur* (Québec: Les Editions Paulines, 1954); *Qui est Jeannette?* (Québec: Editions de Pélican, 1961).

[85]Vinay, *Qui est Jeannette?*, p. 166.

[86]Département de l'Instruction Publique, *Examens Officiels*, 1963, p. 41.

[87]Département de l'Instruction Publique, *Programme des Instituts Familiaux 1956* (Province de Québec: Département de l'Instruction Publique), p. 89.

[88]Département de l'Instruction Publique, *Examens Officiels 1964*, p. 39.

[89]*Ibid.*, p. 49.

[90]The *Programme des Instituts Familiaux 1963* referred to chemistry as "chimie alimentaire" and arithmetic as "compatiblité familiale et arithmétique," pp. 6-7.

[91]Département de l'Instruction Publique, *Programme des Instituts Familiaux 1956*, p. 90.

[92]*Ibid.*

[93]*Ibid.*, p. 96.

[94]*Ibid.*

[95]Département de l'Instruction Publique, *Examens Officiels 1963*, p. 20.

[96]Brown, *Educating Eve*, p. 54.

[97]Llewelynn, *Ecole de Bonheur* 24 (février 1960), 13.

[98]Brown, *Educating Eve*, p. 25.

[99]*Perspectives*, weekend magazine of *Le Nouvelliste*, 22 April 1960.

[100]*Ecole de Bonheur* 18 (mars 1959), 9.

[101]*Ecole de Bonheur* 5 (janvier 1957), 17-8.

[102]*Ecole de Bonheur*, 1 (avril 1956), 12.

[103]Sister Théodore-de-la-Croix, "La direction des instituts familiaux" unpublished thesis for the *Licence en Pédagogie*, Laval University on behalf of the *Ecole de Pédagogie et d'Orientation de Québec*, Outremont, 1960, p. 95.

[104]*Ecole de Bonheur* 9 (septembre 1957), 2.

[105]Sister Théodore-de-la-Croix, "La Pédagogie des instituts familiaux," 68.

[106]Ruth Roach Pierson, "Women's Emancipation and the Recruitment of Women into the Labour Force in World War II," in Susan Mann Trofimenkof and Alison Prentice, eds., *The Neglected Majority* (Toronto: McClelland and Stewart Ltd., 1977), p. 145.

[107]Roland Stromberg shows the persistance of a traditional ideal of woman in American women's magazines *After Everything. Western Intellectual History Since 1945* (New York: St. Martin's Press, 1975), p. 39; A perusal of newspapers after the war reveals the same was true in Canada.

[108]L. A. Fréchette, "Hommage à la mère canadienne-française," *Action Nationale* 21, 2 (février 1943), 132-40.

[109]Mona Josée Gagnon, *Les Femmes vues par le Québec des hommes* (Montréal: Editions du jour, 1974), pp. 89-95.

[110]Report of the *Etats Généraux*, "Atelier sur la Famille et la Politique Familiale," *Action Nationale* 57, 3-4 (nov.-déc. 1967), 335.

[111]*Ibid.*

[112]Jacques Maritain, *Education at the Crossroads* (New Haven: Yale University Press, 1943).

[113]*Ibid.*, p. 97.

[114]*Ibid.*, p.7

[115]Hélène Brulé, *Le Rôle de la femme dans l'Education Familiale et Sociale* (Paris: Les Editions Foucher, 1950), p. 5.

[116]*Ibid.*, p. 27.

[117]Betty Friedan, *The Feminine Mystique* (New York: Dell Publishing Co., 1953), p. 149.

[118]Cited by Donald White in M. A. Tremblay, ed., *Rural Canada in Transition* (Ottawa: The Agricultural Economics Research Council of Canada, 1968), p. 57.

[119]Philippe Garigue, *La Vie Familiale des Canadiens Français* (Montréal: Presses de l'Université de Montréal, 1962), p. xxiii.

[120]Gagnon, *Les Femmes*, p. 18.

[121]Elizabeth Janeway, *Man's World, Women's Place* (New York: Dell Publishing Co., 1971), p. 42.

[122]*Ibid.*, p. 37.

Chapter Twelve

THE LA LECHE LEAGUE: A FEMINIST PERSPECTIVE[*]

Deborah Gorham and Florence Kellner Andrews

In recent years, a defence of 'traditional family life' has been a
central feature of the new right, and anti-feminism has played a
major role in new-right pro-family rhetoric. The supposed
breakdown in the family that new-right activists deplore is often
connected with the rise of the women's liberation movement.

Ironically, the increase in anti-feminist pro-family activism
comes at a time when the feminist movement itself is fragmented,[1]
and feminists themselves disagree about the significance of
motherhood and the value of family life. Only those outside the
movement perceive a monolithic feminist position on these issues.
Twenty years ago, at the beginning of the revival of feminism, such
a unity did appear to exist. Feminists of the sixties did attack the
patriarchal family, with its assumptions of female dependence and
male dominance, and its belief in woman's destiny as nurturer, as
the social structure most responsible for the oppression of women.[2]
But even then there were disagreements among feminists about
explaining the origins of the patriarchal family and defining what
ought to replace it, and these disagreements have become more
evident in the last few years.

Feminist thinking on the family has taken a number of
directions. Socialist feminists emphasize the links between the
patriarchal family and capitalism, and between women's oppression
within the family, and women's exploitation in the labour market.
They see the private oppression of women to be intertwined with
economic oppression, and believe that both can be eradicated only if
class and gender oppression are attacked simultaneously. Some
radical feminists, on the other hand, have perceived women's
oppression in the patriarchal family as having an existence that is
conceptually and temporally prior to any particular economic

[*]We would like to thank the La Leche League Leaders who were interviewed in
the course of this study and who were very generous with their time and with their
information. The interpretations of this information, however, are our own.

238

system. For the most uncompromising among the radical feminists, the only solution seems to be female separatism. And finally, some of the most well-known liberal feminists of the 1960s and early 1970s have in recent years abandoned their attacks on the evils of the family, to come to a defence of family values and of the importance of the experience of motherhood.[3]

In interpreting and understanding motherhood itself, feminist thinking has oscillated between two poles. On the one hand, there are those who emphasize the importance of freeing mothers from the sole responsibility for nurturing the young, and who see this pattern of nurturance as the root cause of misogyny in all human societies.[4] On the other hand, there are those who emphasize woman's special nature as mother, and who wish to strengthen what they see as a unique woman's moral and social culture.[5]

In spite of the fragmentation of feminist thinking, we suggest that it is possible to establish a 'base-line feminist position'[6] on the family. Any feminist analysis of the family will reflect a belief that family forms in the present and in the past have been harmful to women and have supported male privilege. While feminists may not agree on its origins or its functioning, there is a consensus about the existence of patriarchy. In contrast, anti-feminist positions on the family reflect an acceptance of male dominance and of the subordination of women. Such anti-feminist views are often, although not invariably, associated with fundamentalist religious views.[7]

For feminists, anti-feminist pro-family activism is especially disquieting when it is espoused by right-wing women. Male support for anti-feminism can be attributed to male fears about the loss of male privilege: female support for these views undercuts any easy assumptions about a unity of interest among women. If female support, however, for the more extreme anti-feminist views about the values of the patriarchal family represents both a threat and an embarrassment to feminists, it is ultimately of less significance than the fact that a feminist analysis of the oppressive nature of the patriarchal family has failed to attract a broad base of support among women. For while only a tiny minority of women in Canada support an explicitly anti-feminist position, it is still the case that Canadian women who are explicitly feminist make up less than fifty per cent of the female population. The exact size of the remaining 'undecideds', i.e., non-feminists, who reject an explicitly political analysis of women's situation, remains unknown.[8]

The largely white, middle-class origins of the majority of feminists and of feminist ideology may account for the absence of large numbers of working-class women and women of colour from the women's movement.[9] But we must look to other factors to explain the rejection of the feminist analysis of the patriarchal family by women of social origins similar to those of middle-class feminist women. The resistance to feminism displayed by many middle-class women can partly be explained by the fact that in recent years the message of feminism has been distorted by those who control opinions in our culture. Non-feminist women see the image represented by the beautiful, young superwoman of television commercials and mass entertainment, who both manages a successful, lucrative career and serves the needs of a husband and children. It is clear to them that this image does not reflect their own situation, nor does it represent a solution to their deep concerns about the needs of their children, and their own needs as mothers. Many non-feminist women mistake this 'lifestyle feminism' for genuine feminism and fail to see that the television image represents the co-optation of feminist goals by consumer capitalism.[10] They remain unaware of debates within feminism, and do not know that there is an important body of feminist analysis that has been concerned with the devaluation of mothering and with our society's lack of concern with children.[11]

Our intention in this paper is to contribute to an understanding of non-feminist views of mothering and child care through an examination of the La Leche League, an organization whose stated aim--the promotion of breastfeeding--clearly identifies it as a group concerned with mothering. Because the La Leche League, as an organization, has never taken an explicit position on feminism--or indeed on any issue other than the promotion of breastfeeding--we call it 'non-feminist'. Through a historical overview of League activities and League literature, we examine the way in which this explicitly non-ideological organization has been influenced by conflicting ideologies concerning women and the family over the course of its history--a history that antedates the mid-century revival of feminism. Through a study of the League in one North American location in the mid-1980s, we explore the ways in which this organization serves women's needs at the present time, and we examine the way in which League women define themselves in relation to feminist, anti-feminist and non-feminist views about women and the family.[12]

The membership of the La Leche League cannot be considered to be typical of middle-class homemakers, because their attention to breastfeeding and their emphasis upon the importance of the child are articulated much more fully than is or has been the case with most women whose main careers lie outside the labour force. This organization, however, has existed for three decades, actively advocating a style of childrearing and homemaking which definitely conforms to a dominant set of cultural prescriptions in North America.[13]

The La Leche League defines itself as an organization "devoted to providing encouragement, information and support to the mother who wants to breastfeed her baby."[14] The League was organized in 1956 in Franklin Park, Illinois, by seven women, who were all breastfeeding mothers of large families.[15] Founded at a time when the bottlefeeding of infants in North America had become more common than breastfeeding, the League, since its inception,

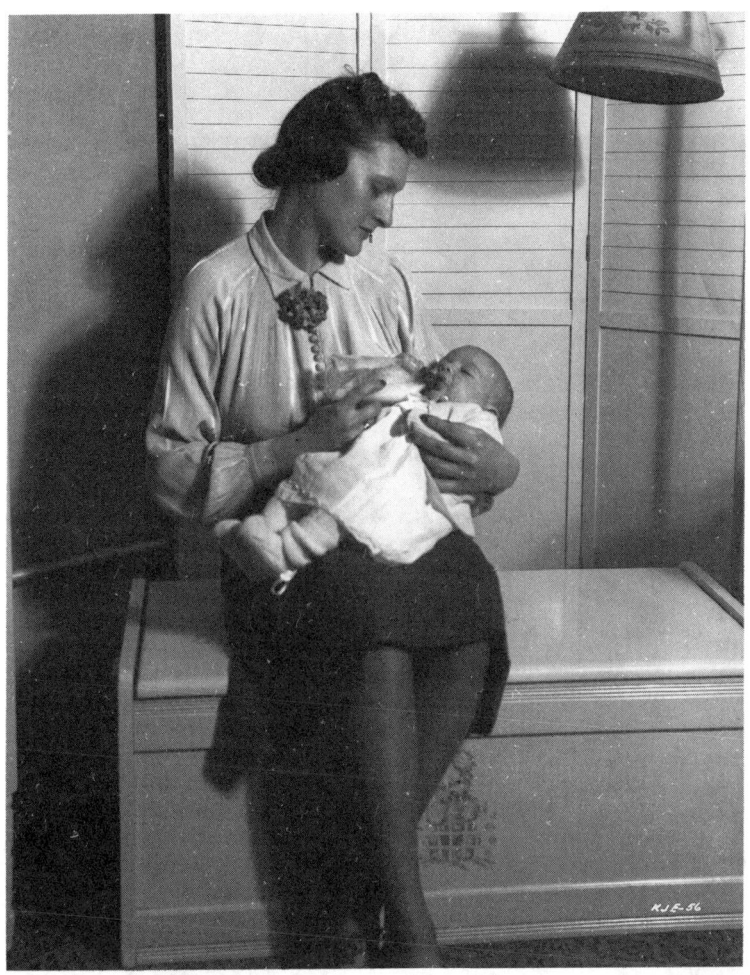

"Wrong way to hold feeding bottle," Ottawa, Ontario, December 1939, photograph by Eugene Michael Finn, C.G.M.P.B. (NFB), for possible use in *The Canadian Mother and Child*.

Source: National Archives of Canada, PA-803170.

'When preparing the formula have everything you require near at hand. It is of the utmost importance that every utensil be scrupulously clean. Wash your hands well before preparing the formula.'' Ernest Couture, *The Canadian Mother and Child* (Ottawa: Department of Pensions and National Health Division of Child and Maternal Welfare, 1940), p. 130. Photograph by Eugene Michael Finn, C.G.M.P.B. (NFB).

Source: National Archives of Canada, PA-163732.

has seen as its main function the provision of support for breastfeeding mothers, and as its corollary, continuous mothering. The League has offered such support through its numerous publications, the most important of which is its manual, *The Womanly Art of Breastfeeding*,[16] and through what the League calls "mother-to-mother" help. The chief group activity that the League organizes on a local level is a series of meetings for mothers, held in the home of one of the local League mothers, and conducted by an accredited League Leader. Local group meetings, which are restricted to women only,[17] are usually held in people's houses, rather than in an institutional setting. The women attending sit informally on chairs or on the floor, and there are always infants and small children present, who are often breastfed as the meeting progresses. All the women present are encouraged to express their views about the topic under discussion.

The informality that characterizes League meetings for mothers reflects the League's wider commitment to a 'womanly' organizational style. It is League policy that the basis for relationships between women involved in the organization should be informal, and League literature advocates "mother-to-mother" contact, rather than contact produced by a rigid organizational structure.[18] According to its own accounts, this commitment to informality goes back to the organization's very beginning. Its seven founders were all full-time housewives and mothers, and they saw themselves, because they were women, as unfamiliar with the sorts of organizational structures established by men. Their early planning sessions were all held in the homes of one or another of the seven, and the first mother-to-mother meeting, which took place in October, 1956, was also held in a private home. As one of the founding mothers put it: "Like Topsy, we just grew, particularly, since the founding mothers were happy as mothers and weren't the 'go-go' organization type. . ."[19]

The League's seven 'founding mothers' did not initially intend to create an organization that would spread beyond the confines of their own community, but the La Leche League had begun to grow before 1960.[20] From its founding in 1956, the League has been a single-issue organization in the sense that the only issues on which it has taken an unequivocal and clearly stated position concern the importance of breastfeeding. It has always been interested, however, in a series of wider but related issues. As its motto--"Good Mothering Through Breastfeeding, the World Over"--suggests, it does not advocate breastfeeding merely because of the nutritional benefits of mother's milk. The League is committed to certain views on motherhood, childrearing and family life, of which breastfeeding forms a central part. These central views may be categorized under four headings: 1) support for "complete" breastfeeding; 2) support for constant and continuous mothering and for a style of baby and childcare which follows the lead of the child rather than of the caretaking adults; 3) support for the family as the most significant unit in society; and 4) support for "natural" as opposed to technological methods of childbirth.

Complete Breastfeeding

When the League was first organized, in the mid-1950s, bottlefeeding of infants was both more common than breastfeeding, and more acceptable.[21] The transformation of birth in North America from a home-centred activity organized by women, to a hospital-centred activity organized by the male-dominated medical profession was complete by 1956.[22] In the technologically dominated maternity ward, breastfeeding on demand was felt to interfere with scheduling. Neither physicians nor nursing staffs encouraged it, and breastmilk itself was thought by physicians to be less reliable than scientifically designed formulae. Moreover, the decline in breastfeeding that had already occurred made further declines likely, since women who wanted to nurse were, each year, less and less likely to be able to find other women they could learn from.

It was out of these concerns that the La Leche League was born. Referring to the beginnings of the La Leche League, Edwina Froelich, one of the founding mothers, stated recently: ". . .the babies belonged to the doctor in those days. . . One of the things we said right from the beginning was, by golly, let's give the baby back to the mother."[23] The League's birth was but one of many symptoms that the unquestioning faith in technological medicine, which characterized both the medical profession itself and its lay consumers in the first part of this century, had reached its crest in the mid-1950s and was about to be challenged by a more skeptical and critical attitude on the part of the consumer. In the area of breastfeeding, that questioning has had its effect: substantial gains have been made in terms of medical and cultural acceptance of breastfeeding.[24]

Accordingly, while there has been no fundamental change in the League's policy--it supported breastfeeding in 1956, and its supports it today--the League in recent years has been more outspoken in its support not merely for breastfeeding, but for what the League calls "complete" breastfeeding. The League firmly advocates exclusive reliance on breastmilk during the infant's early months, and supports extended nursing, until the child is well into the toddler years. League policy today is that, for a healthy, full-term baby, until around the first six months of life, the only nourishment the baby should receive is breastmilk. The use of formula supplements is discouraged, for medical and psychological reasons, and because the introduction of nourishment other than mother's milk might compromise the baby's desire to nurse. Moreover, the League discourages mothers from expressing breastmilk and giving it to the baby later in a bottle: such a practice is condoned only when absolutely necessary, as in the case of premature and hospitalized babies. Mothers are advised to introduce solids only when the baby shows a clear desire for them.

When should a mother stop breastfeeding? The League supports "baby-led" weaning: "To sum up our philosophy of weaning. . .: Let the baby do it. Let him nurse until he wants to stop."[25]

That statement appeared in the first edition of *The Womanly Art of Breastfeeding*, but it is only in recent years that the La Leche League has published extensive literature giving advice and support to women who wish to nurse toddlers.[26] Our local study of League women indicates that the practice of extended and "complete" nursing is, in the 1980s, frequently the practice distinguishing a committed League mother from the majority of Canadian mothers who breastfeed their infants, at least initially, but who stop after a few weeks or months, and who may well give regular supplements from early infancy.

Our study of Ottawa League women indicates that the issue of baby-led weaning presents some difficulties for League mothers, but is also a source of pride. The women who discuss nursing older children (six is the highest age we have heard mentioned) do feel that the practice is a demonstration of good, attentive mothering. But, at the same time, the fact that extended nursing is not accepted generally by society, and is often criticized by the woman's family members, creates difficulties that are assuaged mainly by reinforcing her ties to other League women.

Mothering

One of the La Leche League's ten basic concepts is that "the baby has a basic need for his mother's love and presence which is as intense as his need for food."[27] The League encourages constant mothering and sees mothering as a feminine "vocation." Drawing on the work of Freudian psychology to provide backing for its views, the League opposes any separation of mother and infant. Its position is that the baby needs to have its desires for constant, close contact with its mother met. League literature discourages scheduling an infant's feedings and encourages the mother to respond quickly to the baby's cries. The mother is assured that this will not "spoil" her infant but will, rather, lead ultimately to genuine independence.

The League supports the idea that it is the mother's obligation to respond to the child's needs, and to give her children "loving guidance" rather than to control them with harsh or authoritarian discipline. League literature includes analyses of various stages of a child's development: throughout the childrearing process, mothers are encouraged to respect the child's feelings, and not to push the child to grow up too quickly. League literature assumes that the intense dependence of the child on the mother continues well beyond infancy--at least until the age of three--and should be allowed to diminish at the child's own pace.

The Family

> In helping mothers and fathers to understand the needs of
> our babies, we're helping them to build better families.
> The shape of the family really determines the shape of
> society.[28]

From its first publications to the present, La Leche League
literature has been permeated with a belief that the nuclear family
is the mainstay of society. Implicit in all League and League-
sponsored discussions of family life is a belief that the mother-child
dyad can best flourish in a family setting where the father
wholeheartedly functions as "protector and provider" for his wife
and children. Although its statements about male and female roles
have altered somewhat over the past three decades, the League
stands today, as it did when it was first founded, for separate and
distinct roles for father and mother, but, at the same time, it has
always urged that the father should be intimately involved in
parenthood.

Implicitly, if not explicitly, the League advocates large
families. The message that the family of several children is both
normal and preferable to a family of one or two children is conveyed
through the frequent use of specific examples in its literature,
examples which are often drawn from correspondence with League
mothers. Letters and anecdotes about family management
commonly involve examples of families with three or more children.
The model of the large family has been reinforced, from the League's
earliest days, by the use of the seven founding mothers as
exemplars: the story of the lives and child-rearing experiences of
each of them has figured prominently in League literature during
all the years of the League's history. In 1956, when they founded
the League, not only had all seven nursed at least one of their
infants, they were all committed to being mothers of large families.
The smallest completed family of the seven consists of three
children, and the other six women all had between seven and eleven
children. And it appears that not only did they all wish for larger
than average families, all of them shared convictions about the
nature of family life. Although this fact is not stressed in most
League literature (the League clearly wishes to remain non-
sectarian), all seven were Roman Catholics, and most if not all were
active members of the Christian Family Movement, a Catholic
organization designed to encourage family life.[29]

League literature suggests that the best kind of family is one
in which there is continuous intimacy, closeness, and sharing of
activities among parents and children, and in which family-centred
activities take precedence over all other concerns. In recent years,
one form that the League's advocacy of family togetherness has
taken, is support for the practice of co-family sleeping. Even in its
earliest years, League literature suggested to mothers that it was a

good thing for them to take their infants into bed with them for breastfeeding, or for sleeping. Today League-sponsored literature goes further, and freely discusses the "family bed": a practice in which infants, toddlers and older children are all made to feel welcome in their parents' bed, whenever they wish to come there. League literature maintains that "co-family sleeping" is not only good for children, but strengthens family life.

> Let us therefore, re-unite the family. . .The newborn baby needs his mother, the toddler needs his mother and father, the young child needs his mother, his father, and his siblings. To be one family, we need to touch and to share. Sleep is so wonderful, let's share it. . .with our loved ones, our children.[30]

The Natural Way

"Natural" is one of the most frequently used words in League literature. Breast milk, the League emphasizes, is the "natural" way to nourish infants, and breastfeeding is "basically a natural art. . .possessed by women, and strengthened as it is passed on from mother to daughter."[31] In contrast, "artificial" substitutes, "schedules and bottles" represent an "unnatural approach to the infant."

The League's preference for the "natural" extends beyond breastfeeding to childbirth, birth control and nutrition. The League favours "natural childbirth"--that is, childbirth that is unmedicated, and that takes place with as little medical interference as possible. Indeed, the "natural childbirth" method, as developed by the English physician Dr. Grantly Dick Read, was one of the most important influences on the group of mothers who founded the League: the husband of one of the founding mothers was a physician who followed Dick Read's methods in his own practice. From the organization's inception, its founders not only favoured non-medicated childbirth, they encouraged home birth, although advocacy for this practice was not stressed in the League's early years. In recent years, League literature has made a point of emphasizing the advantages of home birth.

The League also favours "natural" birth control. Although not explicitly opposed to artificial methods of contraception, League literature stresses the benefits of the "natural" spacing that occurs, they say, when the mother "completely" breastfeeds. Recently the organization has been giving support to the "Serena" method, a sophisticated version of the rhythm method of birth control, in which the woman examines her secretions regularly.[32]

As far as health and nutrition are concerned, again, while the League takes no unequivocal stand in its literature, it implicitly and explicitly has given support to the health food movement: for example, it produces a League-sponsored cookbook entitled *Whole Foods for the Whole Family*.

The La Leche League and Feminism

As an organization, the League advocates no explicit position on feminism, nor even on the specific issues--like the right to abortion, or government funding of day care--around which debate over feminism has focussed. League literature and policy, however, do carry with them an implicit set of assumptions about women's nature and about women's role in society, and individual League members are, of course, free to have opinions about issues on which the League remains neutral as an organization. Thus, both from League literature, and from our local study of Canadian League women in the 1980s, it is possible to glean some knowledge of League attitudes towards feminism, both in the present, and over the course of the organization's thirty-year history.

In 1956, when the La Leche League was founded, the feminist movement was in retreat. The successes of the nineteenth and early twentieth century movement--the achievement of legal and political rights and the opening up of higher education and professional training to women--were seen as both a complete victory for feminism, and as mistaken: in the aftermath of World War II, there was an anti-feminist backlash. Powerful voices were proclaiming that "modern woman" was a "lost sex."[33] Such voices were articulating a new version of the ideology of domesticity, a version that Betty Friedan later labelled "the feminine mystique."[34] Reinforced by Freudian psychology, the 'experts' of the 1940s and 1950s were insisting that women could only find true happiness through fulfilling their feminine destiny of selfless motherhood and wifehood; that children who were deprived of single-minded, total motherhood would grow up psychologically disturbed; and that assertive women were threatening and even 'castrating' to their husbands.

If we look at objectively measurable factors, rather than ideology, we see that, in 1956, only a small minority of mothers were employed in the paid labour force[35] and the post-war baby boom was still flourishing. Thus, although the League's seven founding mothers were unusual in some ways for their time--they breastfed their infants, and they had larger-than-average numbers of children--they conformed to most expectations that society then held about women. They were all mothers who put motherhood first. As women, motherhood was central to their identity and they saw no reason to look beyond their families for interest or commitment. As the League itself grew, the seven founders claimed that they always put their "families first," even ahead of the League. And while they encouraged fathers to become involved in parenthood, their views of family life involved support for sharply differentiated gender roles.

We are all in favor of manly men. And La Leche League was formed for no other purpose than to help women become more womanly.[36]

At the time of the League's founding, then, anti-feminism was as strong as it had been at any time during the twentieth century, and the feminist movement was at its weakest. The earliest League literature simply assumes as self-evident the then dominant notion that mothering shapes female identity and that motherhood precludes all other activities, including paid employment.

By the mid-1960s, however, the La Leche League had begun to feel the pressure of a newly revived feminism. Betty Friedan's *The Feminine Mystique* was published in 1963. While its publication was not the sole cause of the rebirth of feminism, it symbolized that rebirth for many and was certainly a central focus. Soon after its publication, the League, along with the rest of North America, began to respond to feminism's new wave.

The League's initial response was to dismiss and denigrate the movement. League literature interpreted the feminist message as a demand that women should put themselves and their own needs ahead of their families, and they assumed that the chief feminist objective was to see all women, including mothers of young children, engaged in full-time employment. The League rejected these ideas, and insisted, instead, that mothering was a career. For example, one of the founding mothers, Mary White, wrote a piece for the *La Leche League News* in 1966, in which she refers to Betty Friedan and the newly revived threat of feminism:

> How can we devote ourselves to this business of mothering our babies and still retain our identities?. . .I suggest we can do it by first of all knowing what our goals are, and then by committing ourselves to the task we've taken on; by accepting the fact that being a wife and a mother is a full-time job in itself and a first-class career, worthy of our very best efforts. . .Isn't this our goal? our special assignment? That is, turning out good children, good people.[37]

Two years later, at the League's third Biennial Convention, Marian Tompson, its president and one of the founding mothers, took a similar tack in her keynote address. She emphasized that the threat of feminism was not a phenomenon which had emerged only in the 1960s; it was there, she says, even in the 1950s, and indeed, was, she suggests, one of the causes contributing to the decline in breastfeeding:

> Even back in 1956 the voice of the extreme feminist was being heard in the land. This was the lady who was telling everybody else that we had to get out of the house in order to really find fulfilment as women. We thought that staying home, taking care of our families, doing things like making bread. . .was something wonderful. But they characterized this as expanding our housework

to fill our empty hours. You couldn't win with people like
this. . .but as a nurse once said to me at a meeting after
one of these women had spoken, "you know a lot of the
things she said were very interesting, but I'm sure glad
she's not my mother."[38]

Tompson goes on to characterize League members as
"homemakers at heart," and she vociferously supports individual
mothers, and the League itself, for insisting that a woman
contributes to society simply by taking care of her family.

Even if we don't have time to run for political office or
teach in the slums or do any other extracurricular work, I
think what we're doing now is terribly important--taking
care of the things that just touch our lives.[39]

Analysis of recent League literature and of the evidence from
our local study of League groups and individuals in Ottawa reveals
that, over the past decade or so, the League has attempted to adapt
to two changing circumstances: 1) the increasing sophistication of
the feminist message and its partial acceptance into mainstream
culture and 2) the very considerable increase in maternal
employment over the last two decades.

The League's adaptation to the partial success of feminism is
reflected in its changing attitudes towards gender roles within the
family. While the League, through its literature and its members,
still views motherhood and homemaking as constituting a full-time
vocation, and believes that men should function primarily as
protectors and providers within the family unit, within this general
framework, there has been adaptation.

During the League's early years, the organization assumed
that it might be very difficult to persuade individual men to be
supportive of breastfeeding or involved in parenthood. Early
League literature also reflects the fact that the League accepted the
principle of male dominance in the making of family decisions. For
example, in one 1968 discussion of fathers' attitudes, it was
acknowledged that, if a husband was unalterably opposed to
breastfeeding, the wife should not attempt it:

If you're clever, and most women are, you may have a way
or find a way to change his mind. The wife who is
confronted with unbending opposition has to keep in mind
what is best for the whole family. She may have to
sacrifice breastfeeding and all its advantages to avert a
severe rupture in her relationship with her husband.[40]

That was in 1968. Since the mid-seventies, however, League
literature has reflected more openness to the sharing of roles and to
an egalitarian relationship within marriage. An early indication of

this was as special issue of the League newsletter devoted to fathering, which included an interview with two fathers, one a university professor, the other a pediatrician. Both these men not only supported involved fatherhood, with considerable sharing of roles, but also suggested that male and female traits might be cultural rather than inborn.[41] The most recent indication of an acceptance of more egalitarian roles within the family is the change in format and direction of the League newsletter, a publication that is sent to all League members. Until 1985 the newsletter was directed exclusively to mothers. But the newsletter's new title, "New Beginnings: A Magazine for Parenting," was adopted with the deliberate intention of placing more emphasis on fatherhood as well as motherhood.

Increasing participation and sharing between husband and wife, while it does represent an adjustment to new social norms, is not at variance with the fundamental principles of the League. The involvement of mothers in paid employment outside the home, however, does conflict with those principles. The continuous presence of the mother that the League's definition of good motherhood entails precludes, for all intents and purposes, active and full-time participation in the paid labour force, for at least six years for each child. And since La Leche League principles involve an implicit commitment to the large family, conducting one's childrearing and family life according to the La Leche League model would involve avoiding labour force participation during half or more of one's working life. As increasing numbers of North American mothers have entered the labour force, the conflict between maternal labour force participation, which entails the use of day care or other alternatives to the mother's continuous presence, and the maternal role that the La Leche League seeks to encourage, has become one of the most difficult issues that the League has had to face over the past decade.

League literature, in the 1960s and 1970s, simply assumed that any good mother would be a "full-time" mother and would not be involved in labour-force participation. In recent years, League literature has sharpened and extended its defence of "full-time mothering," but at the same time, it now acknowledges that the woman whose sole occupation is that of housewife and mother has selected an occupation that is becoming increasingly at variance with mainstream practice. And whereas, in the 1960s, and even in the 1970s, the League, in its comments on the role of the full-time mother, ignored the economic component of maternal employment-- assuming that any mother reading its literature and contemplating working would be doing so only for 'selfish' reasons--today, it is acutely aware of the fact that, for a growing number of families, living on one income is difficult. Its literature reflects an awareness of the fact that, in recent years, not only has the housewife and mother lost status, it is now the case that a woman who decides to stay out of the labour force is often perceived as having selected the 'selfish' option, because she is seen as depriving her family of the extra income she could contribute, were she to enter the paid labour force.

In response to these pressures, the League has adopted a new defensive tone in its literature on the choice of stay-at-home motherhood. Such literature now acknowledges that the choice to stay home is now a difficult one.[42] The solution offered is to put "people before things." Families who choose to live on less, in order that the wife may be a "mother at home," are told that they are engaging in a revolution against contemporary society's excessive obsession with consumerism, a revolution that is difficult and that will involve material sacrifice.

In addition to encouraging what it calls a "new pioneer spirit," League literature directed at women it hopes to persuade to become full-time mothers also attempts not merely to encourage such young mothers, but also to caution them into doing so. League literature has always emphasized the need for close mother-child relationships; in recent years, it has emphasized the dangers of not providing such relationships. In attempting to influence mothers to decide whether or not to work for pay when they have small children, the League relies heavily on one sort of research and no other: on the Freudian and Kleinian research whose purpose is to demonstrate that "maternal deprivation" leads to dire consequences. The implication made is that the woman who leaves her baby with a caretaker or in day care risks producing these dire consequences. Nowhere in League literature have we seen material quoted from the large number of studies which show that good day care does not have these deleterious effects and cannot be equated with "maternal deprivation."[43]

In addition to its new emphasis upon the advocacy of "full-time motherhood," the League has also adopted, to a much more limited extent, a second type of response to the phenomenon of increased maternal employment, a response that represents a radical new departure for the organization, and that runs counter to many of its well-established beliefs. The League, while deeply committed to encouraging its brand of motherhood and family life, does have as it primary objective the encouragement of breastfeeding, even under circumstances it does not consider to be ideal. As a result of its recognition that many mothers are now combining motherhood with paid employment, the League has begun to direct some of its attention to the working mother. For example, a new four-page free handout begins:

> There's a new baby in your life? Congratulations: Have you thought of breastfeeding? You say you'll be working. You can do both, you know! Here's how. . .[44]

Inside, the reader finds helpful, practical advice. This little brochure has no threatening suggestions about the harm that paid work may do to the baby. It concludes by saying: "If you have any questions. . .ask a friend who is happily nursing her own baby. The mothers of La Leche League are friends who want to help you breastfeed. Call or write us!"

The conflicts reflected in current League literature about maternal employment, both the new emphasis employed in discussions of the benefits of full-time homemaking and the adaptation reflected in some of the new literature directed at the working mother, are even more sharply etched in the material produced by our participant observation and interview research at the local level. It is evident that there is strain in the League concerning the issue of maternal employment, and the attitude that the League should take towards it.

The twenty women who have been interviewed as part of an on-going investigation of the League are all League Leaders. These are committed members of the League who do telephone counselling, lead monthly meetings, attempt to maintain close contact with League mothers, and may speak for the League in an official capacity. To become a League Leader, a mother must have breastfed her latest baby for over a year and have demonstrated knowledge of and compliance with the League policy. With very few exceptions, leaders cannot be in the paid labour force; all of our interviewees thus far are full-time homemakers.

Leaders are encouraged--indeed, officially required--to support all mothers who request help regarding breastfeeding. Although a woman whose labour-force activities require that she leave her infant or child on a regular basis represents a position contrary to League policy, leaders are required to support her and to encourage mothering and breastfeeding which is as close to their ideal as is possible under the circumstances. Such support is difficult for some leaders, who are not able to be flexible enough to deal with problems involving nursing and working mothers. As one leader put it:

> Some leaders cannot help 'conflict calls'. They find it difficult to help women who work. This does not mean women who have to work--whose families would be in trouble if they did not. But they harbour resentment towards women who choose to work--who choose to leave their babies. They won't help a conflict call and will take their name and number and have someone else help them.[45]

A partial resolution of the philosophical dilemma encountered by the leaders is to recall that the primary aim of the organization is to help mothers breastfeed. The belief that breastfeeding encourages good mothering enables some leaders and the organization itself to help mothers whose lifestyles run counter to ideology. The League views itself as "the child's advocate," and helping the mother of the child, helps the child.

In short, then, both our survey of current League literature, and our interviews with League Leaders, reveal that the League is making considerable efforts to accommodate to economic and social pressures in the larger society that threaten its message and also its membership in terms both of recruitment and of participation. League Leaders, in dealing with outsiders and potential members, are charged to maintain a rather precarious balance between the communication of League beliefs, and accommodation to mothers whose attitudes and practices may run counter to the League message. In the course of this accommodation, they must come to terms personally with challenges to their own commitment to the League, its beliefs, and their choice of a way of life.

For some League women, part of this adaptation involves coming to terms explicitly with feminism. This is especially true for those whose educational and prior labour-force experiences and present awareness have made feminism a salient issue. In the interviews, two dominant views concerning feminism and feminists emerged. The first view perceives feminism as undervaluing mothering and homemaking. The second reflects a belief that La Leche League women, rather than feminists, have truly understood the message of women's liberation. Participation in the labour force, say these women, is neither necessary nor sufficient for such liberation. As one leader put it, full labour force participation may even undermine the special attributes women can offer:

> I feel the message of the feminist movement is to go out and work, and I disagree with this. . .what I agree with is the idea of women being strong, and being strong for one another. . .You can be very free at home; I think that women have evolved more dramatically than men. In a way, women have evolved more humanistically; women care for women more now than they used to.[46]

And she added that the conventional symbols of success, which 'conscious' women should eschew, are male symbols. Although the respondent does attack 'the feminist movement', the language she uses has clearly been influenced by that strand of current feminist thinking which emphasizes the moral and cultural differences between men and women, and supports a sisterhood based on a shared women's culture.[47]

The following quotation from another leader interviewee is illustrative of ambivalence regarding the feminist movement:

> I'm not against the women's movement. When I was at university, I read a lot and am familiar with the arguments. Women have to find their place in the world, but I'm against a movement which says that women have to find their place in the workplace. The women cannot be at home while the children are young. I believe that it

is important for future generations for some women to be at home and for nurturing to be an activity that is well thought of. It offends me that people think if you are at home, you have to be dumb. If it is 'too boring' at home, it may mean they do not have enough imagination. Sixty or 70 per cent of women are in service jobs--waitresses, or other service jobs. Now you can't tell me some of those are more stimulating than being at home. . .And the models of women at home. I don't like the idea of Mila [Mulroney-- the wife of Canada's Prime Minister] as the representative. She is not exactly a mother at home. I don't like Phyllis Schlafly. At the same time, I wish people would be more understanding.[48]

The respondent does declare that she is not "against the women's movement," and, moreover, she disassociates herself from the anti-feminism of the new right, by her reference to the American right-wing anti-feminist Phyllis Schlafly. Her wish that "people would be more understanding" of her decision to be a full-time homemaker reflects both a sense of isolation, and a belief in her own dignity, and in the importance of her work. It is clear, however, that she is uncomfortable with feminism, and perceives it as the social force most responsible for undervaluing her contribution to society. This is reflected in her statement that she opposes "a movement which says that . . .women cannot be at home while the children are young."

It should also be noted that in quoting statistics on the numbers of women clustered in service occupations, the respondent has assimilated information whose significance has been emphasized by the feminist movement itself. After referring to this information, however, which has played a central role in feminist critiques of gender inequality in the labour market, she does not draw the usual feminist conclusion. Instead of asserting that such inequality hinders women's opportunities, and should be removed, she uses it to buttress her own belief that withdrawing from the labour market to engage in full-time homemaking is a more attractive option for many women.

The extracts just quoted from our interview material reflect the thinking that we have found among the La Leche League leaders and members in the participant observation and interview research. For the most part, League women we have encountered express either antipathy to feminism, or a sense of distance from it. They perceive their form of women's activism to be closer to the real needs of women, and especially of children, than activism they define as feminist. From a feminist perspective, however, some of the language League women use reflects the influence of current feminist thinking, even when that thinking is presented as if through a distorting mirror. And finally, while the League women we have encountered in our study may reject feminism, we have found little support for right-wing anti-feminist views.[49]

Although in our own investigations of current League literature and in our own local study we have found no identification of the La Leche League with feminism, we have encountered one interesting example of a clearly articulated position linking feminism to the League. In March, 1987 the Canadian feminist publication *Herizons* published an article entitled "Women of Conviction: 10 Dynamic Women Share their Views on the Direction of the Feminist Movement." In an introductory section, the editors explained that their purpose was "to mark the diversity of feminism in Canada by exploring the various 'stripes' of feminism that exist within our movement. . .and to find out how women came to be feminists."[50] One of the women interviewed was Irene Todd, who begins her account with the statement "I am a feminist," and goes on to explain that her espousal of feminism began when she was in her early twenties. Then, as a young teacher, she was involved in the Manitoba Action Committee on the Status of Women. At the same time, however, she explains, "I was starting my own family." She decided to give up her job and stay home with her children: "The decision to become a full-time mother was made jointly by my husband and [me] after we had read, observed and discussed various parenting styles." Having made this decision, she says, "I began to feel a growing dissatisfaction with the feminist movement itself. . .my feminist sisters. . .seemed to feel sorry for me because they thought I wasn't able to cope with an outside job--a 'real' career--never acknowledging that motherhood is as valid a career as any." For Irene Todd, the solution to her new feelings of alienation was to join the La Leche League. The League, she says, "gave me the freedom to fulfill my need for growth while not compromising my parenting ideals."[51]

Irene Todd's statement reveals much about changes in the League's position, as well as changes in feminist thinking. Todd defines herself as a feminist, and this self-definition is accepted by the editors of *Herizons* who have chosen to include her in a diverse collection of feminist women. Moreover, she came to the La Leche League from involvement with organizations that are unequivocally feminist. In her brief statement, she does not deal with the question of the League's own position on feminism. She makes it clear, however, that, while she still identifies herself as a feminist, she finds that at the present time the League, rather than feminist women's groups, serves her needs.

Does Irene Todd's case mean that the La Leche League of the 1980s should be regarded as a feminist organization? We don't think so. The line between non-feminist women's activism and feminism has always been difficult to draw, in the past as in the present, and it is a line that is continually shifting. In the case of the La Leche League clearly there has been adaptation, as we have seen: presumably not even the founding mothers themselves would any longer feel comfortable with the anti-feminist stance they took in the 1960s. Yet, we do believe that, in spite of these adaptations, and in spite of the League's long-standing commitment to avoid overt ideological commitment, the League has supported and still supports an ideology that is not in sympathy with feminism. Its emphasis on motherhood and its defence of the nuclear family, dependent for financial support on a male wage earner, supports patriarchal values, the patriarchal family, and a set of limited options for women. From our observations of the current position of the League, Todd represents a rare exception.

Labelling the La Leche League, however, as 'non-feminist' and its underlying ideology as 'anti-feminist' serves only a limited purpose. From a feminist perspective, the feature that is of greater interest is that some of the specific and general concerns of the League, as well as some of the techniques and styles employed by the League, overlap with some of the concerns and styles of the feminist movement. As well, we think that from a feminist perspective it is important to understand why some women feel so much more comfortable with the League than they do with feminist groups.

We will therefore conclude this examination of the La Leche League with an analysis of its views about an issue that has been of central importance to the League itself, to feminist groups, and to anti-feminists, namely the status of housewife, or 'full-time mother'. The League deplores the fact that the status of the housewife/mother has dropped, in recent years, and it believes that mothers are being both enticed and driven into the workforce. For the La Leche League, the chief factor responsible for increased maternal employment is the growth of an undesirable form of individualism, which, for them, includes both feminism and consumerism. Their solution--that women, and men alike, should turn back to the supposedly more solid values of an earlier North American society--is one that is shared by a variety of contemporary groups. For in differing ways, social critics from the left and right have written of a malaise in the personal life of North Americans. In recent years, many commentators have expressed their dismay about the fact that contemporary society appears to offer most of its members a choice of more, and more of less and less. It is a widely held view that contemporary urban society does not fulfill the human need for creativity, for nurturance and for intimacy. Critics of the left believe that the structures of capitalism are responsible for the spiritual barrenness of modern life, and marxist-feminist commentators have perceived urban industrial capitalism as having particularly damaging effects on women.[52] Non-feminist critics of the right, and even those of the left,[53] have tended to blame the feminist movement.

Why does feminism so often bear the brunt of these criticisms? Those who perceive a connection between the rise of feminism and the spiritual barrenness of modern life, are part of a tradition with roots in the past. Nostalgia for a more intimate, nurturing society has been a significant source for a rejection of feminism since the nineteenth century. The fallacy involved in such a rejection is the assumption that if women's work and women's emotional life remain untouched by modern society, a set of older, more humane values will be preserved. That was the basis for the ideology of 'separate spheres' in the nineteenth century, and it is the basis for much contemporary rejection of feminism. Specifically, this nostalgia informs much of the thinking of the La Leche League.

But feminism is not the source of contemporary alienation, and the League's approach to 'consumerism' does not provide an adequate critique of the problems created by urban consumer capitalism. The implicit identification of feminism with selfish individualism that occurs in some La Leche League literature,[54] however, does point to what we regard as the chief danger facing feminism in the 1980s, the danger that the partial success of liberal feminism, and the co-optation of feminist rhetoric by business and government may be mistaken for the achievement of the goals of a truly humanist feminism.

The partial success of liberal feminism, which is reflected mainly in limited legislative change and in the increase in the numbers of young women going into the professions and achieving success in managerial positions, has been seized on by some women as representing the achievement of the feminist goals of the 1960s and 1970s. It has also been absorbed into the ideology and the imagery of mainstream culture, because the present requirements of our economy have encouraged changes in society's ideological position on women. These changes have not been radical enough to create genuine equality between women and men of all social classes and of every race. Instead a limited, pseudo-equality has been fostered, a pseudo-equality which has allowed the system to absorb a few women into the higher reaches of business and professional life. This equality is illusory and not genuine, because its main purpose has been to facilitate and sanction a new form of oppression for the majority of women, one in which they remain responsible for family life and for the rearing of children but in which they are also expected to take on employment in the 'service' sector of the economy, which has needed their labour in increasing numbers.

This shift in mainstream ideology about women's roles has produced the result of which the La Leche League women are acutely aware: the imagery created by the media has made it no longer respectable to be 'just a housewife'. The message of cinema, television and popular magazines is that women are now supposed to be young, sexy, and 'liberated' from any conservative notions of sexual or family morality, but they are also expected to be good mothers and, in addition, to bring in a good salary. Even for the minority of well-paid women, the task of performing all the roles implied by the new imagery demands oppressive amounts of mental, physical and emotional energy. For the majority of women in the greatly expanded female labour force, the possibility of earning a managerial or professional salary is remote. The majority of North

American female wage earners still earn on average 60 per cent of a male wage, and meet discrimination and exploitation in the labour force in greater measure than male workers do. Only a small minority go to work in $400 grey flannel suits, and fewer still wield any real power in the corporate or professional world. As Zillah Eisenstein has so cogently analyzed in her book *The Radical Future of Liberal Feminism*, what has happened is that mainstream society has co-opted part of the feminist message and absorbed it into its prescriptions about women, prescriptions that remain basically unchanged from those of the 1950s. As Eisenstein puts it, the gender identity of the 1950s, the ideology that Betty Friedan labelled "the feminine mystique," is still with us in an expanded, but still oppressive, form.

> What happened throughout the 1960s and '70s was that the demand on women's time and for their labor increased. Instead of simply being mothers, as the "feminine mystique" presented women, today women are supposed to be "working mothers." They are to operate within the patriarchal sexual division of labor in both the public and private spheres. Although women have gained access to the public domain, they have done so while remaining responsible for the private life of their family members. . .As mothers, they have the added responsibility today to work for wages. . .They are simply "working mothers"; the "mystique" of the 1970s and '80s in new form.[55]

In some ways, then, the La Leche League perception of what has happened to the housewife in the 1980s reflects a greater recognition of the real problems facing women today than the programme of shallow bourgeois feminism. Like the socialist feminist Eisenstein, the League recognizes that our society has not provided for the needs of women as childrearers, nor has it displayed sufficient concern from the welfare of children.

Moreover, as our local study of the League reveals, the woman-to-woman contact provided by the organization does offer much-needed assistance to the woman suffering from the isolation, anxiety and other difficulties that housewives who are mothers of young children often experience. As one leader put it, after describing the isolation she felt on moving to a new community, ". . .the La Leche League was my link to survival." Another interviewee stressed that:

> . . .contact is very important for mothers who choose to stay at home with their children. There are feelings of isolation; so much so that the woman might go back to work to escape these feelings and get the social support she would have at work. I guess that was one of the things which kept me going to the League.[56]

In spite of the immediate benefits the organization offers to the mothers who become involved with it, we believe that the League's current solutions to the problems that mothers of young children face are inadequate, and in some ways represent a retreat back to the 1960s version of the "feminine mystique." The inadequacy of the solutions is revealed when one looks at them in detail, as they appear, for example, in *The Heart Has Its Own Reasons*, the book the League has recently produced to help women who wish to be "new pioneers" as full-time housewives and mothers. The book starts off boldly, announcing that "you have made a brave move, but it can be a lonely one. . .if you are a mother who has chosen to stay at home with your children. . ."[57] The book promises to help its readers develop a "pioneer plan," involving a "saving sense" and the ability to "create and innovate," but some of the solutions proposed are not only ineffectual, they unwittingly underscore the fact that individuals alone cannot escape the structures in which we all live. For example, one suggested project to which this book devotes several pages is the saving of the coupons and refunds distributed by manufacturers. "Serious refunders automatically save the box or label from almost any product they use that they think might someday be featured in a refund offer. . .[We recommend]. . .designating a drawer or a box in your kitchen where you can quickly deposit any labels. . ."[58]

While it is possible that a "serious refunder" can, as the book promises, "save hundreds of dollars" a year, what strikes us about this activity is not only its superficiality as a solution for complex economic problems, but also the way in which this "new pioneer" saving is directly tied into and dependent upon the advertising techniques of exactly that "consumer society" that the book professes to oppose.

When La Leche League literature, and individual League members emphasize the benefits of growing their own food, making their own clothes, and baking their own bread, they are attempting to confront a problem that is not unique to the housewife, but is shared by many other productive workers, namely the loss of craft satisfaction that has accompanied the progress of technology. As recent historical analyses of housework have demonstrated,[59] technological change affected household work in much the same way that it affected other kinds of manual work, and the transformation of women's domestic work by technology should be seen as part of a general transformation that has brought with it losses, as well as benefits. Rather than perceiving the problem of the loss of craft satisfaction as a general one, affecting all workers, the League places women's work in the home in a special category, and invests it with a symbolic significance that is not, in fact, appropriate to the work at all.

In short, many of the solutions proposed by the League and other non-feminist groups will not solve the problems women face in urban, industrial capitalist society. Saving boxtops and growing one's own vegetables will not halt a process that appears, at present, to be inexorable, namely the emergence of a presumption that middle, as well as working-class families,[60] are expected to have two wage earners. This presumption has not been produced by feminism, but rather by developments in the economy.[61]

The forces producing these developments are much more powerful than feminism, and they are not concerned with the welfare of individual women, men or children. If we are to ease the burden of the large numbers of mothers with small children who are going into the labour force at an increasing rate each year, we must work for a fair deal for them in the labour force, and for a fair deal for their children. In the short run, this means fighting for equal pay for work of equal value for all women workers, for parental leave, and for good day care. In the long run, it means working for a society in which technology will be used to improve human experience, rather than to produce profits for industrial capitalism. A retreat into the past--a past that was in any case much less pleasant than the images conjured up by rhetoric like that employed by the League's advocacy of "new pioneers"--will not solve women's problems, in the short or the long run.

Conclusion

As an organization of women that has developed and grown over the past thirty years, the La Leche League is unquestionably a success, and for this reason alone, it is worthy of investigation. But as we explained in the introduction, our purpose in this paper was to examine the League not only from its own perspective, but also from the perspective of current debates about the nature of the family and of motherhood. The La Leche League antedates the revival of feminism and, as an organization, has never taken an official position on feminism. Therefore, the evolution of its ideology over three decades offers a way of demonstrating the influence of feminist thinking on women activists, most of whom situate themselves outside the feminist movement. Furthermore, an examination of the League's history, and of the views of the current leadership and membership, provides a way of understanding non-feminist views on motherhood and child care. We believe such an understanding to be of urgent importance, given current feminist debates on the nature of motherhood and family life, and current assaults on feminism from the anti-feminist new right.

When seen from a feminist perspective, the La Leche League, we believe, emerges as an organization with both positive and negative qualities. Its great strength lies in the support that it is able to offer the individual women who seek it out. Not only does it provide support for its stated central concern, breastfeeding, its meetings provide a welcoming space within which women who are caring for infants and children can develop a supportive community.[62] As our research makes clear, the women who find such support through the League do not feel that they would find it in explicitly feminist organizations.

The La Leche League's weakness, from a feminist perspective, lies in its rejection of an explicit, developed, political analysis of women's position in society. As an organization, it has a stated commitment to 'good mothering', and it clearly defines itself as an advocate of good child care. Yet, it avoids an analysis that recognizes the oppression and exploitation that women experience in our society. It is because it eschews such an analysis that the organization itself, and its individual members, frequently resort to woman-blaming as an explanation for what it perceives as evidence of bad mothering. The League, as an organization, should not be confused with new-right anti-feminist groups, but when individual League members blame those they identify as 'feminists' for their 'selfishness' in 'choosing' to work in the labour force, they come perilously close to espousing new-right rhetoric. In short, because of its rejection of feminism, the La Leche League fails to recognize some of the chief causes of our society's failure to nurture not only its children, but also its adult women and men.

Notes

[1]In the 1980s, as the revival of feminism that began in the 1960s has matured, maturation has brought with it fragmentation, as several recent commentators have noted. See, for example, Rosalind Delmar, "What is Feminism?" in Juliet Mitchell and Ann Oakley, eds., *What is Feminism? A Re-examination* (New York: Pantheon Books, 1986), pp. 8-33: "The fragmentation of contemporary feminism bears ample witness to the impossibility of constructing modern feminism as a simple unity . . .", p. 9.

[2]Several commentators agree that this perception, which is the central tenet of radical feminism, was dominant among North American feminists during the early years of the women's liberation movement. See, for example, Alison M. Jaggar, *Feminist Politics and Human Nature* (Totowa, N.J.: Rowman and Allanheld, 1983).

[3]As examples of the socialist feminist perspective see Zillah Eisenstein, ed., *Capitalist Patriarchy and the Case for Socialist Feminism* (New York: Monthly Review Press, 1979); Zillah Eisenstein, *The Radical Future of Liberal Feminism* (New York: Longmans, 1981) and Michèle Barrett, *Women's Oppression Today* (London: Verso, 1980). In our view, radical feminism has undergone radical changes in the last decade, and the analysis of patriarchy to be found in Millett's path-breaking work [Kate Millett, *Sexual Politics* (New York: Avon Books, 1971)] should be distinguished from more recent formulations like that, for example, of Andrea Dworkin in *Right Wing Women* (New York: Putnam, 1983). Betty Friedan is the best known liberal feminist to re-assert the importance of motherhood and the family; Betty Friedan, *The Second Stage* (New York: Summit Books, 1981).

[4]Dorothy Dinnerstein articulates this position in *The Mermaid and the Minotaur: Sexual Arrangements and Human Malaise* (New York: Harper and Row, 1976). Some radical lesbian feminists have taken the position that women should avoid motherhood. See Jeffner Allen, "Motherhood, the annihilation of women," in Joyce Treblicot, ed., *Mothering: Essays in Feminist Theory* (Totowa, N. J.: Rowman and Allenheld, 1984), pp. 315-30. Allen advocates a "philosophy of evacuation," and promotes the collective removal of women from all forms of motherhood.

[5]Adrienne Rich lays the groundwork for this position, through her distinction between motherhood as institution, and motherhood as it could be, if women were free to create a woman's culture. Rich, *Of Woman Born: Motherhood as Experience and Institution* (New York: Norton, 1976). And see also Caroline Whitbeck's discussion of the "Maternal Instinct" (1972) and "Afterword to the Maternal Instinct" (1982), in Treblicot. Whitbeck states that maternal behaviour has its source in biological experiences, such as pregnancy, labour, birth and nursing. Thus, while maternal behaviour is not innate, it is generated initially by biological factors and mediated by cultural factors. See pp. 185-9.

[6]The phrase "base-line definition" is Rosalind Delmar's: "It is certainly possible to construct a base-line definition of feminism and the feminist which can be shared by feminists and non-feminists. Many would agree that at the very least a feminist is someone who holds that women suffer discrimination because of their sex, that they have specific needs which remain negated and unsatisfied, and that the satisfaction of these needs would require a radical change. . .in the social, economic and political order." Delmar, p. 8.

[7]For an analysis of the anti-feminist new right in Canadian context, see Margrit Eichler, *The Pro-Family Movement: Are They For or Against Families?* (Ottawa: Canadian Research Institute for the Advancement of Women, 1986), and Karen Dubinsky, *Lament for a "Patriarchy Lost"? Anti-feminism, Anti-abortion, and R.E.A.L. Women in Canada* (Ottawa: Canadian Research Institute for the Advancement of Women, 1985). Dubinsky's piece provides an insightful analysis of the most visible anti-feminist new-right group in Canada, "Realistic, Equal, Active for Life (R.E.A.L.) women."

[8]A 1986 poll of *Chatelaine* readers asked: "If I had to categorize my position on women's roles and rights as either feminist or traditionalist, I would call myself. . ." Of the 353 women surveyed, 47 per cent responded feminist, 40 per cent responded traditionalist, and the remaining 13 per cent responded neither or both. "Womanpoll: Women's roles and rights," *Chatelaine*, May 1986, p. 42.

[9]From the extensive literature on feminism and social class, we have been especially influenced by Zillah Eisenstein, and Michèle Barrett, and on gender and race, by Bell Hooks, *Feminist Theory from Margin to Center* (Boston: South End Press, 1984).

[10]The phrase "lifestyle feminism" is Barbara Ehrenreich's.

See her "The Women's Movement--Feminist and Anti-Feminist," *Radical America* 15, 1 & 2 (Spring 1981), 93-101.

[11]Adrienne Rich's *Of Woman Born* remains the most important single contribution to this analysis. See also some of the contributions in Treblicot.

[12]This paper is based on an on-going historical and sociological investigation of the La Leche League. The work includes the analysis of some of the League literature over a thirty-year period; participant observation of 10 local meetings; attendance at a regional conference, and at a national conference; and focussed interviews with 20 League Leaders. The interviewees were solidly middle to upper-middle class according to the usual criteria (education, residence, former occupation of the respondents and occupations of their husbands) for class designation. All but one had at least a bachelor's degree and five held university degrees beyond the bachelor's level. The location of the sociological investigation is Ottawa, Ontario, Canada's capital, an urban centre with a population of 300,000. Preliminary analysis of the data appears in two conference papers: Florence Kellner Andrews and Deborah Gorham, "Feminine Pursuits: A Study of the La Leche League," presented at the conference "Deviance in a Cross-Cultural Context: An Ethnographic/Interactionist Perspective," Waterloo, Ontario, 1984; and Florence Kellner Andrews and Deborah Gorham, "Building Trust: A Consideration of Ground-Rules," presented at the conference "Qualitative Research: An Ethnographic/ Interactionist Perspective," Waterloo, Ontario, 1985.

[13]Concerning the issue of the child, the extensive literature on the history of childhood and the family suggests that radical changes in the perception of childhood in Europe and North America took place between the 18th and the 20th centuries. See, e.g., Michael Gordon, ed., *The American Family in Social-Historical Perspective*, 2nd ed. (New York: St. Martin's Press, 1983) and George K. Behlmer, *Child Abuse and Moral Reform in England, 1870-1908* (Stanford, CA: Stanford University Press, 1982). Sociologist Viviana A. Zelizer draws on this historical work to suggest that in North America a dramatic change in attitudes toward children took place between the 1870s and the 1930s. The child who was once useful became 'priceless', and childhood became sanctified, with the result that there are few limits surrounding what parents should do to serve the needs of the child. *Pricing the Priceless Child: The Changing Social Value of Children* (New York: Basic Books, Inc., 1985).

[14]This statement of purpose appears frequently on La Leche League literature, and has done so since the League's earliest publications. For example, see *The Womanly Art of Breastfeeding*, 3rd ed. (Franklin Park, Ill.: La Leche League International, Inc., 1981), p. 339.

[15]The League has published its own history: Kay Lowman, *The LLLove Story* (Franklin Park, Ill.: La Leche League

International, Inc., 1978). Our historical analysis of the League has been based largely on a reading of its newsletter, which has been published since 1958, on conference proceedings, and on other League literature.

[16]In this paper, except where noted, references are to the 1963 edition: La Leche League International, *The Womanly Art of Breastfeeding*, 2nd ed. (Franklin Park, Ill.: 1963). A third edition was published in 1981.

[17]This is certainly the case in English-speaking Canada, as well as in the U.S., although we understand that in francophone groups in Quebec, fathers do attend meetings.

[18]The La Leche League's commitment to an informal style should not be confused with a rejection of a formal organizational structure with clearly delineated lines of authority. The League has, practically since its inception, developed such a structure, through which it maintains strict control over policy and over admission to the status of League officer. And local League meetings, while informal in tone, are in fact highly organized: in each local group, the meetings occur in a series of four, each with a well-defined topic, such as preparing for childbirth, the art of breastfeeding, or adjusting to the newborn. The meetings are led by a League Leader, who carefully guides the discussion according to a format designed, not by the Leader herself, but by official League committees. At the beginning of each meeting, in her words of welcome, the League Leader invariably states, quietly but firmly, that only League Leaders can speak for the League. Thus, while the informal ambiance of a La Leche League meeting is similar in many ways to that of a feminist consciousness raising group, there are significant differences. Much feminist thinking about the establishment of informal structures involves a rejection of hierarchical forms of authority, an assertion that such structures are a product of patriarchal culture, and a belief that feminist structures must exist independently of the masculine world of hierarchy, dominance and subordination. No such articulation of an opposition to authority is involved in the La Leche League commitment to informality.

[19]Comment made by Marian Tompson, one of the founding mothers, at the League's third biennial convention, *Good Mothering through Breastfeeding the World Over*, transcripts, Third Biennial Convention, 17, 18, 19 July 1968, Denver (Franklin Park, Ill.: La Leche League International, Inc., 1970).

[20]"There are some 12,000 LLL Leaders and 4,500 LLL Groups in 45 countries all around the world," according to "Why Breastfeed Your Baby?", current La Leche League information flyer from La Leche League in Canada, Williamsburg, Ontario.

[21]See footnote 24 below, for statistics relating to breastfeeding.

[22]For a study of this process in a Canadian context, see Jo Oppenheimer, "Childbirth in Ontario: The Transition from Home to

Hospital in the Early Twentieth Century," in this volume, pp. 51-74: "Until 1938 most births in Ontario took place at home and after that date most births took place in hospital," p. 51. For a wider survey of this process, as it occurred in the United States, see Richard W. and Dorothy C. Wertz, *Lying In: A History of Childbirth in America* (New York: The Free Press, 1977).

[23]From a taped recording of the conference session, "Affirming Our Beliefs: Differences in Leaders' Perceptions of La Leche League Philosophy," National Conference, La Leche League of Canada, Ottawa, June 1986.

[24]It appears that the decline in breastfeeding, which began in North America in the inter-war period, continued steadily into the 1960s. In the U.S. in the late 1960s and early 1970s, approximately 25% of mothers commenced breastfeeding. The figures were similar in Canada, see, A. W. Myers, "A Retrospective Look at Infant Feeding Practices in Canada: 1965-1978," *Journal of the Canadian Dietetic Association* 40 (1979), 203, 204 and 207. Recent work by Dr. Myers, who is with the Department of Health and Welfare, Canada, indicates that there has been an upswing in the last few years. Dr. Myers did a 1982 survey in which he found that 69.4% of Canadian mothers initiated breastfeeding, and 45% of these were still breastfeeding when their infants were 4 months old. Personal communication from Dr. Myers, May 1984. We would like to express our thanks to Dr. Myers for his generous assistance.

[25]*The Womanly Art. . .*, p. 133.

[26]An example of League literature on extended nursing is Sallie Diamond, "Still Nursing?", La Leche League International Information Sheet No. 97 (August 1982).

[27]The presentation of La Leche League beliefs appears in many of their publications. They are discussed in an article by Betty Crase, "LLL's Image: What is LLL Philosophy and What Isn't?" *Leaven* 22 (1986), 35-6.

[28]From Marian Tompson's keynote speech, *Third Biennial Convention*.

[29]On the founding mothers and their families, see, for example, Lowman, *The LLLove Story*.

[30]Tine Thevenin, *The Family Bed: An Age-Old Concept in Child Rearing* (Minneapolis: Thevenin, 1976). It should be noted that this is not an official La Leche League publication, but it is frequently displayed as part of the members' lending library at League meetings. In the 3rd edition of *The Womanly Art of Breastfeeding*, the family bed is also discussed. See pp. 136-43.

[31]*The Womanly Art. . .*, p. 4.

[32]*Building Relationships for a Lifetime*, La Leche League of Eastern Ontario, Area Conference Program, Gloucester, Ontario, 11 and 12 May 1984. Session E8 was on the "Serena" method of birth control.

[33]The phrase is from Ferdinand Lundberg and Marynia F. Farnham, *Modern Woman: The Lost Sex* (New York: Harper & Brothers, 1947).

[34]Betty Friedan, *The Feminine Mystique* (New York: Dell, 1963).

[35]Twentieth-century trends in the U.S. and Canada have been similar. For Canadian statistics, see Pat Armstrong and Hugh Armstrong, *The Double Ghetto*, 2nd ed. (Toronto: McClelland and Stewart, 1984).

[36]From *The Womanly Art. . .*, p. 115.

[37]Mary K. White, "What's In It for Mother?", *La Leche League News* 8, 5 (September-October 1965), 7.

[38]Marian Tompson, keynote address, *Third Biennial Convention*, p. 2.

[39]*Ibid.*, p. 6.

[40]Quotation from a female speaker at a panel. *Ibid.*, p. 24.

[41]See *La Leche League News* 18, 3 (May-June 1976).

[42]The best example of this new League literature is a book recently written by one of the founding mothers: Mary Ann Cahill, *The Heart Has Its Own Reasons: Mothering Wisdom for the 1980s* (Franklin Park, Ill.: La Leche League International, Inc., 1983).

[43]As an example of this sort of tendentious reasoning, see "Mother-Baby Togetherness," Reprint No. 116 (La Leche International, Inc., Williamsburg, Ontario, August, 1980), a one-page information sheet, which begins by explaining: "La Leche League. . .has always recognized the unique and essential character of the baby's need for his mother, and now--unequivocally stated--we re-affirm this enduring belief. . . .La Leche League International. . . has collected a great deal of background material. . . which strongly supports the importance of mother-baby togetherness. Some of these references have been excerpted here." The excerpts include statements from John Bowlby, Selma Fraiberg, Dr. Joyce Brothers, and Sigmund Freud. The strongest statement about the dangers of maternal employment quoted on this information sheet is from Dr. Rene Spitz, identified as Professor of Psychology, University of Colorado Medical Center: "'Working mothers who return to their jobs shortly after the birth of a baby are endangering the future lives of their children. . .'" See also Cahill, Chapter 2, "Importance of Mothering." Cahill relies heavily on such researchers as John Bowlby and Selma Fraiberg, and nowhere mentions the extensive research and extensive literature which argue that there is little or no objectively perceivable difference in the development of children in day care and those cared for by the biological mother. That research demonstrates that good day care, like good mothering, is good for children. Inadequate day care, like inadequate mothering, can harm them. The quality of the care is the salient feature, rather than the setting. On this point, see the useful survey of the literature and analysis of the bias in many of the sources on which groups like the La Leche League rely, by Kathleen Gallagher Ross, "Group Care and Early Childhood Development," in Kathleen Gallagher Ross, ed., *Good Day Care* (Toronto: The Women's Press, 1978), pp. 25-32. And see also

Sandra Scarr, *Mother Care/Other Care* (New York: Basic Books, 1984).

[44]"There's a New Baby in Your Life? Congratulations!" La Leche League International Publication, No. 58a.

[45]Interview with League Leader, March, 1985.

[46]Interview with League Leader, May, 1985.

[47]The most well-known advocate of the position that women's moral perceptions are different from those of men is Carol Gilligan. See her "In a Different Voice: Women's Conceptions of Self and of Morality," *Harvard Educational Review* 47, 4 (November 1977) and *In A Different Voice: Psychological Theory and Women's Development* (Cambridge: Harvard University Press, 1982). What differentiates the position of the respondents in the interview sample, and cultural feminist theorists, we would suggest, is that even the most extreme cultural feminists do retain some commitment to a political position that emphasizes that women have been exploited and oppressed by a society dominated by men.

[48]Interview with League Leader, June, 1985.

[49]When interviewees were asked about activity in organizations other than the La Leche League, none of them mentioned R.E.A.L. women, and when the organization was mentioned by the interviewer, association with the lobby group was explicitly denied. It is interesting to note that, when interviewing started in 1985, before R.E.A.L. women received the press coverage it has in 1987, some League leaders had only a vague idea of the organization. In short, League Leaders and right-wing activists move in different circles.

[50]See "Women of Conviction: 10 Dynamic Women Share Their Views on the Direction of the Feminist Movement," *Herizons* 5, 2 (March 1987), 18-29. (This was the last issue of *Herizons*.) Of the ten women selected, some were very well-known, like the peace activist Muriel Duckworth, and Rosemary Brown and Flora MacDonald, both active in party politics, and some, like Irene Todd, were less well-known. Our thanks to Ruth Pierson for bringing this article to our attention.

[51]*Herizons*, 28.

[52]Examples of such analysis are to be found in Eisenstein, and Barrett, and, for example, in two historical analyses of housework: Dolores Hayden, *The Grand Domestic Revolution* (Boston: M.I.T. Press, 1981), and Susan Strasser, *Never Done: A History of American Housework* (New York: Pantheon, 1982).

[53]An example of an anti-feminist left-wing critic is Christopher Lasch. See his *Haven in a Heartless World: The Family Besieged* (New York: Basic Books, 1977).

[54]While League literature in the 1980s--in contrast to that of earlier years--rarely challenges feminism directly, criticism of feminism is implicit in much of its literature supporting its view of family life and of the mother's role, and in its statements about the dangers of maternal employment.

[55]Eisenstein, *Radical Future. . .*,p. 190.

[56]Interviews with League Leaders, January and February, 1986.

[57]Cahill, p. 7.

[58]*Ibid.*, p. 151.

[59]For an analysis, see Strasser, and Ruth Schwartz Cowan, *More Work for Mother* (New York: Basic Books, 1983).

[60]The existence of a "family wage" for male workers, which would allow women to remain outside of the paid labour force, has never been fully achieved in practice for working-class families. For an excellent historical discussion of the gap between rhetoric and reality about the "family wage," see Jane Lewis, *Women in England, 1870-1950: Sexual Divisions and Social Change* (Sussex and Bloomington: Wheatsheaf and Indiana University Press, 1984).

[61]On this question, see Margrit Eichler, *Families in Canada Today* (Toronto: Gage, 1983); Paul and Erin Phillips, *Women and Work: Inequality in the Labour Market* (Toronto: Lorimer, 1983); and Kathleen Gerson, *Hard Choices: How Women Decide about Work, Career and Motherhood* (Berkeley: University of California Press, 1985).

[62]It is especially supportive for those women who become most actively involved, as leaders and as office-holders in the League. Ironically these are the very women who might otherwise have been involved in feminist organizations. To quote Irene Todd again: "As my involvement with LLL increased (and my time with feminist organizations correspondingly decreased) I was able to develop many skills which will serve me a lifetime--chairing meetings, research, public speaking, empathetic listening, counselling, and perhaps most importantly for me personally--how to continue to trust my own feelings and do what I believe is right, even if the majority of society doesn't share those views." *Herizons*, 28.

Chapter Thirteen

ELLEN KEY: MATERNALISM AND PACIFISM[*]

Ruth Roach Pierson

Currently maternalism as a theory of women's specificity is enjoying a comeback, not only among male sociobiologists[1] but among women pacifists, feminists and feminist pacifists. The feminist theorist Sara Ruddick, for instance, locates a major source of opposition to war in the mothering experience of women, above all the "preservative love" of women as mothers.[2] Meanwhile, in Canada, "home-loving," pro-family R.E.A.L. Women are lobbying members of Parliament with home-baked muffins[3] to oppose such standard items on the feminist agenda as a woman's right to abortion, no-fault divorce, universal free child care, enforced affirmative action, and equal pay for work of equal value.[4] Given the present resurgence of maternalism, in both feminist and anti-feminist camps, it maybe useful to take an historical perspective on the question of maternity as a basis for women's pacifism. As a first step in such a project, what I propose to do in this chapter is to look at the maternalism of the Swedish theorist Ellen Key in its relation to her ideas on women and peace.[5]

Ellen Key was born in 1849 into a cultured and liberal-minded family of Swedish gentility: her mother was of "an old and noble family," and her father, possessor of a country estate, represented radical liberal views in Sweden's parliament.[6] The world might never have heard of Ellen Key had not the loss of much of the family fortune necessitated her going out to work as a teacher at age thirty. Before that she had read widely in European literature, philosophy and history and, as the personal secretary of her father, travelled widely through continental Europe, particularly France and Germany. Only in middle age did she begin to write and then prolifically, producing a steady stream of books and articles before she died in 1926.[7]

[*]Earlier versions of this paper were delivered at the Eighth Annual Conference of the U.S. National Women's Studies Association at the University of Illinois (Urbana-Champaign) in June 1986 and at the Centre for Cross-Cultural Research on Women, Queen Elizabeth House, University of Oxford, in January 1987.

She saw the labour movement and the woman movement, "the emancipation movements of labouring men and of women," as "the great forces of the time."[8] Her thought was most visibly shaped, however, by Darwinist evolutionary theory combined with eugenics (the sociobiology of her day), and sex radicalism. Against enforced monogamy, the "whited sepulchre of lawful wedlock,"[9] she set the 'free love' ideal of a monogamous heterosexual union sanctified by the comingling of souls as well as bodies. Not a mother herself, although rumours credited her with a child born out of wedlock, she became one of the most influential proponents of maternalism in the English and German-speaking worlds before the Great War.[10] The "right to motherhood", and the rights of motherhood, the supreme importance of childhood, and the sanctity of the mother-child relationship, as well as women's right to heterosexual fulfillment in a relationship based on love, were the central and recurring themes of her many books and articles.

In her own day she was a controversial figure, as she continues to be in ours. To the British radical feminist and sex libertarian Rebecca West, "Miss Key" was an anti-feminist and the author of "eroto-priggery."[11] To the sexologist Havelock Ellis, acclaimed as "one of the finest English minds" by the same Rebecca West,[12] Ellen Key was a reasonable and temperate feminist who sought to rescue the Women's Movement from those women who "sometimes seemed anxious to be emancipated from their sex."[13] According to her defender Ellis, Key's writings were "often rather informal in method and personal in style, but freely following the author's thought and feeling, full, not only of ardent enthusiasm but of fine intuition and mellow wisdom."[14] In the words of her detractor West: "At the least provocation her sentences gush into fountains of italics, and every now and then they tangle into an elaborate pattern of contradictory parentheses as though she were trying a new crochet stitch."[15] The German radical suffragist Hedwig Dohm also designated Key as an anti-feminist and "ruthlessly exposed" her "numerous contradictions,"[16] while the German utopian maternalist Ruth Bré, a great admirer of Key, founded the *Bund für Mutterschutz und Sexualreform* (League for the Protection of Motherhood and Sexual Reform) in 1904 to implement the ideas of the Swedish social reformer concerning unmarried mothers and the 'new morality'.[17]

Opinions on Ellen Key remain divided to this day. Whereas certain of Key's reform proposals are being hailed as the antecedents of the maternal welfare policies of contemporary Sweden's social democracy, the lesbian feminist historian Sheila Jeffreys denounces Key's role in helping the pro-motherhood movement of the 1910s and 20s to undermine and arrest the drive of the earlier feminism for equality between the sexes.[18] Certainly Key's works are capable of evoking conflicting responses from contemporary feminists. What feminist could quarrel, for instance, with Key's insistence that women should have a "right to motherhood" independent of patriarchal morality and marriage?[19] And, when in Canada and the U.S., the number of sole support mothers living in poverty has risen steeply in the last ten years,[20] matched only by the number of fathers defaulting on child maintenance payments, one cannot help but be struck by the pragmatism of her plan, in anticipation of Aleksandra Kollontai's,[21] for "a paternity assessment upon society" into which all gainfully employed would contribute for "the maintenance of children and a compensation" to mothers from the state for the socially necessary and valuable labour they perform. Were such a plan in place, Key proposed, there would be "no more illegitimate children" and "no fathers who avoid their economic duties toward their children." Nor would there be, she sensibly pointed out, "mothers who for the sake of their own and their children's maintenance need to stay with a brutal man."[22]

Not all of Key's ideas appear so progressive, however. One is dismayed, for instance, by her sweeping condemnation of any kind of collective child care[23] and corresponding advocacy of full-time motherhood for the individual mother during the first seven years of every child's life.[24] Furthermore, while she applauded women's "unwillingness to produce children by the dozen or score," she deplored the 'new woman's' disinclination for motherhood as evidenced by her "sick" desire to stop after one or at most two. In Key's view, the number of offspring should "not fall short of three or four."[25] In Kollontai's view, "the talented though erratic" Key had "too loving a regard" for "the obligations of maternity" and "the isolated family unit."[26]

But whether Key should be regarded as progressive or reactionary, feminist, non-feminist or anti-feminist is not at issue here.[27] What is, instead, is the question of the soundness of her maternalism as a basis for women's pacifism. Key made the association between maternal and pacific qualities in her pre-war writings as a part of her general idealization of motherhood. The most sustained attention that she gave to the subject of women and peace appears in her 1916 *War, Peace, and the Future.*[28]

Key in no way challenged, but rather subscribed wholeheartedly to, the sex differences orthodoxy of her day. In *Love and Marriage* (1912) she specifically refers her readers to Francis Galton, the father of eugenics, to Patrick Geddes and J. Arthur Thomson's *The Evolution of Sex* (1898) and to Havelock Ellis' *Man and Woman: Sex in Relation to Society* (1894).[29] As a gender essentialist and a eugenicist, Key held that motherhood was the highest and most important vocation for women both as individual members of their sex and as "mothers of the race."[30] Key was rather fond of thinking in terms of abstract dualisms, particularly those expressive of an opposition between self and society, like egoism versus altruism, or individualism versus socialism. She also had a penchant for advocating a middle position between, or the reconciliation of, such opposites. The beauty of motherhood for Key was that it brought self-realization and self-renunciation into perfect harmony: the individual woman's feminine (or womanly) nature attained self-fulfillment in motherhood at the same time that she as mother performed her self-sacrificing duty to the evolutionary betterment of the race.[31]

The vocation of motherhood, however, involved more than the performance of a biological function; that is, the work of mothers included the rearing as well as the bearing of children. For the former, particular psychological qualities were required, the crucial combination of which Key called "motherliness." In *The Woman Movement*, Key defined the "spiritual attributes" composing "motherliness" as: "protecting tenderness, gentle patience, glad readiness to help, the interest embracing each one in particular, the fine and quick vibration in contact with the feelings of others which we, in a word, call 'tact'."[32] The most salient of these qualities was "the feeling of tenderness," acclaimed by Key as the greatest virtue in woman as "the sense of justice" was in man. The "so much greater significance" that "enhancing and preserving life" had "for woman than for man" was traceable to this "feeling of tenderness in woman."[33] When, in 1916, Key came to reflect on woman's relation to war and peace as distinct from man's, the concept of "motherliness" figured prominently, albeit problematically, in her reflections.

In 1916, the year of the Battle of the Somme in which the British lost approximately 420,000 casualties, the French nearly 200,000, and the Germans some 450,000,[34] Key saw "the inmost strength of woman's nature" as providing the "only gleam of hope for the future."[35] It seemed inevitable that women as mothers would have to rise up in revolt against the male-exclusive politics that called for and countenanced the wanton slaughter of sons whom women had so painfully borne and painstakingly reared. "If the motherliness of women is not so incensed by this war that it causes a mass-rising against the injustice of woman's position, then I don't know from what source we may expect salvation," Key wrote.[36]

To bring an end to that senseless cycle of women giving life in order for men to take each other's, Key endorsed women's struggle for enfranchisement and eligibility for public office. In the tradition of maternal feminists, Key maintained that, when women had a voice in the affairs of state, the eugenic aim of protecting, increasing, and improving "the living human material that is now ruthlessly sacrificed for so-called purposes of state" would become "the foremost object of statecraft."[37] Key's assignment, according to a sexual division of traits, of tenderness of feeling to women and sense of justice to men did not prevent her from asserting that her own sense of justice was offended by men expecting women, "as a matter of course," to make endless sacrifices for war, "without dreaming of granting them, as citizens, the logical recompensation, suffrage."[38] To end that injustice, Key argued, it was essential that women acquire a share of the decision-making power of the state. Only then could women fulfill their cultural mission both to inject the qualities of motherliness into the governing of society and to restore the state to a eugenic course. "The citizenship of women is thus," Key concluded, "the first condition for enabling them...to lift the race out of the stage of the beast of prey."[39]

While women's ability to work effectively "to humanize humanity"[40] was dependent on their gaining the right to vote and hold public office, that public activity, in Key's view, ought not supplant but only supplement women's equally important service for peace, the education of the young. It was Key's conviction that, during the years when children were still in the home, a mother's duty to them must take precedence over sitting in parliament or occupying public office.[41] Despite her identification of protective tenderness as the salient feature of motherliness, Key knew of women who wished "to abolish war" but still believed "that the souls of children are to be cleansed like mats, by beating."[42] She therefore felt constrained to admonish mothers against the use of corporal punishment if they wished to educate their children "to detest brutal methods as a means."[43] "In order to overcome the spirit that creates war," Key reasoned, "mothers must begin in the tender years of childhood to teach children that right must be the foundation of all might."[44]

Working against the placement of hope in women as the humanizers of humanity in both the public and the private spheres, however, was the indisputable fact, as Key well knew, that "millions of women have greeted a war in which their sons and husbands have been killed with enthusiasm."[45] Key recognized that women had fallen prey to jingoistic nationalism and war enthusiasm in much the same way as men; indeed that the majority of women in the belligerent nations had "completely made the point of view of the man their own" and were "willing to continue the war to a 'glorious victory'."[46] Key had even heard of German women who were "proud of the sinking of the Lusitania."[47] She had evidence of women directly involved in combat, "Russian and Polish women who have dressed as men and entered the ranks."[48] Exaggerated and largely unfounded stories had also reached Key of Englishwomen who were enlisting "by the hundreds in [a] women's reserve corps," arming themselves and receiving a "cold blooded training to kill."[49]

Key was most appalled by women's willingness to participate directly in warfare: such women, she held, transgressed against their true nature and forfeited their claim to a voice in the politics of the public realm. "To everybody with any depth of insight," Key intoned, "the warring woman must seem a painful contradiction in terms. To be a woman implies the giving and protecting of life, and the whole future significance of woman's increased rights is dependent on her reverence for this mission and her abhorrence of all destruction of life, especially of the mass destruction of war."[50]

In Key's view, to deserve the right to vote and hold public office, women had to put themselves back in touch with peace-loving "motherliness." She heartily endorsed the opinion that the "'Woman's movement must be pacifistic or cease to be'."[51]

What was this elusive "motherliness," then, if it could be contradicted and betrayed by so many women, most of whom were mothers? If, as Key expounded in *The Renaissance of Motherhood*, "*Das Ewigweibliche* (the eternally feminine) is nothing but the well of maternal tenderness,"[52] did she understand "motherliness" to function like a Platonic archetype, embodied in individual mothers at best to varying but inevitably limited degrees? Perhaps, as Key definitely viewed women and men as stratified from low to high, common to noble, and their status, in her eyes, was more dependent on culture and "refinement of feeling" than on economic class.[53] Nonetheless, however much "motherliness" operated in Key's thought as a normative concept, evolutionary eugenics and not Platonism is the context in which her use of the term needs to be understood.

Certainly Key did not equate "motherliness" simply with women's biological capacity to give birth. On the contrary, as a eugenicist, she regarded some women capable of giving birth or already having given birth as 'unfit' to be mothers. Key defended the right to motherhood of unmarried women who were idealistic, strong, and healthy. Moreover, she advocated state support for such 'fit' mothers and their children, but not for weak and sickly mothers and their offspring, whether born within marriages or not. At the same time, while claiming that motherhood was "the fountainhead of altruistic ethics,"[54] Key herself gave eugenics precedence over altruism when she called for withdrawal of state support from "all the miserable human progeny which, married as well as unmarried, mothers cast upon society." Indeed, she clearly favoured steps to ensure that "this class" of "vicious human offscum" be prevented from propagating "its kind."[55] Did such outcast women possess a maternal instinct? Presumably Key believed not, for she stated as an established fact in *The Renaissance of Motherhood* "that there existed women without motherly instincts."[56]

Key thus drew a line between the biological capacity for motherhood and the maternal instinct. She would have denied the promised fulfillment of motherhood to all 'unfit' women. Key also distinguished between the maternal instinct and "motherliness," but in this case she placed the two phenomena on an evolutionary continuum. In *The Woman Movement* of 1912, Key extolled "the development of the mother instinct into motherliness" as "one of the greatest achievements in the progress of culture." Moreover, she denied that "motherliness" was "a spontaneous natural instinct," categorizing it instead as "the product of thousands of years not merely of *child-bearing*, but also of *child-rearing*."[57] According to Key in *The Renaissance of Motherhood* of 1914, "motherliness. . .in the beginning was but the animal instinct for protecting the young" and had only over time evolved into "helpfulness, compassion, glad sympathy, far-thinking tenderness, personal love." Nevertheless, Key believed that "the feeling of duty" which motherliness entailed "had come to possess the strength of instinct."[58]

For someone who put so much faith in the pacifying potential of "motherliness," Key's conception of its ontological status is maddeningly unclear. On the one hand, Key wrote as if "motherliness" were not a natural endowment of women,[59] but only a female aptitude that had taken centuries of cultural evolution for its development. Even within a single lifetime cultivation was required to develop blind maternal instinct into enlightened motherliness.[60] From this perspective it made sense for Key to advocate, as she strongly did, state-supported education for motherhood. Key consistently pressured for "a year of compulsory state service for women," analogous to the military service required of men, for the purpose "of preparing young women for the duties of motherhood and home making."[61] In other passages, on the other hand, Key assumed the voice of a gender essentialist and identified "motherliness" as the essential characteristic of woman. In *The Woman Movement*, for example, she spoke of woman's spiritual "fitness and readiness" for motherhood, that is, her adaptation to and desire for motherhood in soul as well as in body. She saw this predisposition as having developed over at least "one hundred thousand years" into "the normal condition" of womanhood. This was so much the case, Key held, that if one were searching for the essence of "womanliness" it was to be found in "motherliness."[62]

If "motherliness" were practically coterminous with womanhood, and had so many thousands of years of evolutionary development behind it, why was it so precarious? In 1912 Key felt obliged to warn her readers "that motherliness is not an indestructible instinct."[63] In the pre-war period, Key clearly believed it was under attack from, and needed to be defended against, the "zealots of feminism." Led by Charlotte Perkins Stetson (later Gilman), these "cerebral, amaternal women" had "begun to strengthen the tendency to celibacy" by espousing co-operative housework, collectivized child care, and paid work outside the home as the only guarantee of women's independence.[64] These "amaternalists" were the advocates of a future in which "both sexes shall have the same duty of work and the same protection of work, while the children are reared in state institutions."[65] To Key, however, for a woman to work outside the home during her reproductive years was a case of "'women's misused energy'."[66] Although hailed as promoting the principle of individual freedom for women, Key questioned just how liberating wage labour was for the proletarian woman "employed in hard agricultural labour" or in industrial work

in which lead, quicksilver, phosphorus or tobacco poison

the workers, or those branches of work where inhaling
dust at the weaving loom or in spinning, breathing gas
and coal smoke, and damp, they contract tuberculosis and
other diseases. . .[67]

But the debilitating effects of seeking "'Full equality of woman with
man'"[68] in the field of labour were also visited upon the middle-
class woman. In her case they took the form of nervous exhaustion.
"Here we are faced," Key expounded, "by the fundamental cause of
modern woman's nervosity. She lives year in and out above her
powers."[69]

The truly innocent victims of this 'one-sided' pursuit of
woman's right to work, in Key's judgment, were the children. She
pointed to the infants who were born "dead or sick or crippled" and
the children who became "scrofulous, rickety, [or] idiotic" as a result
of the conditions of their mothers' employment.[70] But no matter at
what the mother worked, her absence from the home would have a
deleterious effect, for "the bringing-up of a child demands the same
undivided attention as the production of a work" of art, Key
maintained.[71] It is on this point that Gilman and Key parted
company. While they both agreed that the job of child care required
training, Gilman would have reserved it for those women uniquely
suited to become specialists in the education of babies in
nurseries.[72] Censuring the isolated, privatized home for its anti-
social tendencies, Gilman sang the benefits to children of having
"playmates of exactly their own age" in communal child care
settings.[73] In contrast to Gilman's contention that "Direct,
concentrated, unvarying personal love is too hot an atmosphere for
a young soul,"[74] Key argued that

each young soul needs to be enveloped in its own mother's
tenderness, just as surely as the human embryo needed
the mother's womb to grow in and the baby the mother's
breast to be nourished by.[75]

Maternalists both, Gilman's "social" motherhood and Key's
"individualized" motherhood stood in diametric opposition.[76]

Important as winning the woman "back to the home" was for
the welfare of the individual child, it was even more crucial in Key's
eyes for the future of the human race.[77] The qualities of
motherhood were nurtured, Key believed, only in the one-to-one
relationship of mother to child, and society risked losing these
qualities altogether if the sexual division of labour were not strictly
enforced. The only major shift in that division sanctioned by Key
was for women to have a "voice in the ruling of the country for
which they bear and bring up the coming generation." Altering the
sexual division of labour any further would be, Key warned,
"detrimental to the race," deflecting women from their cultural
mission to preserve the values of motherliness and assert them in

the public sphere.[78] For that reason, she pronounced "*the work of the mother outside the home* in and for itself. . .an evil."[79] In this context, the qualities of "motherliness" hardly appear to possess even the status of innate predisposition, so dependent are they on the perpetuation of women's confinement to the home.

The confusion as to whether "motherliness" is inherent in the nature of woman or culturally created and socially enforced persisted into Key's 1916 reflections on women and war and peace. In *The Woman Movement* of 1912, Key had castigated the "amaternal advocates" for having championed woman's right "to emancipate herself from the heresy that motherliness should be the ethical norm for the 'being' or 'essence' of womanhood."[80] By 1916, "motherliness" had begun to function in Key's own thinking more and more as the normative standard for, rather than the normal condition of, women. Notwithstanding her continued talk of woman as the giver of life who "uses her strength to preserve life, not destroy life,"[81] Key returns again and again to a need for woman's spiritual, cognitive development in order for her to align herself on the side of peace. So long as the majority of women succumbed to narrow-minded patriotism, "they have not the faintest idea how to wage war against war," Key wrote.[82] Before women could begin to work for peace in the post-war world, she added, "the minds of women must be really transformed by the impressions of war."[83] Those already committed to peace, like Rosika Schwimmer and Helena Swanwick, were, Key knew, but a minority, and they apparently came to their commitment, she implicitly recognized, by education and culture or by political consciousness, not "motherliness."[84] Key noted that "The most passionate protests against war. . .have come from the socialistic women."[85]

A further, perhaps even more fundamental, contradiction in Key's association of women with peace concerns the nature of the pacifism Key herself espoused. Key was an internationalist and advocate of collective security, not an absolute pacifist. Scoffing at those who put their faith in "the magic of fantastic peace-Utopias," she supported what she called "scientific pacifism" that looked to the slow building up of a system of international law and international justice administered through an international court of appeals.   The goal was a world organization safeguarding international peace.[86] Until that far-off day, probably centuries hence, when humanity "by conscious effort" had overcome "the madness of a world at war," such an international system was dependent on arms to enforce its verdicts.[87] To believe otherwise, as did the principled pacifists, was, in Key's view, "building castles in the air."[88] Key distinguished between an imperialistic, war-conducive nationalism and a sound love of country that respected international law and regulations. She further allowed that "true" nationalism as well as the collective security of nations had to be backed up by military force, for, Key averred in 1916, "even patriotism demands the defence of the mother-country."[89]

On close examination, then, Key's maternalism proves a shaky foundation for pacifism. While women were to advance peace by infusing society with motherly qualities, the "motherliness" that Key upheld in some passages as "the distinguishing characteristic" of woman,[90] she treated in others as a precarious cultural artifact not to be sacrificed to women's selfish pursuit of individual freedom and the right to work. Moreover, Key arrived at her own advocacy of internationalism by dint of "conscious effort" not maternity. Finally, Key, while believing in women's greater respect for life than men's, also believed in the justice and necessity of defensive war for love of country. Therefore, committed as she was to maintaining the sexual division of labour in order to preserve "motherliness," and abhorrent as she found the notion of woman as combatant, Key was a "feminine pacifist"[91] who would leave men to shoulder the burden of arms bearing as well as to assume the role of potential killer for the foreseeable future.

Notes

[1]Ruth Hubbard, "Have Only Men Evolved?," in Ruth Hubbard, Mary Sue Henifin and Barbara Fried, eds., *Women Look at Biology Looking at Women* (Cambridge, Mass.: Schenkman Publishing Co., 1979), pp. 7-36.

[2]Sara Ruddick, "Preservative Love and Military Destruction: Some Reflections on Mothering and Peace," in Joyce Trebilcot, ed., *Mothering: Essays in Feminist Theory* (Totowa, New Jersey: Rowman and Allanheld, 1983), pp. 231-62.

[3]Linda Hossie, "Muffin-loving lobbyists attracting new admirers," *The Globe and Mail*, May 19, 1986, p. A-4. R.E.A.L. is the acronym for Realistic, Equal, Active for Life.

[4]Karen Dubinsky, "Lament for a 'Patriarchy Lost'? Anti-feminism, Anti-abortion and R.E.A.L. Women in Canada," Canadian Research Institute for the Advancement of Women Papers on Feminist Perspectives, no. 1 (1985), 31.

[5]For a somewhat different retrospective look at Ellen Key's maternalism and pacifism, see Berenice A. Carroll's review essay "Ellen Key on Women, War, Peace and the Future," *Peace and Change* 2, 1 (Spring 1974), 53-5.

[6]Havelock Ellis, Introduction to Ellen Key, *Love and Marriage*, trans. from the Swedish by Arthur G. Chater (New York: G. P. Putnam's Sons; London: The Knickerbocker Press, 1912), p. vii.

[7]Louise Nystrom-Hamilton, *Ellen Key: Her Life and Her Work*, trans. from the Swedish by A.E.B. Fries, with an Introduction by Havelock Ellis (New York: G. P. Putnam's Sons, London: The Knickerbocker Press, 1913).

[8]Ellen Key, *The Woman Movement*, trans. by Mamah Bouton Borthwick (New York: G. P. Putnam's Sons; London: The Knickerbocker Press, 1912), p. 218.

[9]Key, *Love and Marriage*, p. 14.

[10]In the United States, articles by Ellen Key appeared regularly in the *Atlantic* and *Harper's Weekly* between 1912 and 1916. (My thanks to Flora Clark for copies of these articles.) In Canada she was read by promoters of Home and School Clubs (Parent-Teacher Associations). See Terry Crowley, "Ada Mary Brown Courtice: Pacifist, Feminist and Educational Reformer in Early Twentieth-Century Canada," *Studies in History and Politics* 1 (1980), 76-114. For an excellent discussion of Ellen Key's wide ranging influence on both the bourgeois and proletarian women's movements in Germany, see Kay Goodman, "Motherhood and Work: The Concept of the Misuse of Women's Energy, 1895-1905," in Ruth-Ellen B. Joeres and Mary Jo Maynes, eds., *German Women in the Eighteenth and Nineteenth Centuries: A Social and Literary History* (Bloomington: Indiana University Press, 1986), pp.110-27.

[11]Rebecca West, "The Sin of Self-Sacrifice," *The Clarion*, 12 December 1913; "Literary Pulp: A Comment on August Strindberg," *Daily News*, 25 August 1916, reprinted in James Marcus, ed., *The Young Rebecca: Writings of Rebecca West 1911-1917* (New York: The Viking Press in association with Virago Press, 1982), pp. 235, 320.

[12]Rebecca West, "War and Women," a review of *Essays in Wartime* by Havelock Ellis, *Daily News*, 20 December 1916, reprinted in *The Young Rebecca*, pp. 332-33.

[13]Havelock Ellis, Introduction to Ellen Key, *The Woman Movement*, p. xvi; Ellis, Introduction to *Love and Marriage*, p. xiv. Strangely enough there is no mention of Ellis' promotion of the writings of Ellen Key in Phyllis Grosskurth's excellent and otherwise exhaustive reconstruction of the British sexologist's life. Grosskurth, *Havelock Ellis: A Biography* (Toronto: McClelland and Stewart, 1980).

[14]Ellis, Introduction to *Love and Marriage*, p. xii.

[15]Rebecca West, "Eroto Priggery," *The New Republic*, 13 March 1915, p. 150. I am indebted to Flora Clark for this reference.

[16]Goodman, pp. 111, 113

[17]Richard J. Evans, *The Feminist Movement in Germany 1894-1933*, SAGE Studies in 20th Century History, vol. 6 (London and Beverly Hills: SAGE Publications, 1976), pp. 120-1.

[18]Torborg Lundell, "Ellen Key and Swedish Feminist Views on Motherhood," *Scandinavian Studies* 56 (1984), 351-69; Sheila Jeffreys, *The Spinster and Her Enemies: Feminism and Sexuality 1880-1930* (London: Pandora Press, 1985), pp. 137, 140.

[19]Cheri Register, "Motherhood at Center: Ellen Key's Social Vision," *Women's Studies International Forum* 5 (1982), 604; Key, *Love and Marriage*; Ellen Key, *The Renaissance of Motherhood*, trans. from the Swedish by Anna E. B. Fries (New York: G. P. Putnam's Sons; London: The Knickerbocker Press, 1914).

[20]In Canada, "Over the period 1966-1986, the number of lone-parent families rose 130%, while husband-wife families

increased only 42%." In 1986, more than 82 per cent of all lone parents were women. "Lone-parent families headed by women had the highest incidence of low income of all family types." Maureen Moore, "Women Parenting Alone," *Canadian Social Trends* (Winter 1987), 31-6.

[21]At the time of the marriage law debate in the Soviet Union in 1926, Aleksandra Kollontai proposed that alimony be replaced with a General Insurance Fund, built on the contributions of the entire adult working population, for the support of mothers in need and their children. Beatrice Brodsky Farnsworth, "Bolshevik Alternatives and the Soviet Family: The 1926 Marriage Law Debate," in Dorothy Atkinson, Alexander Dallin, and Gail Warshofsky Lapidus, eds., *Women in Russia* (Stanford, CA: Stanford University Press, 1977), pp. 149-60.

[22]Key, *The Woman Movement*, p. 150.

[23]While Key and Kollontai shared the view that the state should administer society's collective responsibility to see that the work of mothering receive adequate remuneration, their positions diverged on the issue of collectivized child care. Kollontai's proposed General Insurance Fund would have supported "the establishment of day nurseries and homes for children." Farnsworth, p. 151.

[24]Key, *The Renaissance of Motherhood*, p. 133.

[25]Key, *Love and Marriage*, pp. 226-8; *The Renaissance of Motherhood*, p. 115.

[26]From *The Social Basis of the Woman Question* (1909) as reproduced in Alix Holt, ed., *Selected Writings of Alexandra Kollontai* (New York: W. W. Norton, 1977), pp. 70-1.

[27]For such an appraisal, see Pearl Dykstra, "Ellen Key: Motherhood for Society," *Atlantis: A Women's Studies Journal* 9, 1 (Fall 1983), 49-57.

[28]Ellen Key, *War, Peace, and the Future: A Consideration of Nationalism and Internationalism, and of the Relation of Women to War*, trans. by Hildegard Norberg (New York: G. P. Putnam's Sons; London: The Knickerbocker Press, 1916), p. 18. Rebecca West panned this book as "Woman Worship." Rebecca West, "Woman Worship," a review of *War, Peace and the Future*, by Ellen Key, *Daily News*, 13 April 1917, reprinted in *The Young Rebecca*, pp. 338-40. Even more than by Key's maternalism West was offended by a neutral's spreading the blame for the war among the four major belligerents, Germany, Russia, France, and England.

[29]Key, *Love and Marriage*, p. 226.

[30]Ellis, Intro. to *Love and Marriage*, p. xiv.

[31]Key, *The Woman Movement*, p. 28; Key, *The Renaissance of Motherhood*, pp. 104-5.

[32]Key, *The Woman Movement*, p. 18.

[33]Key, *Love and Marriage*, p. 265.

[34]A.J.P. Taylor, *Illustrated History of the First World War* (New York: G. P. Putnam's, 1964), p. 105.

[35]Key, *War, Peace, and the Future*, p. 100.

[36]*Ibid.*

[37]*Ibid.*, pp. 96, 149, 99, 100.

[38]*Ibid.*, pp. 112-3.

[39]*Ibid.*, p. 142.

[40]*Ibid.*, p. 142.

[41]Key, *The Woman Movement*, p. 131.

[42]Key, *Love and Marriage*, pp. 278-9.

[43]Key, *War, Peace, and the Future*, p. 154.

[44]*Ibid.*, p. 93.

[45]*Ibid.*, p. 221.

[46]*Ibid.*, p. 168.

[47]*Ibid.*, p. 104.

[48]*Ibid.*, p. 200.

[49]*Ibid.*, p. 198.

[50]*Ibid.*, p. 199.

[51]Key, *War, Peace and the Future*, p. 246.

[52]Key, *The Renaissance of Motherhood*, p. 99.

[53]Key, *War, Peace, and the Future*, p. 55.

[54]Key, *Renaissance of Motherhood*, p. 91.

[55]*Ibid.*, p. 73.

[56]*Ibid.*, p. 97.

[57]Key, *The Woman Movement*, pp. 185, 191.

[58]Key, *The Renaissance of Motherhood*, p. 103.

[59]Key, *The Woman Movement*, p. 28.

[60]Key, *The Renaissance of Motherhood*, pp. 119-20.

[61]Key, *War, Peace, and the Future*, p. 217; *Love and Marriage*, p. 206; and *The Renaissance of Motherhood*, p. 161.

[62]Key, *The Woman Movement*, p. 58.

[63]*Ibid.*, p. 190.

[64]*Ibid.*, pp. 192, 176, 189, 173, 180.

[65]*Ibid.*, p. 32.

[66]Key first articulated the concept of "*Missbrauchte Frauenkraft*" at a women's conference in Copenhagen in 1895. She published an essay with that title in Germany in 1898. Goodman, pp. 111-12.

[67]Key, *The Woman Movement*, pp. 35, 38-9.

[68]*Ibid.*, p. 32.

[69]Key, *Love and Marriage*, p. 218.

[70]Key, *The Woman Movement*, pp. 38-9.

[71]Key, *Love and Marriage*, p. 219.

[72]Charlotte Perkins Stetson (Gilman), *Women and Economics* (Boston: Small, Maynard & Company, 1898), pp. 277-94.

[73]*Ibid.*, p. 288.

[74]*Ibid*, p. 292.

[75]Key, *The Renaissance of Motherhood*, pp. 136-7.

[76]Key and Gilman waged their debate in the pages of the New York publication *Current Opinion* in 1913. See "Ellen Key's Attack on 'Amaternal' Feminism," *Current Opinion* 54 (February 1913), 138-9, and "Charlotte Gilman's Reply to Ellen Key," *Current*

Opinion 54 (March 1913), 220-1. My thanks to Flora Clark for these references.

[77]Key, *Love and Marriage*, p. 213.

[78]Key, *War, Peace and the Future*, p. 97.

[79]Key, *The Woman Movement*, p. 41.

[80]*Ibid.*, p. 178.

[81]Key, *War, Peace, and the Future*, p. 220

[82]*Ibid.*, pp. 168, 94.

[83]*Ibid.*, p. 118.

[84]*Ibid.*, pp. 110, 142, 241.

[85]*Ibid.*, p. 223.

[86]*Ibid.*, pp. 140, 123, 23, 56, 114. Key's position is typical of the legal internationalism that predominated among women peace activists in Europe before the First World War. See Sandi E. Cooper, "Women's Participation in European Peace Movements: The Struggle to Prevent World War I," in Ruth Roach Pierson, ed., *Women and Peace: Theoretical, Historical and Practical Perspectives* (London: Croom Helm, 1987), pp. 51-75.

[87]Key, *War, Peace and the Future*, pp. vii, 32, 57.

[88]*Ibid.*, p. 57.

[89]*Ibid.*, pp. 17, 16.

[90]Key, *The Woman Movement*, p. 179.

[91]". . .feminine pacifism is easily eroded because it arises from a false view of masculinity and femininity, the Victorian ideology of separate spheres. To assert that women are intrinsically opposed to war is to condone war for men and to make opposition to war part of woman's separate sphere of activity." Deborah Gorham, "Vera Brittain, Flora MacDonald Denison and the Great War: The Failure of Non-Violence," in Pierson, ed., *Women and Peace*, p. 140.

Chapter Fourteen

DESPERATELY SEEKING BABIES:
NEW TECHNOLOGIES OF HOPE AND DESPAIR*

Rona Achilles

Motherhood, in the last decade, has moved from a peripheral to a central position in feminist thought. The publication of Adrienne Rich's *Of Woman Born* in 1976[1] marked the beginning of a now prolific literature addressing the diverse issues and questions raised by women's roles as mothers.[2] The shift that occurs with *Of Woman Born* is not just one of focus--it is also a shift towards recognition of more positive features of mothering. Rich, who distinguishes between the "experience" and the "institution" of motherhood attributes the negative aspects of mothering to the patriarchal system in which women mother. The experience, she argues, contains the potential for tremendous joy and creativity. Dinnerstein argues that the current arrangements for parenting in which women are dominantly responsible for the nurture of children contains both the origins of misogyny and the equation of women as nature. This combination, Dinnerstein suggests, could lead to the annihilation of the planet.[3] Chodorow asks why, given the social devaluation of the mothering role, do women continue to mother? She concludes that, among other influences, it is women's greater "relational potential" which continues to reproduce the mothering role.[4]

Simultaneously--in an entirely different arena--recent medical advances in the field of reproductive technology have irreversibly altered both the cultural meaning and the experience of motherhood. While numerous feminist thinkers are attempting to discern the defining features of modern motherhood, these very features are being radically transformed by the discovery,

*This chapter is a revised and updated version of "Artificial Reproduction: 'Hope Chest or Pandora's Box?'," which originally appeared in Sandra Butt, Lorraine Code, and Lindsay Dorney, eds., *Changing Patterns: Women in Canada* (Toronto: McClelland and Stewart, 1988). I would like to thank Mark Lippincott for his assistance and our continuing dialogue on the subject of artificial reproduction.

refinement, and promotion of new reproductive technologies. The introduction of new reproductive technologies (commonly referred to as NRTs) will require us to draw upon our diversity of perspectives and deepest resources to critically grasp their impact. Both female biology--those (once) seemingly immutable processes of conception and gestation--and the social and historical role of mothering take on new meaning in this context.

This chapter is devoted to two projects. The first is to achieve technical literacy--comprehension of what NRTs actually involve through explanations and descriptions of the technical procedures. Secondly, an analysis is provided of actual and potential psychological and social ramifications of NRTs.

Reproductive technology is actually a very broad term. It can refer to something as simple and user-controlled as a diaphragm, to technologies as complex and physician-controlled as *in vitro* fertilization (IVF). For purposes of clarification we can divide reproductive technologies into three basic categories: those that inhibit the development of new life, those that monitor the development of new life, and those that involve the creation of new life. Reproductive technologies involved in the inhibition of new life are the most familiar--all forms of birth control, sterilization, and abortion. Medical advances in the monitoring of new life are more recent and involve techniques such as ultrasound, amniocentesis, chorionic villi sampling, foetal monitoring, and foetal surgery.[5] Developments in both of these spheres have a tremendous impact on women's reproductive autonomy. Foetal surgery, for example, creates a situation where the foetus still in a woman's uterus can be potentially defined as a patient separate from the carrying mother. The capacity to monitor, "correct," and artificially sustain foetal life at increasingly earlier stages of pregnancy may, in practice, work against the individual mother's reproductive autonomy. Kolder et al. document that court-ordered obstetrical procedures are on the increase in the U.S. and that there is substantial support for the practice among physicians surveyed.[6] In Canada, there have been two incidents so far this year (1987) of court-ordered foetal protection.[7] The checkered health record of the Pill and the intrauterine device (I.U.D.) further illustrate the extent to which the technological 'hope chest' for reproductive autonomy and choice may become a 'Pandora's Box' under the prevailing social, economic, political, and medical conditions. The central question is not simply 'choice' but 'choice for whom' and under what conditions?

Feminist efforts in relation to reproduction have largely been devoted to our right *not* to mother or to plan and space pregnancies. The availability of safe and effective birth control and equal access to legal abortion have been major concerns for feminists in the past two decades.[8] More recently the right to control the conditions of birth and access to midwives have emerged as feminist issues. All of these remain important arenas for feminist analysis and action. However, even before we have available safe and effective birth control measures, midst the volatile and unresolved abortion debate, and the ongoing controversy over the legality of midwifery, we are moving into an era that has and will continue to have an unprecedented impact on women's reproductive choice. The developments in the realm of artificial reproduction, those involved in the creation of new life, are our central concern in this chapter.[9]

Artificial insemination, sperm banks, surrogate motherhood, *in vitro* fertilization, frozen embryos, and surrogate embryo transfer are some of the developments in the field of artificial reproduction. This is a field of very rapid medical advances; ten years ago they would have been considered to be the stuff of science fiction. Although the reporting of many of these techniques has moved beyond the medical journals to front-page news coverage, the actual procedures and the implications of their development are sometimes difficult to grasp. The media tend to sensationalize their coverage and label every new development as "test-tube" babies. An authentic "test-tube" baby would require conception, gestation, and birth to occur completely outside of a woman's body--the technical term for which is ectogenesis. The technology for an authentic "test-tube" baby has, as far as we know, yet to be fully developed although it may not be too far off in the future. The inaccurate description in the media of current procedures, however, has sown the seeds for its public reception. Adrienne Rich's "one, unifying, incontrovertible experience shared by all women and men..." will no longer be the case.[10]

Reproductive autonomy, previously limited to concerns about when, how, or not to mother is an issue that takes on new meaning through the use of artificial reproduction procedures. New dilemmas, choices, and responsibilities accompany their introduction into society. Shulamith Firestone, a radical feminist theorist, in the early 1970s proclaimed pregnancy "barbaric" and "the freeing of women from the tyranny of their reproductive biology by every means available..." as the first, among other, structural imperatives for women's freedom.[11] Although Firestone was not lacking in imagination, she did not foresee the complexity and depth of women's role as mothers and its links to both emancipation and domination. In concert with the issues surrounding the freedom from motherhood, feminists must now analyze and understand the need to mother expressed by women who will utilize these technologies.

There is a striking absence of social and psychological research on the impact of infertility on either men or women.[12] Infertility is very simply the inability to reproduce oneself biologically. In the past, the 'barren' wife constituted grounds for divorce, public sympathy and social stigma. The quest for fertility through artificial reproduction, which is usually taxing emotionally, physically, and sometimes financially, testifies to the strength of the 'motherhood mandate' still pervasive in our culture. Increased participation in the paid labour force and progress, limited as it may be, for women to enter professions has not eliminated motherhood as central to women's identity and self-esteem. The reasons for this are complex--family pressures, full adult status, gender identity, and the importance of biological continuity or lineage are some of the factors which induce women (and men) to seek fertility through these costly measures. "It hurts to be infertile..." as Barbara Menning states in her defence of *in vitro* fertilization.[13]

Before we can fully comprehend the implications of these procedures for women and for society in general, it is important to understand what they actually involve, who will use them, and for what reasons. Ultimately they will have an impact on all women although they are currently used only by a small number of women. One of the questions that we need to ask in relation to these developments is whether they expand or reduce women's reproductive choices. Definitely these technologies do provide the opportunity for some women to have children who perhaps otherwise could not do so. On the other hand, these technologies close down some choices, while introducing new pressures and dilemmas for women. A woman confronted with infertility today will likely feel the pressure to pursue every possible avenue to overcome or circumvent her (or her partner's) infertility. As with the pre-natal diagnostic techniques of amniocentesis and ultrasound which have become commonplace for many 'high-risk' women, the mere availability of various reproductive technologies may foreclose the option of *not* using them. Furthermore, the causes of infertility may be ignored since they can be technologically by-passed.

Infertility is estimated to affect up to 15 per cent of couples and is considered to be on the increase. At present, approximately one-third of all cases of infertility are attributed to women, one-third are attributed to men and one-third are either unexplained or shared by both partners. In Canada, infertility is defined as one year of attempting to achieve pregnancy without success. The definition of infertility varies in different countries. France, for example, defines infertility as five years of trying to achieve pregnancy without success. The definition of infertility itself therefore is socially defined and structured. Currently, artificial reproductive technologies are only used to assist couples who have fertility problems or, in some instances, women without a male procreative partner. The potential exists, however, for these technologies to be used for other reasons. For example, we can imagine a woman or couple wanting to hire another woman to bear their child for a number of reasons--for convenience, economic considerations, or simply to avoid the discomforts and health concerns of pregnancy.[14]

As well as the prevalence of infertility, there are a number of social factors which indicate that the market or demand for these procedures is assured and will likely increase. Furthermore, the causes of infertility may be socially rooted to some extent in occupational health hazards, environmental pollution, food additives, and the use of pharmaceutical drugs like Diethylstilbestrol (DES) and devices like IUDs. These include: the decline in availability of children for adoption,[15] the strong emphasis in our culture on having genetically related children (which is possible with some of these technologies but not with others), late child bearing which sometimes incurs fertility problems, the use of vasectomies or tubal ligations[16] with individuals who later change their mind about childbearing, and the increase in genetic counselling which may forewarn potential parents about possible genetic defects in their offspring. In addition, the increase in single women and lesbian couples who want children without contact with a male promises to increase the demand for some techniques such as artificial insemination by donor.

Putting aside temporarily the complex matrix of social questions and consequences, artificial reproduction technologies can be broken down into two basic categories--artificial insemination and *in vitro* fertilization. A fundamental difference between these two technologies is that with artificial insemination conception occurs inside a woman's body whereas with *in vitro* fertilization conception occurs outside a woman's body in a petri dish. (*In vitro* is Latin for "in glass.") Within each of these two categories there are numerous possibilities of different procedures and in some cases they overlap and are used together. Each procedure must be explained and analyzed individually.

Artificial Insemination

Artificial insemination is the oldest, least visible, and most widespread of what we now call artificial reproduction technologies. It is arguable, given the simplicity of the procedure, whether it is appropriate to call artificial insemination a technology since it is very simply a replacement for sexual intercourse. Sperm, obtained through masturbation, is inserted into a woman's vaginal canal at the time of her ovulation. Sometimes a small cap or diaphragm-like device is used to keep the semen in place. Although most artificial insemination takes place in clinical settings, the simplicity of the procedure makes it possible for women to inseminate themselves without the assistance of physicians. Self-insemination groups who organize the transfer of sperm from donors to women are springing up in various countries, including Canada.[17] Since conception, gestation, and birth occur through natural processes (or as 'naturally' as pregnancies that occur through sexual intercourse), the term 'artificial' is slightly misleading. Lahey argues that a more appropriate term is "alternative insemination."[18]

There are three distinct types of artificial insemination--artificial insemination by husband or male partner (AIH), artificial insemination by donor (AID), and what is popularly referred to as surrogate motherhood.[19] Artificial insemination by husband is used when a man's sperm count is very low. The sperm is concentrated through a process of centrifugation which is intended to increase the likelihood of pregnancy occurring. Technically speaking artificial insemination by donor (AID) is the same procedure. The only difference is in the relationship between the man who donates the sperm and the recipient. If the man who donates sperm is not the recipient's husband or partner, the procedure is called artificial insemination by donor.

Artificial insemination by donor is not a new procedure and has a surprisingly long history. The first recorded instance of AID occurred in 1884. When a local merchant and his wife were unable to conceive a child, they requested help from a Philadelphia physician, Dr. William Pancoast. After testing both the husband and the wife the doctor concluded that the problem of infertility was on the part of the husband. While the woman was anaesthetized, Dr. Pancoast and some of his medical students decided to inseminate the woman with the sperm of "the best looking member of the medical class." The woman became pregnant, but she was never informed about the procedure by her husband or Dr. Pancoast. Arguably, as Corea suggests, this incident was a form of rape.[20] Twenty-five years later, in 1909, a physician, presumably the former "best looking member of the medical class," wrote an article for a medical journal and exposed the whole incident. This aroused an enormous debate in medical journals about the ethics of the procedure. Opponents of the procedure argued that it was against the laws of God and nature, that the use of another man's sperm was adulterous, that the legitimacy of the child was questionable and the procedure was dishonest and immoral. Advocates perceived the possibility of improving the quality of the species (an early form of eugenics) and that the source of the sperm was irrelevant.[21] Over one hundred years later we have yet to resolve some of these dilemmas. The Roman Catholic Church, for example, still considers donor insemination to be adulterous. The issue of secrecy is unresolved and the eugenic potential of AID remains problematic.

Since there is no regulation or monitoring of the procedure, the actual incidence is unknown. Estimates in Canada range from 1,500 to 6,000 babies born a year through artificial insemination by donor alone. Since these estimates were made several years ago and do not include women inseminating themselves outside of clinical settings, the numbers are probably conservative. In the United States in 1981, it was estimated that there were a total of 250,000 births through AID with an annual rate of 10,000.[22]

Donors are solicited from a variety of sources--a common assumption is that most donors are medical students or medical personnel. My own study of participants in donor insemination indicates a broader spectrum, varying from postal workers to accountants.[23] Donors are usually paid approximately $25 for time and expenses and Annas argues that sperm donors are more accurately called sperm vendors.[24] After all, we do not pay blood donors in Canada and there is evidence to indicate that the quality of blood is lower in countries where blood is bought and sold.[25] The issue of payment for reproductive capacities becomes even more problematic when we look at the practice of surrogate motherhood. At present, there is no consensus on the number of children one donor can biologically father. The risk of individuals conceived through AID meeting and marrying a half-sibling (unknown to each other as such) increases with the number of AID children produced by each donor. One donor in my study estimated that he had donated approximately 240 times. Another issue concerning donors is the extent of screening for genetic abnormalities or sexually transmitted diseases. This issue is currently exacerbated by the existence of Acquired Immune Deficiency Disease (AIDS).[26] Curie-Cohen, Luttrell, and Shapiro conclude in their study of artificial insemination practice in the U.S. that screening of donors for genetic diseases was inadequate, there was little concern for the possibility of incestuous matings and that record-keeping was haphazard.[27]

How the procedure is practised informs us about our attitudes toward it. Although the specifics may vary from physician to physician, the common ad hoc practice (which is supported by most legal, medical, and ethical reports) is that donors and recipients remain unknown to each other. Anonymity, it is argued, is essential to avoid emotional complications, to ensure "the stability of the family and the welfare of the child."[28] The fear that conflicting emotional ties might arise if anonymity is not protected is based on the assumption that biologically linked individuals may develop curiosity or feelings about each other which could threaten the coherence of the family unit. For example, AID offspring may become interested in the identity of their biological father, the AID mother might become curious about the man who is the biological father of her AID child, or the infertile husband may feel threatened by the sperm donor who was able to impregnate his wife when he was unable to. Consequently, the recipient(s) usually have no information about the donor and the donor is generally not told whether a pregnancy or birth has occurred. Frequently there is an attempt to 'match' the physical characteristics of the sperm donor to the AID mother's partner (if present) or to herself. Women using self-insemination (outside of clinical settings) may choose to know or not know their donors.

This, in itself, is a momentous shift in reproductive relations. Although neither marriage nor parenthood has always been based on individual choice--our choices are socially structured in any event--to neither know nor choose the biological father of one's child is an unprecedented social act. In the case of donor insemination, physicians are choosing the reproductive partner, the man who will be the biological 'father' of an AID mother's child.

The practice of AID is surrounded by secrecy, anonymity, and the confidentiality of the doctor-patient relationship. Most physicians advise the parents that there is no reason to tell the children or any other family members about the child's origins through AID. In this respect, AID anonymity is reminiscent of early adoption practice. Unlike adoption, however, AID anonymity holds out the possibility to heterosexual couples of 'passing' as biologically linked parents. (Single or lesbian AID mothers will usually have to explain their child's origins in some way. The explanation of AID may be preferable to the assumption of a 'one night stand'.) There is a collusion among participants in the procedure to protect the social father and the couple from the stigma of male infertility as well as an attempt to protect the child from feeling 'different'. Problems arise, however, for a variety of reasons. In some instances, the offspring of AID find out about their origins and usually not under the best of circumstances. As with most secrets, they are most likely to be divulged during periods of emotional stress and conflict (e.g., marital crises, divorce, death).

Already in the United States there is a group called "Donors' Offspring" who are asserting their right to know the other half of their biological heritage. This is generally problematic because there is no legal responsibility for the physician to keep records linking the donor, recipient(s), and offspring. Even when records are kept, they are defined as medical records, and hence, are the property of the physicians. In Canada access to medical records is guided by the principle of best interest of the patient. In addition, sperm donors participate in AID with the understanding that their identity will remain anonymous. There are, as yet, no laws to protect the participants in AID, with the exceptions of Quebec where the child is legally considered to be affiliated with the social father and the Yukon where donors are protected from possible legal suits by offspring or recipients. Recently the Ontario Law Reform Commission (1985) undertook a major study of the legal problems posed by artificial reproduction and proposed amendments to legislation.[29] Despite the fact, however, that their study purports to protect the "best interests of the child," the report agrees with most other reports in viewing donor anonymity as essential to the success of the procedure. Some individuals conceived through AID may have no interest in knowing the identity of their biological father. Given the current increase in genetic counselling, however, access to medical information regarding sperm donors may be considered important by some participants, and increasingly by recipients.

Secrecy about a procedure as significant as this can be experienced as a burden.[30] Among the married AID mothers who participated in my study and adhered to secrecy, all described a cost to keeping the donor insemination secret. Although generally described by respondents as 'liveable', feelings of isolation, a desire to know about the experience of other AID recipients and painful reminders (usually through comments about physical resemblance of their AID children) were reported. The majority, however, found that secrecy was not feasible and were faced with difficult questions about who, how, and when to tell about their use of AID. For example, one woman's husband had been institutionalized (for mental illness) shortly after the birth of their AID son. Under stress she had quickly told friends and family that her husband was not the 'real' father. Her son (aged eight at the time of the interview) was now asking questions about this unknown but somehow 'real' father. Understandably, this AID mother was confused and frightened by her son's interest in knowing more about his biological father and was uncertain whether any information could be obtained.

In the medical literature, AID is described as a treatment for male infertility. It does not, however, cure infertility but circumvents it through the use of another man's sperm. Ironically, but not surprisingly, it is the fertile woman who becomes the patient! Despite the simplicity of the procedure, when it is practiced in clinical settings, it is frequently accompanied by other medical procedures to increase efficiency and the success rate. The presumably *fertile* woman may undergo a series of tests to ensure that she is fertile and that sperm is not 'wasted' on a woman with her own fertility problems. These can include, hysterosalpingograms (a procedure in which dye is injected into the fallopian tubes and uterus), endometrial biopsies, drugs to regulate her ovulation, and possibly drugs to sustain the pregnancy. Several of the AID mothers that I interviewed described the testing as the "worst part." In addition, the insemination itself was described as difficult. Finding a physician, arranging to take time off work, and co-ordinating the schedules of potentially four individuals (donor, if fresh sperm is used; partner, if present; mother; and physician) to ovulation time was reported consistently as stressful. If pregnancy was not achieved within a few months, the pressure and stress were described as intolerable. Women who choose to inseminate themselves outside of clinical settings avoid additional medical procedures. What all AID mothers share, however, are the legal and social ambiguities arising from this shift in reproductive relations.

Surrogate Motherhood

Surrogate motherhood is a much more socially visible procedure than the version of artificial insemination that we have just examined. This is partially because paternity is a less visible event than maternity.[31] It is also a more controversial social arrangement since biological motherhood is a more complex and involved relationship than biological fatherhood. Therefore, it has captured the attention of the media more than any other artificial reproduction technology. It is also a much more problematic practice for the future of all women in relation to reproduction.

Surrogate motherhood is generally used by couples when the wife is infertile. The husband's sperm is used to artificially inseminate a woman (the surrogate) who agrees (contractually) to surrender the child at birth and is generally paid a fee for her 'services'. It has the potential, however, to be used by anyone willing and able to pay a woman to bear a child for them for any reason. Surrogate motherhood is actually a misnomer for this arrangement since an authentic surrogate would be a woman who uses donor eggs and provides the uterine environment for a child surrendered at birth to the contracting couple or individual.

Innumerable questions are raised by the practice of surrogate motherhood. It is somewhat reminiscent of wet-nursing when poor women were used to provide breast milk for babies of wealthier women. By logical extension, it sets the groundwork for some women to become essentially breeders for others--with some surrogates being more highly valued according to the current standards of beauty or intelligence. Margaret Atwood's novel *The Handmaid's Tale* provides a dystopian vision of this possibility.[32]

As an organized practice, surrogate motherhood is just a little more than ten years old.[33] So far there are no organized surrogate services in Canada; media reports indicate, however, that these services exist as an underground practice and that Canadians are participating in surrogate arrangements (both as surrogates and commissioning couples) through U.S. organizations. In 1984, there were sixteen organizations in the United States offering surrogate services and currently, surrogates are paid approximately $10,000 for their 'services'. However alarmed we may be at the idea of women bearing children for a fee, it is the lawyers involved in arranging these services who profit and charge approximately the same amount, ($10,000) for co-ordinating the arrangement.[34]

In contrast to donor insemination, the recipients of surrogate services generally pick their surrogate out of a catalogue and may have contact with the surrogate during the pregnancy. (This varies according to the particular organization.) Also, in contrast to sperm donors who are apparently difficult to find, there is an abundance of women who want to become surrogates. There has been a mixed response from the feminist community toward surrogate motherhood but in either case it has been strongly stated. On the one hand, it is argued that it is exploitation, similar to prostitution or concubinage and the surrogate is acting as a surrogate wife to the biological father. On the other hand, some feminists have said, "It's about time someone gets paid for nine months gestation--blood, sweat, and hard delivery."[35]

Any discussion of surrogate motherhood must be grounded in the facts of women's status in the labour force and their role as childbearers and caretakers. That is, most paid work for women remains low status, low paid, and with little opportunity for advancement. The fee of $10,000--although if we calculated it on an hourly basis is less than the minimum wage--is still a substantial amount of money that could alter the short-term economic circumstances of most people's lives. Additionally, surrogates say it provides "all the magic of pregnancy" without the responsibility of rearing a child.[36]

In order to separate themselves from the child they will surrender at birth, the surrogates describe themselves as "vehicles" or "vessels." Nevertheless, there is frequently a grief reaction (termed "transient grief") after the child is given to the contracting couple or individual.[37] There are already self-help groups for surrogates organized to provide support after the child is surrendered. Susan Ince posed as a surrogate applicant to gain insight into the workings of one surrogate organization from the surrogate's perspective. Her documentation of the experience is chilling. She reports the inadequacy of screening (medical and psychological) procedures, how she was discouraged from seeking independent counsel and, in short, the company's complete control over the surrogate.[38]

Although it is as yet unclear to what extent surrogate arrangements are enforceable, current contracts potentially divest the surrogate of her rights over her body throughout the terms of the contract.[39] This includes extensive controls over diet, lifestyle, and activities. There is already one instance in the United States of a surrogate being charged with a misdemeanour for taking drugs during her pregnancy. It may also involve undergoing medical procedures, such as ultrasound or amniocentesis, to ensure a "quality product." If the foetus is discovered to be 'defective' (by whose standards?), she may be asked to undergo an abortion late in the pregnancy and forfeit the majority or all of her 'payment'. There is also the question of what happens if the surrogate decides that she does not want to give up the child. In current adoption practice the birth mother generally has a period of approximately two weeks after birth to make her final decision.[40] There have already been several instances of surrogates changing their minds about 'surrendering' the child after birth. In addition, since the ideal surrogate is married with children of her own (a good track record), the impact of the arrangement on other family members, such as her other children, her husband (or partner), and grandparents, is unknown.

In the recent New Jersey case of 'Baby M', the issues which emerged exemplify the inevitable dilemmas inherent in surrogate arrangements. The surrogate, Mary Beth Whitehead, *did* change her mind about giving up her baby. The contracting father, William Stern, decided to fight for custody in the courts and he won.[41]

The trial of this heart-wrenching scenario went on for months and was reported in detail in several media. At the time of the contract, Mary Beth Whitehead was married, a full-time homemaker and mother of two children; her husband was a sanitation worker. Despite Whitehead's initial claim that she entered the surrogacy agreement because her sister was unable to conceive and she felt "empathy for childless couples who were infertile," the $10,000 must be regarded as a substantial sum for this single-income working-class family.[42] The Sterns, the contracting couple, were earning an estimated $90,000 between them--William Stern as a biochemist and his wife, Elizabeth Stern, as a pediatrician.

The arrangement was transparently class-bound. It is difficult, if not impossible, to imagine wealthy women having babies, fee or no fee, for poorer couples. Beyond the obvious, however, this case was loaded with class issues that stem directly from having or not having money but are less apparent than the capacity to pay $10,000 for someone to bear a child. The Sterns' money also bought them knowledge, respectability, and an excellent lawyer. They never gave a press conference without their lawyer present and projected a public image in this highly volatile and emotional case as controlled, sensible, and cool. In stark contrast, Mary Beth Whitehead "spilled her guts" to the media, appeared 'hysterical', 'out of control', and hot-headed. She looked crazy, i.e., to be an unfit parent. The Sterns 'looked good', i.e., to be fit parents. The class-bound nature of this construction was not explored. The Sterns might well have been equally hysterical in the privacy of their home but had the 'good sense' not to damage their public image.[43]

The outcome of the case was predetermined in another dimension as well. Mary Beth Whitehead cared for her baby for the first four months of her life and named her Sara. The Sterns named her Melissa. When the judge ordered temporary custody to the Sterns (four months after birth and for the duration of the extended trial), the child was named by the court 'Baby M'. Why 'M'? Why not 'Baby S' or more neutrally 'Baby J'? As Annas points out, temporary custody orders almost always become permanent orders.[44] The Sterns had this temporary decision on their side from the beginning of the trial.

As well as the custody of the child, at issue in this case was the enforceability of surrogate contracts. Mary Beth Whitehead signed a contract which required her to undergo amniocentesis at the request of William Stern (which she did against her own and her doctor's wishes) and have an abortion if the foetus were deemed by the physician to be "physiologically abnormal," or determined by tests to be "genetically or congenitally abnormal." If she had conceived an "abnormal" child and aborted, she would have received $1,000. If she had refused to abort, Stern's obligation to her would have "ceased forthwith," as would his obligation had she miscarried within the first five months. Judge Sorkow's decision confirms the North American way that, in fact, 'a deal is a deal' even when it clearly contravenes social values and legislation against exchange of money for body parts or human beings. Trafficking in humans was outlawed with slavery.[45] The fact that Whitehead, as would any other surrogate, receives her $10,000 only upon delivery of a healthy newborn eliminates any confusion about whether payment is for "services" or for the "product"--and the product is a child.

Finally, of particular interest, in the context of this anthology is the manipulation of maternal ideology that accompanies the practice of surrogate motherhood and this specific legal precedent. The very success of the procedure is dependent on women conceiving, gestating and relinquishing their children without any messy emotions like attachment, bonding, affection and/or love. One's historical vision need not be too lengthy to recall that these are precisely the qualities required of women to be good mothers-- not very long ago, if not currently, in other contexts. Women who leave their child(ren) wear this century's scarlet letter. One mother's virtue, in other words, is another mother's crime. Surrogate motherhood is a practice that challenges these values and it is precisely these values that were re-examined, reneged, and tossed out as outmoded and a 'mistake' in the New Jersey courtroom. Mental health experts, some of whom had written passionately in the 1950s about the importance of maternal bonding, were called to the stand to testify that maternal bonding was really non-existent or not that important after all. Whitehead was reported to play 'patty-cake' incorrectly with her daughter and also (incorrectly) gave Sara teddy bears rather than pots and pans to play with.[46]

The entire trial is the stuff of a best-seller and undoubtedly several will be forthcoming. Whitehead handing her baby out the back window to her husband when the Sterns arrive with the police, Whitehead fleeing to Florida with her baby, the police breaking into her mother's home there and delivering the child back to the Sterns, Stern taping telephone calls from Whitehead in which she threatens to commit suicide and take her child with her, Whitehead's ten-year-old daughter begging the police to be taken away instead of her little sister.... Another round in a higher court is about to begin (at the time of writing).[47] Sara/Melissa has already been passed back and forth between her biological mother and biological father and will, no matter who finally gets custody, be labelled for life as a surrogate child. The 'best interests' of this child have already been violated, although her own response to her origins will be unknown for years to come.

In Vitro Fertilization

In vitro fertilization (IVF) is the second major form of artificial reproductive technologies. In this method the process of conception moves firmly into the hands of physicians. IVF is distinct from artificial insemination in that it involves very sophisticated medical technology and medical expertise. The process for recipients is stressful, invasive, and financially and emotionally draining. What we don't read in the newspapers reporting with awe the birth of another IVF child is that the success rate is actually very low.[48]

The history of IVF is short, with the first successful IVF child born in Britain in 1978. Nevertheless, this is definitely a growth industry within the medical profession as there are already nine IVF clinics in Canada, all of which have very long waiting lists--indicative both of the prevalence of infertility and the desperation of couples for their own genetically linked children.

IVF was initially used when the problem of infertility was on the part of the woman, usually because her fallopian tubes were blocked. Yet, there is already evidence of the expansion of its use to couples where the male partner has a low sperm count. Williams, in a preliminary study of IVF candidates, also found IVF being used as a diagnostic tool to further define the source of infertility.[49]

This procedure is not simple. The first step is the retrieval (or "harvesting"--note the language of animal husbandry, where all of these techniques were developed first) of the eggs which involves taking drugs to stimulate egg production, daily blood tests, pelvic examinations, and ultrasound. Then there is the removal of the eggs. Usually since drugs have been used to stimulate the ovaries to produce more than one egg at a time, between two to six eggs are removed surgically through a laparoscopy.[50] The second step is when the eggs and sperm (usually the woman's partner's sperm but not necessarily) are joined in a culture dish where fertilization may or may not take place. If fertilization does take place, the third step is the transfer of the fertilized eggs into the woman's uterus in the hope that implantation and pregnancy will ensue. Usually more than one fertilized egg is transferred to increase the possibilities of implantation. This is why IVF births frequently involve twins, triplets, or quintuplets. If the eggs are transferred back into the same woman from whom they were removed, the procedure is referred to as embryo replacement. If they are implanted in another woman, the procedure is referred to as embryo transfer. Fertilized eggs, technically referred to as concepti, may also be frozen and stored for future use by the genetic mother or another woman.

A more recent development in artificial reproduction is called surrogate embryo transfer (SET) which combines artificial insemination with a later stage of IVF, embryo transfer. Similar to IVF, SET is used with heterosexual couples when the problem of infertility is on the part of the woman. With this method, a woman, the surrogate, is artificially inseminated with the sperm of the husband. If successful, the fertilized egg is flushed (also called "lavage") from the surrogate's uterus and implanted in the uterus of the biological father's wife. At least one birth through this method has already occurred. Although this method of artificial reproduction is argued as less invasive than IVF, problems can occur if, for example, the lavage technique is not successful. The surrogate risks an unwanted pregnancy and the decision to abort or carry the foetus to term. If she carries the child to term, conflicts may arise about whom the child belongs to. Other risks include pelvic infection and ectopic pregnancies which could potentially result in sterility.[51]

Social Implications

There are numerous medical, legal, and governmental reports that attempt to identify and resolve the problems raised by the use of all these procedures.[52] We know very little, however, about who actually uses them and what their experience is. The legal questions alone raised by these technologies are overwhelming.[53] There is currently a wealth of legal literature which identifies these problems and attempts to resolve them. Resolution of legal issues, however, will not entirely settle the social problems created by the use of these procedures. Since most of these procedures are still in experimental stages, much is unknown about their short or long-term social implications. At least four social issues can be identified: 1) the further medicalization of the reproductive process, 2) the impact on family structure, 3) the commercialization of reproductive capacities, and 4) the potential eugenic uses of artificial reproduction technologies.

Medicalization

Among the most obvious social processes involved in the use of artificial reproduction technologies is the further medicalization of women's reproductive experience. Although reproduction requires the biological contribution of both sexes, it is notable that all of these technologies involve women becoming patients--even in the case of AID where the woman is presumably fertile. Medicalization is the expansion of medical expertise and influence into previously non-medical arenas of society.[54] The medicalization of women's reproductive experience is an ongoing social process. The introduction of artificial reproduction technologies, therefore, is not a bold leap into Huxley's *Brave New World*. Rather, it is a significant furthering of already existing social trends. The medical profession is already very involved in numerous decisions surrounding reproductive matters, including the choice and distribution of most birth control methods, pre- and post-natal care, and birthing, all of which increasingly involve reproductive technologies. The development of artificial reproduction technologies may be perceived as a logical (but extreme) extension of the 'planned parenthood' mentality pervasive in our culture. Their further involvement provided by the development of artificial reproduction, however, raises new levels of control and, therefore, new levels of responsibility and influence. In short, these new techniques may precipitate a host of hybrid social consequences which reflect, in a heightened manner, already existing social forces.

Society has always attempted to regulate, to some extent, who has sexual intercourse with whom, where, and under what conditions. Informal and sometimes formal sanctions govern sexual behaviour according to, for example, age, race, religion, class, and marital status. Prior to the development of artificial reproduction, conception itself occurred through the private interaction of two individuals--through sexual intercourse between a man and a woman. All of these technologies separate the act of sexual intercourse from reproduction. This in itself is not necessarily problematic. With the exception of self-insemination, however, artificial reproduction technologies as practised in clinical settings move conception out of the private and into the public realm, and medicalize it. Members of the medical profession, in other words, are now deciding who will have access to these services and, therefore, who will or will not become parents. This is not a realm of decision making for which physicians are trained. Furthermore, the movement of conception into the public realm raises the question of whether every individual has a fundamental right to procreate and whether this right includes access to these services. The potential for discrimination exists on grounds of class (those who can afford to pay for these services), race, marital status, and sexual preference. Most physicians will presumably attempt to uphold cultural standards that designate a heterosexual married couple the best possible parents for a child.[55]

Family Structure

The diversity of current Canadian family structures has been documented by Eichler.[56] Few Canadian families conform to the presumed cultural norm of a married heterosexual couple who rear their biological offspring to adulthood. Nevertheless, this image/norm of the family persists. When we use the term parent, we generally assume that the biological and social components of the role merge in one person. Exceptions to this are families formed through adoption, foster parenthood, and step-parenting. In these situations, the term 'parent' is modified by an additional descriptor indicating some deviation from the presumed cultural norm. With adoption, for example, biological parents are referred to as birth parents and social parents are referred to as adoptive parents.

Artificial reproduction technologies facilitate further diversity in possible family configurations. This assortment of parental roles is reflected in the current linguistic and conceptual confusion in describing these roles. With AID, fathering is split into two roles--the generally unknown biological (sperm donor) father and the social or rearing father. This family configuration presumes the recipients are a heterosexual couple. If the AID mother is single, there will be no rearing or social father. If she is part of a lesbian couple, then the second parent will be another mother (a co-mother) who is not biologically linked to the child.

The term 'mother', a role which traditionally refers to the genetic, uterine, and social mother of a child, is potentially fragmented into six different roles through the use of one or a combination of artificial reproduction technologies: 1) an egg donor--

a woman who provides an egg but does not carry or rear the child (this is possible through egg donations with IVF and through SET); 2) a uterine mother--a woman who provides the gestational environment for a child who is not hers genetically and whom she will not rear (this is an authentic surrogate or host mother); 3) an egg and uterine mother (popularly referred to as a surrogate mother)--a woman who is the biological mother but will not rear the child (this situation is somewhat analogous to a birth mother who gives up a child for adoption at birth); 4) a uterine and social mother--a woman who is the recipient of an egg donation; 5) an egg (or genetic) and social mother--a woman whose fertilized (*in vitro*) egg is carried and birthed by another woman and then returned to her; 6) a social mother not genetically related to the child--the recipient of a surrogate motherhood arrangement. This situation is similar to adoptive or step-mothers or any woman who raises children to whom she is not genetically related. Although not all of these roles are socially unprecedented, the manner in which they are created is new. Six new roles of mothering! The implications of this fragmentation of women's reproductive and mothering experience is yet to be realized.

A child conceived through a combination of these procedures could potentially have five parents--two fathers and three mothers. The two fathers are the sperm donor or biological father and the social father, similar to the situation with artificial insemination by donor. The three possible mothers include potentially an egg donor, uterine mother, and the mother who will rear the child (the social mother). Again, these family constellations are based on the presumption that recipients are a heterosexual couple. An even more complex picture of possible family forms emerges when the recipients are single or in lesbian couples.

The practice of freezing eggs, sperm, or embryos, technically referred to as cryopreservation, further complicates our common understanding of the process of reproduction. Conception, for example, could occur in a petri dish in Australia. The embryo could be frozen, stored, and transported to Canada where it could be implanted in a woman who (if successful) could give birth to a child, conceived many years earlier, to whom she has no genetic ties and whose genetic parents may no longer be alive. These possibilities alter both our temporal and geographical assumptions about the boundaries of the reproductive process, as well as the common cultural assumption that the parents of a child are genetically linked.

The rights and responsibilities of gamete (sperm or egg) donors, uterine donors, surrogates, and social parents can be legislated. Yet, the image of family as constituted by biological links is strong in our culture. The consequences for participants in artificial reproduction procedures who are linked solely through biological ties is unknown. The feelings, for example, of a woman who provides an egg, her uterus, or both (as in the case of surrogate motherhood) to create a child she may not have a social relationship with is unknown. The 'Baby M' case indicates that a surrogate mother can change her mind about relinquishing her child. Anecdotal evidence about other surrogate arrangements shows that some surrogates develop a relationship similar to that of an aunt, and others, depending upon the policy of the surrogate agency, have no contact with the child after birth. The feelings of the infertile wife in a couple who utilize a surrogate are also unknown. She may feel jealous of her husband's 'surrogate wife' who can fulfill his need for his own biological child or the two women may develop a close relationship if the arrangement is successful.[57] A woman who donates an egg for another woman who will carry and rear a child takes on a role somewhat similar to that of a sperm donor.[58] The potential exists, therefore, for women to 'father' children by providing only genetic material similar to men who donate sperm or biological fathers who do not assist in rearing their offspring.

Research on children who are adopted indicates that they frequently desire information about their biological heritage and may search for their biological parents in order to complete their sense of identity. Individuals conceived through one or a variety of artificial reproduction procedures that disassociate their biological and social parentage may react similarly. If accurate records are kept linking biologically related individuals, and if participants have access to these records (both of which are questionable at this time), the maze of bureaucratic and social dilemmas is formidable. Other issues include the unknown responses of other family members, such as the biological grandparents of AID or surrogate children (the parents of the donor or surrogate), aunts, uncles, and siblings of children in both the recipient and donor families.

The success of families created through artificial reproduction rests, to some extent, not on the technologies themselves but on our capacity, as a society, to redefine what constitutes family. In concert with other changes in family forms, artificial reproduction technologies challenge the sanctity and increasingly mythological image of the biologically linked nuclear family as normative. If the emphasis on the blood-tied nuclear family persists, it is likely that a preference will develop for technologies which preserve the genetic links of parents and offspring wherever possible. This could result in the use of more expensive and invasive methods over simpler less costly procedures. For example, in the case of a male with a low sperm count, IVF may be used instead of AID to preserve the genetic link and, when donor gametes are employed, they will likely be used on an anonymous basis. The issues are complex and volatile; the consequences of these procedures are unknown.

Commercialization

Sperm donors are paid approximately $25 per ejaculate, surrogate mothers are paid $10,000, and surrogates participating in SET are paid approximately $250. Putting a price tag on reproductive capacities has profound social implications. The children created through these technologies will eventually become adults and have to come to terms with their origins. They may feel special and particularly wanted or they may feel like a commodity, bought and sold. In any case, their creation through a commercial transaction is likely to affect their identity and is potentially stigmatizing. Surrogate motherhood has been described as another version of prostitution--the expansion of exploitation of women's sexuality into the reproductive realm.[59]

There are partial social precedents for payment in relation to body parts, organs and blood. Furthermore, despite legal restrictions, baby-selling does exist. Insurance companies establish a 'price' for the loss of an arm, leg, or other body parts. All of these analogies, however, are limited since there is a crucial distinction among the maintenance of a life already in existence, the loss of a body part, the use of women's bodies for sexual services, and the payment for reproductive capacities involved in the creation of new life. The result of the latter is a new human being accompanied by new social roles for family members and consequently new social responsibilities. Commercialization of reproductive capacities, therefore, although not totally unprecedented, is similar to the issue of medicalization. It is the significant furthering of already existing social trends.

In the United States a private company is attempting to patent the technology for SET. In a recent television programme, the company's directors reported that egg donors, essential for the success of the company, are available in "cost effective abundance."[60] The very language used by these entrepreneurs signals a change in our relationship to the reproductive process. Commodification entails a process of evaluating and assessing a human activity or the product of a human activity according to current market forces. It also disguises the presence of the human being involved in the labour required to produce the product. Treating reproductive capacities as commodities commercializes and brings market values and processes into a realm which has previously been immune to these influences.

Eugenics

The final area of concern is the issue of eugenics. Eugenics is the practice of selective breeding intended to 'perfect' the human species. It is generally distinguished by two different methods--positive eugenics and negative eugenics. Positive eugenics is the attempt to increase the number of children born with 'good' genes.

Negative eugenics is the attempt to reduce the number of children born with 'bad' genes. Although a useful dichotomy, an obvious problem arises in deciding what is valued as 'good' or 'bad' and who is to make these decisions.

At first glance, negative eugenics would seem overall to be a worthwhile project. Genetic screening can increasingly detect carriers of diseases such as Huntingdon's chorea, muscular dystrophy, and cystic fibrosis. Decreasing the incidence of these agonizing diseases is seemingly socially advantageous; grey areas, however, abound. Activists in the disabled rights movement have pointed out that screening or aborting for "defects" further devalues individuals considered by society to be "defective."[61] One particularly contentious area is the use of pre-natal diagnostic techniques, such as ultrasound, chorionic biopsy, or amniocentesis to identify the sex of a foetus, followed by an abortion if the sex does not accord with parental preference. Roggencamp documents the incidence of this phenomenon in India where female foetuses are overwhelmingly aborted.[62]

Although the extent of this practice is unknown in western industrialized countries, we can speculate that wherever males are valued more highly than females, female foetuses would be aborted more frequently. Research on parental sex preferences overwhelmingly indicates a preference for male over female offspring, a view held more frequently by men than women, and particularly in relation to first borns.[63] The desire for a child of a particular sex is in itself sexist and could potentially institutionalize sexism at a new level, since, for example, first borns are known to be high achievers.[64] Other concerns include alterations in the sex ratio with fewer females born than males. The consequences of this possibility can only be speculated about[65] and include feminist concerns about gynocide.[66]

Pre-conception sex selection techniques are an example of positive eugenics. These are less invasive methods than post-conception techniques and usually involve theories about the timing of intercourse with ovulation or the separation of X and Y bearing spermatozoa.[67] What was once the substance of folklore is increasingly the subject of scientific study. A U.S. company is marketing a package called "GenderChoice" which is available over the counter in drugstores. The most extreme example of positive eugenics is the existence of a Nobel Prize Winner sperm bank in the U.S. from which women or couples of 'superior' intellectual capacities can order sperm.[68] Surrogates and gamete donors may be chosen for socially valued traits perceived as genetically inherited. The underlying assumption is that genetics are the key factor in determining personality traits or capacities, such as intelligence, athletic abilities or musical talents. Australian IVF physicians are already claiming that children conceived through IVF are superior to those conceived 'normally'.[69] Statements such as these neglect to consider the obvious influence of environment--

including the specialized treatment and care these desperately wanted children most likely receive from their parents. The twentieth century has seen the rise of experts advising women how to rear perfect children.[70] Artificial reproduction technologies provide the opportunity for a different level of 'quality control' in the parenting process. As well, pre-natal diagnostic techniques provide information about a foetus previously unavailable before birth. A woman in her fifth month of pregnancy may have to choose on the basis of this knowledge whether to have an abortion or carry to term and give birth to a child she knows will be disabled--in a society that devalues the imperfect. This instance of choice posed by the new reproductive technologies is a burden that will be carried largely by women.

Commercialization of reproductive capacities is inextricably linked to eugenic issues. Through commercialization the child becomes a commodity, the recipient parents become consumers and gamete donors and surrogates become suppliers. Damaged or defective 'products', babies who are not 'perfect', will likely be unacceptable to the consumer. In a surrogate arrangement in 1983, a handicapped child was rejected by both the contracting (presumably) biological father and by the surrogate. Eventually a paternity test proved the surrogate's husband to be the biological father (this destroyed any validity the contract might have had) and the surrogate and her husband agreed to keep the child.[71] Despite the inevitable increase in the use of reproductive technologies to prevent the likelihood of this situation, other problematic instances are bound to arise in the future.

Social policy already lags far behind these rapidly developing medical advances. As the technologies become more sophisticated, the social dilemmas posed by them become more complex. The crucial question is who is going to control these technologies and under what conditions? Medical control over these technologies is already well established and is solidified by recommendations in government reports. Public debate on these issues, at least in Canada, has been quite limited.[72] Since it is unlikely once a technology is introduced that it will be withdrawn, all of these technologies are probably here to stay.[73] The project for feminists is neither to embrace nor to reject their use. The first crucial step is to monitor and assess the impact of their implementation and lobby for the least abusive practices. In cultivating a critical approach to reproductive technologies an important point to consider is that already scarce health resources are being utilized to develop these technologies. As a result it appears that fewer health resources are being channelled into research about the causes of infertility.

As with any new social process or technology, we are granted an opportunity to rethink and reorganize some of our most deeply embedded assumptions. Consequently, the alterations in our traditional assumptions about parenting facilitated by artificial reproduction may have a hidden blessing. It has the potential to force us to reflect on and further our understanding about the meaning and task of parenting. This potential can be lost, however, if we allow the use of these technologies to be divorced from a thorough and open discussion of the social context and consequences of reproduction and mothering. Isolated and unquestioned, they may only serve to reinforce and exacerbate the traditional hopes and despairs of women as childbearers. As the limits of the possible change, so must our understanding of choice and the desirable.

Notes

[1] Adrienne Rich, *Of Woman Born* (New York: W. W. Norton and Co., 1976).

[2] Earlier theorists, such as Simone de Beauvoir, *The Second Sex*, trans. and ed. by H. M. Parshley (New York: Alfred A. Knopf, 1953) and Shulamith Firestone, *The Dialectic of Sex: The Case for Feminist Revolution* (New York: William Morrow and Co., Inc., 1970), also regarded motherhood as central to understanding women's subordination, but their discussions are more negative about the possibilities for satisfaction.

[3] Dorothy Dinnerstein, *The Mermaid and the Minotaur: Sexual Arrangements and Human Malaise* (New York: Harper and Row, 1976). Issued in Great Britain as *The Rocking of the Cradle and the Ruling of the World* (London: The Women's Press, 1987).

[4] Nancy Chodorow, *The Reproduction of Mothering: Psychoanalysis and the Sociology of Gender* (Berkeley: The University of California Press, 1978).

[5] Ultrasound involves the use of high frequency sound waves to produce an image on a video screen of the foetus (or other body parts). Increasingly, particularly in urban centres, it is used routinely in pre-natal care and presumed to be safe though no long-term follow-up studies have been undertaken. Amniocentesis is a pre-natal diagnostic technique used to detect certain chromosomal abnormalities (for example, Down's syndrome). A needle is inserted into the abdomen of a pregnant woman to extract a sample of the amniotic fluid. Amniocentesis cannot be used until the second trimester of pregnancy, is becoming standard practice for pregnant women over 35, and can be used to detect the sex of the foetus. Chorionic villi sampling (CVS) or chorionic biopsy is a newer, still experimental method of pre-natal diagnosis to detect foetal abnormalities (it can also detect the sex of the foetus). A sample of foetal cells is removed through the pregnant woman's cervix. CVS can be performed in the first trimester of pregnancy and the results are obtainable more quickly than with amniocentesis. Foetal monitoring is a method of measuring the foetal heartbeat during pregnancy or labour. Foetal surgery is a form of micro-surgery directed towards the correction of foetal defects within the womb.

[6] V. E. B. Kolder, J. Gallagher, and M. T. Parsons, "Court-Ordered Obstetrical Interventions," *The New England Journal of Medicine* 316, 19 (7 May 1987), 1192-6.

[7]Dorothy Lipovenko, "Protecting the Fetus: How Far Can the State Go?" *The Globe and Mail*, 1 August 1987, pp. D1-D2. For more information and critical discussion of this vital issue--see also, Ruth Hubbard, "The Fetus as Patient," *MS* (October 1982), 31-2; G. J. Annas, "Forced Caesarians: The Most Unkindest Cut of All," *The Hastings Centre Report* (June 1982), 16; W. Ruddick and William Wilcox, "Operating on the Fetus," *The Hastings Centre Report* (October 1982), 10-14; and, G. J. Annas, "Pregnant Women as Fetal Containers," *The Hastings Centre Report* (December 1986), pp. 13-14.

[8]This is also true of the women's movement historically but less so of Canadian feminists. See Angus McLaren and Arlene Tigar McLaren, *The Bedroom and the State* (Toronto: McClelland and Stewart, 1986) for an historical view of the politics of contraception and abortion in Canada.

[9]The typology of reproductive technologies suggested here--the inhibition, monitoring, and creation of new life--is useful to distinguish the variety of reproductive technologies currently available. It is important to note, however, that they are frequently used in combination with each other and are not necessarily distinct. For example, women who conceive through IVF, artificial insemination (AI), or surrogate motherhood arrangements may utilize diagnostic techniques such as amniocentesis, ultrasound, or chorionic villi sampling as do women who conceive 'normally'. The focus here on artificial reproduction is a pragmatic one due to limitations of space. Other developments, however, such as the routine use of amniocentesis for women over the age of 35, are also important issues in considering new choices available for women in their reproductive and mothering roles. See, for example, Barbara Katz Rothman's excellent book *The Tentative Pregnancy* (New York: Penguin, 1987).

[10]Rich, p. xiii. The title of Rich's book *Of Woman Born* is presumably derived from Shakespeare's *Macbeth*.

[11]Firestone, p. 206.

[12]See, for example, Ralph Mathews and Anne Martin Mathews, "Infertility and Involuntary Childlessness: The Transition to Nonparenthood," *Journal of Marriage and the Family* 48 (August 1986), 641-9.

[13]Barbara Menning, "In Defense of In Vitro Fertilization," in Helen B. Holmes, Betty B. Hoskins and Michael Gross, eds., *The Custom-Made Child?* (Clifton, New Jersey: Humana Press, 1981), p. 264.

[14]For example, in the recent and highly sensationalized 'Baby M' trial, the counsel for the surrogate mother attempted to reassert her custody rights on the basis that the contracting mother was avoiding pregnancy for minor or convenience concerns. See Robert Hanley, "Doctor Disputes Pregnancy Risks in Baby M Case," *New York Times*, 15 January 1987, p. B2.

[15]The decline in children for adoption more specifically involves the decline in availability of 'perfect' white babies.

[16]Vasectomies and tubal ligations are sterilization procedures (permanent contraception) and are designed to be irreversible. A vasectomy is a simple medical procedure in which the vas deferens is cut so that sperm cannot mix with seminal fluid. It can be done in a doctor's office with a local anaesthetic. Tubal ligations are more complex procedures (there are several methods) in which the fallopian tubes are blocked or cut so that the sperm and egg cannot join. Usually a general anaesthetic is employed.

[17]For further information on self-insemination see: Nancy Adamson, "Self-insemination," *Healthsharing* 6, 4 (1985), 8-9; Francie Hornstein, "Children By Donor Insemination: A New Choice For Lesbians," in Rita Arditti, Renate Duelli Klein, and Shelley Minden, eds., *Test-Tube Women: What Future For Motherhood?* (London: Routledge and Kegan Paul, 1984), pp. 373-81; Renate Duelli Klein, "Doing It Ourselves: Self Insemination," in *Test-Tube Women*, pp. 382-90; Gillian E. Hanscombe and Jackie Forster, *Rocking the Cradle* (London: Peter Owen, 1981); Cheri Pies, *Considering Parenthood: A Workbook for Lesbians* (San Francisco: Spinster's Ink, 1985); Susan Robinson and H.F. Pizer, *Having a Baby Without a Man* (New York: Simon and Schuster, Inc., 1985); Joy Schulenberg, *Gay Parenting* (Garden City, N.J.: Anchor Press, 1985); Kathleen Lahey, "Alternative Insemination: Facing the Conceivable Options," *Broadside* 8, 1 (1986), 8-10.

[18]Kathleen A. Lahey, "Reproduction, Male Technology and 'Lifestyle' Conflicts: The Lesbian Challenge," paper presented at the Sixth National Biennial Conference of the National Association of Women and the Law, Ottawa, 21-24 February 1985.

[19]See Menning for a description of treatments for infertility that are utilized before artificial insemination is attempted, p. 265.

[20]Gena Corea, *The Mother Machine* (New York: Harper and Row, 1985).

[21]A. T. Gregoire and Robert C. Mayer, "The Impregnators," *Fertility and Sterility* 16, 1 (1965), 130-4.

[22]G. J. Annas, "Fathers Anonymous: Beyond the Best Interests of the Sperm Donor," *Child Welfare* 60, 1 (1981), 161-74.

[23]Rona G. Achilles, "The Social Meanings of Biological Ties: A Study of Participants in Artificial Insemination by Donor," unpublished Ph.D. thesis, University of Toronto, 1986.

[24]Annas, "Fathers Anonymous."

[25]Richard Titmuss, *The Gift Relationship* (London: George Allen and Unwin, 1970).

[26]Two Australian AID mothers have already contracted AIDS through donor insemination. See D. Zagury *et al.*, "HTLV-III in cell cultured from semen of two patients with AIDS," *Science* (1984), pp. 226-449.

[27]Martin Curie-Cohen, Lesleigh Luttrell, and Sander Shapiro, "Current Practice of Artificial Insemination by Donor in the United States," *New England Journal of Medicine* 300, 11 (1979), 589.

[28]Ontario, Ministry of the Attorney General, Law Reform

Commission, *Report on Human Artificial Reproduction and Related Matters* (Toronto, 1985), p. 103.

[29]The Ontario Law Reform Commission was requested by the Attorney General for Ontario (at the time, November, 1982, Roy McMurtry) to "inquire into and consider the legal issues relating to the practice of human artificial insemination, including 'surrogate mothering' and transplantation of fertilized ova to a third party...[and] report on the range of alternatives for resolution of any legal issues that may be identified." The legal issues suggested in the terms of reference for the report included: "1) The legal status and legal rights of the child and the safeguards for protecting the best interests of the child. 2) The legal rights and legal duties of each biological parent. 3) The legal rights and legal duties of the spouse, if any, of each biological parent. 4) The nature and enforceability of agreements relating to artificial insemination and related practices. 5) The nature and enforceability of agreements respecting custody of the child. 6) The legal rights and liabilities of medical and other personnel involved in performing artificial insemination and other related practices. 7) The legal procedures for establishing and recognizing the biological parentage of children born as a result of these practices. 8) The applicability of present custody and adoption laws in such cases. 9) The availability of information to identify the child and the parties involved. 10) Such medical and related evidence as may have a bearing on the legal issues raised in these cases." Ontario, Law Reform Commission, *Report*, p. 1.

[30]The AID mothers who participated in my study included women who were married at the time of insemination, single women and lesbian couples. Single or lesbian AID mothers consistently adopted an attitude of openness about their AID child(ren)'s origins. The absence of a male partner made it impossible for them to attempt 'normalization' to the conventional image of the family.

[31]Donor insemination for male infertility has been practised for over a century with very little public awareness of its existence. However, surrogate motherhood has existed for a little over ten years (in an organized fashion) but has immediately become a well-covered news item.

[32]Margaret Atwood, *The Handmaid's Tale* (Toronto: McClelland and Stewart, 1985).

[33]Evidence exists that women have borne children for other women before the practice became organized as a profit-making enterprise for lawyers and physicians in the latter part of this century. For millennia elite, powerful families threatened with the dying out of the patrilineal line have resorted to the practice of surrogate motherhood. See, for example, Im Kwon Taek, (director), *Surrogate Mother* (Seoul, Korea: Shin Han Motion Pictures Co. Ltd., 1987), for a film account of the institutionalization of surrogate motherhood for the service of noble families in 14th-century Korea. For a Biblical reference to this practice, see the account of the

conception of Ishmael. Abraham's wife, Sarah, was unable to bear children and therefore bid her husband to have intercourse with her handmaid, Hagar. Abraham "went in unto Hagar, and she conceived." *The Bible*, King James Version, Gen. 16:4.

[34]Lynda Hurst, "Time to Ban Surrogate Motherhood," *Toronto Star*, 17 January 1985, p. D1.

[35]Laura Sabia, "Why The Fuss About Surrogate Moms?" *Toronto Sun*, 17 November 1982, p. A4.

[36]"Surrogate Mothering," television programme, "Speaking Out," *TV Ontario*, 10 February 1983.

[37]*Ibid.*

[38]Susan Ince, "Inside the Surrogate Industry," in *Test-Tube Women*, pp. 99-116.

[39]Note the contrast between the screening of sperm donors and the controls imposed on a surrogate.

[40]A crucial, particularly in the legal sense, difference between birth mothers and surrogates is that surrogacy involves a pre-conception agreement.

[41]Whitehead has appealed the decision and the case will go to a higher court in September, 1987.

[42]Whitehead has reportedly separated from her husband since the trial ended due to "the stress from losing her custody battle" (*Globe and Mail*, 5 August 1987, p. A2). This is interesting in light of Judge Sorkow's assessment that "despite many moves, job problems, and financial and alcohol-related difficulties in the past, the Whiteheads 'have a stable marriage now'." Cited by G. J. Annas, "Baby M: Babies (and Justice) for Sale," *The Hastings Centre Report* (June 1987), 15.

[43]"Surrogate Mom Suicidal over baby, trial told," *Toronto Star*, 7 January 1987, p. A3; "Surrogate mother threatened to kill baby, self, court hears," *Globe and Mail*, 5 February 1987, p. A12.

[44]Annas, "Baby M."

[45]Michele Landsberg, "Baby M decision gives legal backing to inhumane practice," *Globe and Mail*, 4 April 1987, p. A2.

[46]Katha Pollitt, "The Strange Case of Baby M," *The Nation*, 23 May 1987, pp. 1, 682-8.

[47]As this book goes to press (February 1988) the decision by the higher court, the Supreme Court of New Jersey, was reported. Chief Justice Robert Wilentz overturned all aspects of the earlier court's ruling with the exception of the custody decision. Although the custody decision was not overturned, Mary Beth Whitehead's parental rights were restored which will allow her to seek a new custody hearing. Most significantly, this ruling which will likely have impact in other jurisdictions, rules that the contract between Whitehead and Stern was illegal because it violated the state's adoption laws concerning payment for a child. "'This is the sale of a child, the only mitigating factor being that one of the purchasers is the father,' the courts said." Robert Hanley, "Surrogate Deals for Mothers Held Illegal in Jersey," *The New York Times*, 4 February 1988, pp. 1, 14.

[48]Estimates range anywhere from 5 to 20 per cent for success rates with IVF. Conseil du statut de la femme, *Dilemmas when technology transforms motherhood* (Quebec: Les Publications du Québec, 1987).
[49]Linda S. Williams, "Who Qualifies for In Vitro Fertilization? A Sociological Examination of the Stated Admittance Criteria of Three Ontario IVF Programs," paper presented at the annual meeting of the Canadian Sociology and Anthropology Association, Winnipeg, Manitoba, 7 June 1986.
[50]A laparoscopy is a surgical procedure requiring a general anaesthetic by which eggs can be suctioned out through a fiberoptic tube.
[51]Robyn Rowland, "A Child at Any Price?" *Women's Studies International Forum* 8, 6 (1985), 539-46.
[52]In Canada, the following reports are available: British Columbia, Royal Commission on Family and Children's Law, "Artificial Insemination," *Ninth Report* (Vancouver, May, 1975); Institute of Law Research and Reform, *Status of Children* (Edmonton, Alberta: University of Alberta, June, 1976); Saskatchewan, Law Reform Commission, *Tentative Proposals for a Human Artificial Insemination Act* (Saskatoon, 1981); Canada, Health and Welfare, Advisory Committee to the Minister of National Health and Welfare, "Storage and Utilization of Human Sperm," *Report* (Ottawa, 1981); Ontario, Ministry of the Attorney General, Law Reform Commission, *Report on Human Artificial Reproduction and Related Matters* (Toronto, 1985). In the U.S., the most recent medical report has been published by the American Fertility Society, The Ethics Committee of the American Fertility Society, "Ethical Considerations of the New Reproductive Technologies," *Fertility and Sterility* 46, 3 (1986). In Britain, the most recent report is Mary Warnock, *A Question of Life. The Warnock Report on Human Fertilization and Embryology* (Oxford: Basil Blackwell, 1985). Other international reports of interest are listed and briefly summarized in the Ontario Law Reform Commission, *Report* (1985).
[53]Yet to be clarified are the legal rights and responsibilities of all the participants in artificial reproduction. Traditionally, rights and responsibilities for offspring are assigned to biological parents unless otherwise legislated as with, for example, adoption. In the practice of artificial insemination by donor, the husband of the AID mother is named on the birth certificate as the father of the child despite the fact that the biological father is the sperm donor. Further complications arise from the biological and socially defined differences between maternity and paternity. Is an egg donation, for example, the legal equivalent of a sperm donation? What rights do gamete (egg or sperm) donors have over their genetic materials? Can they be used for research, frozen, and used for another couple? Who owns the extra embryos that are not implanted? Can physicians, lawyers, or surrogate organizations be liable for

inadequate screening procedures or 'damaged goods'? For a more thorough discussion of legal issues, see Ontario, Law Reform Commission, *Report* (1985).

[54]Ivan Illich, *Limits to Medicine* (New York: Penguin Books, 1976).

[55]Two of the lesbian mothers who participated in my study described difficulties acquiring access to AID due to their single and/or lesbian status.

[56]Margrit Eichler, *Families in Canada Today: Recent Changes and Their Policy Consequences* (Toronto: Gage, 1983).

[57]Noel Keane and Dennis Breo, *The Surrogate Mother* (New York: Everest Press, 1981).

[58]The procedure for an egg donation is much more medically invasive than sperm donation, but it is possible that women donating eggs will do so during surgical procedures for other medical problems, or simply donate extra eggs removed during the initial phase of IVF. Genoveffa Corea, "Egg Snatchers," in *Test-Tube Women*, pp. 37-51, also points out that "egg donations" may occur unknown to women during surgery.

[59]"The borrowed-womb debate," *Globe and Mail*, 2 August 1982, p. A8; "White slavery or a gift of life?" *Globe and Mail*, 3 August 1982, p. A8.

[60]"High-Tech Babies," television programme, "Nova," PBS, 4 November 1986.

[61]See Anne Finger, "Claiming Our Bodies: Reproductive Rights and Disabilities," in *Test-tube Women*, pp. 281-97, for a fascinating discussion of how words like "defect" or "unfit," once adjectives, are now nouns and the implications of this linguistic and structural transformation for the disabled.

[62]Viola Roggencamp, "Abortion of a Special Kind: Male Sex Selection in India," in *Test-Tube Women*, pp. 266-77.

[63]Nancy E. Williamson, *Sons or Daughters? A Cross-Cultural Study of Parental Preferences* (Beverley Hills: Sage Publications, 1976); Nancy E. Williamson, "Sex Preferences, Sex Control, and the Status of Women," *Signs* 1, 4 (Summer 1976), 847-62; and Nancy E. Williamson, "Parental Preference and Sex Control," *Population Bulletin* 33, 1 (1978).

[64]Robyn Rowland, "Motherhood, Patriarchal Power, Alienation and the Issue of 'Choice' in Sex Preselection," in Gena Corea, *et al.*, eds., *Man-Made Women* (Bloomington and Indianapolis: Indiana University Press, 1987).

[65]See Neil G. Bennett, ed., *Sex Selection of Children* (New York: Academic Press, 1983).

[66]Rowland, "A Child at Any Price?"

[67]See Jalna Hanmer, "Sex Predetermination, Artificial Insemination and the Maintenance of Male-Dominated Culture," in Helen Roberts, ed., *Women, Health and Reproduction* (London: Routledge and Kegan Paul, 1981), pp. 163-90, for a more complete discussion of these methods.

[68]In *Not An Easy Choice*, Kathleen McDonnell refers to this sperm bank, known as the Repository for Germinal Choice, which "was set up a few years ago by California entrepreneur Robert Graham to house the sperm of Nobel Prize winners and other high achievers." In 1984, when the book was written, McDonnell noted that the bank had already "'produced' several babies." Kathleen McDonnell, *Not An Easy Choice: A Feminist Re-Examines Abortion* (Toronto: The Women's Press, 1984), p. 105.

[69]Fiona Whitlock, "Test-tube Babies are Smarter and Stronger," *The Australian*, 17 May 1984.

[70]Barbara Ehrenreich and Deirdre English, *For Her Own Good: 150 Years of the Experts' Advice to Women* (Garden City, New York: Anchor Press/Doubleday, 1978).

[71]Roger Rosenblatt, "The Baby in the Factory," *Time*, 14 February 1983, p. 72.

[72]In contrast to, for example, Great Britain where publication of The Warnock Report (1985) caused a flurry of public discussion.

[73]At least until further technological developments replace them.

INDEX

Abortion 10, 14, 15, 84, 155,
157
    and eugenics 303, 304
    and the medical
profession 141-6
    and single women 109
    Supreme Court ruling
on xviii
Abortion deaths xviii,
    in British Columbia
126-46
    case of Mrs. R ____,
Vancouver 141-4
    legal records of 136-41
    medical reports of
128-30
    rates 133, 127-8, 135,
137
    vital statistics on
128-35
Achilles, Rona xx
Act for the Protection of
Infant Children 55
Adoption 116
Advice literature
    on crying 199,
    emphasis on doctor
xvi, 193, 195-6
    on feeding 199, 241-2
    impracticality of 201,
202
    for mothers xix, xx,
190-210
    and scientific child care
196-200
    on sleep 197, 199

    on toilet training 197
    women's response to
193
AID
    see Artificial
insemination
American Board of
Obstetricians and
Gynaecologists 79
American College of
Surgeons 79, 81, 87
American Gynaecological
Association 80
*American Journal of
Obstetrics and
Gynaecology (AJOG)* 79
Amniocentesis 305
Andrews, Florence Kellner
xxi
Arnup, Katherine xix
Artificial insemination
288-92
    anonymity 290, 291
    donors 289-90
    effects on women 291,
292
    methods 288-9
Artificial reproduction
technologies
    see New reproductive
technologies
Association of Pharmacists
42

The Baby 193, 195, 197, 199
Baby's Milk Dispensary

313